REA's Book

They have rescued ... grades and more!

(a sample of the hundreds of letters REA receives each year)

"Your books are great! They are very helpful, and have upped my grade in every class. Thank you for such a great product."

Student, Seattle, WA

"Your book has really helped me sharpen my skills and improve my weak areas. Definitely will buy more."

Student, Buffalo, NY

"Compared to the other books that my fellow students had, your book was the most useful in helping me get a great score."

Student, North Hollywood, CA

"I really appreciate the help from your excellent book. Please keep up your great work."

Student, Albuquerque, NM

"Your book was such a better value and was so much more complete than anything your competition has produced (and I have them all)!"

Teacher, Virginia Beach, VA

(more on next page)

(continued from previous page)

"Your books have saved my GPA, and quite possibly my sanity. My course grade is now an 'A', and I couldn't be happier."

Student, Winchester, IN

"These books are the best review books on the market. They are fantastic!"

Student, New Orleans, LA

"Your book was responsible for my success on the exam. . . I will look for REA the next time I need help."

Student, Chesterfield, MO

"I think it is the greatest study guide I have ever used!"

Student, Anchorage, AK

"I encourage others to buy REA because of their superiority. Please continue to produce the best quality books on the market."

Student, San Jose, CA

"Just a short note to say thanks for the great support your book gave me in helping me pass the test . . . I'm on my way to a B.S. degree because of you!"

Student, Orlando, FL

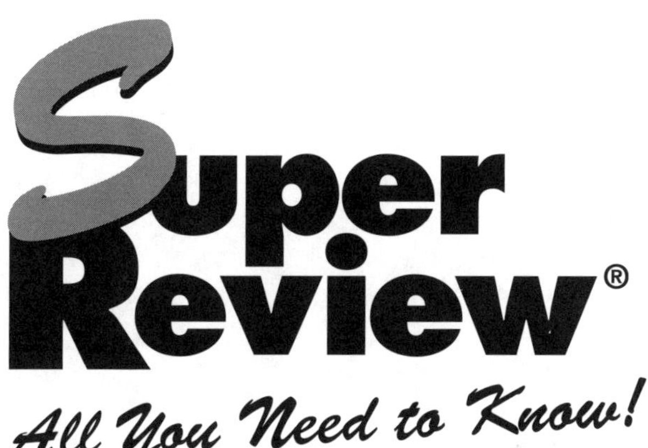

DRAWING

Charles Lederer
Artist and Teacher of Drawing

and the Staff of
Research & Education Association,
Carl Fuchs, Chief Editor

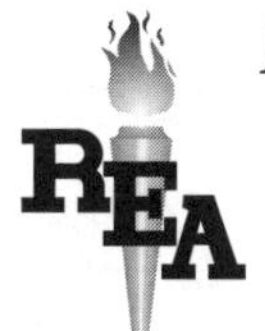

Research & Education Association
61 Ethel Road West
Piscataway, New Jersey 08854

Dr. M. Fogiel, Director

SUPER REVIEW®
OF DRAWING

Printed in the United States of America

Library of Congress Control Number 2003103995

International Standard Book Number 0-87891-432-3

I-1

WHAT THIS Super Review WILL DO FOR YOU

This Super Review provides you with the practical skills and all you need to know to perform successfully in a drawing course. Practical applications of the rules of drawing with easily understood illustrations are presented throughout this review book.

The book focuses on the core aspects of drawing and helps you to grasp the important elements quickly and easily.

Outstanding Super Review features:

- Topics are covered in logical sequence
- Topics are reviewed in a concise and comprehensive manner
- The material is presented in student-friendly form that makes it easy to follow and understand
- Individual topics can be easily located
- A glossary of commonly used terms in the field of art and drawing is included
- Written by professionals and experts who function as your very own tutors

Dr. Max Fogiel, Director
Carl Fuchs, Chief Editor

CONTENTS

PREFACE

Knowledge of drawing of a practical kind is of more use and is the least apt to be forgotten of any form of study not in constant use. Aside from the fact that the study of art encourages and fosters a love for the beautiful, as expressed in form and color, it has its every-day practical value. Information of various kinds can be imparted more readily to others by means of pictorial illustration than by the description of words, written or spoken.

More can be told by a few correctly placed lines than by many words. What geographical truth can be told by words alone? Pictures have ever told more than words. Facts are more easily impressed by pictures than by words. The date may be forgotten when William Penn signed his treaty with the Native Americans, but the fact that an agreement was made, which is the most important feature of the event to know, will stand by one for life if the culminating or most important scene connected with that transaction has, by means of a picture, been impressed on the mind. A person may not know the latitude and longitude of the Pyramids of Egypt, but if one has seen a picture of them the conception so obtained will be more lasting and precise than could be given by pages of print. Art is the handmaid of every-day knowledge. There is no trade, no profession, no business of any kind, in fact, whose follower is not benefited if he has a knowledge of how to convey intelligently to others a pictorial message.

Pictures! Where can you go nowadays to escape them in some shape? Nowhere; so why not learn something about them and the way to make them? Certainly such knowledge may be found *at least* as useful as that of algebra, Greek, Latin, or a dozen other seldom-applied parts of higher education.

The real reason why drawing is not taught more frequently, and especially more successfully in the schools is because there is a scarcity of practical teachers and manuals of drawing. There are words a-plenty. There is theoretical art a-plenty. Of the practical application of the rules of drawing with easily understood illustrations there is a famine.

In the schools, as a general thing, drawing is made an almost incomprehensible task. It should be and can be made a relaxation, a recreation, without in the least degree losing its value as an educational feature. Drawing in the schools would not then be considered a fad but a most important, useful and sought-for branch of instruction.

Anyone who can learn to write can learn to draw—and draw well. To become a great artist is another matter. Success,—fame,—cannot be guaranteed.

It is not the design of this work to supply a "complete art education." Indeed the author knows of no one who possesses such. Many years of diligent study and patient labor would be necessary to attain even such knowledge of matters appertaining to art as would be requisite for a career in the highest paths of art. Many necessary branches have barely been broached in these pages. The subject of artistic anatomy for instance, if pursued to anything like completion, would alone entail the study of a bulkier volume than this. Likewise, a full knowledge of the laws of perspective would require a volume by itself. Many other subjects that are treated in the present work have been the themes of exhaustive series of books written by specialists. The information conveyed by them cannot be successfully abridged to a few pages. Therefore it would be impossible for such a humble work as this to supply more than a smattering of the knowledge necessary to understand the rudiments of art. The student of art who is desirous of taking up the more ambitious branches of even black-and-white illustration must constantly go to Nature, including the living model. Exhaustive works on art, each devoted to a single topic, must be read and the rules they contain put into constant practice for months at a time. If one possesses the means, attendance at one of the art institutes will be of immeasurable value.

Assurance is given that sufficient instruction is contained in this volume to impart to the reader all knowledge of drawing that should be required on an elementary level.

Because of the author's many years' experience as a practical teacher of drawing and in the field of illustration, he believes that he can teach many things in the way of drawing in the EASIEST WAY. He has divulged many useful "tricks

of the trade." He has brushed aside some of the popular notions of the difficulty of learning to draw well, especially if the pupil possesses the slightest talent in that direction.

Having been jack-of-all-trades in a pictorial way, the author feels that he does not display undue egotism when he says that the knowledge he has gained—at the hands of that hardest of task masters, Necessity, and that most thorough of teachers, Experience—and which he now places at the disposal of the reader should meet all requirements for gaining competence in drawing.

CHARLES LEDERER.

CHAPTER I

INTRODUCTION

The beginner should not make undue haste in his or her studies; it is necessary to focus attention on the simplest examples before attempting to experiment with those more intricate. Beginners have a natural tendency to work out their own fancies in direct opposition to the laws that cover drawing. By example and adherence to precept, one should avoid giving rein to misdirected fancies.

In choosing models for early work do not select subjects intricate in design or highly polished. Choose subjects simple and with little detail. An abnormal desire to make rapid progress is a detriment to the person learning to draw.

Simplicity and directness should prevail wherever the subject will permit of such treatment. Risking the charge of reiteration the claim is made that in the illustrations and accompanying text the principles by which a considerable fund of knowledge of drawing, of a simple but practical character, may be found.

Anyone who can learn to write can learn to draw. The latter may take longer than the former, yet any person with a fair stock of patience and perseverance who is equipped with the use of at least one hand and one eye can, by going about it in the right way, learn not alone to copy, but to transfer to paper many of the things he or she sees, and the ideas, in the way of form, that come to the mind of every intelligent being.

The professional is apt to overlook the difficulties of the beginner. That which may seem ridiculously simple to the former often staggers the inexperienced mind. For this reason, the authors have striven to make each step in these studies so plain and practical that it may seldom be necessary to retrace it. Yet it can only be helpful to refer to some parts of the early lessons.

The study of drawing is almost sure to become more and more attractive as it is continued.

Success depends largely on perseverance and the cultivation of habits of observation. Bear in mind that a keen discernment will impart more knowledge than any number of text books or rules of practice. Manuals and rules alone never produced ability to draw. Genius itself teaches us that the "methods of genius are ever changing." The highest purpose of the great masters of art and the working out of their loftiest ideas resulted from mind concentration coupled with close observation of nature.

Imitators and copyists are born of rules made by others. The strict adherence to rules would bind genius as the chains of captives. Rules alone would shackle originality of idea and bar advance into new fields of art and beauty. But until the student has mastered certain fundamental laws and has advanced beyond the limit of instruction given in this work, he would be wise to be guided by the rules herein set forth.

The greater the regularity with which the study of drawing is attended the better will be the results. Perseverance and patience should be allied to a precision in the matter of time. The hour allotted to the study of drawing should be given up to nothing else. Neither should the time be unduly extended, so that the practice of drawing becomes distasteful —irksome. The study of art in any form should not be considered as a task and should not be made such by overexertion. The drawing hour should be a pastime and a pleasure for anyone endeavoring to draw.

Many beginners are prone to choose subjects too complex in character. As mentioned before, one should be deterred from such exercise, though not discouraged in efforts to be original. It is simple enough to find the difficulties attending complicated subjects and to discriminate.

Notwithstanding the generally accepted rule that it is necessary for the student to have some knowledge of the rudiments of drawing before being permitted to exploit the composition of a picture, one should indulge one's fancies in arranging groups comprised of many figures and scenes embracing wide areas.

A student of music would hardly attempt the composition of a sonata before he or she had even an inkling of the meaning of a single note. To a certain extent the same restriction applies to art. Yet one's natural inclination

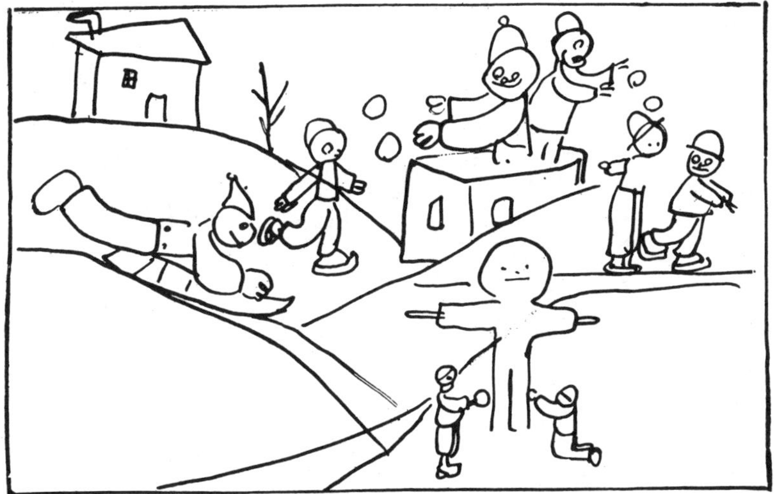

Fig. 1

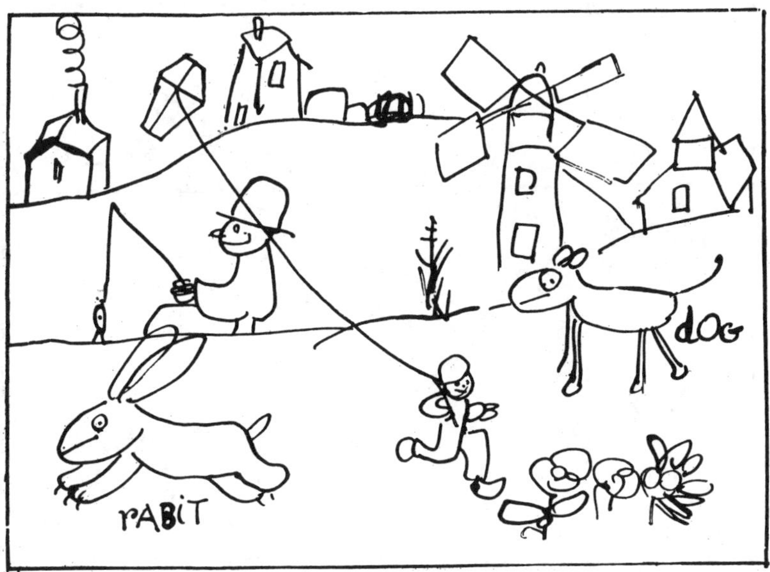

Fig. 2—Drawn Without Instruction

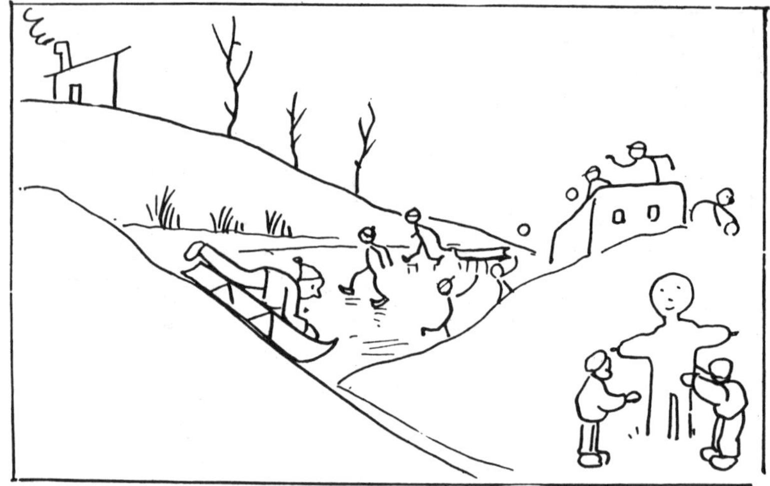

Fig. 3

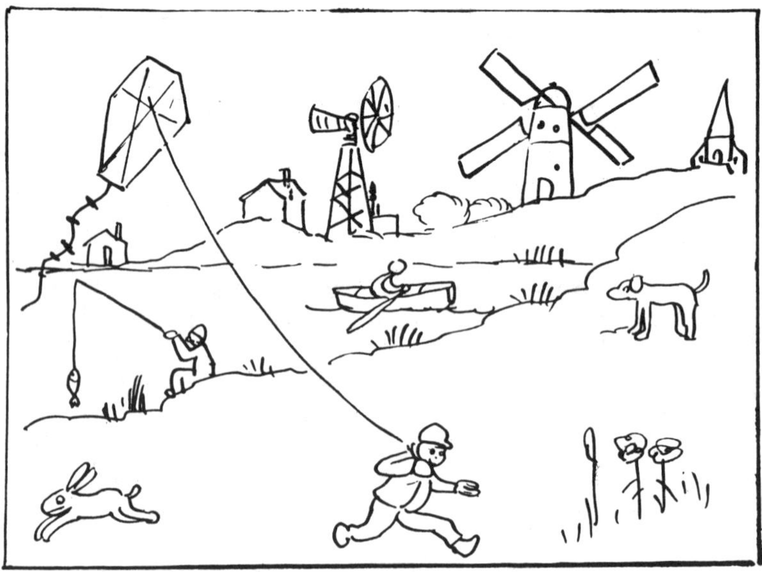

Fig. 4—Drawn After a Little Instruction

must be taken into consideration. In early attempts to draw, one's tendency is to stretch one's fancy too wide. Hence the challenge is to balance one's desire to display the fruits of one's unfettered imagination and ingenuity with one's desire to depict the subject accurately.

The best technique is to draw each object correctly rather than to distribute so many distorted objects over a wide field. Figs. 1 and 2 show two infantile scenes where the figures are clearly not in proportion; the figures in the background are too big, in proportion, to those nearer to the eye. Figs. 3 and 4 show improvement.

Keeping proportion in mind, take the component parts of the rudimentary composition, rendering them in single studies each one more accurate than the last—conforming more with the objects as actually seen in nature.

CHAPTER II

MATERIALS FOR DRAWING

Aside from the slate and blackboard, black-and-white drawing requires the following materials:

Drawing paper (in sheets or tablets) and cardboard.
Pencils,
Pens,
Erasers (pencil and ink),
Drawing board,
Thumb tacks,
Brushes,
Straight edge and other
Drawing instruments,
Scrap book,
"Finder."

Drawing Paper for Pencil.—Take some pains in selecting drawing paper for pencil drawing if an assortment is at hand, for there is one thing that may be depended on and that is that it is almost impossible to do satisfactory work on very smooth or very soft paper. Pencil drawing requires a grained surface to work upon, that is to say, a rough finished paper. Rough-surfaced manila paper is well adapted for the pencil, especially for practice work.

Drawing Paper for Pen Work.—Smooth paper is generally to be preferred, nevertheless, it should not be so highly finished as to repel ink, neither should it be so coarse as to absorb it. The paper should be sufficiently firm to withstand erasures of the pencil marks after the pen lines are dry, or erasures of the pen lines themselves by means of the ink eraser. If there is a fuzzy appearance on the surface after the rubber eraser has been passed over it it is an indication that the paper is too soft. On the other hand, if the ink lines dry unevenly, as if on an oily surface, it is a sign that the paper is too smooth—that the ink does not take hold. Should it be necessary to use one kind of paper for both pencil and pen, procure medium rough linen paper. The so-called "bond" and "ledger" papers are excellent for pen-and-ink work.

The main objection to drawing books is the difficulty of maintaining a flat surface. Tablets or blocks are preferable, but separate sheets are the best. These should be fastened upon drawing boards of sufficient area to allow an inch at the bottom and each side. If too close there is not room for the hand to move while guiding the pencil.

Pencils are graded in numbers from the softest, No. 1, to the hardest, No. 5. In letters a greater range of extremes is found between the softest 6B and the hardest 9H. Of these, the intermediate letters are the most valuable for school purposes, in the following order: In numbers running from soft to hard—Nos. 2,1, and 3. By letters 1B, 2B, HB, F and H. Further gradations may be required for more advanced work. Soft pencils with flat but rather long points are better for general sketching than hard, sharply pointed pencils. By slightly turning the flattened point the angle pressed against the paper serves for the sharpest of lines.

The drawing paper (and copy, if not too large) should be tacked to the drawing board; ordinary tacks may be used. Thumb tacks, however, are better, and as now made in one piece of steel are quite inexpensive.

Eraser for Pencil Marks.—For erasing small parts on a firm drawing paper, ordinary India rubber, or Artgum may be used. If the paper is not firm, soft or kneaded rubber is the best. For cleaning large surfaces, a "sponge" rubber is good, although dry bread crumbs gently rubbed over the surface will answer the same purpose.

Pens.—For elementary pen work ordinary pens will suffice, but there are pens suited for the more advanced exercises.

Erasers for **ink marks** are a combination of India rubber and emory powder. A sharp-bladed knife is used for the same purpose, especially for erasing very small spaces.

Ink for Drawing.—Ink that is as black as possible is essential, even for the beginner, in any kind of pen work. Pale ink is a positive detriment to advance in study. While India ink, whether in stick or liquid form, is best, any so-called jet black will admirably suit ordinary purposes. India ink in sticks is the cheapest. In fact, many artists prefer India ink in stick form to the prepared liquid India inks. The latter is apt to "cake" on steel pens, making frequent cleaning necessary. It is more expensive than the stick ink.

To prepare stick India ink for use, place a little water in a saucer. Then, place the flat end of the stick in the water and grind with a rotary or twisting movement. The ink should be ground until it appears quite black, but not until it is as thick as the consistency of cream. If ground too much it may not flow readily from the pen. If such is the case, the ink may be diluted with water before using it. The ink should be tested by making a heavy line on a sheet of paper and allowing it to dry. If the line appears brown or gray the grinding should be continued. After the stick is used it should be wiped dry. This will prevent its cracking. Grind only enough for present purposes, as the ink will not keep well, even if bottled, for more than two or three days without giving forth an offensive odor. A drop of carbolic acid or oil of cloves may, however, prevent the decomposition of the vegetable matter (of which the ink is composed) and which cause the disagreeable smell.

If the liquid ink is preferred, procure any of the ready prepared waterproof liquid inks sold in bottles by art material dealers. Should the ink become too thick dilute it with soft water.

Chinese White.—In using Chinese white in tubes, squeeze a little on a slab or saucer, and then dilute with very little water—just enough to make it flow readily. It should be used much thicker than ink. If used with a pen, it should be thinned. The pen must be quite clean.

Drawing Instruments.—No valid reason can be given for the entire prohibition of the use of drawing instruments. The straight edge and the compass are implements frequently necessary to every student of art whether beginner or professional.

One should never cease freehand exercise of straight and curved lines, constructing by these means nearly all the examples shown in this work. When, however, the accuracy of the final drawing depends on the correctness, for instance, of a square or of a circle, the boundary or perimeter of which encloses or establishes the form of some object, the assistance of the simple instruments mentioned is greatly appreciated. Even the most accomplished artist cannot depend on his hand and eye to construct a perfect circle, or an exact vertical or horizontal line: then why should the inexperienced be hampered by the prohibition of such aids as will make his or her drawing accurate? From another standpoint—the aid of drawing instruments will eventually be necessary, so why not become proficient in their use? There can be no reasonable negative answers to these questions, at least such is the conviction of the author of this humble volume. Therefore, it is advised that each beginner at least practice with a straight edge and a pencil compass, for occasional use. Furthermore it is deemed quite safe for advanced drawing students to have dividers, T-squares, triangles and protractors. Their straight edges should be in the form of inch-rules.

Even in elementary mechanical and working drawing exercises, such as described in this work, the use of the ruling-pen and pen-compasses is helpful when the drawing is to be made in pen-and-ink.

The T-square is a straight edge with a cross piece at right angles securely fastened at one end. The latter slides along one end of the drawing board while the blade is used for marking horizontal and perpendicular lines.

T-squares with movable heads are made for the purpose of permitting the main blade to pass over the surface in such manner as to permit oblique parallel lines to be made.

Triangles are made with various angles. To draw parallel lines with triangles two triangles are necessary, except that one triangle may be used in conjunction with the T-square—either with fixed or movable heads. The triangle may be used for making parallel lines and for making opposite angles, as shown in the diagrams.

Compasses are used for drawing circles and arcs of circles. Pen and pencil points are usually provided to be used interchangeably. A lengthening bar is sometimes provided to extend the radius of the compass.

Dividers are similar to the compass but both legs are provided with points. Dividers are used for laying off distances in the drawing, or from scales, or from other parts of the drawing. They are excellent for dividing a line into equal parts. A compass can be used as dividers for ordinary work.

Bow-pens and bow-pencils are compasses fitted with permanent pen or pencil shanks and have screw arms to retain the adjustments of distance between the legs. A drawing pen, or ruling pen, as it is also termed, consists of two blades with a handle, the former joined by a thumb screw to adjust the distance between the blades by means of a brush or ordinary pen used as a feeder.

Loose Leaf Scrap Books

It's a good idea to preserve illustrated clippings. The best manner of keeping them in an orderly way is as follows:

Get a quire of very heavy manilla paper and have it cut up in sheets to suit. Sheets nine by twelve are the usual size.

The sheets can be kept together in a homemade portfolio constructed of "Pressboard," a very firm article that can be procured from any printer or bookbinder. The boards should be half an inch wider and longer than the sheets.

Number each sheet as you would the pages of a scrap book, and paste the scraps to the sheets. Leave enough margin around the pictorial part of the scrap so that the corners can be pasted to the sheet. If the *corners only* are pasted, each scrap can be detached without defacing the picture or unduly marring the sheet.

Paste the scraps of subjects relating to different matters by themselves. That is, keep one or more sheets for animals; for landscapes, seascapes; comic figures, costumes, children, etc. Let the sheet (or page) numbers run along consecutively. Keep one page for an index, with a list of subjects and pages opposite. For example, thus:

	Sheet No.
Animals	3, 14, 20
Botany	8, 16, 30
Cartoons	17, 23
Children	1, 4, 9

and so on.

When quite an accumulation of sheets has been acquired, bring the various subjects together, in sequence, re-number the sheets and make a new index.

Copying is frequently necessary.—The artist cannot always go to nature. It happens frequently something has to be introduced in a picture for which the artist cannot conveniently go to nature, and which, even if he had the most prodigious memory, he fails sufficiently to bring to mind. Suppose the artist should want to introduce a camel into a picture. He may remember the general outlines sufficiently to render the shape so that it would not be mistaken for a giraffe or a billy goat. What does he do? Why, he goes to his scrap book, into which he has pasted his pictures of animals, clipped from illustrated periodicals, and perhaps he will find the animal he wants exactly in the required position. He adopts the camel into his picture. He has simply borrowed a camel without permission, knowing the counterfeit quadruped will not be missed.

How to Stretch Paper

There are several methods of stretching paper, of which the following two are the simplest.

A simple frame of wood is used, an inch or so wide, and about three-quarters of an inch in thickness, according to the size of the drawing. This is covered with muslin, tightly stretched and tacked at intervals of one inch all along the sides, turning the muslin over to the outer edges, not on the face of it, which should present a perfectly smooth, flat surface.

The paper should be cut the proper size, that is, as large as the muslin has been cut, and then dampened on the wrong side by means of a sponge or clean cloth dipped in cold water. There should be just enough moisture in the sponge or cloth to enable one to pass it rapidly over the surface of the paper, wetting it evenly. The sponge, or whatever is used, should not be dripping with water. Before this is done, however, have at hand some good flour paste or prepared library paste (many prefer the liquid glue) and put this all around the edge of the paper to about the width of the frame. Next spread the paper while still damp upon the muslin covered stretcher. starting at the bottom and working upward, carefully smoothing out all creases or air bubbles. Turn the frame over and press down the edges of the paper, which have been covered with the paste, holding them until they stick to the cloth. Cut a V-shaped piece from each corner of the paper, so that it will fold over neatly. This operation requires time and experience to do well, but is worth the trouble.

The second method is the same as the first, except that no frame is required, the paper being pasted directly on the board. The outer edges of the paper should be pasted along the edges from a half to one inch in width, according to the size of the drawing.

Erasing Mask

Take a piece of cardboard, a business card is excellent for the purpose; cut slits in it of varying sizes and use them as stencils (only in this case the pigment is removed instead of applied). If a larger surface is to be erased the part to be preserved may be protected

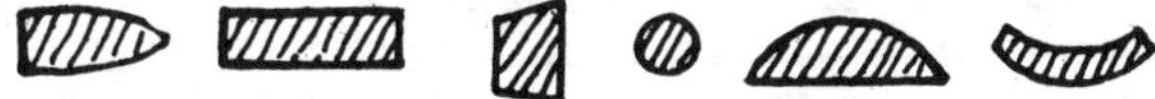

by using the card as a shield, simply placing the card over that part and cleaning up to the edge of the latter. The eraser should not be used too rapidly. Its correct use is such as not to smudge the drawing nor wrinkle the paper.

Notes.—Materials for charcoal, pastel and crayon, see page 191, 192, 194 and 198; for pastel-stenciling, 191, 192, 194 and 198; and for water color work, 315, 316 and advertising pages.

CHAPTER III

CLAY MODELING

Clay, being a plastic material, is a suitable medium by which one can express a thought. Modeling soon becomes a delight, a recreation, and at the same time ideas of form are received. By its means, dexterity in the use of the fingers is gained. An object can be copied in form while, at the same time, the mental image is stored in memory or imagination and becomes an actuality.

To a certain extent, at the outset, the choice of subjects is open. First, however, become familiar with the material and with its use. Try familiar subjects, such as a ball or an apple, and mold objects in clay that appear similar. After that, select simple forms, such as the sphere, cube and cylinder, and imitate them in the clay. Model the general form rather than the minor details. Do not insist on smoothness or minute attention to texture of substance. The appearance of the general mass, or effect, is the thing most desired from the beginner.

The Models.—If the modeled article is a rectangle, say four inches wide and a half an inch in thickness, it should be built up by packing and pressing the clay firmly together with the thumbs, while the edges and sides are made straight and firm by packing the clay against one thumb with the other. No attempt should be made to have the tablet smooth like a paper box. The evidence of the human hand should be apparent. The tablet may be the base upon which other objects may be placed.

More ambitious subjects may now be attempted, such as a simple leaf. Of course, the clay leaf will be much thicker than the natural one, but it should be curved to follow Nature's lines. A few of the veins may be shown with occasional indentations on the edges.

Decorative Form.—The next step is the modeling of single decorative forms. These should be built on the tablet and gradually pressed down until the ornament and tablet are connected as one. Care should be taken to keep the clay sufficiently moist to prevent its drying very quickly in the hands of the children. The Spring and Fall are better seasons for modeling exercise than the dryer months of the winter. Should the clay become too wet, roll it in a clean cloth and knead it until it is of the proper consistency. On the contrary, should the clay become too dry, it may be placed in a vessel and covered with water where it may be allowed to stand for two or three days. After this, the water may be poured off and the clay wedged—wedged being a technical term, meaning to cut, divide, and work together a mass of wet clay, in order to drive out air bubbles and to render it more plastic. The clay may now be formed into bricks, wrapped in wet towels, placed in an earthen jar, for further use.

Quantity of Clay.—A mass of soft clay about three inches in diameter will be sufficient. Each piece should be placed on a small piece of heavy writing paper and placed on the desk.

Cubes, spheres, cylinders and prisms may now be made into models.

Materials.—A small wooden board, a piece of the oil stencil board or a slate will answer for a molding board. A little trouble may be experienced at first in getting the clay of the right consistency to work with. It should be neither too soft nor too dry. The clay may be used again, the models being broken up.

Modeling Tools.—Most of the work should be done by kneading and molding with the hands. Sticks of wood, shaped like small, pointed paper cutters, some of them curved, may be used for detail.

Subjects.—A wide range of subjects is offered for modeling. Almost any of the simple objects that are used for drawing models are suited for work in clay. Among these are simple geometrical forms, vegetables and fruits, leaves and even flower forms, toys, etc.

Notes.—Subjects for clay modeling will be found on the following pages: 28 (turnip), 38, 39, 48 (the first toy), ABCD, (snails), 50 (the pumpkins), 111 (the apples and toadstools), 113 (simple leaf forms), 117 (simple leaf forms), 119 (simple leaf forms), 120 (vegetables), 222 (leaf forms), 229, 232, 233, 235, 245, 265.

CHAPTER IV

PRELIMINARY INSTRUCTIONS

Position of the Drawing Board.—It is essential that the drawing should be held as near as possible at right angles to the direction at which it is seen.

Position.—Assume an erect, easy attitude, neither inclined to the right nor the left, facing the desk. The latter rule should not be made rigid, nor, on the other hand, be deviated from with great frequency.

Measurements.—In free hand exercises, from copy or objects, actual measurements *before* completion of drawing should be avoided. Otherwise, the entire object of free-hand drawing is defeated. This objection does not refer to the pencil measurements made by holding the pencil at full arm's length, referred to in the next paragraph.

Eye Measurement.—The best aid to eye-measurement is to hold the pencil at any angle required, the pencil meanwhile being parallel with the erect body and at right angles to the extended arm. Then raise or lower the thumb to the point required. The angles of objects to be drawn can be obtained also by the extended pencil. (See Chapter X.)

Guide Lines.—Guide lines as an aid to writing are prepared in advance. In drawing, owing to the complexity of form used in the exercises, ready-made guides would be manifestly impractical if not impossible.

There is as good a reason to learn to draw with the aid of guide lines as there is to learn to write that way. And there certainly is a good reason for the little blue lines in the copy books in the schools that keep the pupils from writing like this:

See the boy run

instead of like this:

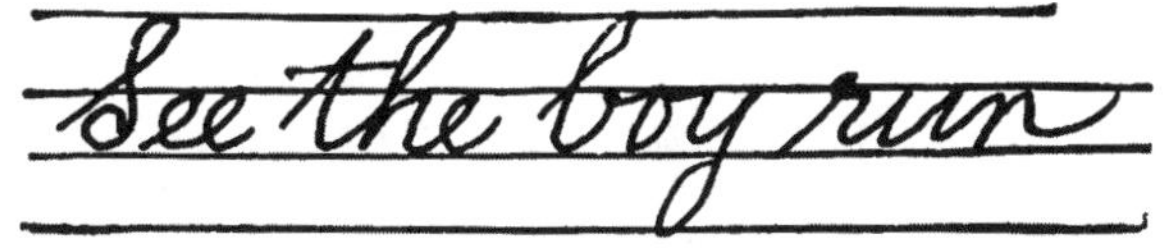

Hence the guide lines—and long may they flourish.

Elementary Practice in Form.—It is important to control the hands before proceeding far. It is best to begin with straight lines. The next step is to draw curved lines and, from this, to proceed to draw angles, circles, squares, and other such forms and outlines until the muscles of the hand become fairly under control. The foundation of technical skill in drawing, whether with charcoal, crayon, pen and ink or pencil, depends upon the ability to make lines with correctness and dexterity. Later one learns to see form rather than the lines themselves, yet the early training of the hand is responsible for firmness and surety of touch in the future.

The Point of the Pencil.—This is a very important point. The point, including the lead and wood, should be fairly long and tapering, not short and blunt, as in Fig. 1, or ragged, as in Fig. 2, or too tapering, as in Fig 3. The right point is shown in Fig. 4. The lead should not be sharpened to a fine

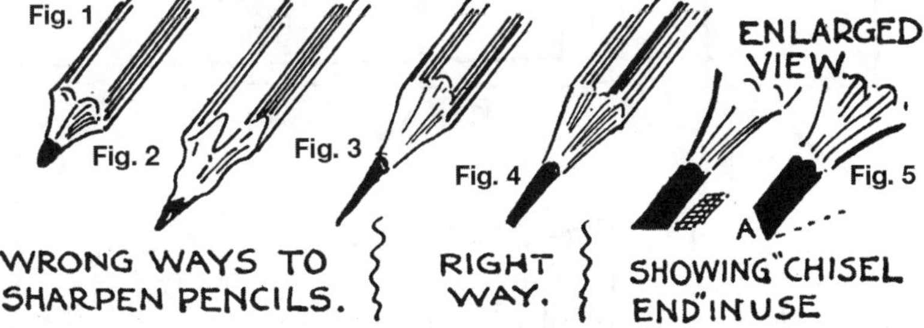

point. By holding the pencil at an angle without turning it, making broad lines, the pencil wears away to a chisel point, as in Fig. 5. By a slight twist the angle A can be brought to play for the purpose of making a fine line. Illustrate this by making a number of broad lines, holding the pencil rigidly, and then giving the pencil a half turn.

CHAPTER V

OUTLINES FOR BEGINNERS

During the earliest period of exercises no attempt should be made to produce other than flat drawings, that is to say, the front faces of the objects presented. Unaided, the beginner scarcely could do this, but simple instructions here suggested can overcome the difficulty.

Try this method: Prop up a slate against some books. The slate now presents the form of an oblong containing additional parallel lines. Draw a picture of a slate, first drawing an oblong within an oblong, shading the latter, then adding the corners and rounding them. (See Fig. 1.)

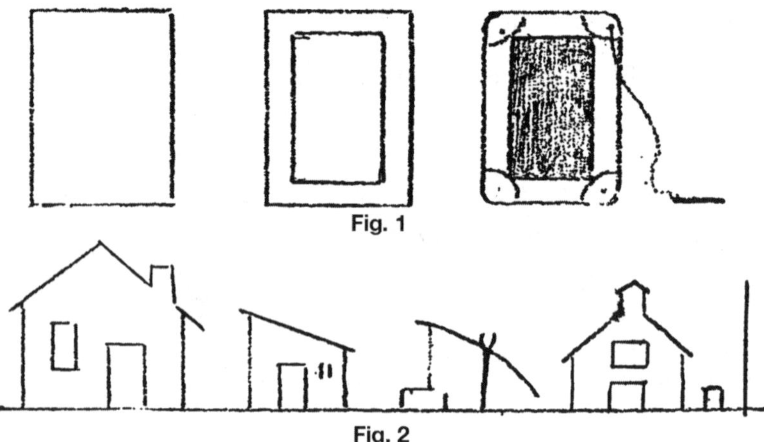

Fig. 1

Fig. 2

Next, draw a simple picture of a house—just the front view. Then the adjoining shed, the well, the barn, etc. To render the entire subject simple, draw a horizontal as a base line for all the buildings (see Fig. 2).

The youngest beginners usually find difficulty in drawing objects by means of parallel lines; therefore, the examples in single line exercises on this page are given. Make additional drawings of familiar objects, enclosing each object in a square.

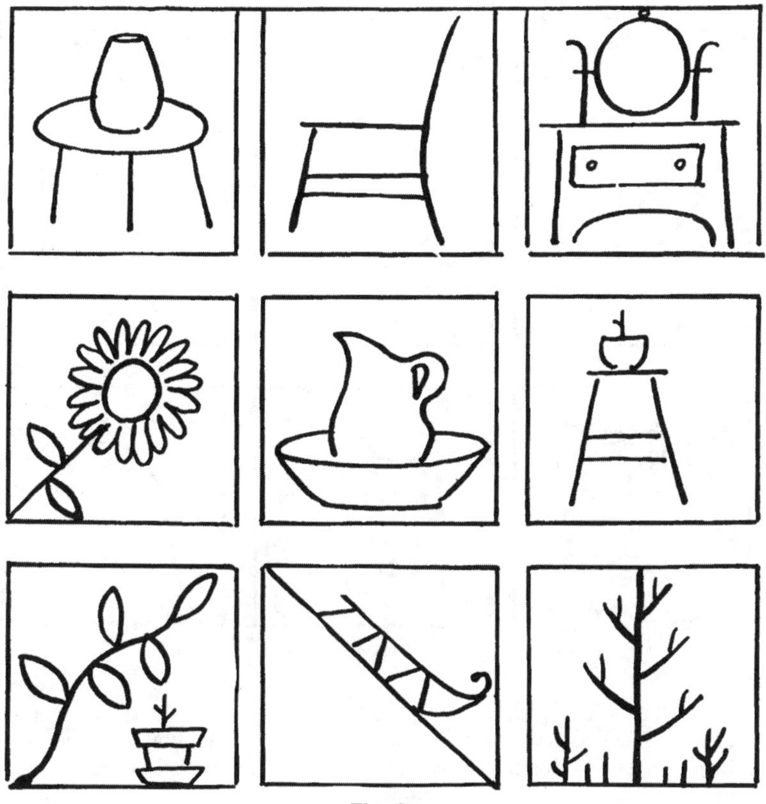

Fig. 3

Simple Composition

Drawing from Imagination.—The following exercises will develop the imagination. The subjects are merely suggestive and others may be substituted. Care should be taken to select objects simple in outline and construction.

Draw a box—just the front of it. Now add wheels and a

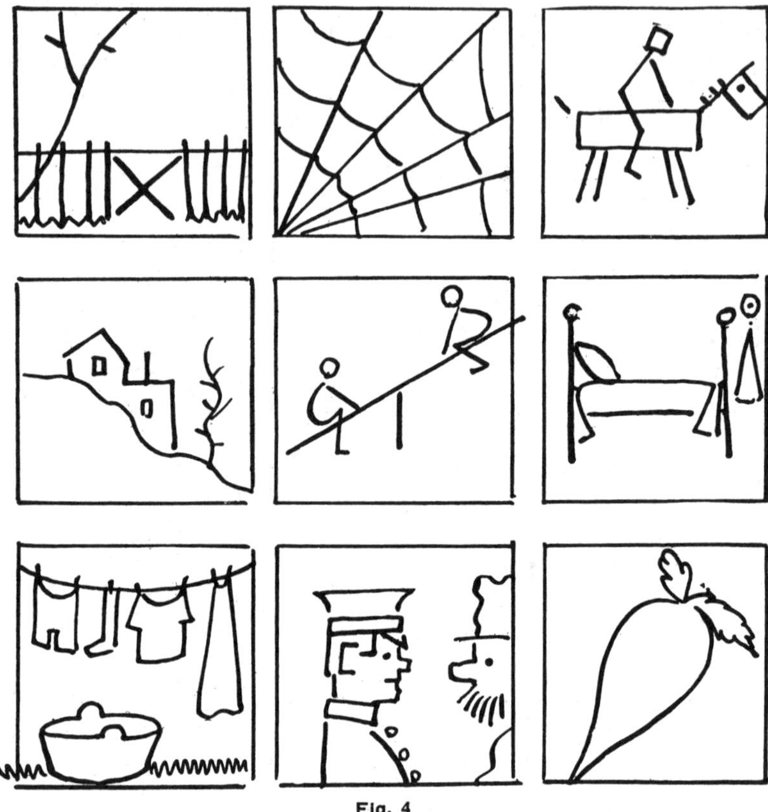

Fig. 4

handle, thus making a wagon out of it. Put a doll in the wagon. Now draw a boy or a girl pulling the wagon. Write a line under it, descriptive, for instance, as to where they are going.

Draw the box again—just the front—put a flower pot on it. Now put a long stem with a flower in the pot. Add leaves to the stem. Next put a butterfly or a bird flying near the flower. Write under the drawing a line about birds (or butterflies) and flowers.

Draw a box; put a cage on it; put a bird into the cage. Draw a cat near the box, looking at the bird. The cat is fond of the bird. Write under the drawing what the cat says about it.

Draw a log on a bank; put a boy or a girl on the log; put a fishing rod, with line and hook, in the hands of the boy. Draw a line showing the surface of the water. Now show a fish under the waterline, getting ready to bite at the hook.

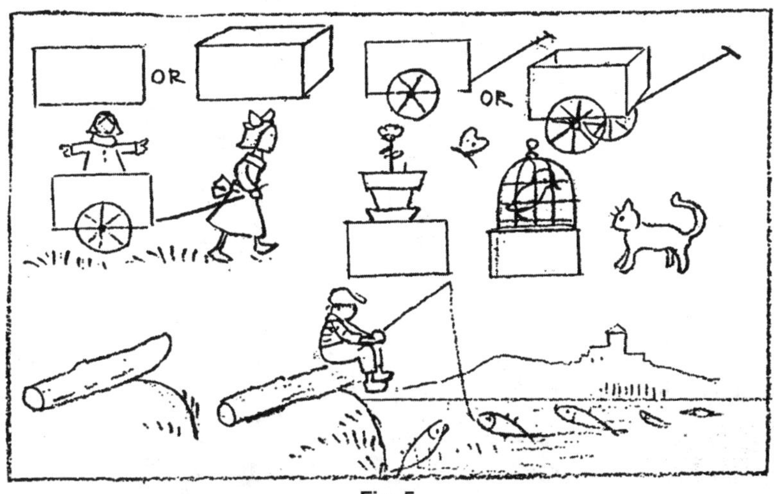

Fig. 5

Effect by Suggestion.—By combination and juxtaposition, we are enabled to establish the meaning of lines that by them-

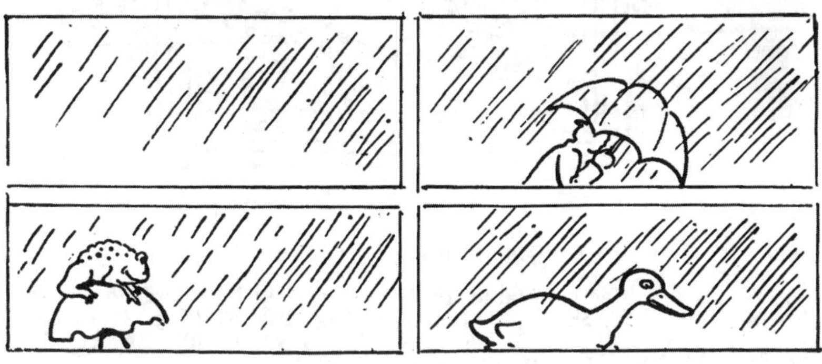

Fig. 6

selves would not be recognized in the way intended. For instance, the lines in the upper left hand corner of Fig. 6, by themselves, would not be understood as representing rain. But place an open umbrella in connection with the lines, and the eye interprets them as portraying rain. For practice, draw plain lines and add figures as here suggested.

In A of Fig. 7, the scallops, by themselves, represent nothing in nature. Invert them and place a sketch of a sailboat and waves as suggested.

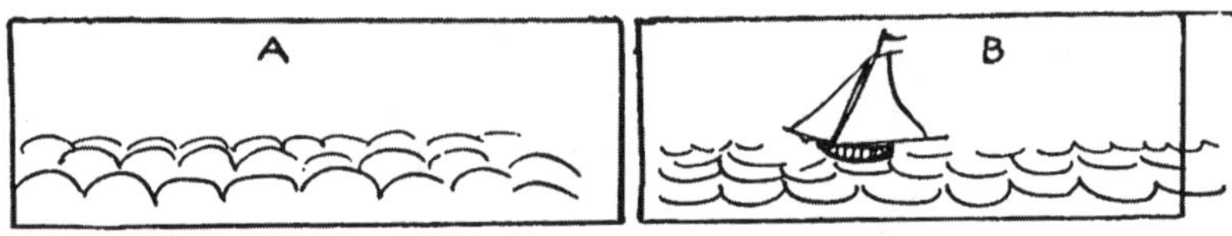

Fig. 7

The lines inside the frame, by themselves, would hardly be recognized as representing glass, but draw objects beyond, partly hidden, and the meaning becomes clear.

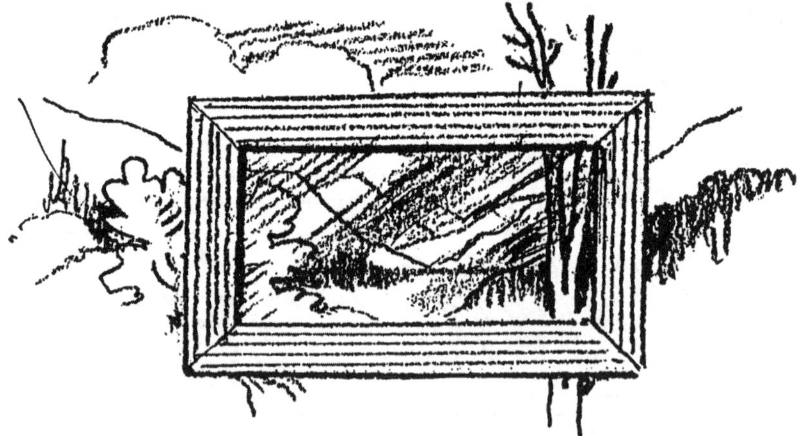

Fig 8 – The Oblique Lines Suggest Glass.

Notes.—Subjects suitable for beginners will be found on the following pages: 55, 58, 59, 60 (parts of Fig. 16), 63 (Fig. 21), 64, 65, (Fig. 25), 75, 76, 82, 83, 85, 86, 90, 93, 95, 96, 97, 99, 102, 108, 110, 111, 112, 119, 134 (Fig. 6), 135, 136 (Fig. 9), 140, 141 (Fig. 2), 144 (Fig. 8), 145, 146 (Fig. 11), 150 (Figs. 1 and 2), 158, 161, 163, 165, 169, 170 (Fig. 3), 181, 182 (Fig. 1), 189, 202, 204, 207, 208, 218, 219, 224, 226, 227, 229, 230, 233, 234, 235, 236, 245, 246, 255 (Fig. 2), 264, 265, 267, 268, 269, 275, 276.

CHAPTER VI

ELEMENTARY LINES

Lines in drawing are made in several ways. The smallest lines are made by means of the medium (pencil, crayon, pen, or brush), held so as to be controlled principally by the fingers, wrist, elbow, or even by the arm at the shoulder socket. In a sitting position, the two former are most used; the latter two movements are more frequently used while standing, as at the blackboard. Small details are usually

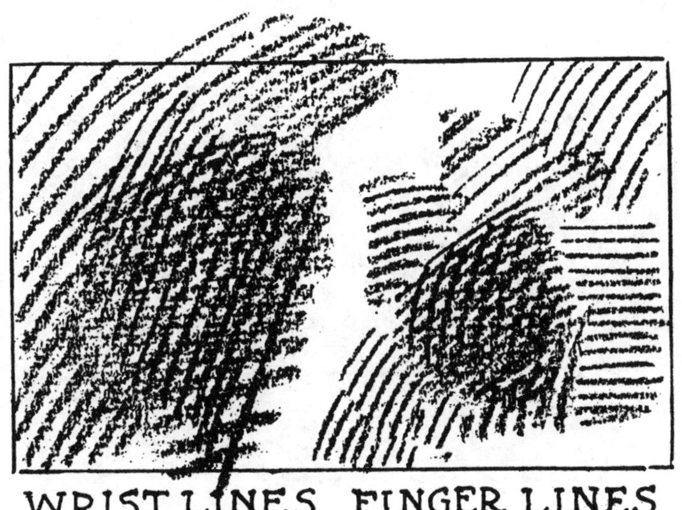

Fig. 1

executed by the control of the thumb and first and second fingers.

Broad Effects.—More freedom and broader effects are produced by the movement of the fingers and the motion of the hand radiating from the wrist. Still more sweeping effects are secured by holding the hand nearly rigid and obtaining actions by means of the forearm swung from the elbow. A still greater radius may be had, though infrequently required, by swinging the full length of the arm, as, for instance, in describing a circle on the blackboard several feet in circumference.

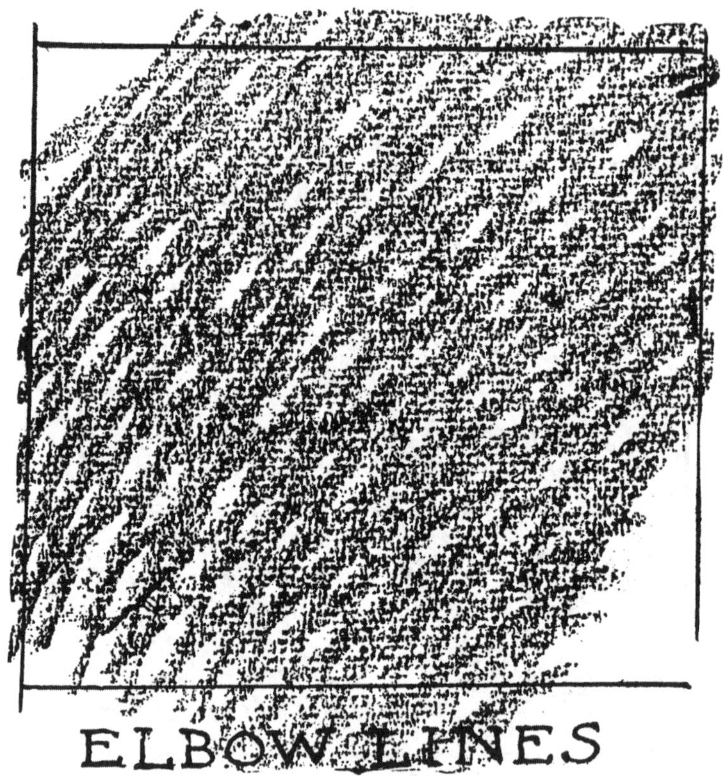

Fig. 2

Scratchy and Unevenly Spaced Lines, with few exceptions, such as when drawing grasses, etc., are to be avoided The upper lines in Fig. 3 are of the scratchy and uneven kind, while those below are more deliberately and carefully placed. In Fig. 4 the difference between the correct lines and the reverse is made apparent.

Fig. 5 shows practice lines that should be repeated over and over again until you become quite expert in their use. To avoid tiresomeness, they are introduced with frequency into other examples in which interest is obtained by enclosing the practice lines in various forms. In A, the lines are about as evenly placed as could be expected from someone after several months of training. In B, the lines are such as would be made by the absolutely untrained hand and eye.

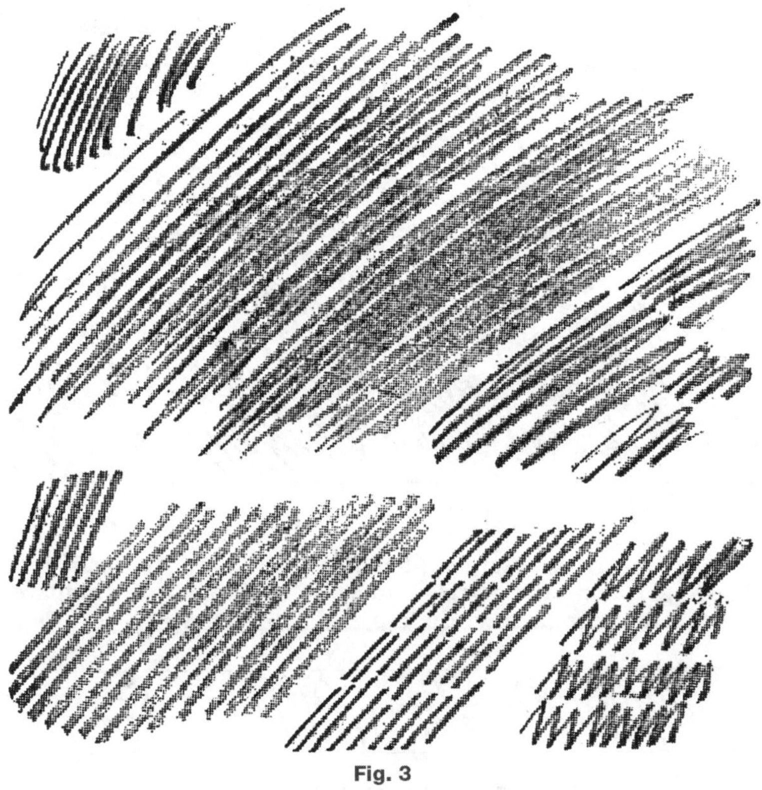

Fig. 3

In Fig. 6, C shows lines enclosed in order to train oneself to stop the lines within prescribed limits.

Also in Fig. 6, at D, the lines are drawn backward and forward quickly without removing the pencil.

E consists of lines drawn quickly, but by lifting the pencil at the end of each stroke.

At F the lines are broken, but firmly and evenly placed.

Even Pressure Desirable.—Keep in mind that it is most

desirable to learn to make a line with an even pressure, from the moment the pencil or crayon touches the paper until it leaves it; that is, the making of a line that neither presses into the paper at the beginning nor drops off at the end.

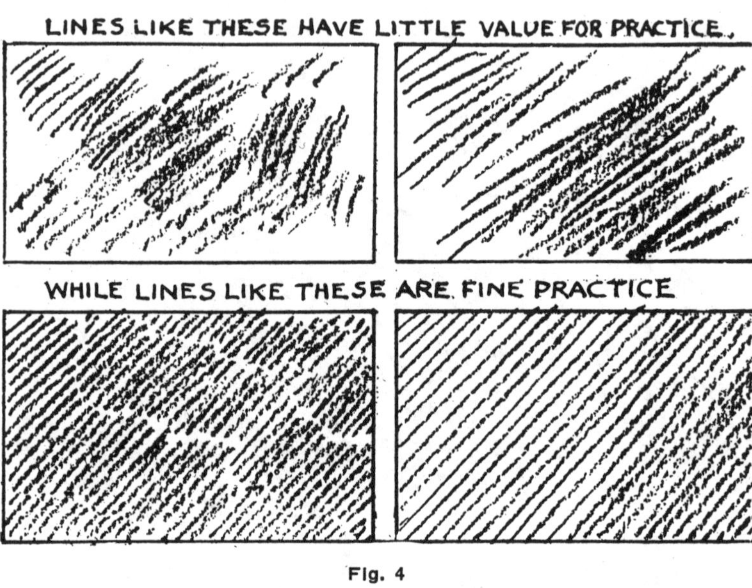

Fig. 4

Fig. 7 gives practice lines that are used in nearly all drawings, from the parallel lines at the top, the graduated lines in the second row, the cross-hatch lines near the bottom

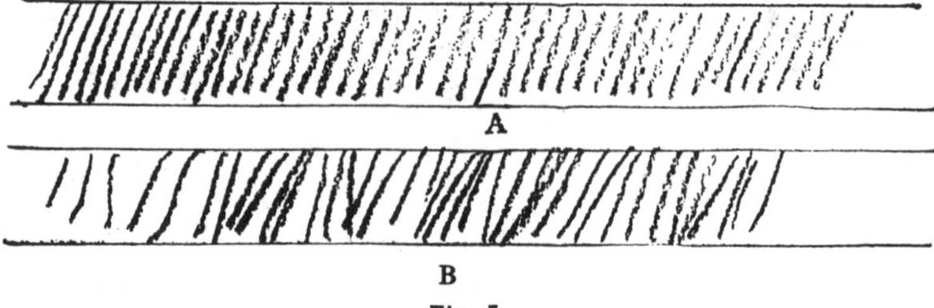

Fig. 5

and, lastly, the solid shading in which the lines are placed so closely together as to nearly or quite lose their identity.

Repeated Practice.—Fig. 6 shows practice lines that should be repeated over and over again until you become quite expert in their use. To avoid tiresomeness, they should be introduced with frequency, only a short time, however, being devoted to each exercise.

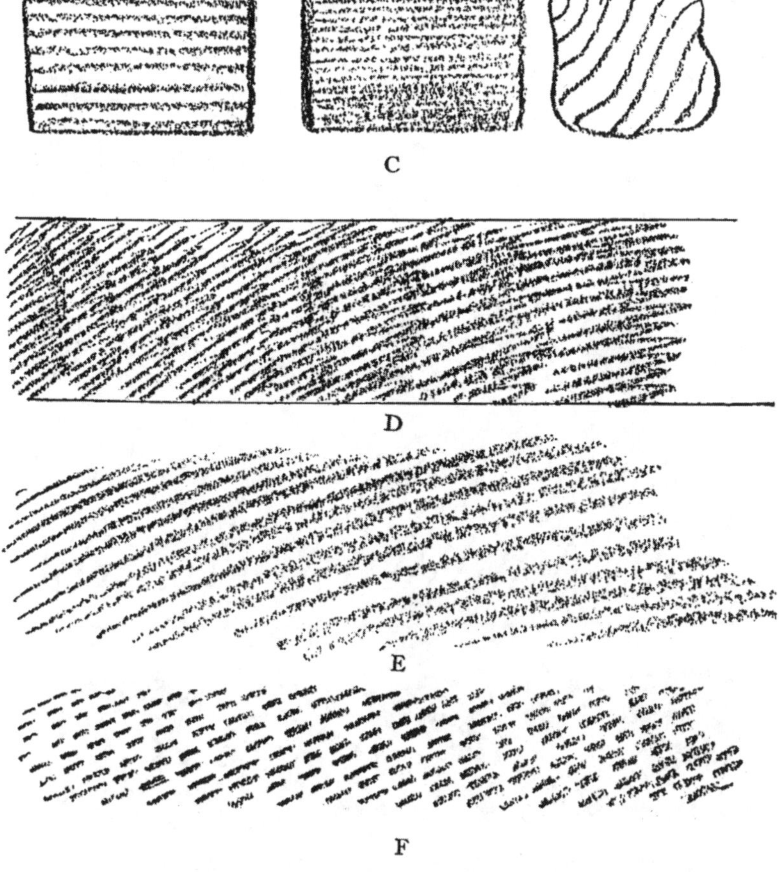

Fig. 6

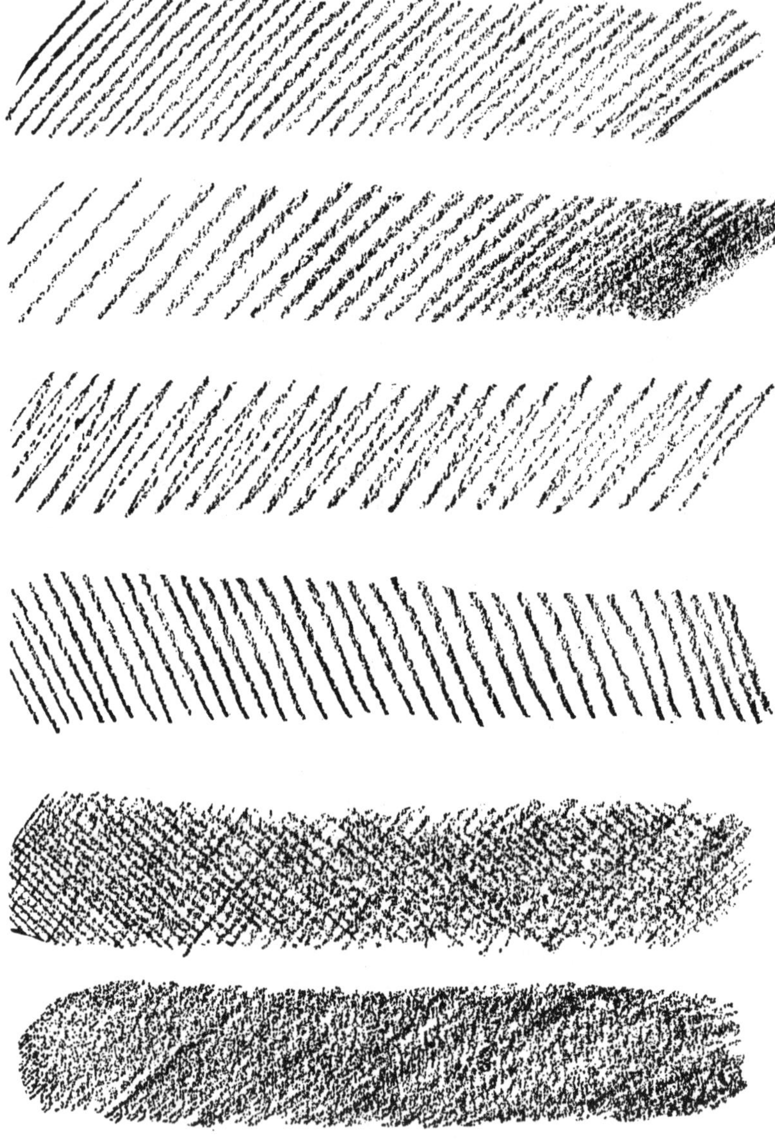

Fig. 7—Simple Line Exercises

CHAPTER VII

EARLY EXERCISES

Application of Elementary Lines.—The reason for placing the exercise lines in the early exercises in enclosures of various shapes, rather than in formal squares (which are wearisome and uninteresting, and therefore hurriedly practiced if not altogether slighted through a desire to get at something that is interesting) seems sufficiently apparent. It is just as well and easy at the outset to encourage and cultivate a taste for form while engaged in the necessary practice of making flat tints. There is no use in making the study of drawing a treadmill. Drawing should, right from the start, be along the lines of pictorial art; therefore, the use of different forms, of more or less interest and beauty, in connection with practice exercise has been adopted. Experience has shown that this method is of benefit to those learning to draw and does not result in the usual weariness and impatience engendered by the use of simple square spaces.

Odd Shapes Preferable.—Besides, the use of odd shapes found in the enclosures teaches a greater control and adaptability in the use of pencil or pen than would be gained by the stopping of lines within unvarying angular borders.

In Figs. 1, 2, 3 and 4 the various practice lines are used in connection with the simplest forms that may be copied or drawn from memory or imagination. Fig. 4 is an exercise in copying aided by means of twelve squares of equal size. To obviate any difficulty that may arise, for the beginner, in drawing this example, draw what is seen in a single square, irrespective of what appears in the other. For instance, draw all the lines in a single square, as if it were a separate picture; for example, make the square marked A or B.

Simple Landscapes.—Fig. 5 presents five simple landscapes in which the economy in lines used is a leading fea-

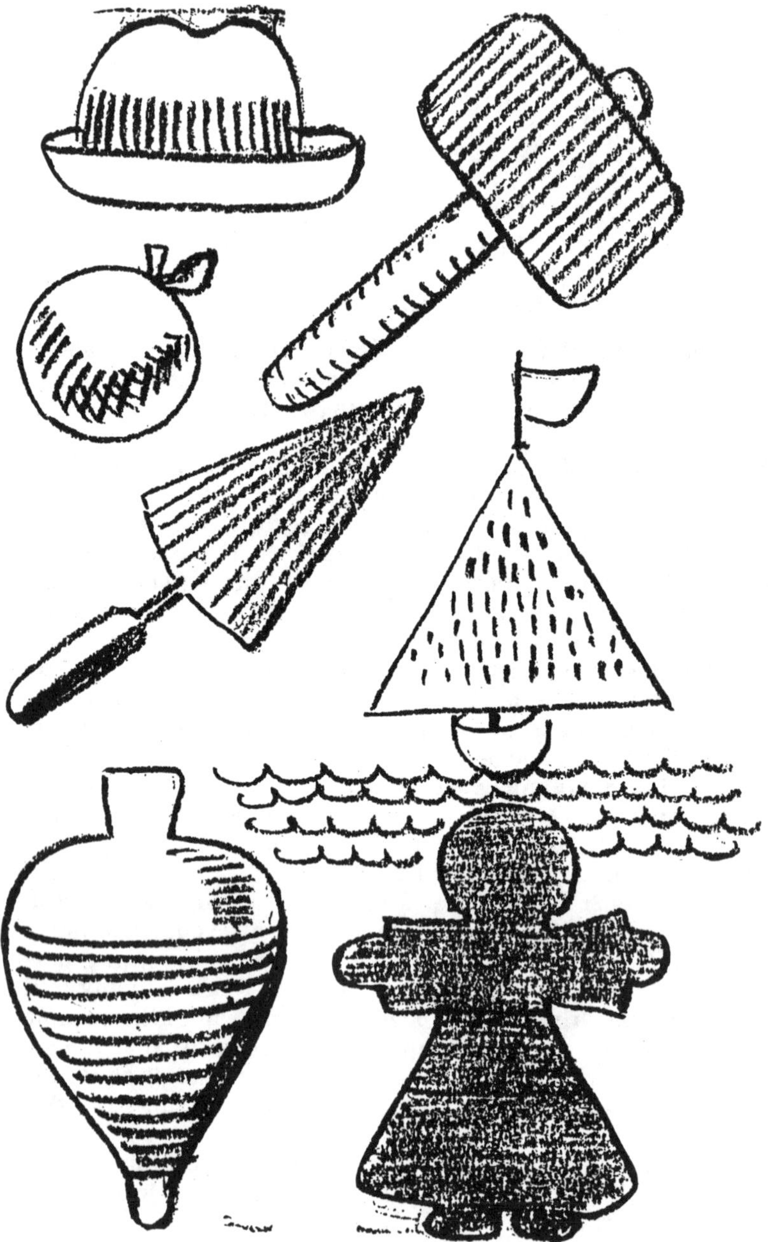

Fig. 1

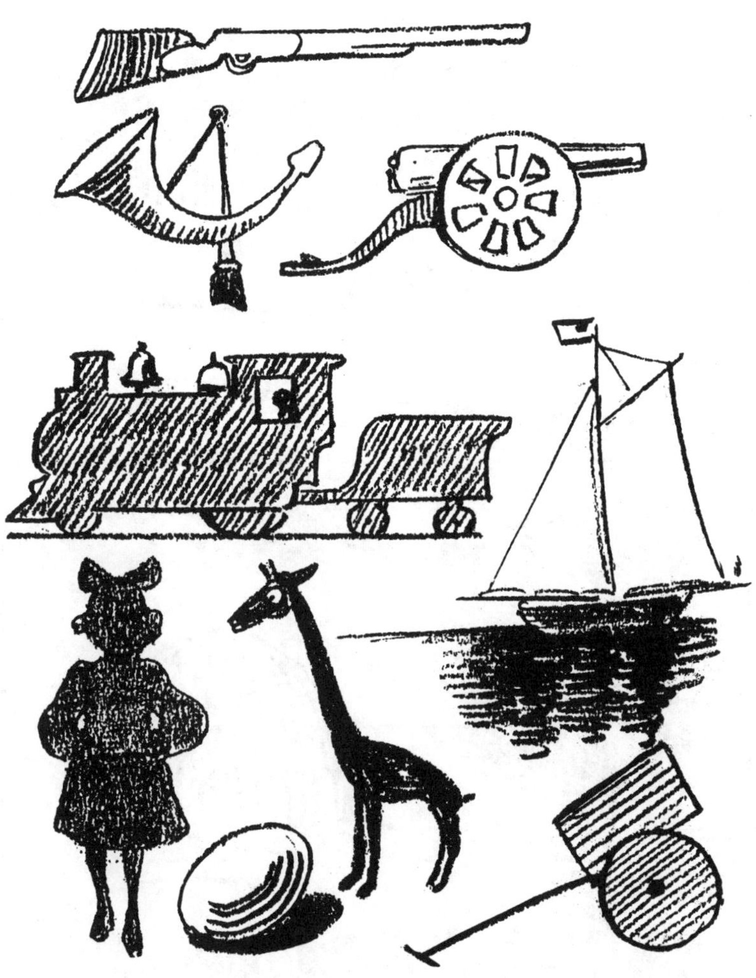

Fig 2

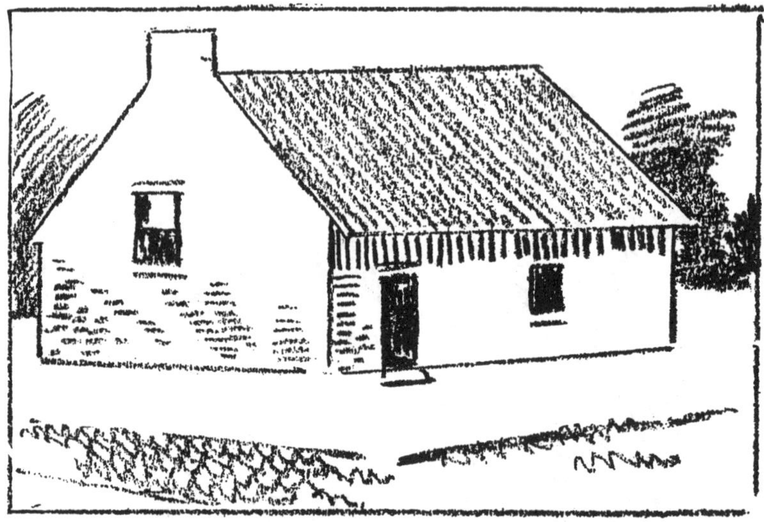

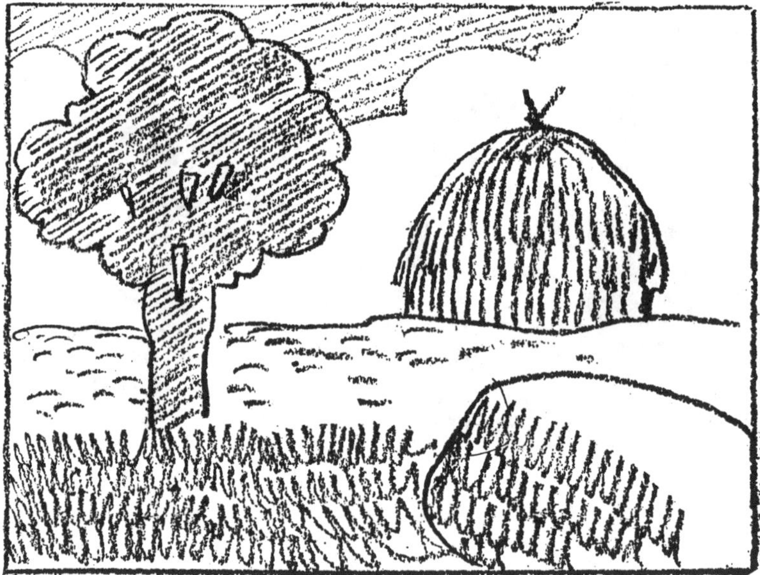

Fig. 3

ture. One will derive benefit from the study of such examples. The fewer lines that can be used to produce the general effect the better.

Rapid Line Exercises.—Fig. 6 comprises subjects suitable for pencil sketches. They are examples in rapid line effects where strength of execution is aimed at rather than detail, of which there is a conspicuous absence. The introduction of color into this will be easy.

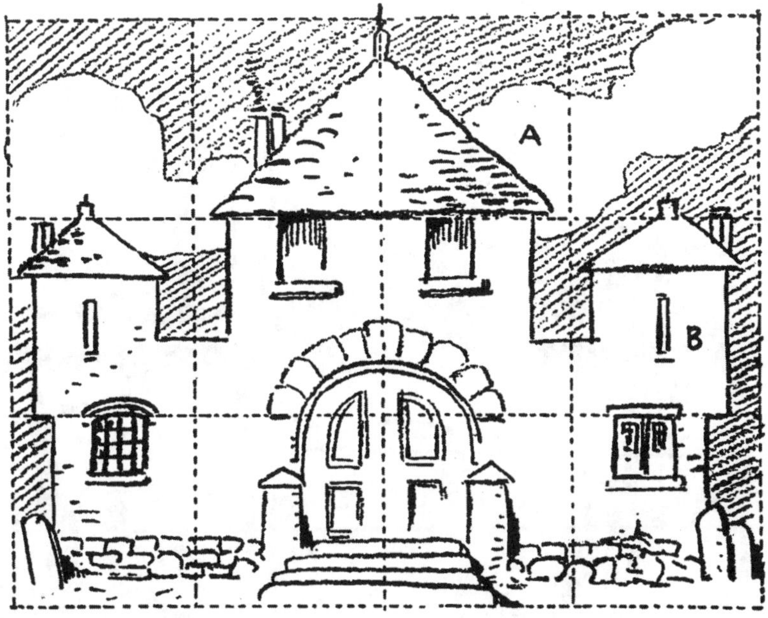

Fig. 4

Further Application of Lines.—In the simple landscape, Fig. 8, will be found many of the lines which enter into nearly all practice work. First, as in Fig. 7, faintly sketch the general masses, so they can be easily erased if they are not properly placed. The cut on page 44 shows how this is done. The little figures at the right may be introduced into the finished picture. If used, their placing is to be left subject to your individual taste and ingenuity. Should they be used in the foreground, they should be enlarged con-

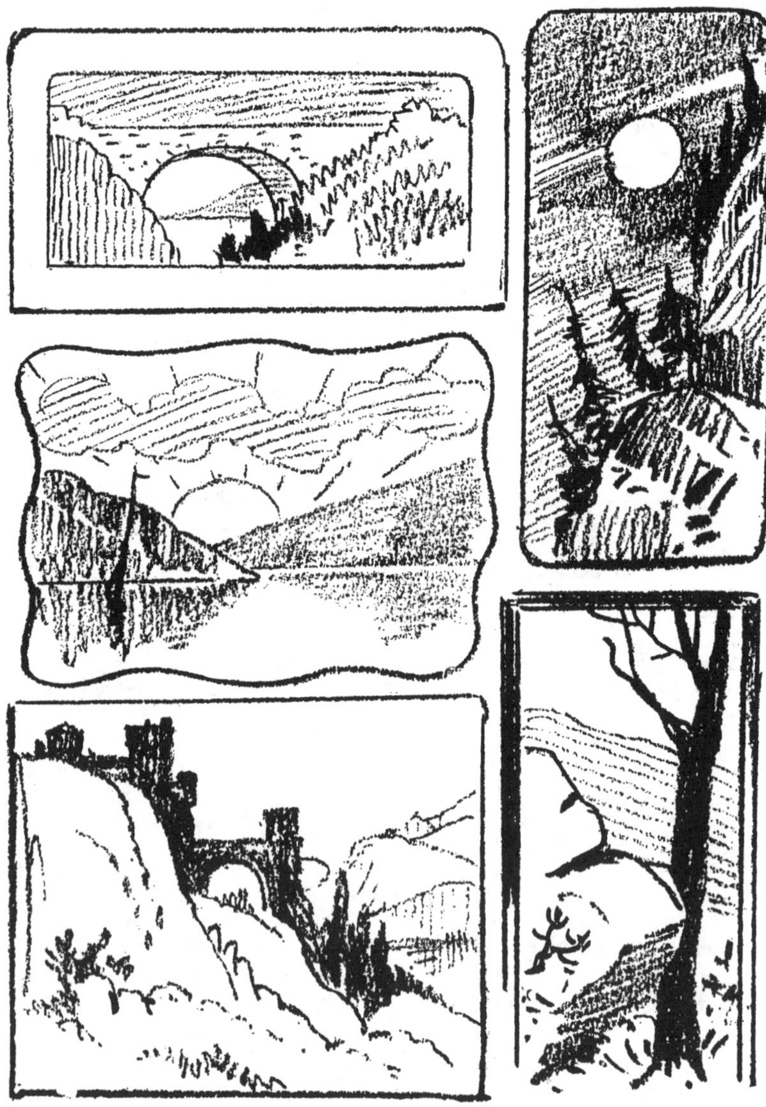

Fig. 5

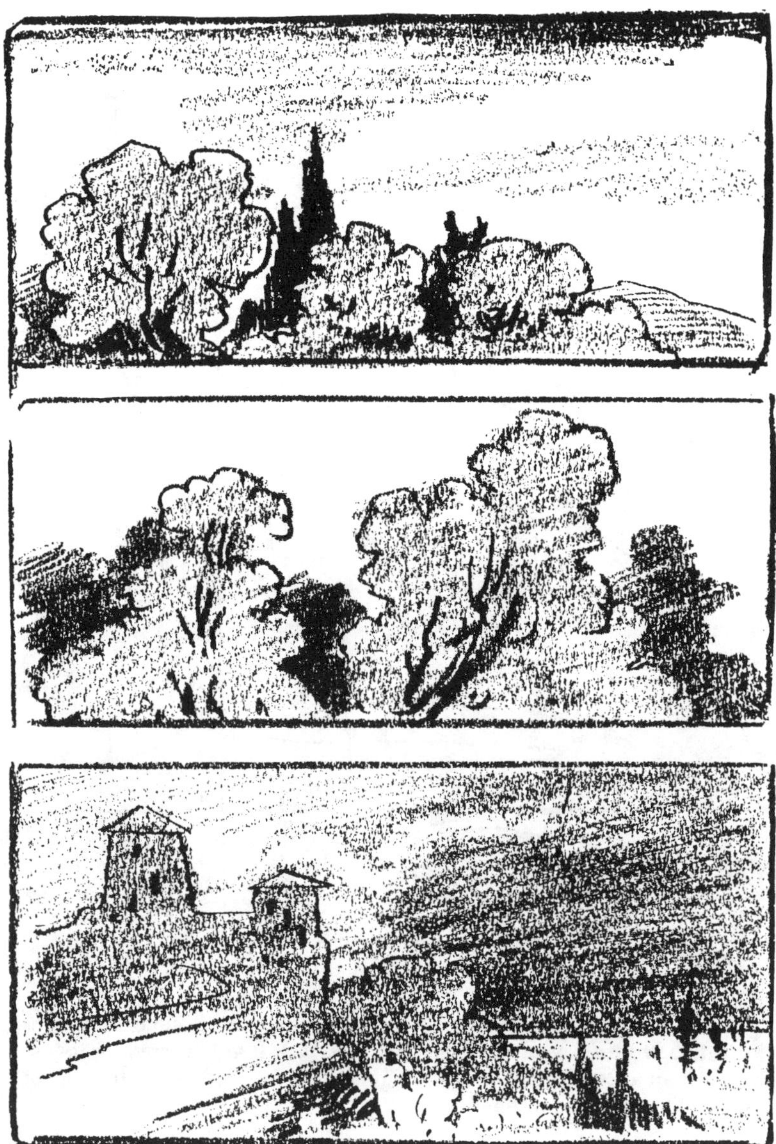

Fig. 6

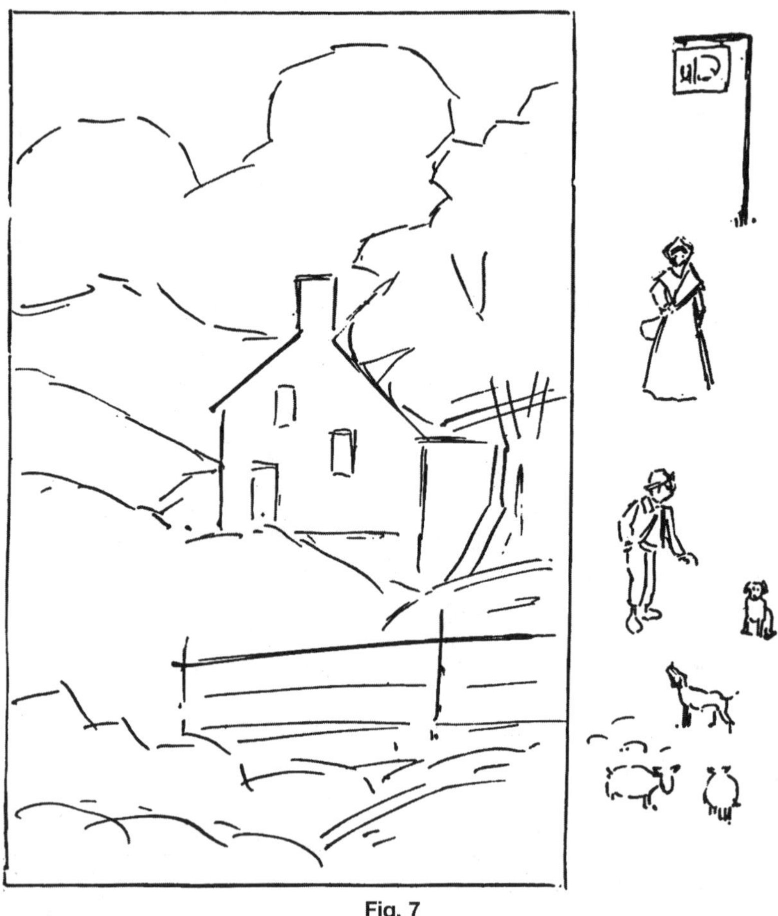

Fig. 7

Your drawings should be as neat in appearance as possible. Nevertheless, it is better to have a mussy-looking drawing that is correct in its essentials than a clean, spickspan drawing full of inaccuracies in the way of misplaced lines, tones or shadows.

siderably. The letters locate the corresponding lines in Fig. 8 and are not for use in your sketch, but are placed to show where the corresponding lines and tints are to be found.

Drawing Actual Objects

Subjects for Simple Drawings.—Draw the front of the house in which you live. If it is a simply constructed building this will not be difficult. If it is somewhat ornate in its facade, draw only a part of the detail, such as the front door or a window or two. Draw any of the outbuildings, such as the barn, the shed, or a chicken coop, or garage.

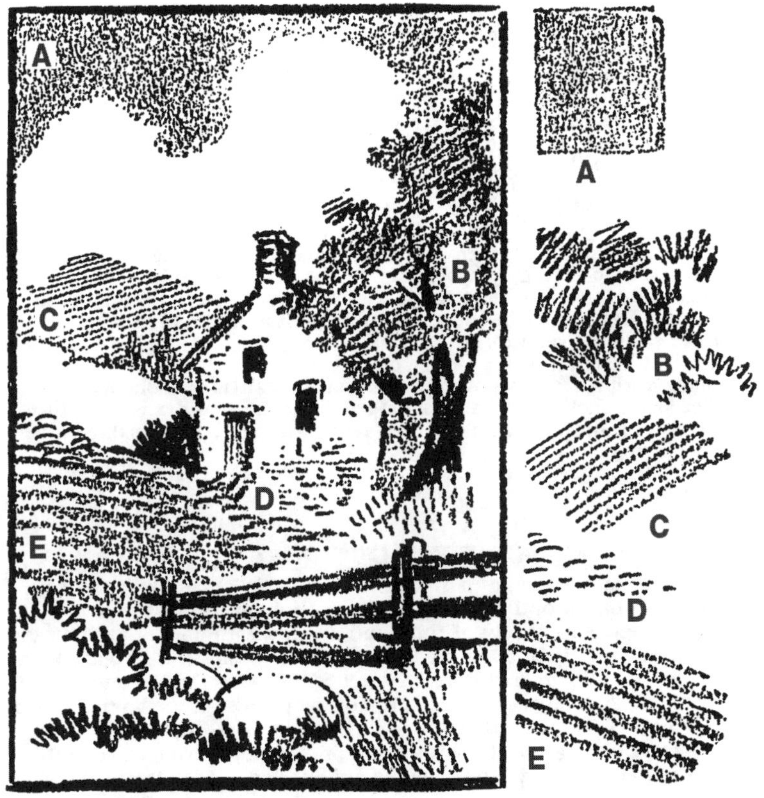

Fig. 8

As mere suggestions from memory subjects, the following are offered. Many others will suggest themselves according to the surroundings:

SUBJECTS

Draw
The house you live in.
The barn door.
The barn.
The shed.
The dog house.
The wheel of the wheel-barrow.
The wheel-barrow.
The handle of the hatchet.
The hatchet.
Draw a wagon or a buggy from memory.
Draw the wheels of an automobile.
The automobile itself.
Draw any piece of furniture.
Anything used in the kitchen.
Any simple garden tool.
Any carpenter's tool, such as a saw, plane, chisel, mallet, hammer, etc.
Draw any tool used by a blacksmith, shoemaker, or other artisan.

Draw any article of clothing: A hat, cap, slipper, boot, or shoe. (Coats and dresses may be found rather difficult at first and may be omitted from the earliest exercises.)

Draw a barrel, a pail, a dipper or cup.

Show with a few lines what a lamp or a flashlight looks like.

The pupil should not be discouraged if he fails to draw more than a few of these subjects. If he can do a few fairly well, he is making a very good beginning.

CORRECT OUTLINES.

One should become as perfect as possible in one's ability to depict things by means of outlines. The outline is important always. Even in a drawing composed entirely of tints and shadows, the areas of light and shadow have their definite outline and they must be accurately placed. The limit of one's ability to draw correctly an outline is the limit of one's ability to reproduce, with any art utensil, be it brush or pencil, the boundaries of given objects. To do the latter well is a great part of all that can be learned from instruction in art. Unless one can represent form by means of outline one will not be able to do so by means of light and shade effects alone.

Notes.—Other exercises will be found on following pages: All in chapter VIII (except Fig. 4 and 5), pages 56, 60 (Fig. 17), 62 (Fig. 20), 77, 78, 87, 88, 91, 92, 93, 101, 106, 111, 113, 114, 115, 116, 117, 118, 119, 120, 122, 124, 125, 150 (Figs. 3 and 4), 164, 166, 167, 170, 173, 174, 175, 180, 187, 188, 190, 193, 196, 197, 199 (Fig. 7), 206, 214 (Figs. 25 and 26), 220, 232, 238, 243, 243, 255 (Fig. 2), 257. Selections from 259, 260, 269, 276, 277 and 278.

CHAPTER VIII

SIMPLE STORY PICTURES ILLUSTRATING THE MONTHS

The value of these exercises consists largely in fostering one's inventive faculty in bringing out individual ingenuity. Depend on your own imagination entirely, and afterwards evaluate and improve the most palpable errors.

The Subjects.—The stories illustrated may be original, or from suggestions offered by simple nursery tales and rhymes. For instance:

John flew a kite, but the wind was so strong that the string broke and the kite fell towards the ground. But it never reached the ground. It was caught in a tree and stayed there for a long time, so long, indeed, that there was nothing left of the kite except a few rotting sticks. Did John cry? No, he went home and made another kite.

To illustrate this, one or more pictures may be made.

Examples: A boy flying a kite. The kite falling (upside down). The kite lodged in a tree.

Reverse the Operation.—For instance, draw a picture and write a little story about it.

As for example: A picture of a bird feeding a little bird in a nest. The story: "One day a bird fed its little one and then flew away to get another meal, but the mother bird never came back. A bad boy threw a stone at it just as it was picking up a nice little worm for the birdling's luncheon. Wouldn't the bad little boy feel sorry if he knew that the little bird in the nest starved to death because its mother never came back?"

Many of the Mother Goose Melodies provide easy, yet interesting, material for simple illustrations, thus:

MOTHER GOOSE MELODIES SIMPLY ILLUSTRATED

Anniversaries.—On holidays, national anniversaries and other seasonable occasions, or rather for some days preceding

MERRY
CHRISTMAS
LITTLE JACK HORNER
PUSSY-CAT, PUSSY CAT
GOOSEY, GOOSEY GANDER
RIDE A COCK-HORSE.
JACK AND JILL
POST NO
BILLS
HUMPTY DUMPTY.
TOM, THE PIPER'S SON.
A
B
C
D
A, B, C, TUMBLE DOWN D.
SIX LITTLE SNAILS.

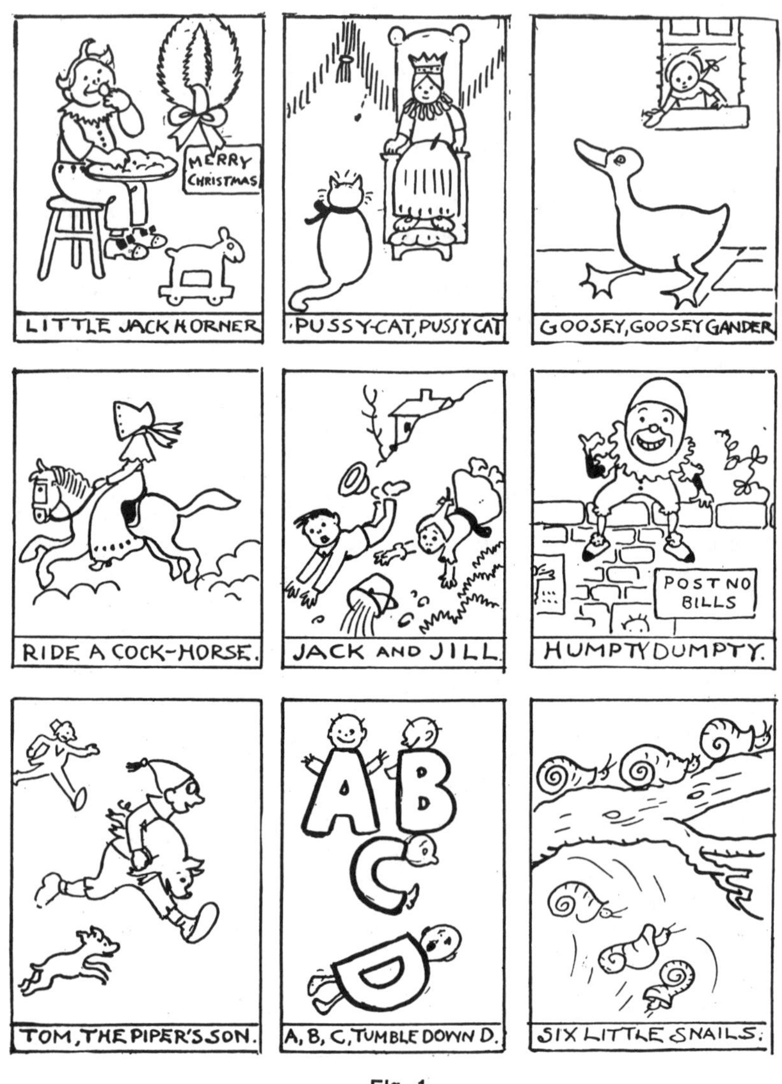

Fig. 1

them, it is well to direct the pupil's energies toward the symbols and pictures by which these events and persons are commemorated.

New Year's Day suggests Father Time, his scythe and hour glass. The New Year itself, as portrayed by a child, illustrating the new born year with the date thereof made prominent. Good resolutions—someone writing in a diary, etc.

February presents Washington's and Lincoln's birthdays as subjects, besides Valentine's day. Events in the lives of the two great patriots are good subjects, or simply their portraits surmounted by or surmounting, for instance, a hatchet and a cherry tree trunk, or a rail fence or broken shackles, made into a frame—as the case may be.

SEPTEMBER.—Draw Autumn flowers, such as the golden-rod, sunflower, and others found in your locality, grasses, grains, bushes and trees.

OCTOBER—Draw fruits, Autumn leaves, pumpkins and Jack-o'-lanterns.

NOVEMBER.—Draw objects suggested by Thanksgiving—The Mayflower, Native Americans, wigwams, turkeys and corn.

DECEMBER.—Subjects suggested by Christmas, Hanukkah, or Kwanzaa, such as trees, stars, holly, Santa Claus and reindeer, monorahs, dreidels, kinaras, toys of all kinds.

JANUARY.—Eskimo huts, snow forts, snow men, snow crystals, skating and coasting.

FEBRUARY.—Subjects suggested by Lincoln's and Washington's birthdays and Valentine Day.

MARCH.—Draw kites, windmills, boats and pussy-willows.

APRIL.—Draw buds and twigs, tulips and other early Spring flowers, umbrellas, ducks.

MAY.—Draw May-baskets, birds and their nests and eggs, trees, flowers and simple landscapes.

JUNE.—Draw flowers, vacation scenes, landscapes.

The Months.—The next page offers a suggestion for each month of the year. The designs are intended for those who are well advanced as well as for beginners. The latter may use them as copies, while the former may find in them bases for improvement in form and idea.

HAPPY NEW YEAR
JANUARY
FEBRUARY
MARCH
APRIL
MAY
SCHOOL
CLOSED
TO THE PICNIC
JUNE
JULY
AUGUST
SEPTEMBER
OCTOBER
MAYFLOWER
NOVEMBER
DECEMBER

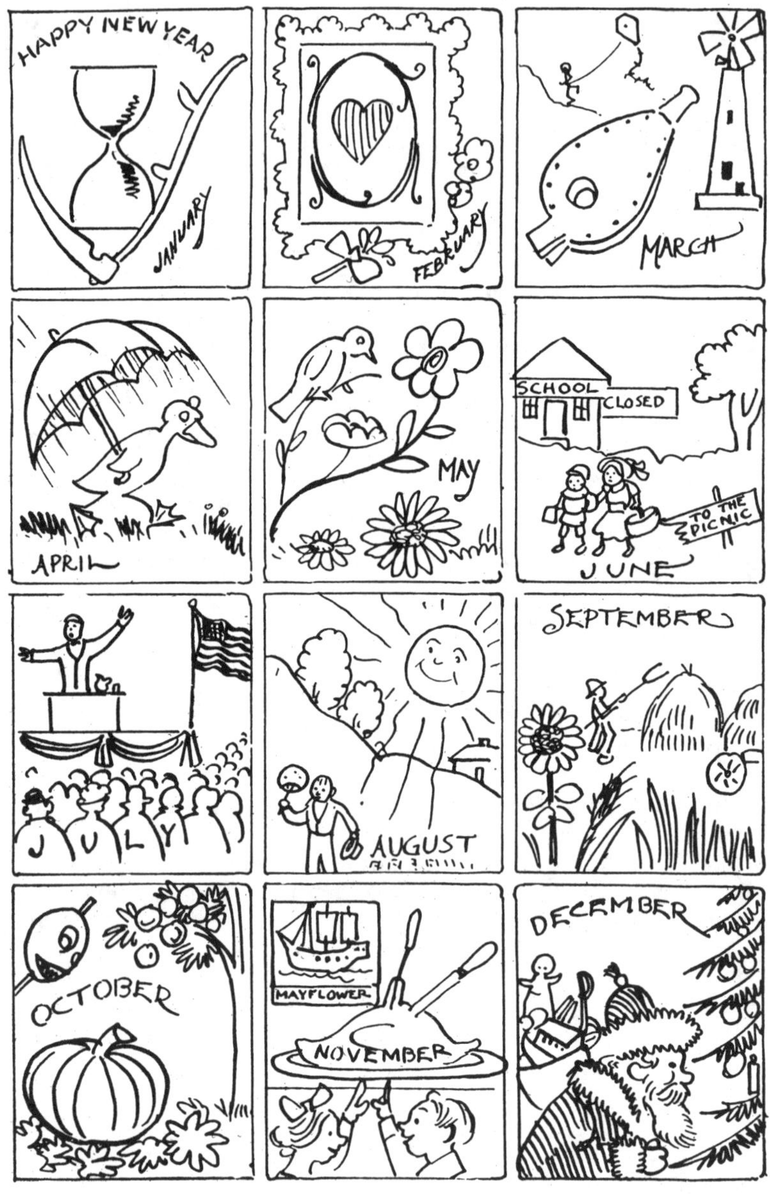

Fig. 2

Here are two suggestions for simple story pictures:

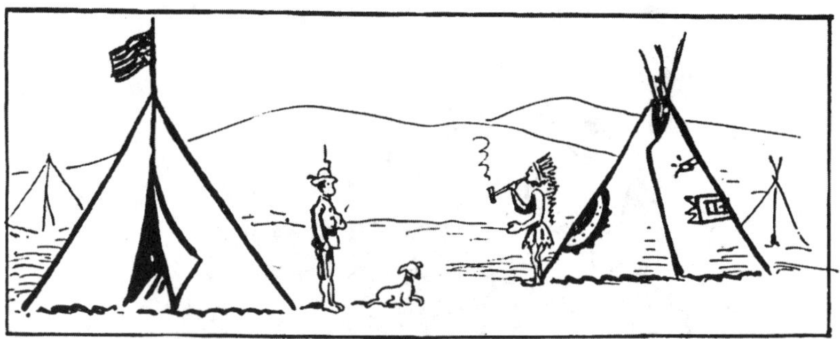

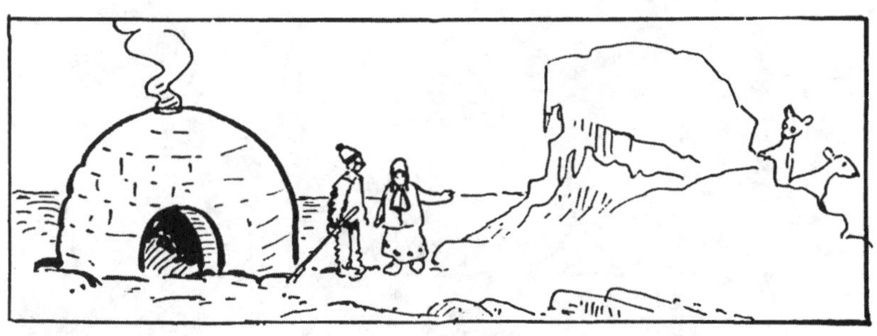

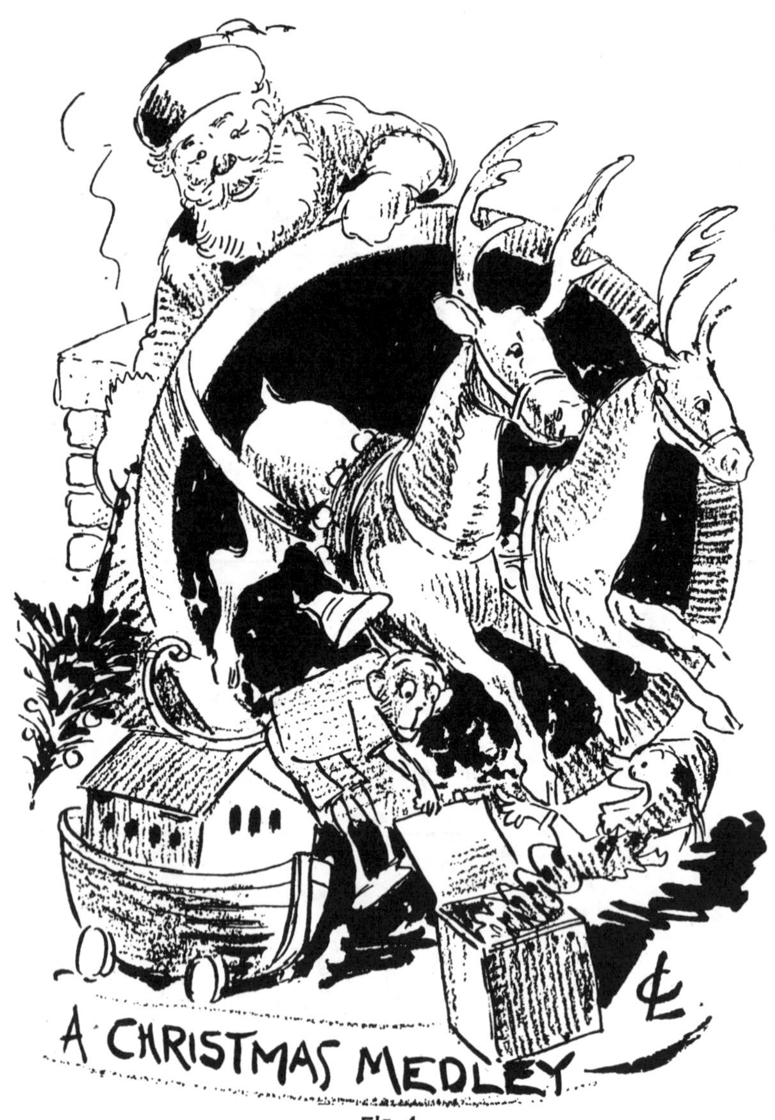

Fig. 4

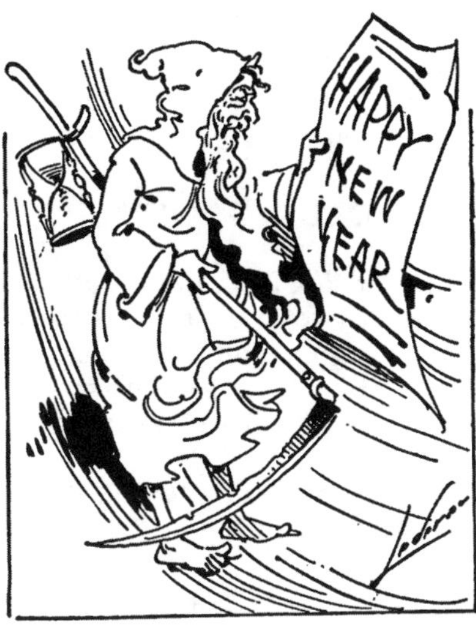

Fig. 5

MEMORY DRAWING.

Practice drawing from memory. Take a single figure, a simple subject, and, having drawn it two or three times from the original, lay both aside and then, by no aid except that of your memory, draw the object once more. Then compare it with the original and see how near it you have made the sketch. This is an interesting as well as a practically helpful exercise.

CORRECTING ERRORS.

There are many benefits to frequently criticizing your own work. Thus only is improvement possible.

It is a mistake to suppose that it is necessary to have separate instructions for drawing each form or even each group of forms. Certain fixed rules govern drawing, and, once these are mastered, they can be applied to almost anything that can be represented by pen, pencil or brush.

Notes.—As you progress you may take up the following exercises: pp. 52, 53, All in chapter IX; pp. 67, 69; All in chapter X; 73, 74, 75, 79, 87 89, All in chapters XIV, XVI, XVII, XVIII, XIX XX, XXI, pp. i76, 178, 186, 209, 222, 224 238, 243, 244, 251, 256, 257 Selections from pp. 258, 259, 260, 270, 271 272, 273, 274, 283, 292 (Fig. 16), 294, 295.

Pen-drawing, the study of perspective, composition, light and shade, nature sketching, charcoal and crayon work, and other studies may be taken.

CHAPTER IX

PAPER FOLDING AND CUTTING

Paper folding and cutting is a valuable adjunct to the study of drawing and adds greatly to one's resources for acquiring form knowledge, besides being a delightful phase of manual training. Almost unconsciously one gains familiarity with geometrical figures, which, later on, will tend to lessen difficulty in studying geometry itself.

Paper folding and cutting adds to one's interest in drawing, because of the intimate conception of giving form from which the drawing is produced.

Paper in Strips.—Procure paper in strips or in squares. Scratch pads, about 4 by 8 inches square will answer the purpose. In addition to this, you should supply yourself with 6-inch squares of Manila paper.

If the paper is not square, place the shorter edge on the longer, then fold over at the corner, even with the edge, as in Fig. I.

Creative Ability.—Much of this work will depend on creative ability. Besides merely learning the folding and cutting, it is essential to do so with care and precision.

Paper folding adds greatly to one's resources for acquiring one's own knowledge.

Once you have obtained paper from which squares from three to four inches in width may be cut, observe the following directions: (See Fig. I.)

Oblongs.—Place the shorter edge on the longer, fold at the corner and cut even with the edge folded over from b to a (Fig. 1). Fold the lower edge of the square even with the upper edge. This divides the square into two *oblongs* (Fig. 2).

Right Triangles.—Fold another square from corner to corner (Fig. 3). This gives the diagonal. It also divides the squares into two right triangles.

To Form an Equilateral, or equal-sided triangle, fold a diameter at right angles to the lower side of a square, as in Fig. 4, for the angles of an equilateral triangle are always in

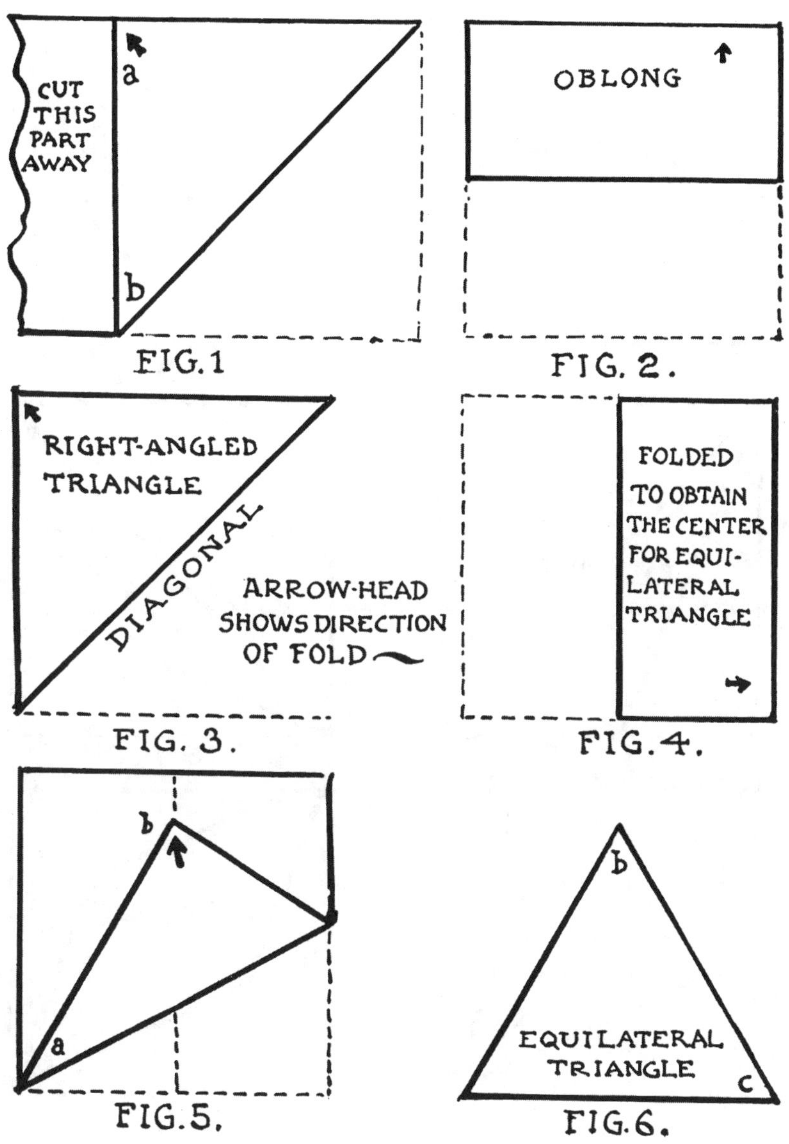
CUT
THIS
PART
AWAY
a
b
FIG. 1
OBLONG
FIG. 2.
RIGHT-ANGLED
TRIANGLE
DIAGONAL
ARROW-HEAD
SHOWS DIRECTION
OF FOLD
FIG. 3.
FOLDED
TO OBTAIN
THE CENTER
FOR EQUI-
LATERAL
TRIANGLE
FIG. 4.
b
a
FIG. 5.
b
EQUILATERAL
TRIANGLE
c
FIG. 6.

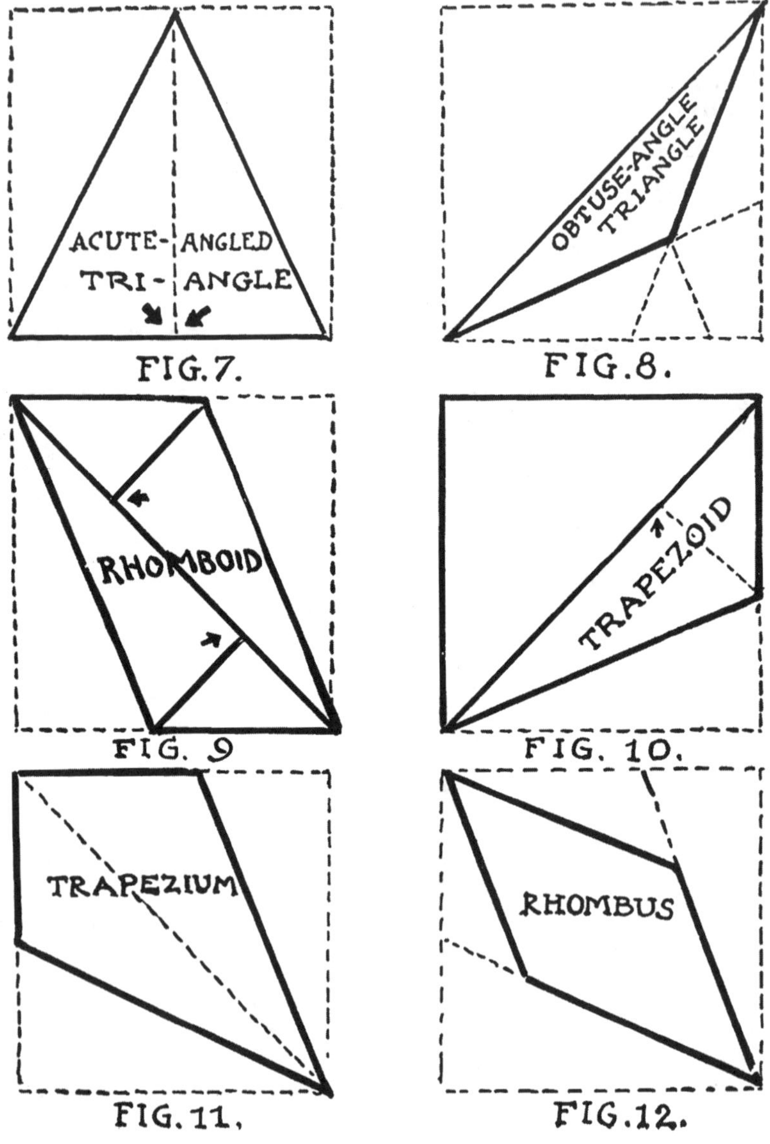
ACUTE-ANGLED
TRI-ANGLE
FIG.7.
OBTUSE-ANGLE
TRIANGLE
FIG.8.
RHOMBOID
FIG. 9
TRAPEZOID
FIG. 10.
TRAPEZIUM
FIG.11.
RHOMBUS
FIG.12.

a line that would bisect the opposite side. Since the angles of this triangle must be equal, we fold the lower edge until one angle touches the diameter, as in Fig. 5. Then cut along the line a b. By duplicating this operation with the opposite corner, an equilateral triangle is formed.

To Form an Acute Triangle.—Fold at right angles to the lower edge of the square, as in Fig. 4, to get the center; now fold from the upper end of the diameter to each of the lower angles, as shown by arrows in Fig. 7.

To Form an Obtuse Triangle.—Fold one diagonal of the square, then fold the lower edge over until it touches the same line. Next cut the diagonal and the two folds to their point of intersection, as shown by dotted lines in Fig. 8.

To Form a Rhomboid.—Take a square, fold a diagonal, then fold the left edge of the square so it will coincide with the diagonal. Then fold the right edge to coincide with the diagonal. Cut the last two folds, as indicated by the heaviest lines, as in Fig. 9.

To Form a Trapezoid.—Fold one diagonal of the square, then the lower edge so it will fall on the diagonal. Result, Trapezoid, Fig. 10.

To Form a Trapezium.—Fold one diagonal. Then fold so that the lower edge of the paper will coincide with the diagonal. Now fold again so that the right edge will be on the diagonal. Cut the last two folds. Result, a Trapezium, Fig. 11.

To Form a Rhombus.—Fold square same as for Trapezium. Then fold the shorter sides of the Trapezium over until they coincide with the diagonal. Cut the folds as indicated by the heavy lines, as shown in Fig. 12.

Combination Form as Model.—Cut out of cardboard a combination form composed of a square and an equilateral triangle, as in A, Fig. I3. Bend it at the dotted ines.

The way to bend it straight is to cut *slightly,* the cardboard with a knife and straightedge. Do not cut *through* or even half way through, just a dent-like cut is sufficient. Then bend away from the dented line.

Cardboard bent properly.—Cardboard is composed of three or more (seldom less than three) sheets of paper pasted together. The effect of the bending of the cardboard, when a slight cut has been made, is to cause the *outer* sheet to break (see Fig. 14), leaving the other sheets bent but intact. Should a thick piece of cardboard be bent as described, and then bent in the opposite direction, the sheet is readily divided.

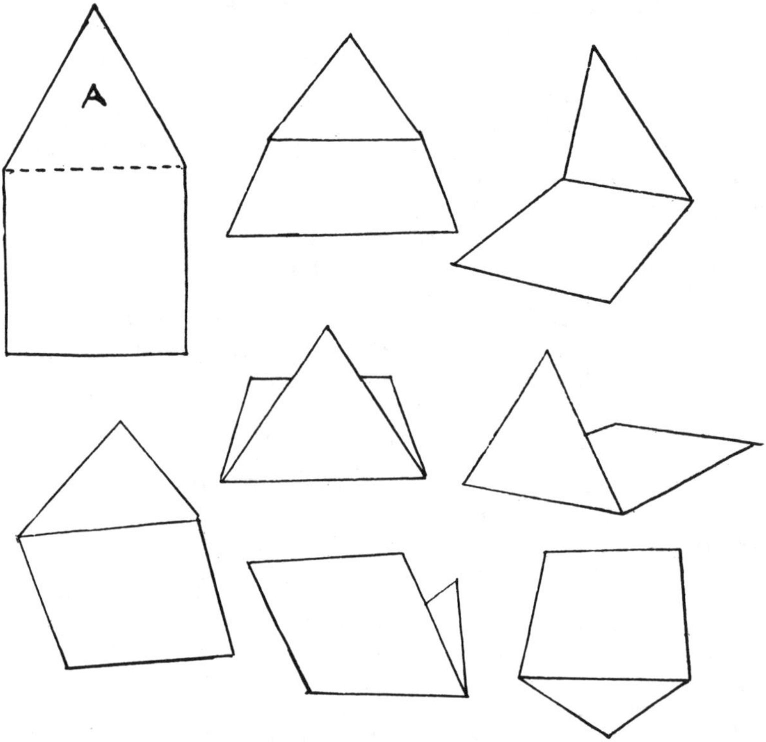

Fig. 13

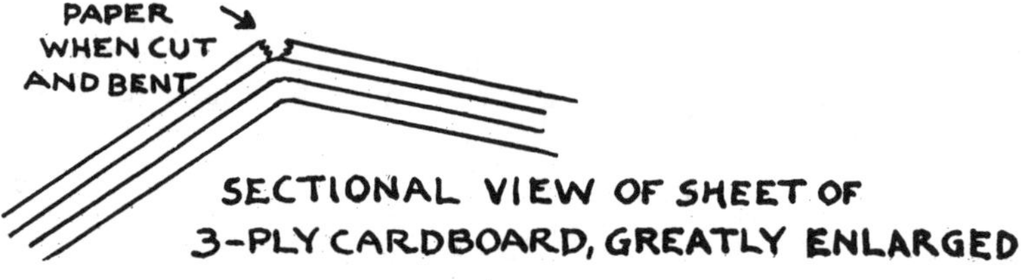

PAPER WHEN CUT AND BENT
SECTIONAL VIEW OF SHEET OF 3-PLY CARDBOARD, GREATLY ENLARGED

Fig. 14

Using the Model.—Having drawn, cut, and properly bent this form, proceed as follows: Hold the bent cardboard in your left hand, between the thumb and fourth finger. Then draw the form as seen by moving it in various directions, as indicated in Fig. 13.

For Two-Handed Exercise.—The angle at which the cardboard is bent may be varied also.

For ambidextrous exercise, hold the cardboard in the right hand and draw with the left.

Whether for right or left hand drawing, the paper on which the drawings are made should be tacked firmly.

A Christmas Tree.—Fold a piece of paper about five inches square. Draw half of the Christmas tree and the pot. Without unfolding the paper, cut the outlines of the pot. With the paper still folded, tear the jagged outlines of the tree. Now unfold paper. Cut out of white paper the shapes of the candles. Same for the candles' flames, but for these use red and yellow paper. Paste the candles and flames, alternating red and yellow flames.

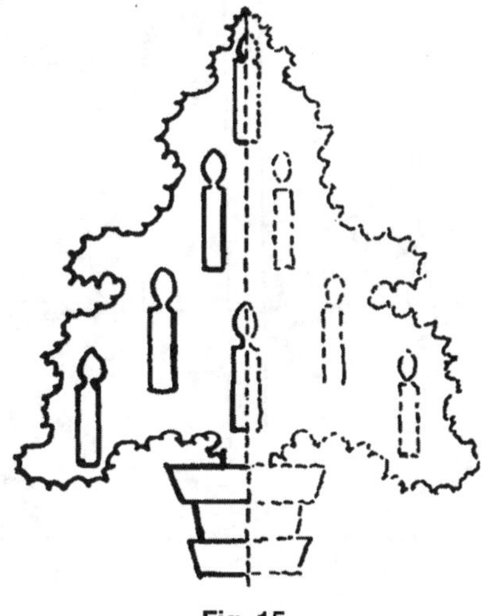

Fig. 15

Multi-Colored Cut-Out Pictures

A form of exercise, entertaining as well as instructive, is the use of multi-colored papers, in connection with paper cutting and drawing. The method which follows will be found much easier in application than the instructions would indicate.

The Materials.—Thin, colored paper of the tints indicated, cardboard, scissors and paste. If suitable colored paper is

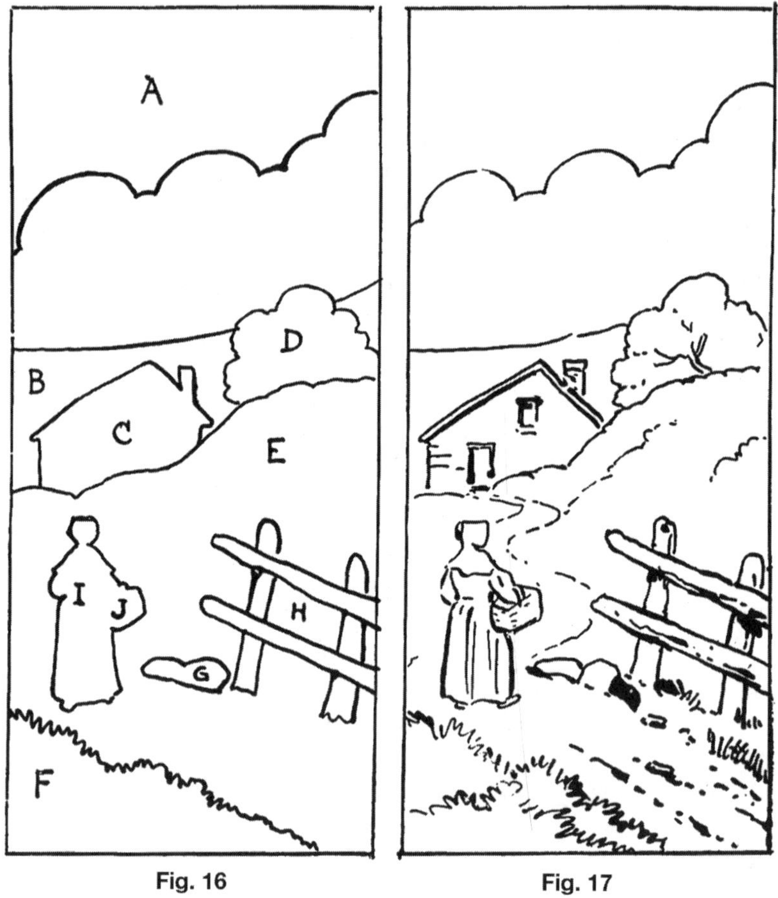

Fig. 16 Fig. 17

not available, white paper may be used and colored according to requirements.

The necessary materials for producing the scene described in Fig. 17: A piece of heavy, white cardboard, or mounting board, the latter preferred, size 4x8 inches; pieces of manila paper, yellow, green, blue, red, gray and brown paper.

Cut them out in the forms and according to the colors indicated in Fig. 18. The outlines may be drawn on the re-

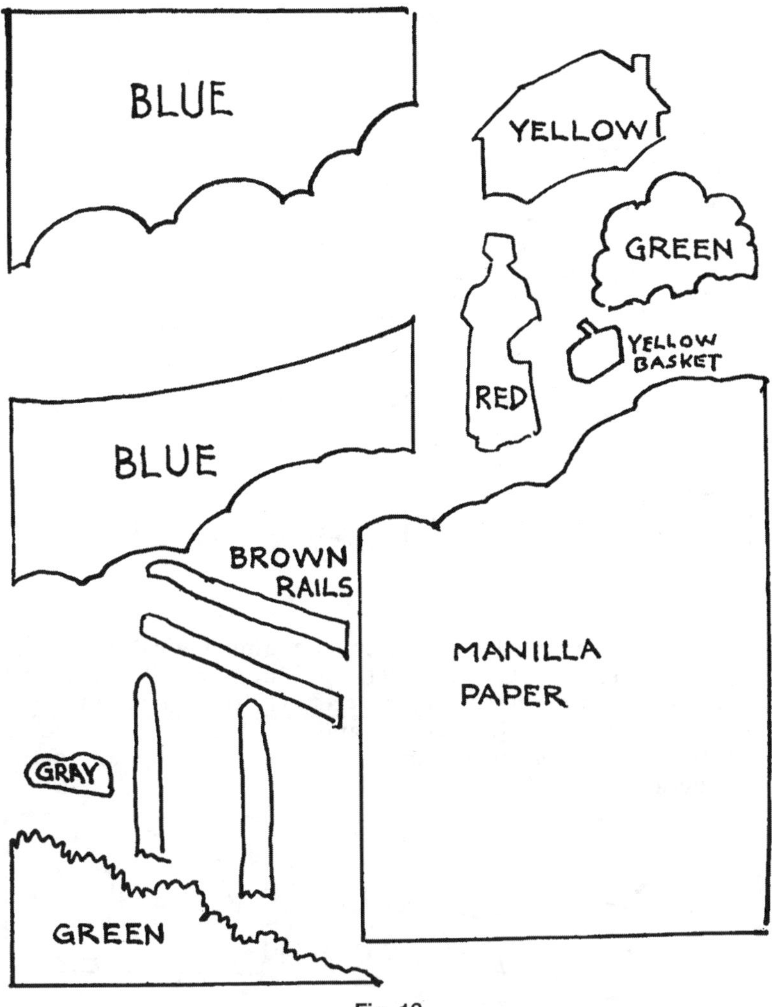

Fig. 18

verse side of the paper. Paste them carefully, as in Fig. 16, and finish them up with a fine brush or coarse pen, as described in Fig. 17.

Pasting the Pieces.—Paste the pieces in the alphabetical order, according to instructions regarding Fig. 16.

The landscape in Fig. 21 is made as follows: Take a piece of the white board and cut the figures in Fig 19 out of colored paper.

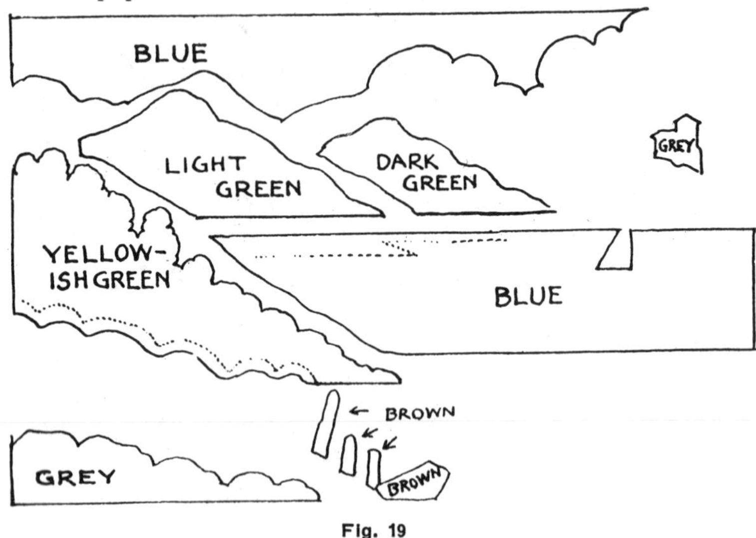

Fig. 19

Paste these on the board in the alphabetical order, as shown in Fig. 20. Thus: First, the blue A and B; then, the dark green C; next, the light green D; then, succcessively, the pieces of paper, E, F, G, H and I. With a fine brush or coarse pen, add the necessary detail to give character to the production, as in Fig. 21.

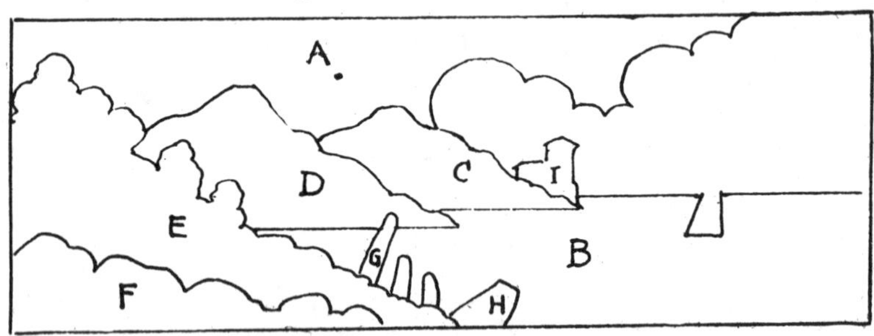

Fig. 20

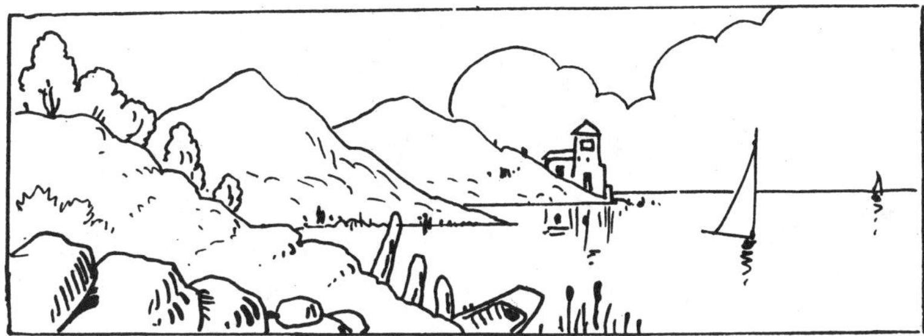

Fig. 21

To produce Fig. 22, take a piece of black cardboard or, if that is not at hand, paint with an even coat of black, on a piece of white cardboard, covering a surface about four by five and one-half inches; then paste the pieces of colored paper, as shown in Fig. 23.

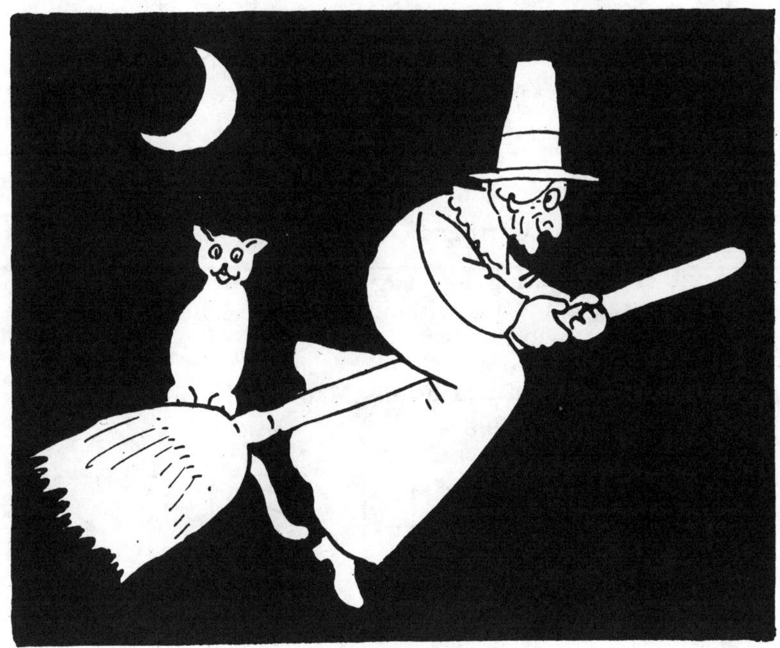

Fig. 22

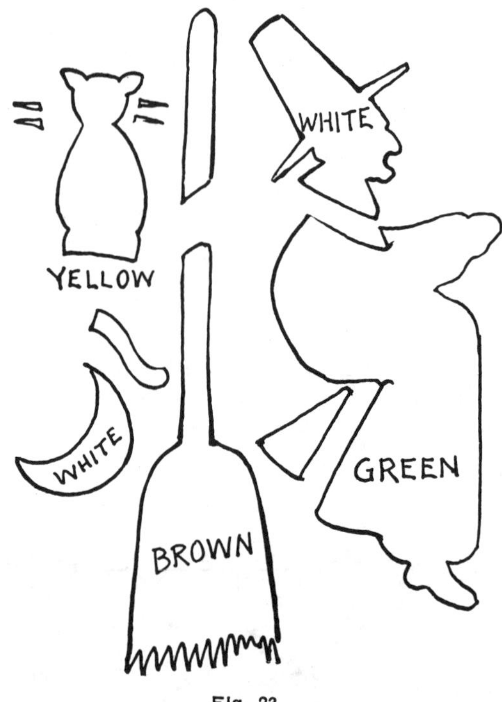

Fig. 23

Cutting Forms by Eye

Another Interesting Form of Paper Cutting is to cut out simple geometrical forms without guides, except squares made according to previous instruction. Some of the forms are shown in Figs. 24 and 25.

For Other Geometrical Forms Made by Folding, see chapter on Working Drawings.

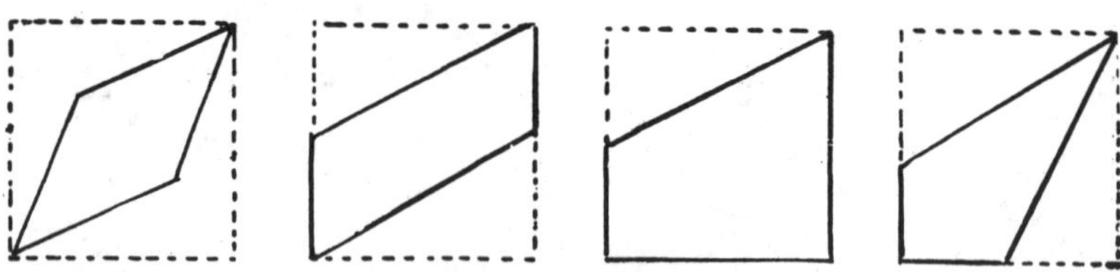

Fig. 24

x
a a a a IDENTICAL
IN LENGTH.
a
a
B
A
e
e
c
d
c
c
ccc ½ width of d.
d ½ width of ee.

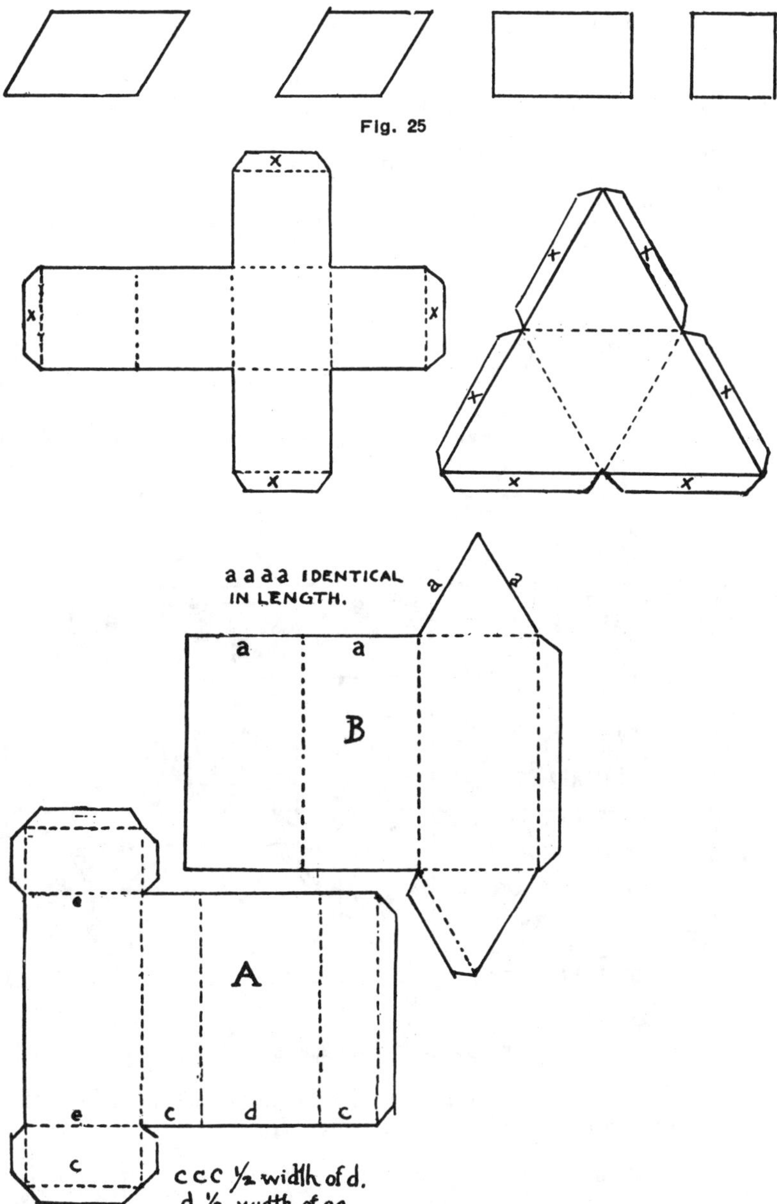

Fig. 25

Fig. 26

Quadrangular Prism and Triangular Prism, Etc.

Draw the diagrams in Fig. 26. Use heavy ledger paper or cardboard; if the latter, dent or slightly cut the dotted lines, as described in Fig. 14.

The Greek cross will fold into a cube.

The triangle will form a pyramid.

The parts marked "X" are to be covered with mucilage or paste for the purpose of fastening the adjacent surfaces of the solids.

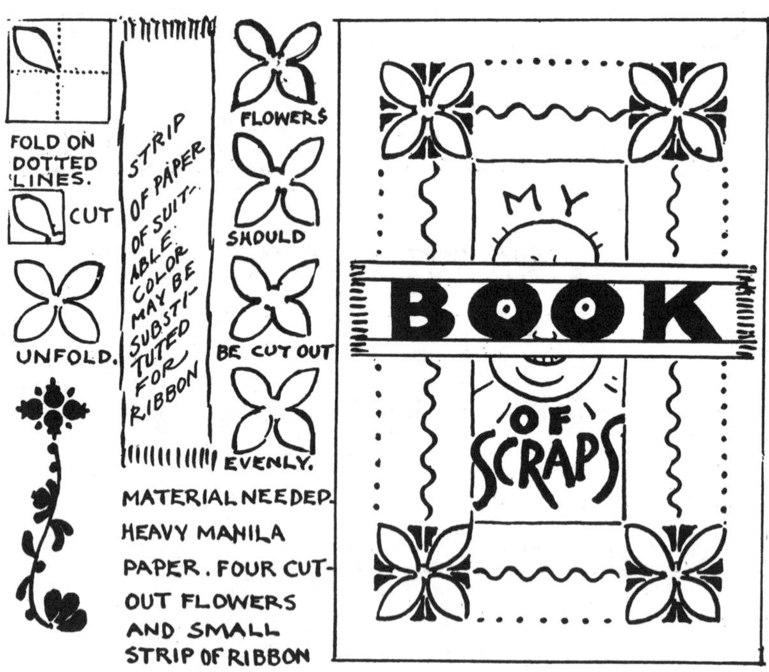

Multi-Colored Book Covers

Book covers may be made by the same means used for producing the multi-colored cut-out pictures.

Notes.—Subjects suitable for paper folding and cutting will be found on pp. 101, 106, 108, 111, 112, 117, 122 (Fig. 1), 227, 229, 233, 234, 236 (lines to be drawn in triangles), 245, 246, 251, 252, 269, 275.

CHAPTER X

USE OF MODELS—MEASUREMENTS AND PROPORTIONS

Imitation or copy drawing is valuable at the outset, as it imparts style or method of handling. To an extent it reveals the personality. By its use the pupil gains accuracy of eye-measurement, errors in that respect being more readily shown than when drawing from model.

Drawing from copy also trains the eye by giving it some means of correcting its mistake in the estimate of lengths and values of lines.

Perspective or object drawing gives a knowledge of form, color, and construction. Ideas of relation and relative sizes are thus acquired.

Imaginary and memory drawings enable one to express thought and impart ideas.

Intermingling parts of all three supports, helps and explains the others.

In copying one is shown how.
In object drawing one sees how.
In imaginative drawing one thinks how.

Eye Measurements

Measurement Exercise.—As you progress, greater accuracy in eye-measurement will become apparent. This can be hastened by frequent practice exclusively in this direction.

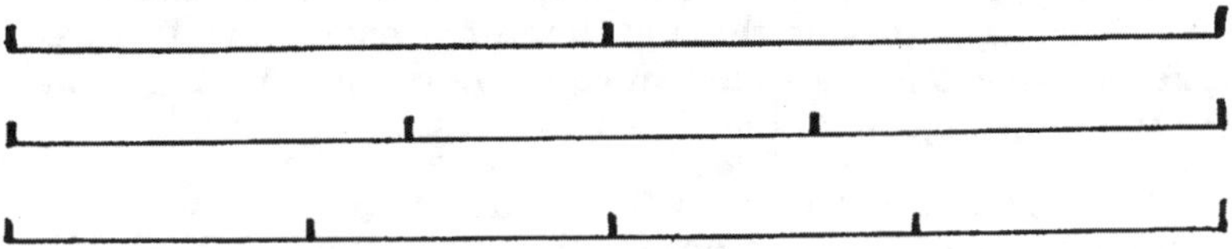

A good plan is for you to draw straight lines of the various determined lengths, and then bisect, trisect and quadrisect them at regular intervals. Thus, draw a line four inches long to be divided in half. Then the same line in three equal divisions; then into four equal divisions.

Proportion

Proportion, and What Is Meant by Out of Proportion.— For example: If a picture of a man were drawn with the head twice as long as the head should be, as is shown in Fig. 1, Chap. 19, that would be called out of proportion, because it would be unnatural.

It should be in "good proportion," which means it should be near the natural size as compared with other parts of the body. The ability to draw the figure in proper proportion requires considerable practice, close observation and accurate eye-measurement.

Varying Proportions.—In drawing the head of a child, the same proportions as adults does not exist; the child's head being larger in proportion to the body than in the case of adults. There are also further variations. Putting a very small head on the body of a child would make the drawing appear as much out of proportion as in the case of the over-large head referred to. In caricature, lapses from true proportion are permitted. Then it is done purposely to produce a ludicrous effect.

Relative Proportions.—Ability to represent the relative size or proportion of one object to another is an essential element in correct drawing.

An effective method of learning this is to choose some object for a unit of measure or comparison, and place others beside it, one or several at a time.

Any well-known object will do, as, for instance, a piece of fruit, such as an apple or an orange—or a ball.

Exercise in Proportion.—Make a drawing of the object selected and compare it with some other object of about the same size. Then place beside them still another object, two or three times as large, such as a book or cap. Now make a drawing showing the three objects in their relative sizes.

Any small wooden or cardboard box may be used in connection with other small boxes to demonstrate proportionate sizes.

Place the apple (or whatever object is selected) on a box and draw both in proportion.

Proceed with the exercise by drawing from imagination (or copy) some other object with which you are familiar and draw the object in proportion. The subject may be a bird, a mouse, a rat, a cup, mug; in fact, any object that is not larger than the box itself.

How to Measure

How to Measure.—When drawing from any object the proportion can be measured by holding up a pencil and meas-

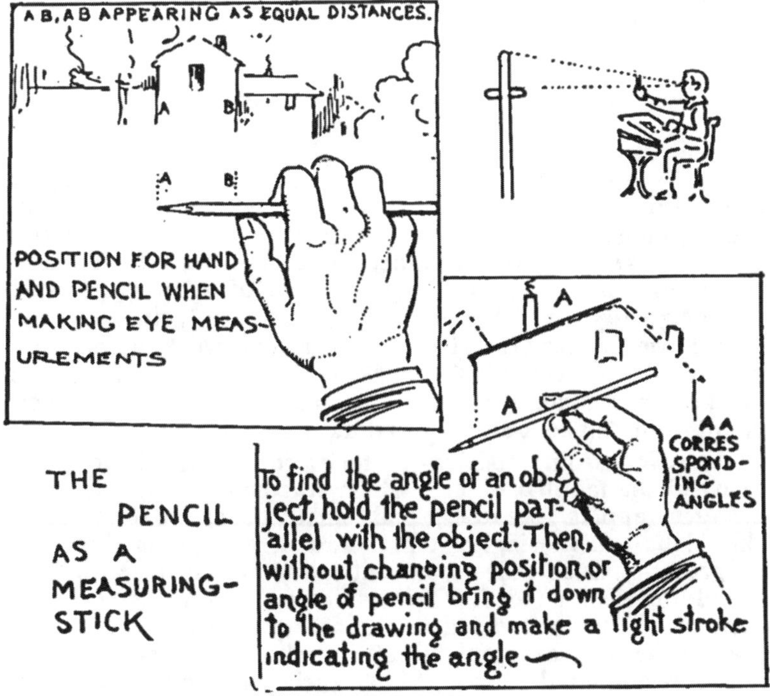

uring or gaging on it with the thumb, and comparing the length of one point with another, as shown in the accompanying diagram.

To insure accuracy the pencil must be held at arm's length and at right angles to the line of vision.

Hold the pencil so that the end comes between the eye and some certain point on the object to be drawn; for instance, in drawing a house, the height of the chimney might be taken as a standard of measurement. Hold the pencil upright, the top on a line with the chimney top. Now move the thumb downward until the end of the thumb comes between the eye and the bottom of the chimney. Then draw the chimney. Repeat the measuring operation, finding where the length of the chimney corresponds to other parts of the building.

That is to say, the pencil may be moved between the object and the eye and by using the chimney length as a standard, corresponding length and width thereof may be estimated.

The Scale on Which Drawings Should Be Made

One of the greatest faults of the beginner, and a very natural fault, is to draw on too small a scale. In copying from printed pictures, taken from periodicals of any kind, the beginner very naturally imitates the pictures as he sees them, not knowing that in ninety-nine cases out of a hundred the picture is the reduced reproduction of a drawing which was originally much larger than it appears in print.

It is well to vary the size of the drawing. Working long on a very small scale would in time make one acquire a cramped style; on the other hand, working for an extended period at a blackboard would make it difficult to draw on a more minute scale.

Drawing from Models.—Material for models is found in many of the familiar objects which surround us, such as balls, oranges, apples, potatoes, and small paper boxes. These should be drawn singly at first and in groups as the study progresses. Such objects present fairly dull surfaces and are therefore recommended. Objects having very glossy or shiny surfaces are to be avoided in all early practice. Models with dull surfaces present only light and shade in varying degree and cast simple shadows. Shiny surfaces receive and reflect complex lights and shades, hence the objection to their use.

Avoiding Confusion.—In order not to confuse the eye of the pupil objects of a single color are best. The eye is centered then on form and outline rather than color. The simplest way to effect this when plaster casts are not available is to prepare a basin one-quarter full of whiting to which a small quantity of glue has been added and mixed with water until the consistency of cream is obtained. Then dip in this pigment articles to be used for models, such as a brick, a potato, a carrot, a turnip or even an old shoe.

When dry these objects will serve temporarily nearly as well as clay or plaster models. Draw these singly or in groups. For the earliest exercises more than one object at a time is not desirable.

Placing the Model.—Unless there is contrast in light or color it is difficult for the eye to discern the shape of an object. For example, if you were to place a piece of cardboard against a blackboard, its outline would be easily distinguished. On the other hand, place the same piece of paper flat against another and larger piece of cardboard of the same color, and its form can scarcely be perceived. Keep this experiment in mind when drawing from any model. If the latter is dark, place it against a light background, if you wish the best effect. Reverse the process if the article used is light in color.

Light and Shade.—For models for early work in light and shade, small objects with simple outlines should be selected. They should be free from polished surfaces. Select, instead, any piece of dull earthenware or wooden object; or, best of all, something made of plaster of paris. A small wooden or paper box is good; anything, in fact, that has a well defined outline with a fairly dull surface.

Place the object selected before you on a sheet of white paper and, if possible, in such a position that it receives the light from one direction only. If the object receives light from more than one direction, multiplicity of undefined shadows will cause a confusing effect.

Shoes as Models.—Shoes, the older the better, are excellent models. Their study leads to more natural appearance to the clothed human figure in subsequent drawings from memory or imagination. Feet are generally considered very difficult things to draw—meaning feet enclosed in the usual footwear of mankind. In drawing shoes, it is well to place them well below the eye, since that is the position in which they are generally seen.

The drawings should be blocked-in as indicated in the sketch shown in chapter on Blocking-in.

Notes.—Other subjects suitable for models will be found on pp. 91, 92, 120, 173, 180, 222, 223, 225, 232, 235, 243, 244, 246, 247.

CHAPTER XI

METHOD OF COPYING BY TRIANGULATION

(From an illustrated article by Charles Lederer in the South Dakota Journal of Education.)

To enlarge or reduce one may resort to any of the following methods:

(1) Photography.

(2) The mechanical instrument known as the pantograph.

(3) The mechanical instrument known as the proportional dividers.

(4) Free hand drawing. Good practice, but not conducive to accuracy.

(5) Squaring the original by means of intersecting horizontal and vertical lines. This requires great care in preparation and use. The squares must be *square* and usually require numbering along at least two sides of the original and of the copy.

(6) Triangulation. An old and simply made geometrical form which I have adopted for the purpose of enlarging and reducing.

In my practice it has, since my discovery of its new use, entirely superseded the laborious, if time-honored, methods. By its use ordinary care produces accurate work, no measurements being required except when laying out the perimeters.

In the squaring method even an ordinary reduction or enlargement requires from 16 to 64 squares, the latter with boundary numbers 1, 2, 3, 4, 5, 6, 7 and 8 on at least two sides of both original and copy. In this maze the draftsman is apt to become "lost." In the method I have adopted, the triangulation forms a pattern which aids the eye to keep within the proper corresponding spaces. That is, each triangle, in the original and in the drawing under way, occupies a distinctive and individual position not observable in the squares.

I have not space here to describe the numerous applications and advantages of the triangular method, nor even to describe its operation beyond giving a diagram of its most primitive, simplest form, as shown in the accompanying figures.

A square or other parallelogram is drawn first, the oblique, vertical and horizontal lines being added.

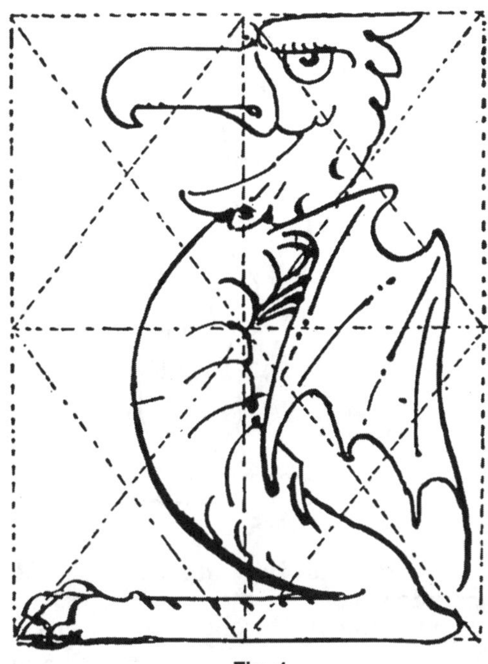

Fig. 1

In a drawing in which the detail is complex, the triangles are easily subdivided, both in the original and in the drawing to be made from it.

Not alone is this method superior in every way to the "squaring" process, but it provides a sure and easy way to make regularly proportional distortions.

Not long ago an engraver on old gold and silver ware came to me. He was distressed. An order had been given to him in which it was required that certain heraldric devices should appear on some silver plate. The devices included the pleasant-looking creature shown in Fig. 1.

The engraver's trouble was that the mythological animal had to be reproduced in narrow vertical and horizontal panels,

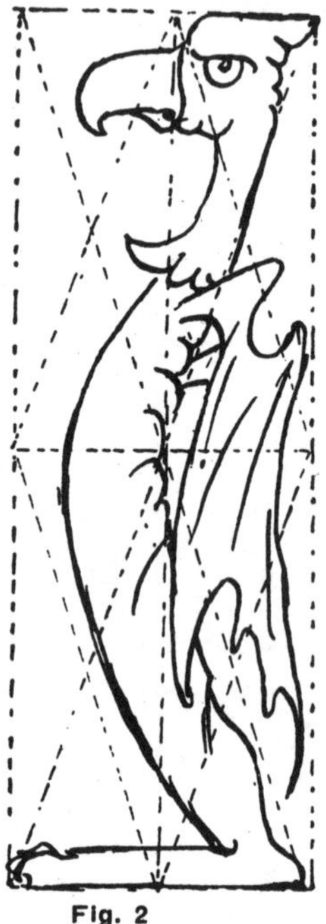

Fig. 2

respectively, of certain definite dimensions. My engraver friend did not know how to get the "critter" squeezed and distended into anything like proper proportions.

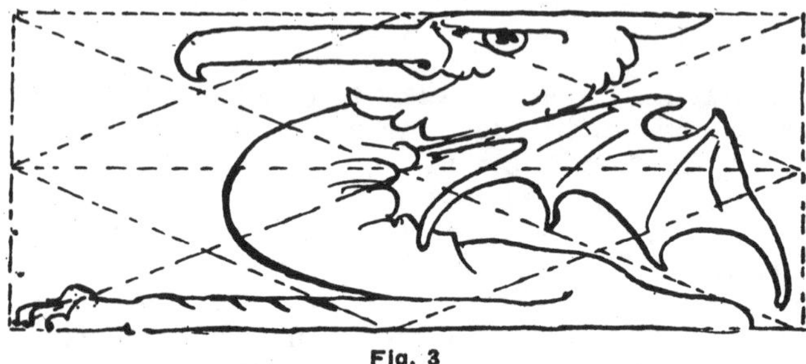

Fig. 3

Figs. 2 and 3 show the engraver's purpose was satisfactorily accomplished.

It is to be hoped that the result pleased his customer. It was my conjecture that the griffons might be intended for evolutional ancestral portraits and if my surmise was correct the two distortions might serve as portraits of two of his

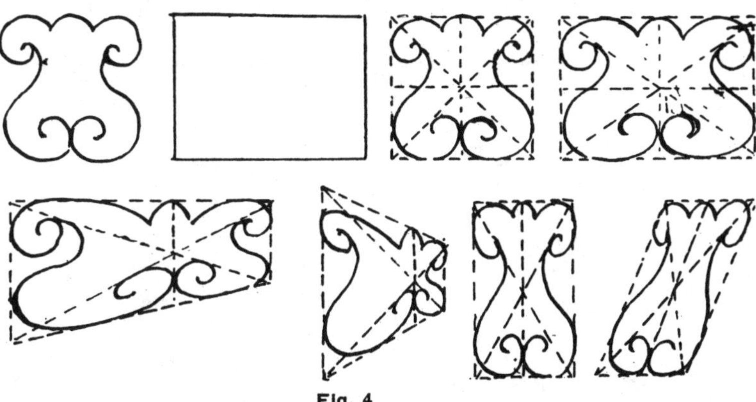

Fig. 4

ancestors—one attenuated and the other obese. Anyway, I would as soon trace my origin to a fine official and officious-looking griffon—or whatever it is—as to a grinning, chattering chimpanzee.

Another Example.—Fig. 4 is another example of what may be done in the way of varying the form of an area in which any design may be placed.

The Start of the Diagonal Method of Enlarging and Reducing

Only one drawing, about 4x6 inches in size, not four drawings, as indicated, are to be made. Proceed thus: draw a rectangle as in A. Intersect with diagonals as shown in A and B.

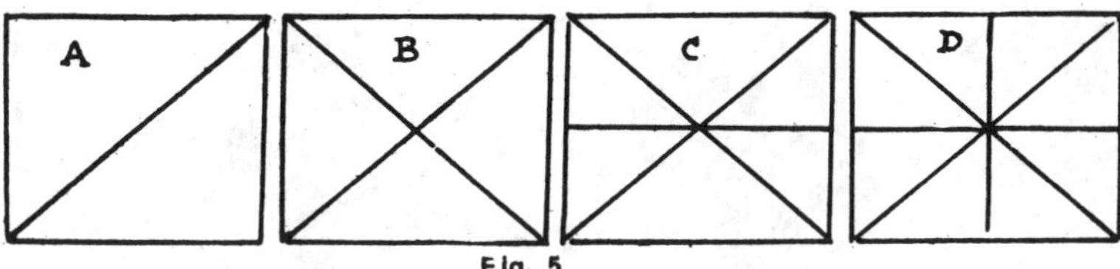

Fig. 5

Intersect the diagonals with a horizontal line as in C and finally with a vertical intersecting line as in D. All lines inside of the rectangle should be made very light. They are merely guide lines to be erased when the drawing is completed.

Blackboard Exercise.—Copy the images in Fig. 6 by means of the triangular guide lines. The first one by the aid of a single oblique line; the second by the aid of two oblique lines; the third with two oblique lines and one hori-

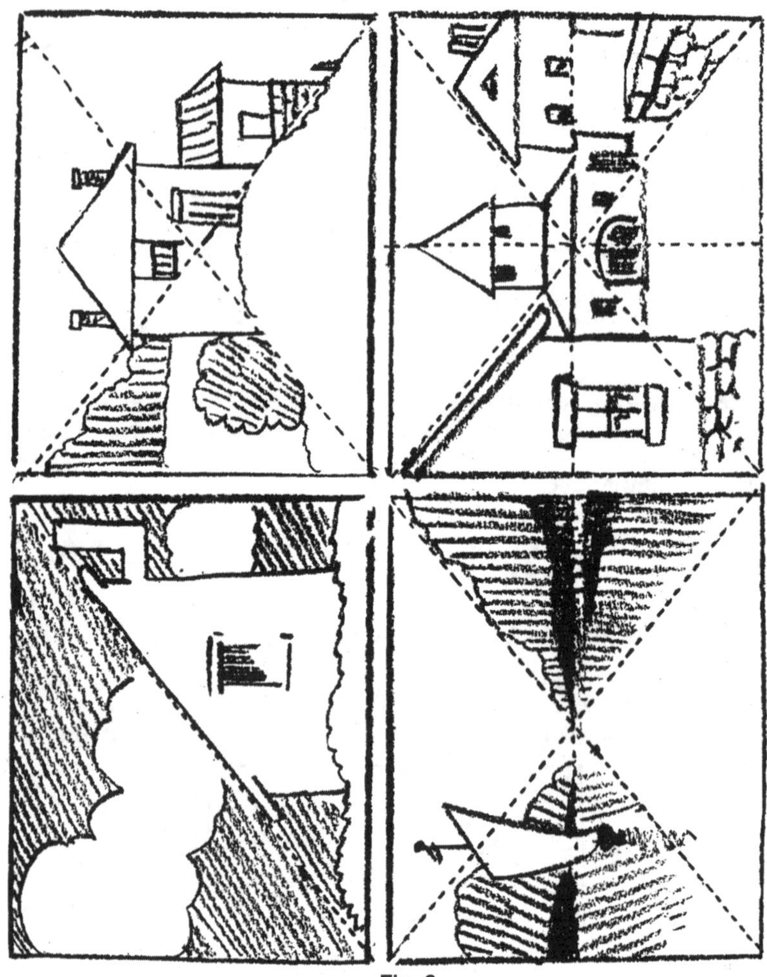

Fig. 6

zontal line; the fourth aided by the addition of a vertical line.

Errors Quickly Noted.—For the beginner, even a common vase or teacup is a difficult subject. Straight, upright and oblique guiding-lines are helpful in drawing curved objects. The following diagrams will make the method clear. By this means, as will be observed, the several parts are balanced with ease, and errors quickly noticed and corrected. The use of these lines accustoms one to judge the relative proportions of the different parts of an object as related to the whole.

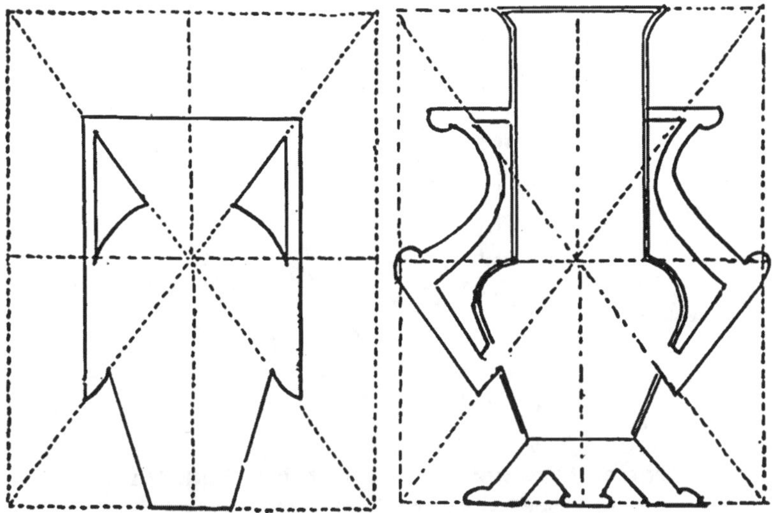

Fig. 7 – Exercises in Vase Forms

Fig. 8 – Additional Divisions

The divisions made by vertical, horizontal and oblique lines will greatly aid you in your work. Thus, you will be able to become methodical and accurate in your measurements, and will cultivate what is known as the "true eye" for drawing.

Do not, however, depend on or permit yourself to be crippled by the constant application of mechanical methods or appliances, or allow the use thereof to interfere with free-hand drawing. They are intended for occasional use. To avoid this, frequently lay aside the guide line methods and trust more to the eye.

Whenever desirable more divisions can easily be made. The additional spaces need not be made over the entire surface, but the surface may be subdivided indefinitely in whole or in part, according to the intricacy of detail in the design to be copied, same size, enlarged or reduced.

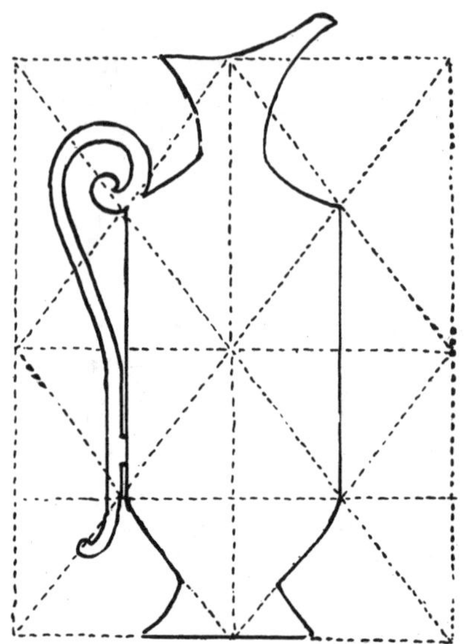

Fig. 9—Showing Divisions

General Directions for Triangular Guide Lines

Triangular guide lines are particularly adapted for the purpose of enlarging or reducing portraits.

In this exercise a small pencil sketch of the Father of His Country is offered as an example, showing the start of an enlarged drawing of the sketch.

The guide lines should be made as faintly as possible.

After the main outlines of the features and forms of the principal shadows are indicated with lines considerably stronger than the guide lines, the whole drawing may be rubbed over with dry bread crumbs. By this means the guide lines will be nearly, if not quite, obliterated, while the outlines of the features and shadows will remain sufficiently visible as a means by which to finish the drawing.

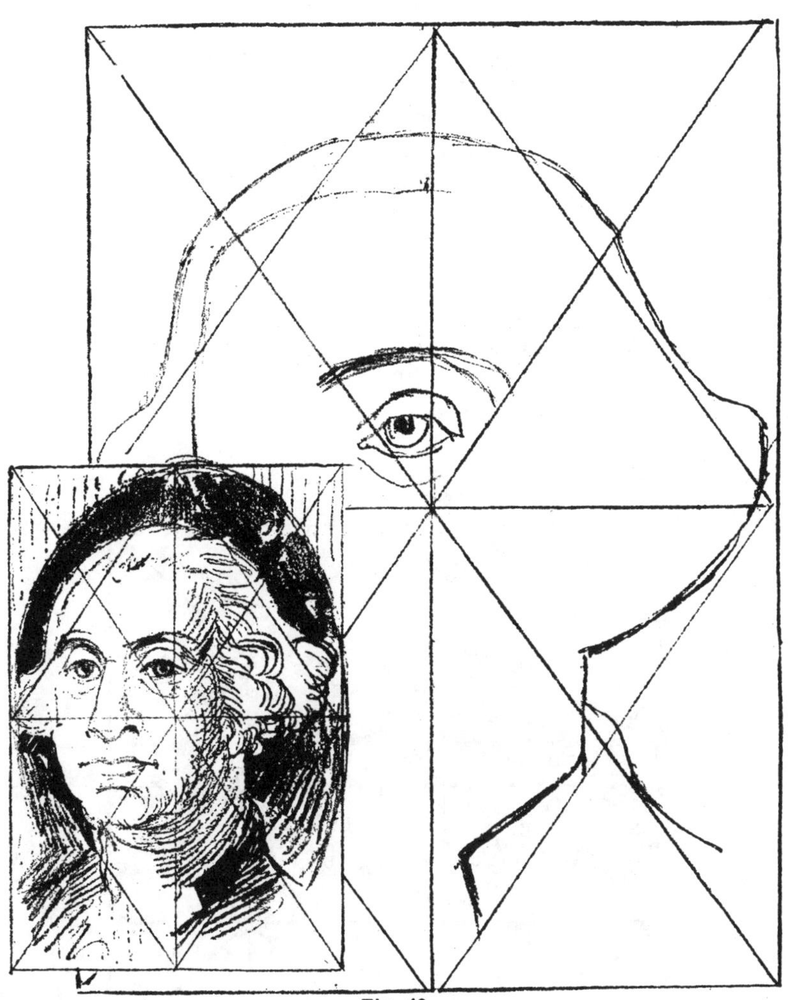

Fig. 10

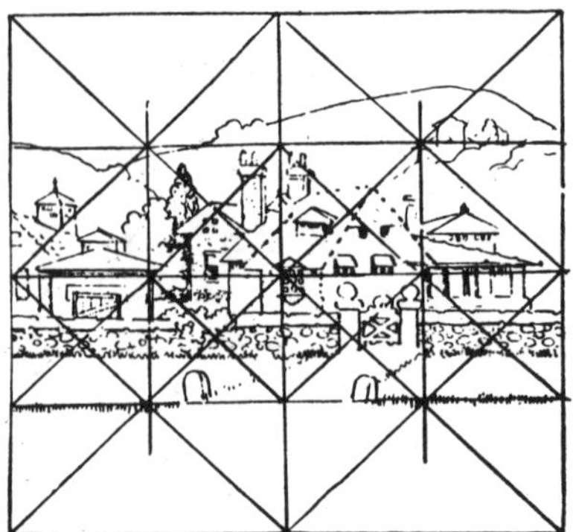

Fig. 11—The Original with Triangulation Lines

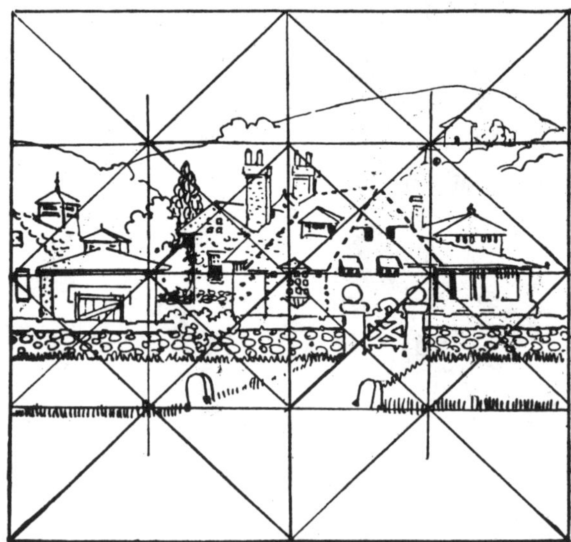

Fig. 12—Enlarged Copy of Original with Triangulation Lines

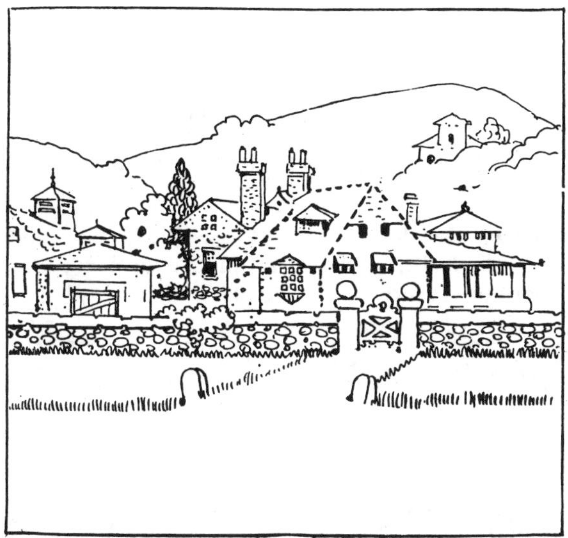

Fig. 13—Enlarged Copy of Original with Triangulation Lines Erased

If the original is one that is to be preserved, and might be marred by the guide lines, one of these methods should be used:

(1) Tack a piece of very transparent tracing paper (the vegetable tracing paper is preferable for this purpose) over the original and place the guide lines on the tracing paper.

(2) Use tracing gelatine instead of paper and a steel point instead of a pencil, and with the latter scratch the guide lines on the gelatine. A coarse needle fastened into a cork as a handle makes a good tracing point.

(3) If the copy is very large pins may be placed at the points where the usual vertical, horizontal and oblique lines intersect the outer lines and thread carried from one point to the other instead of marked lines.

Notes.—Instances in which the method of triangulation is shown in practical form will be found on pp. 159, 279 and 280.

CHAPTER XII

TWO-HANDED EXERCISES

Value of Two-Handed Exercises.—Skill, speed, and grace are acquired by the rhythmical two-handed exercises, and for this the blackboard is the most effective place. Use two pieces of chalk.

Fig. 1

In each of the previous and following examples the starting point is indicated by a Λ.

If possible two-handed work should be continued until you become, in fact, ambidextrous, but each exercise should be about five minutes long. The exercise may be alternated by two-handed pencil work at the desk.

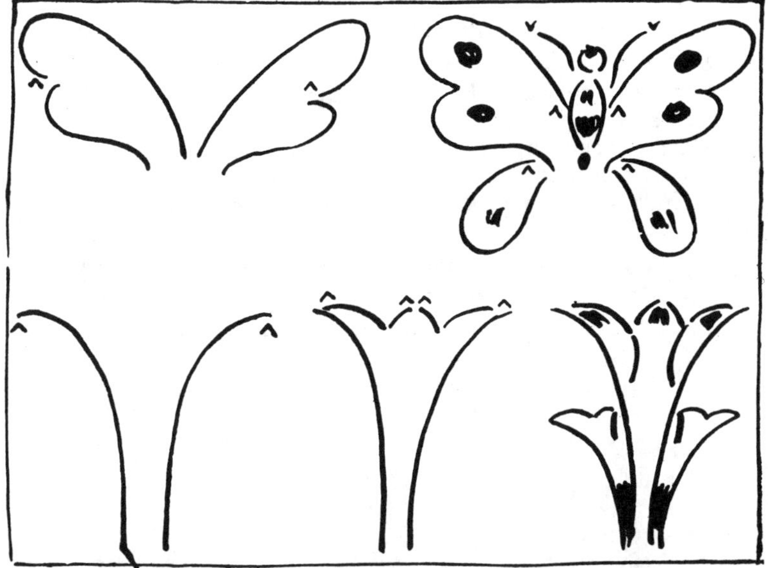

Fig. 2

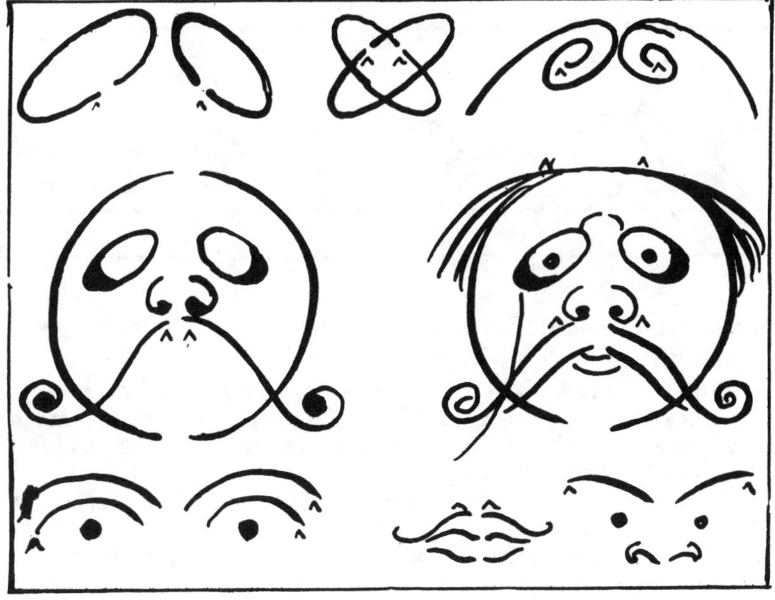

Fig. 3

Erase with slow downward strokes. This will prevent the raising of clouds of chalk-dust.

The best movements at first are the quarter circles, reversed; starting at the top in Fig. 1.

After continued exercise in the lines at top of Fig. 1 proceed with the more complex lines below.

In Fig. 2 the lines cause freedom of movement and train the muscles.

Fig. 3 consists of two-handed exercises intended to try one's ingenuity by adapting one to more intricate designs modeled on

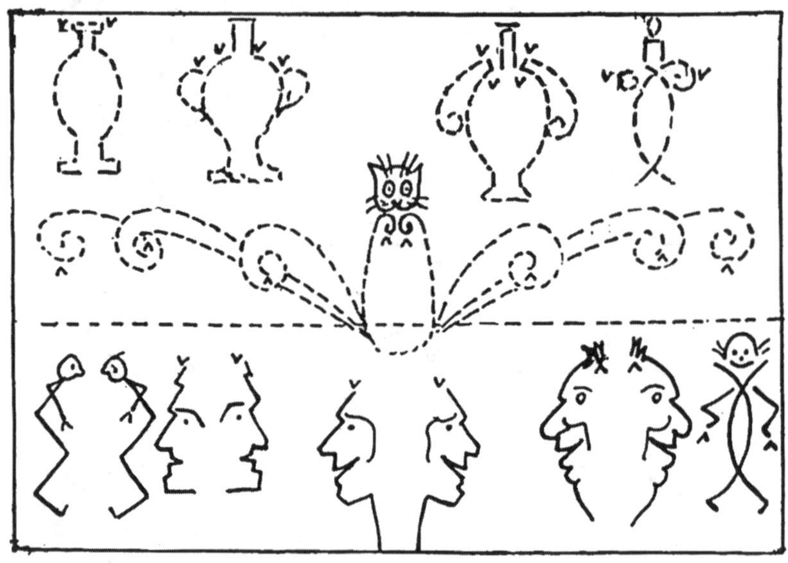

Fig. 4

these examples. Add details to these and also other figures given in earlier examples of simple forms.

For two-handed exercises on the blackboard broad, sweeping lines are to be recommended. The lines should be started at about the height of the head, the converging points at about the middle of the chest

Fig. 4 contains suggestions for two-handed exercises, in which the hands work independently.

The lines on the right-hand side of each object are to be

drawn first with the right hand; immediately afterward the opposite half is to be completed with the left hand. Short strokes, as indicated, should be made in the upper figures, and will be found to act as an aid to accuracy. These exercises are adapted for blackboard and pencil.

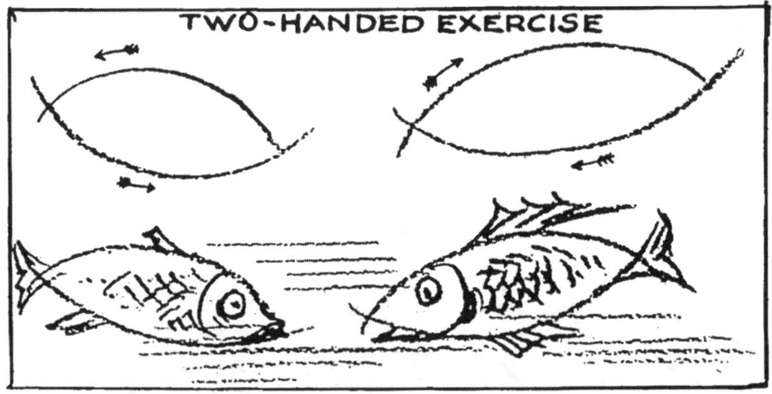

It is natural to be discouraged because your drawings look wrong to your own eyes. But this dissatisfaction is evidence of your ability to criticize your work.

Having made a drawing, put it aside, and, after a period, look at it carefully and see where you can improve a line here, or strengthen or lighten a line there to the betterment of the whole drawing. This sort of practice means real advancement.

Notes.—Subjects suitable for two-handed exercises may be found on pp. 86. 112, 158 (Fig. 2), 236, 238, 245, 246, 250, 251, 252, 253, 264 (Fig. 2), 267, 268, 269, 271, 272, 274, 275, 276, 277, 278.

CHAPTER XIII

EXERCISES STIMULATING IMAGINATION

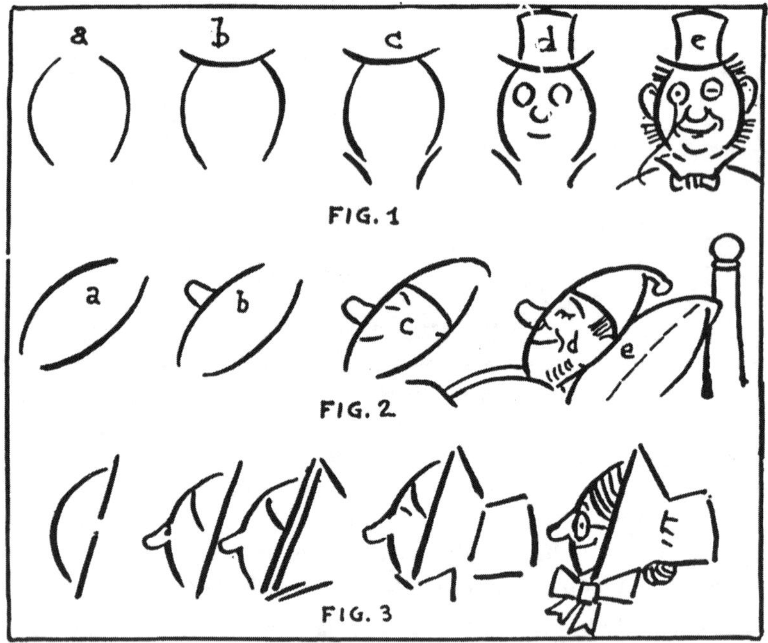

The Progression of a Drawing.—In this exercise the progression of a drawing is shown. A, B, C, D and E in Fig. 1 are not intended as separate drawings. A is the start, B the next step, and so on until the completion E.

In Fig. 2 the lines in A are partly repeated in the final drawing D E. The examples are given to show how the pictures are to be started and the order in which they should be finished. These are only suggestions and you should base other subjects, either serious or comic, along similar lines.

Incentive to Ingenuity.—In this interesting exercise (Figs. 5 and 6) the curves on which the subjects are based are shown in heavy lines as keys to the original motif. As the exercise is intended as an incentive to the display of ingenuity, mere accuracy in execution should not be required.

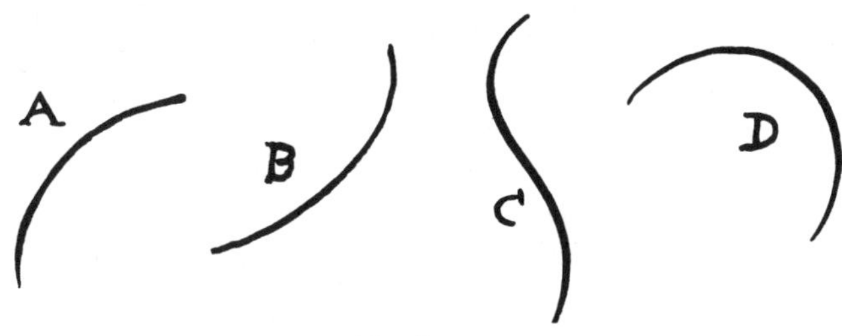

Fig. 5

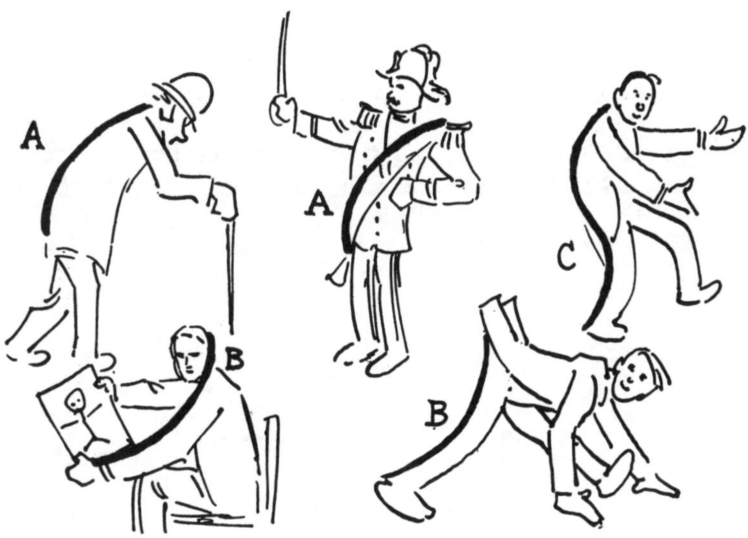

Fig. 6

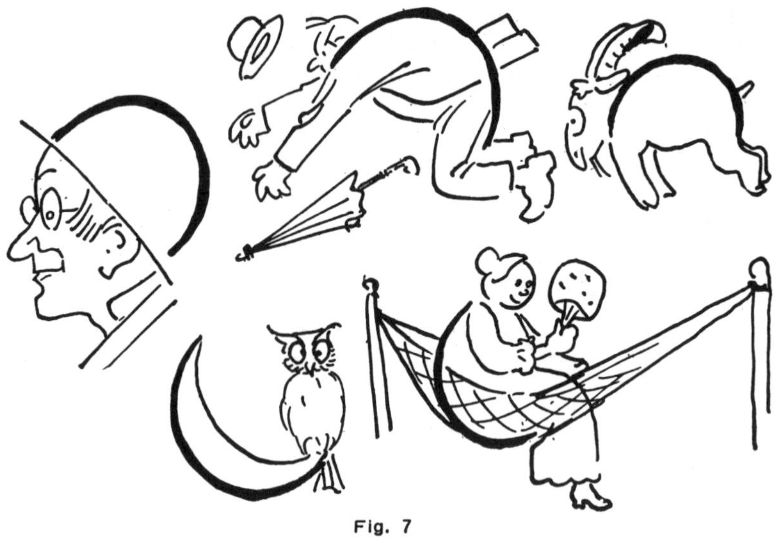

Fig. 7

Further Advanced Exercises.—These are exercises similar to Figs. 5 and 6, but are farther advanced. Draw any desired curves and angles and then construct human figures based on these lines. Subjects of a humorous character will be found the easiest to produce.

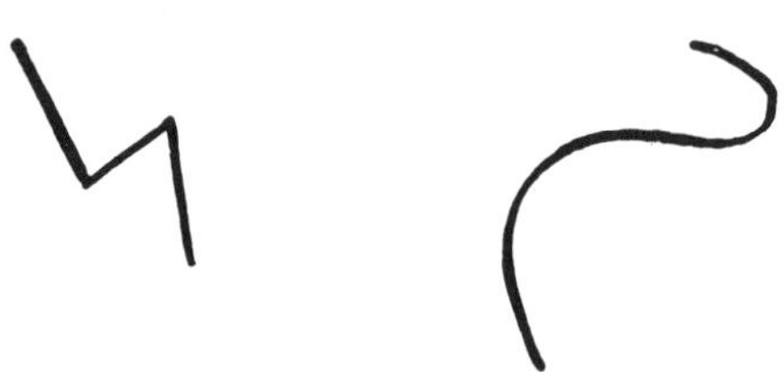

Fig. 8

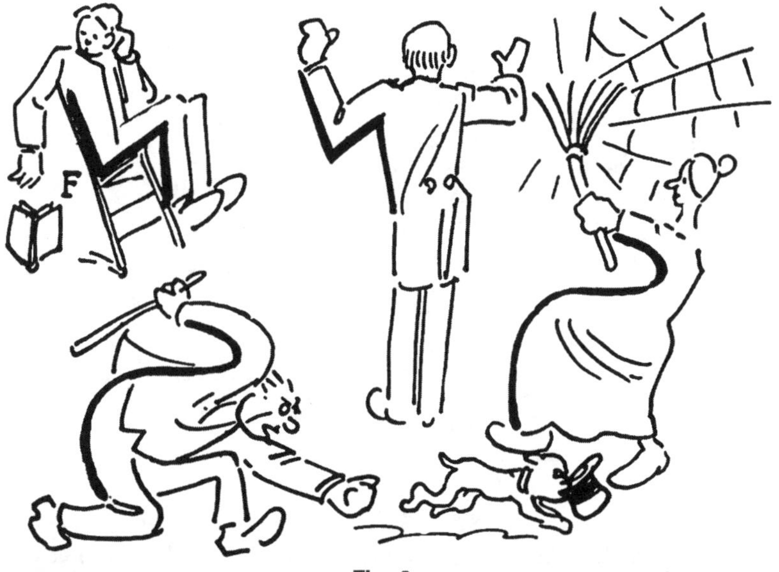

Fig. 9

Circle Exercises.—Make several circles and curves and then dispose of them in the composition of a figure. The examples in Fig. 10 will serve to show what can be accomplished in this direction.

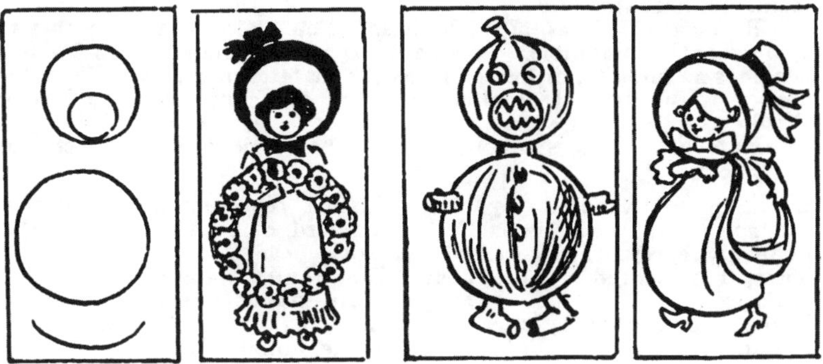

Fig. 10

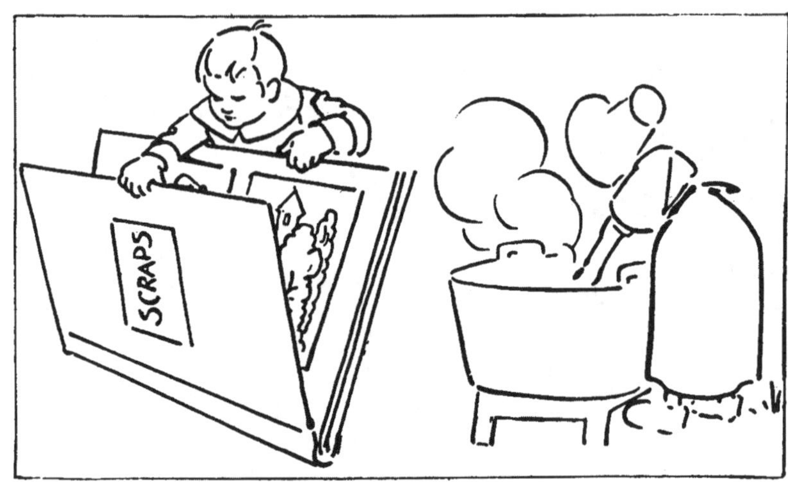

An Exercise in Line-Economy

SUGGESTIONS.

In a drawing that presents a pleasing aspect to the eye much is left to the suggestion and to the imagination of the observer. For instance, in drawing the stones in a stone wall it is only necessary, as a usual thing, to suggest a few of the stones. In the same manner, a few bricks are all that need be indicated in a brick house to show that it *is* a brick house. A few leaves, sometimes, in the foreground of a drawing contain all the detail of that sort that is required to indicate the foreground foliage.

By pictorial means, we suggest or indicate things, some of which have neither form, quality, visible appearance, or in fact, any physical manifestation whatever.

By means of lines, aided by association of ideas, we are able to symbolize the intangible. In time the symbolic definition of an object becomes as familiar, or nearly so, as the material meaning. Thus, the anchor is the symbol of Hope; the key of Knowledge; the owl of Wisdom.

Here are a few symbolic objects that make good subjects for exercises:

Learning represented by the lamp.
Bondage, represented by shackles.
Time, represented by the hour glass.
Peace, represented by the olive branch.
Justice, represented by scales or sword, or both together.
Dove, peace.
Dog (bull), watchfulness.
Mule, stubbornness.
Lion, royalty and dignity.
Eagle, domination.

Notes.—Other subjects and suggestions correlated with this chapter will be found on pp. 48, 49, 51, 52, 53, 60, 62, 63, 66, 73, 83, 84, 95, 96, 97, 99, 107, 111, 113 122, 124, 125, 126, 137, all of chapter XXI, 168, 251, 253, 254, 257, 258, 259, 260, all of chapter XXXI. (Look up symbols.)
(Chapter XIV)

CHAPTER XIV

BLOCKING-IN

The Necessity of Blocking-in.—It has ever been a difficult matter for teachers of drawing to instill in the minds of beginners the value and importance of blocking-in; that is to say, getting the general shape and relative proportions of the component parts of the picture before endeavoring to describe, in line or tint, any of the minor details or even main characteristics of the picture. The group or figure as a whole, rather than the objects in a group or the minor details in a figure, are the points to be fixed at the outset, with guide-lines, as few and faint as possible. Every change in direction should be thus indicated. The purpose of this may be made clear when it is stated that it would be advisable to get the general shape of a tree before drawing the individual leaves thereof.

Blocking-in has more than an immediate value to the pupil, for its use as a method of initial procedure induces a correct habit of observation. It maintains and increases the tendency to look at the whole before the parts, to seek mass rather than detail. For all time it broadens the style of the artist.

Example of Blocking-in.—The manner of blocking-in, as shown in Fig. 1, is the way to start a copy of Fig. 2. Pick out the general direction of the lines in the original where

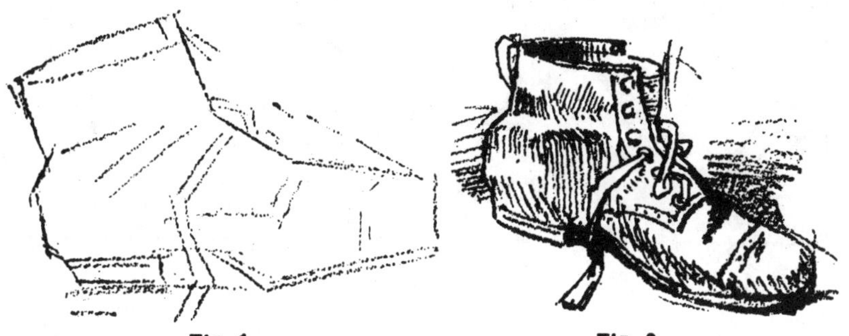

Fig. 1 Fig. 2

simple geometrical figures may be formed. After the exercise of a little imagination the eye can form lines that correspond with forms with which he is familiar, such as the square, the triangle, trapezoid, etc. It may be well to reiterate that the blocking-in lines always should be represented in the drawing by pencil marks so faint that they can be easily erased as soon as their presence is no longer necessary.

Figs. 3 and 4 are additional examples of the blocking-in method.

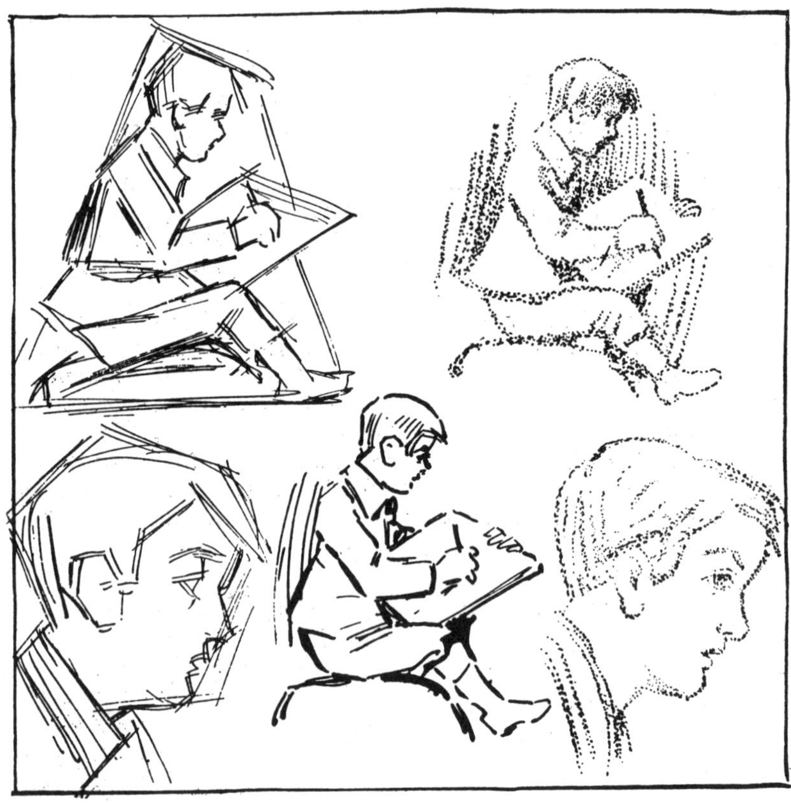

Fig. 3

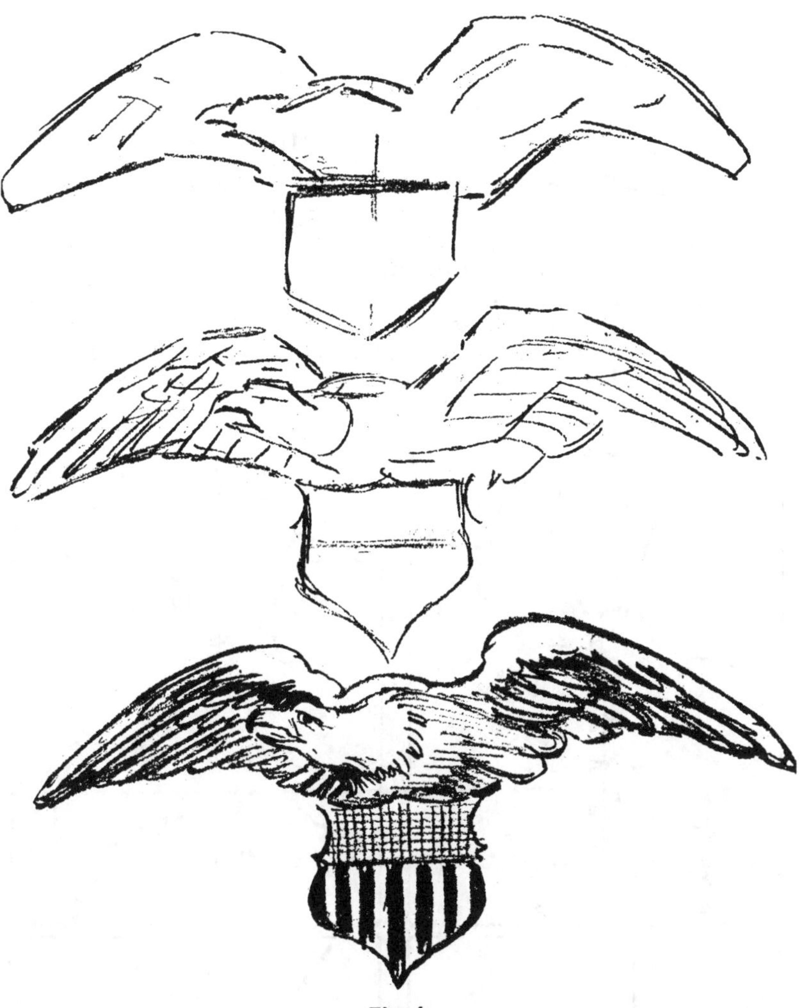

Fig. 4

Notes.—Examples where blocking-in is applicable are found on pp. 40, 41, 42, 43, 44, 45, 46, 47, 52, 53, 59, 60, 62, 63, 90, 95, 111, 114, 115, 116, 117, 118, 119, 120, 126, 130, 131, 132, 134 (Fig. 5), 135 (Fig. 8), 136, 141, 146, 147, all illustrations in chapters XXI and XXII, pp. 174, 176, 177, 178, 181, 182, all illustrations in chapters XXV and XXVI, pp. 223, 257, 258, 259, 260, 281, 282, 286, 289, 290, 292, 293, 294, 295, 296, 299, 300, 301, 302, 304, 323, 325, 327.

CHAPTER XV

ACTION DRAWING

Action.—When the vital element of action enters into the drawing interest is quickened in the mind of the beholder. Generally speaking, action in pictures simply drawn is shown most frequently by lines diverging from the horizontal and vertical. Thus, in Figs. 1 and 2 the lines on the left at the bottom, including the curved ones (which are resting horizontally) convey the impression of rest; whereas, similar lines at the right, being inclined, indicate unrest, or action.

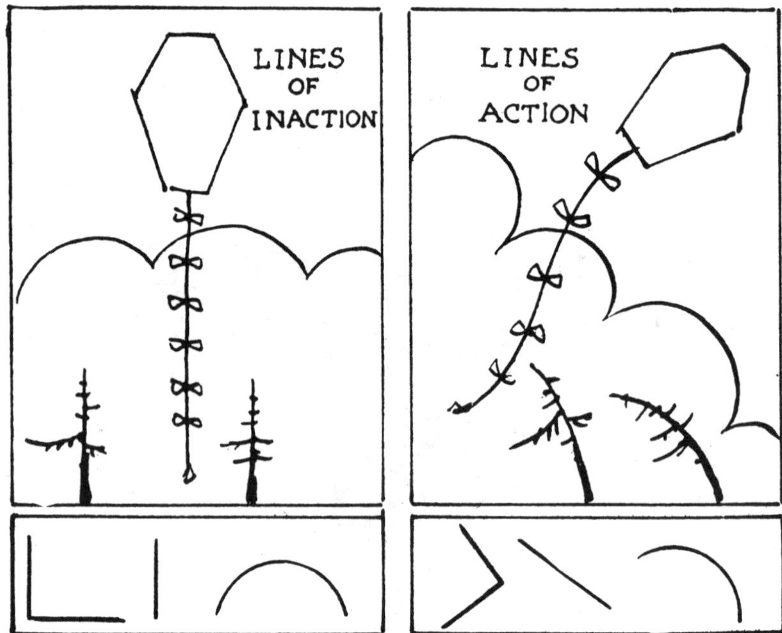

Fig. 1

In Fig. 3 none of the lines are at rest; action is shown throughout. In Fig. 4 there is the same divergence from the upright and the level.

For exercise draw objects that convey a sense of action, based on lines similar to those shown here. Beginners may copy these.

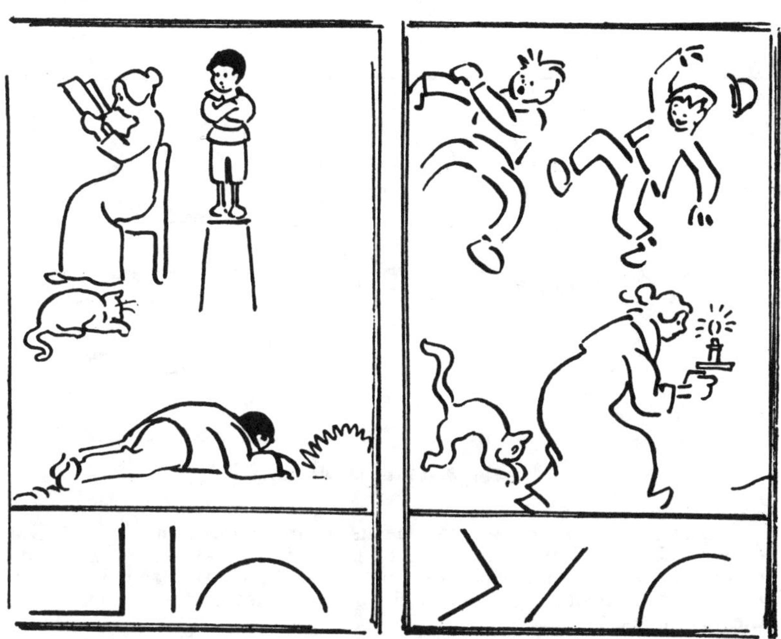

Fig. 2

Value of Lines.—Lines have *direction* and *quality*. Quality is of secondary consideration just now. On the correctness of direction will depend the completeness of the impression conveyed.

The eye of the beginner cannot grasp the direction of the lines of an object in action. Therefore, he must depend on copies to assist him in his early efforts.

This gives him practice in expressing action. It will aid him also in his memory work.

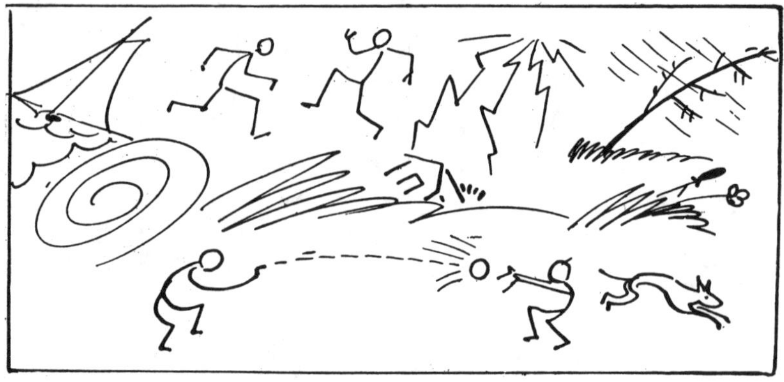

Fig. 3—Lines of Action

Drawing, in its elements, means form, color and action. Not only to the untrained mind, but to many far advanced in the study of art, form and color are subservient to action. If action is absent, interest is transient. Of course the drawing itself does not move but the idea does.

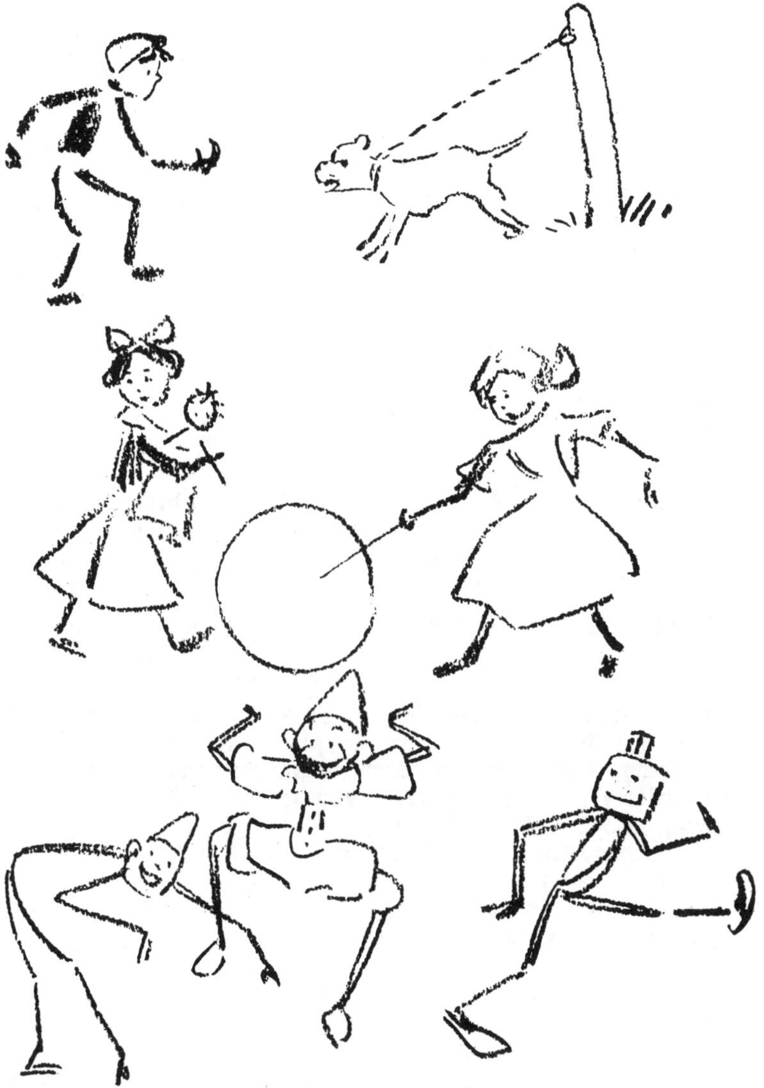

Fig. 4—Action Exercises

Memory Work

After the simple lines of the action exercises have been learned, they should be adapted and connected with little stories and language lessons.

Suggestions for subjects:
Man running from policeman.
Ship riding before a storm.
Boy chasing a dog.
Dog chasing a boy.

Single Line Action Exercises

Imagination Exercises in Action Drawing.—Fig. 5—

Show the wagon, and the boy falling off. Show the first boy standing on the sled.
Show the second boy dragging his sled up hill.
Show the boy with the pail, pumping water into it.
Show the boy with the rake gathering hay.

Border Exercise in Action Drawing.—Fig. 6—In the border below the circle the exercise looks rather difficult. It will be made easy if these directions are followed:

First, draw the guide lines, then draw all the black dots on the hats, first being careful to place them the proper distance apart—each one a little less than half the entire width of the border from each other, seven in all. Make the entire drawing about eight inches wide.
Then draw the hats—all seven.
Then the arms.
Then their legs in the air.
Then their legs on the ground.

Note.—For other examples in action drawing, see Figs. 6 and 7 in the chapter on Drawing Men, Women and Children.

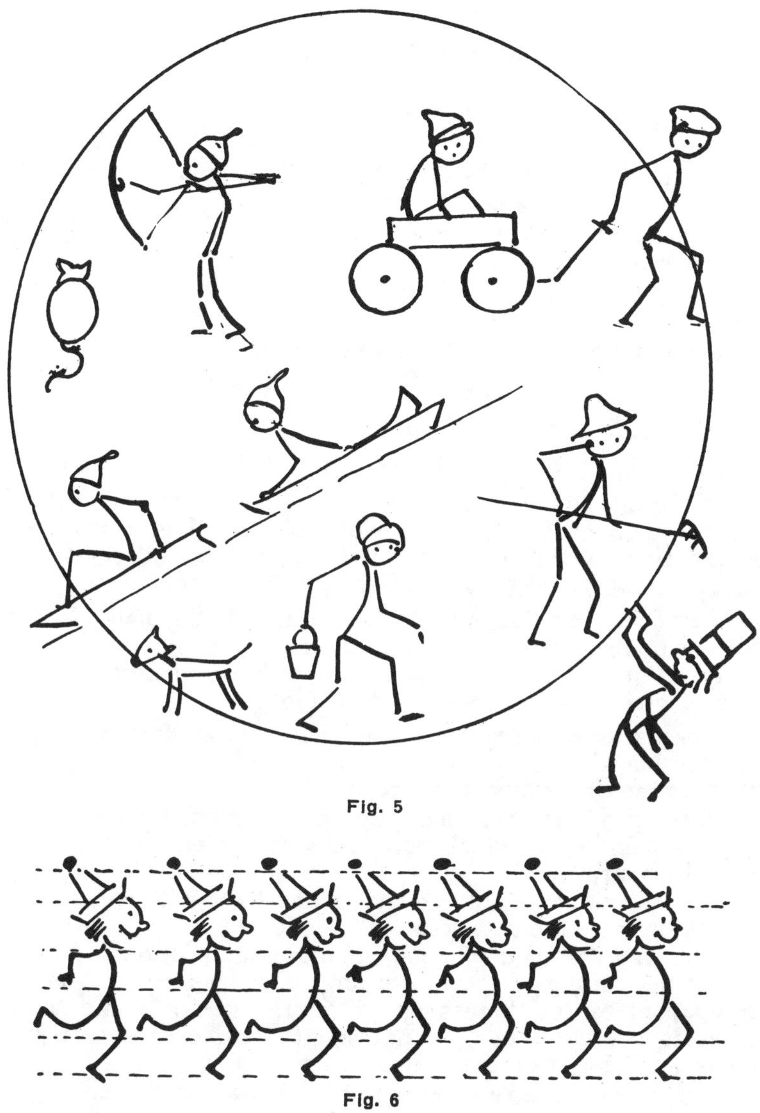

Fig. 5

Fig. 6

Notes.—Subjects in which action is introduced will be found on pp. 48, 52, 84, 87, 88, 89, 134, 135, 136, 141, 144, 146, 147, 152, 153, 154, 156, 157, 158, 161, 163, 165, 259, 260, 290.

CHAPTER XVI

PASTEL-STENCILING

Pastel-stencil work is an exceedingly fascinating line of art work invented by the author of this work.

As its name indicates, it is a dry stencil process, easy and cleanly in operation.

For beginners, it is better than any other method of stenciling. It is reversible, and by its use the most complex geometric, ornamental and other forms become simple.

One great advantage is that both sides of the stencil can be utilized, because:

(1) The stencils are self-cleaning.

(2) Pigment never adheres sufficiently to cause smudging.

Blending Colors.—In making designs by means of pastel stenciling one is enabled to blend colors and give variation to the lines and tints transferred, making modulations that cannot be obtained by any other stencil process.

Parts May Be Taken Out.—By means of this method, with the use of the rubber or similar eraser parts of the design may be taken out, in the case of decorative design, gaining the effect of one ornament placed upon another.

The materials used are these: A sheet of drawing paper (or the blackboard).

A sheet of oil stencil board.

A pencil for making the design on the stencil.

A pen knife, of which only the extreme end of the blade need be sharp.

An assortment of colored chalks or crayon. These must be soft to produce the best results.

The wax crayon can be used to a modified degree.

Rather strange to say, working with wax crayons is accompanied by less "mussing up" of the person using them, whereas the work itself is not so productive of neatness in effect as the use of the soft crayons.

Adapted for the Younger Artists.—Work with pastel-stencils is admirably adapted for children because by this means the study of form becomes peculiarly interesting instead of tiresome.

As an example, cut stencils in shapes shown in Fig. I. By making them in various colors, color as well as form can be learned with a minimum of effort and a maximum of interest.

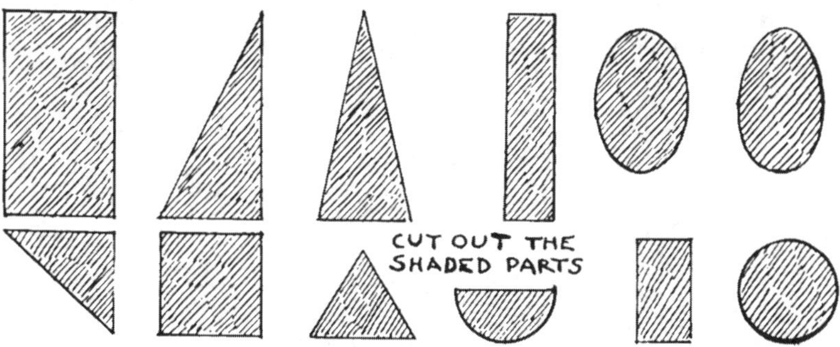

Fig. 1—Stencils for Early Exercises

The sauce crayon mentioned in Chapter XXVI is excellent for pastel stenciling where soft gray and white effects are desired.

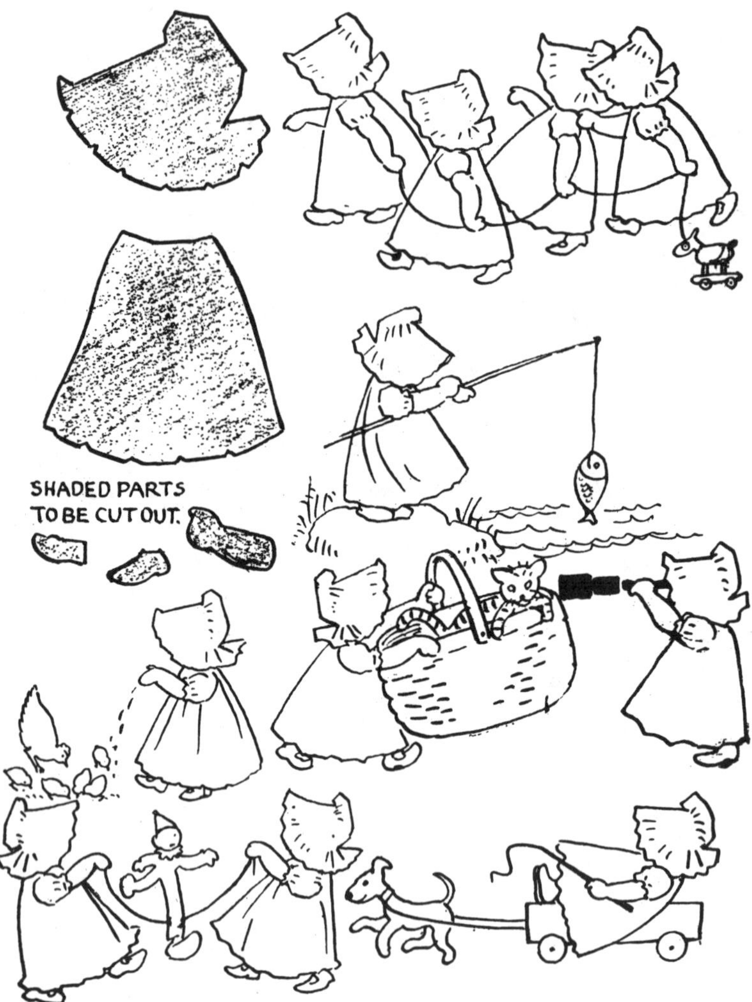

Fig. 2—Sun-bonnet Babies made with the help of the pastel-stencils.

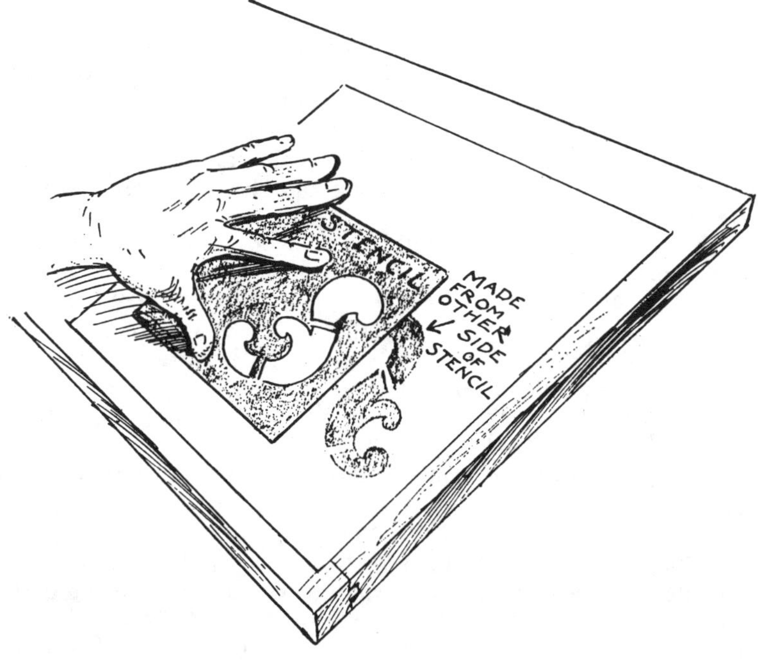

Fig. 3

After making a stencil impression from one side of the stencil it may be reversed and an opposite impression made. This is the manner in which the vase in Fig. 4 was made.

The color can be applied in several ways.

(1) By means of powdered crayon taken up on a rag or "pouncet."

(2) By means of crayon applied to the rag or "pouncet."

(3) By means of the crayon applied directly to the paper through interstices or openings in the stencil, and then distributed over the required surface with the rag.

Varying Degrees of Color.—The last method is an important one, as it permits of variation and blending of tints and gradations or softening of detail when such are indicated. Thus, if a leaf is being stenciled, one side may be made lighter than the other, placing blue on one side of the interstice and yellow on the other. Then by gently rubbing with the rag or pouncet (the former is better for this purpose) the result may show a light green running into dark.

Autumn tints are easily produced by this means.

In the case of a vase or butterfly beautiful ranges of color can be secured with scarcely any effort.

High Lights Taken Out.—High lights can easily be taken out without removing the stencil. Little dabs of very brilliant color can also be added after the blending before removing the stencil.

A hardwood board should be placed under the oilboard when cutting the stencil. For obvious reasons, do not use a desk or table, or even the drawing board for this purpose.

Separating the Parts.—Usually it is not necessary to cut quite through the stencil, for the material is rather brittle, and when the design has been cut nearly through a gentle pressure will usually separate the parts. When they cling together a little added cutting will be necessary.

Margins.—Enough margin should be left around the designs to prevent the colors from being rubbed beyond the margin. About an inch will suffice.

Where Only Half Stencil Is Needed.—If the design to be stenciled is one that can be formed of two or more parts quite alike, though reversed, like a vase or a quarterfoil, only one section need be cut out (see Fig. 4). In the case of a vase, make a stenciled impression from one side of the stencil and then from the other. In the case of the quartrefoil stencil one-quarter; reverse and stencil an adjoining quarter, and so on. This method insures greater accuracy or balance than if the entire design were cut out.

Conformity a Requirement.—Stenciling should not be done at random. Each unit should be placed with a definite purpose. To do this lay out on the paper some design to which the units will conform—just as if in laying out a garden you were to mark the spots where trees, shrubs or plants were to be set out.

If, for instance, the design is to consist of a poster with a border, lay out the border lines as guides and stencil even with these lines, first, however, placing the corner designs. Next in order is the background design which should be, usually, low in tone, in order that when human or other figures or lettering is added, the latter will stand out distinctly. The background should never conflict or be confused with the main objects in the design.

Use of Eraser.—Should there, nevertheless, be such conflict, portions that are the cause can be removed with the eraser. In making such erasures one of the advantages of this system of stenciling will be observed. It is almost as easy to take something out as it was to put it in.

If, however, the background design has been put in dark tones, and, for instance, a line of lettering is to be placed over this, the letters, by means of suitable stencils and the eraser, can be made to appear white, or at least light, and outlines added to cause them to stand out well defined and bright against the background.

Lines Should be Added.—Stenciling alone is usually unsatisfactory and is only a step in the final design. After the patterns have been stenciled lines should be added. These may be in the form of outlines around each unit, or accented lines on one side of each. Besides these, connecting lines uniting the disconnected parts are often required. In other instances details may be added, harmonizing and contrasting. The veins of the leaves, in some instances, may be shown, stems added, and here and there tendrils may be drawn.

In addition to this, the spaces left blank, because of lack of openings in the stencil, should be filled in, and in doing this the effect of the stenciling should be closely matched.

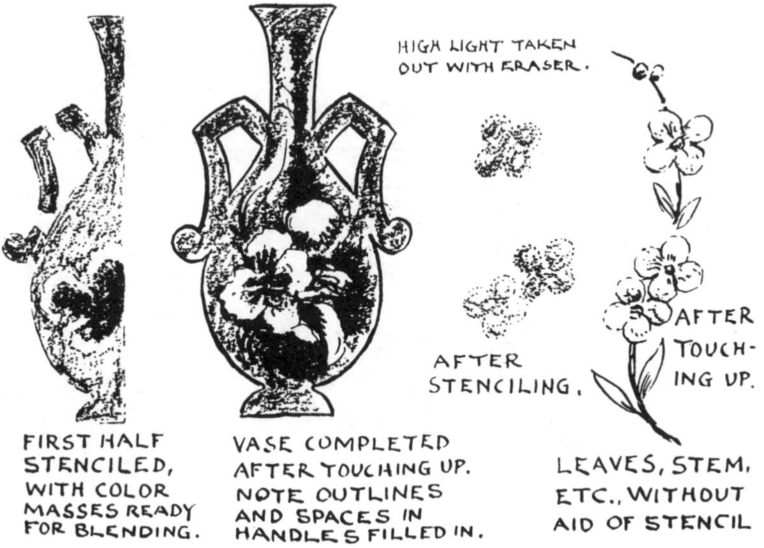

Fig. 4

A disadvantage in the use of the wax crayons is that the markings made by the wax crayon cannot be erased or defects readily remedied.

Cut stencils of half butterflies similar to those indicated in Fig. 5. Use any bright tints and add detail in accordance with Fig. 9 in the chapter on Tracing and Transferring.

Cut a stencil as in Fig. 6. Repeat it as shown in Fig. 10 in the chapter on Tracing and Transferring. The white dart-shaped part, marked A, should be cut as a separate stencil and erased after the larger stencil-transfer has been made.

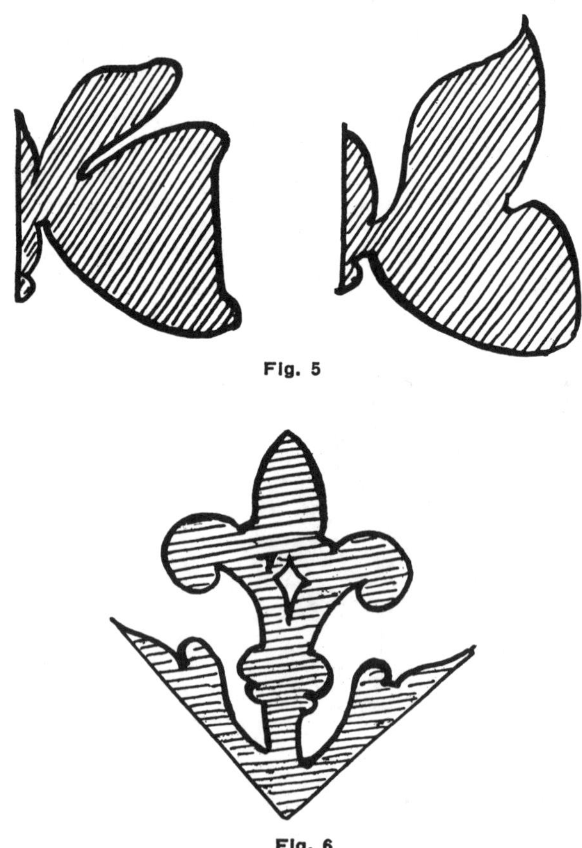

Fig. 5

Fig. 6

Stenciled medallions are easily made by the following method: Cut the unit stencil A in Fig. 7. B is a pinhole. Divide with guide lines a piece of paper as at C. Fasten the stencil with the pin in the center of C. Repeat the stencil eight times as at D. Make the additions shown in black in D. A pretty effect will be had by using two colors, alternating them. E, F, G, H and I show other unit designs that may be used.

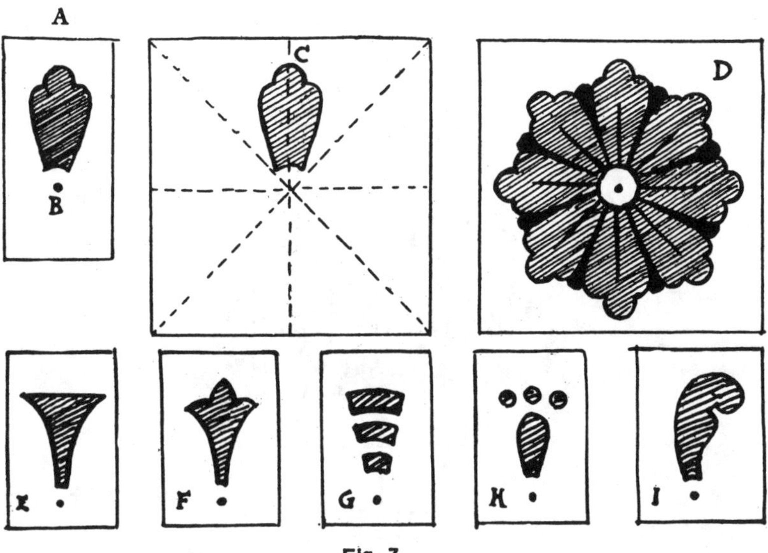

Fig. 7

Always keep your drawing materials at hand, and when putting them away, keep them all in some one place provided for that purpose.

Cut a stencil of half of the Christmas tree and the pot. Stencil one side and then reverse. Use dark green applied evenly. Cut a few stencils for the candles, toys, etc. Use them with the eraser, taking out the indicated spaces. Leave the candles white, but color in various tints the toys, etc., on the tree. The pot should be colored a bright red.

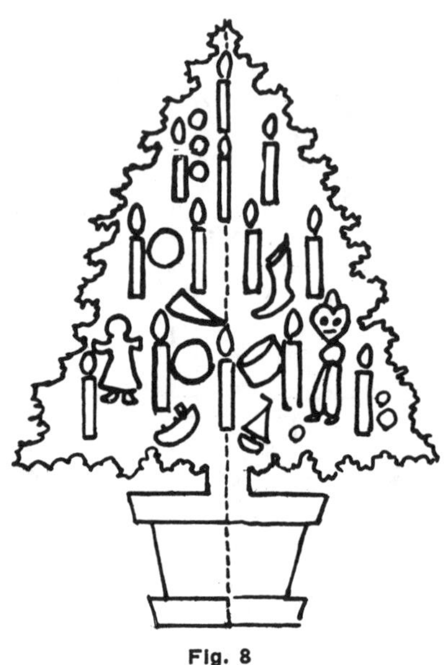

Fig. 8

Directions for Cutting Out and Using the Stencil Sectional Alphabet

Outline and then cut out the shaded parts. Leave more space between the characters than in the copies given on next page. Both sides of the stencils may be used, as they are intended for *dry stenciling*. Oiled stencil board is recommended for this purpose since dry colors do not adhere to its surface.

When stenciling a line of lettering, make one guide line in pencil on the paper on which the stencil is to be made. The guide line may be at the top or bottom of the letters.

The letters are formed in the following manner:

A—Stencil No. 1 use twice, with No. 4 for the cross-bar. Very little space is needed between A and any letter placed next to it.

B—Stencil No. 1 with No. 2 used twice. Leave ample space between B and all "crowded" letters.

The "crowded" letters are B, C, D, E, G, H, I, K, M, N, O, Q, R, S, U, X and Z. Leave less space between B and all other letters when an "open" letter is the next one.

The "open" letters are A, F, J, L, P, V, W and Y.

C—Stencil No. 3, and No. 6; the latter used twice—once as seen in the copy and once reversed.

D—Stencil No. 1, and Stencil No. 3 reversed.

E—Stencil No. 1, and Stencil No. 4 for top and bottom. Use No. 5 for center cross-bar.

F—Same as E, leaving out lower cross-bar.

G—Same as C, with the cross-bar No. 5 added, using it reversed.

H—Stencil No. 1 use twice; cross-bar No. 4.

I—Stencil No. 1.

J—Stencil No. 4 used vertically, and No. 2 turned half around.

K—Stencil No. 1, and No. 4 used twice, obliquely.

L—Stencils Nos. 1 and 4.

M—Stencil No. 1 used twice, and No. 4 used twice, obliquely.

N—Stencil No. 1 used twice, once obliquely.

O—Stencil No. 2 used twice, turned half around.

P—Stencil Nos. 1 and 2.

Q—Same as C, with stencil No. 7 added.

R—Same as P, adding cross-bar No. 4, used obliquely.

S—Stencil No. 8 used as seen in copy for the upper part; using other side for the lower part.

T—Stencil No. 1 for main stem, then use No. 4 or 5, as is seen in copy, for right half of cross-bar, turning it around for the left half.

U—Stencil No. 2 turned half around for lower part; No. 4 for upper part.

X—Stencil No. 1 used twice.

Y—Stencil No. 4 used twice obliquely; No. 5 for lower part.

Z—Use No. 4 twice and No. 1 used obliquely.

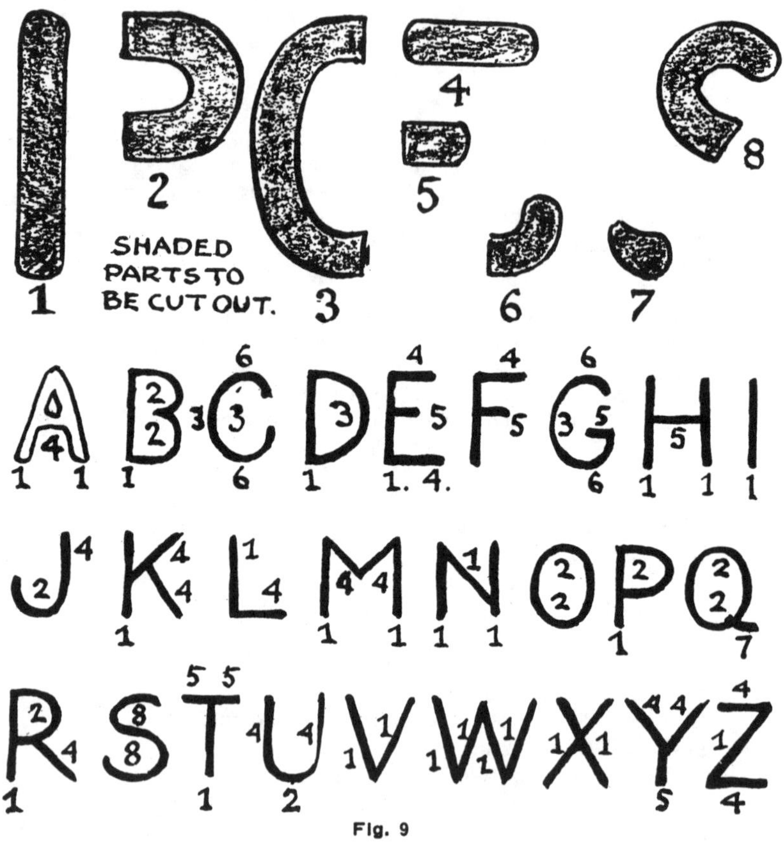

Fig. 9

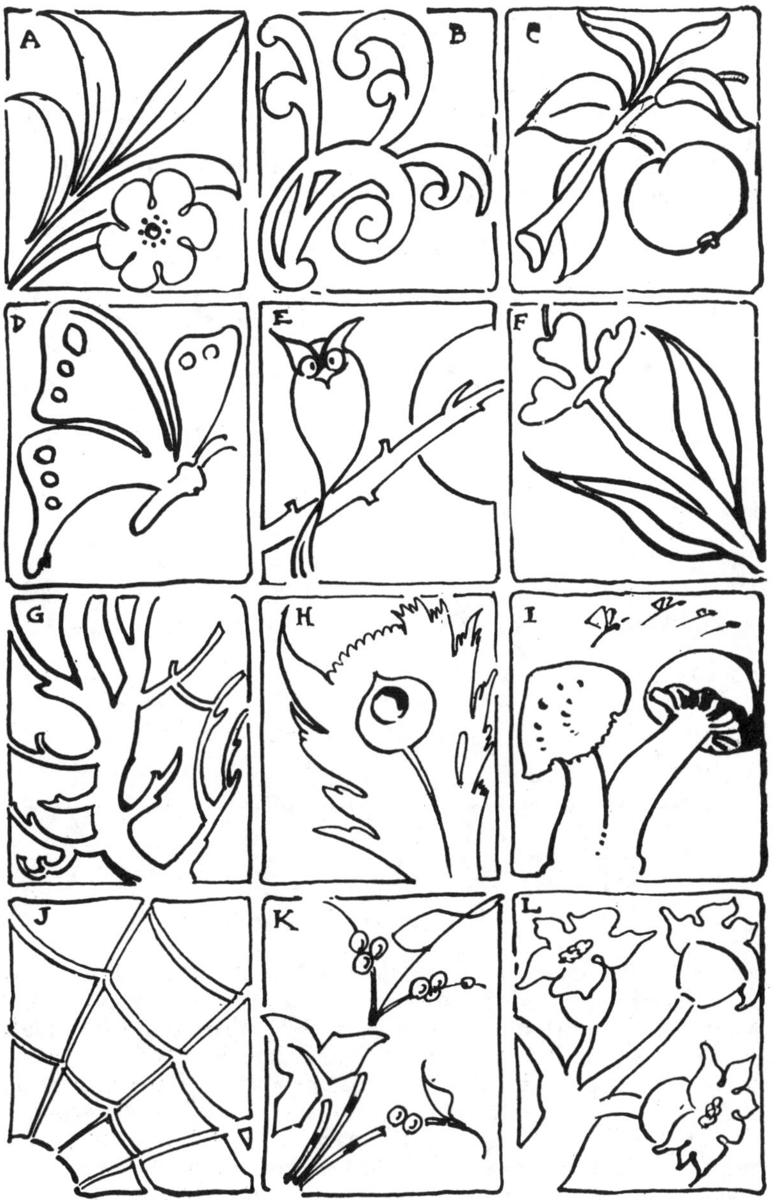

Fig. 10

Fig. 10 contains simple designs which are adaptable for a variety of purposes, such as pastel-stenciling, as, for instance, B, D, E, F, G and I.

The above-mentioned designs are also suitable for paper cutting.

A, C, F, J, K and L may be adapted for decorative purposes by repetition for borders, etc.

How to Use the Stencils in Fig. 11

The stencil patterns 1 to 14 in Fig. 11 should be made double the size shown here. The dotted lines in 1 and 3 indi-

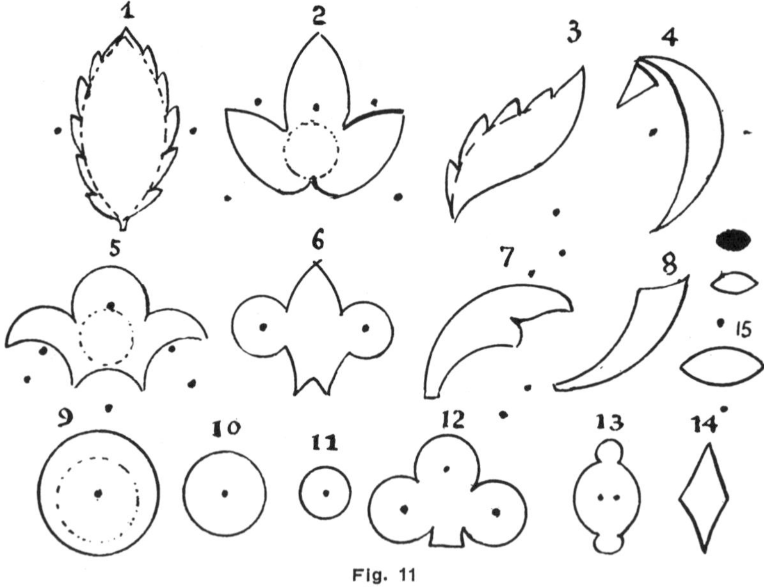

Fig. 11

cate that the cutouts are to be made along those lines, and the serrations or notches of the leaves are to be cut afterwards. The dotted circles in 5 and 9 mean that the small spaces are to be erased after the main spaces have been filled with color. Nearly all the forms, or parts of them, can be cut out by means of a pair of dividers. The board need not be cut entirely through. The board being brittle, the pieces can be pushed out when the board is partly cut through. The black dots indicate where the point of the dividers is to be placed. All the designs in Fig. 12 can be formed mainly by the use of the stencils. Then Nos. 1, 2, 3, 4, 5 and 14 in Fig. 11 correspond with the figures in Fig. 12. The dotted line at the side of No. 5 is a guide line, such as should be made whenever a border or other straight line of units of design is intended.

Fig. 12

Notes.—Objects adapted to pastel-stenciling will be found on pp. 27, 38, 39, 42, 48, 59, 60, 61, 62, 63, 65, 78, 83 (Fig. 2), 84, 85, 93, 117, 118, 119 (Fig. 6), 122 (Fig. 1), 124, 125, 126, 142, 161, 165, 181, 193, 196, 199, 217, 229, 230 (Fig. 7), 233, 234, 245, 246, 251, 252, 253, 264 (Fig. 2), 265, 267, 269, 270, 271, 272, 273, 274, 275, 279, 280, 283.

CHAPTER XVII

DRAWING FLOWERS

Models for drawing flowers and like forms of vegetation are so easily procurable that it seems unnecessary to give many examples in these pages. Real flowers, etc., are better than copies. For purposes of a model one flower is as good as another; one leaf is as good as another. The only advice

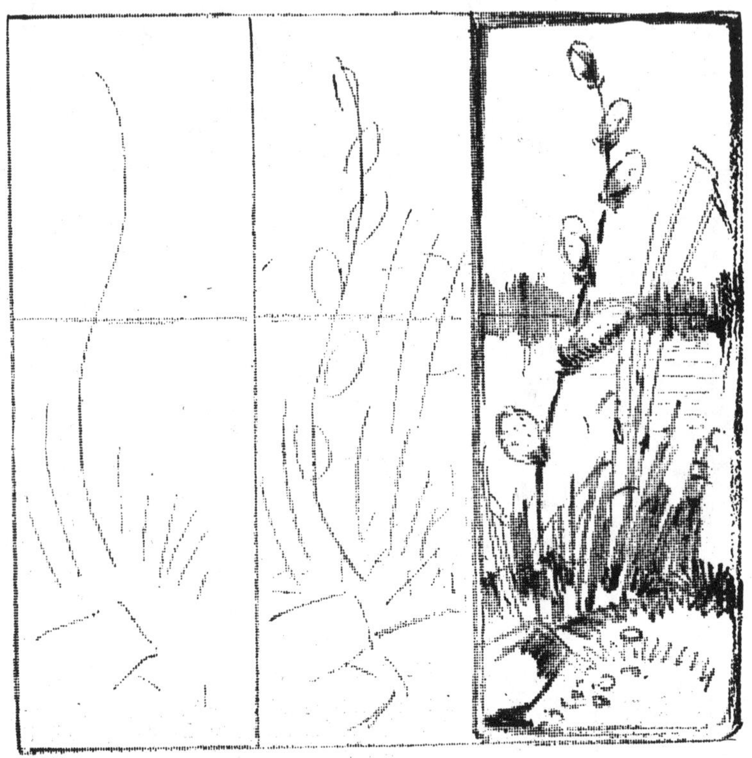

Fig. 1

to be given is that the beginner should be given a simple flower or leaf. Afterward the more complex flora may be studied and drawn, from nature preferably. A daisy, a dande-

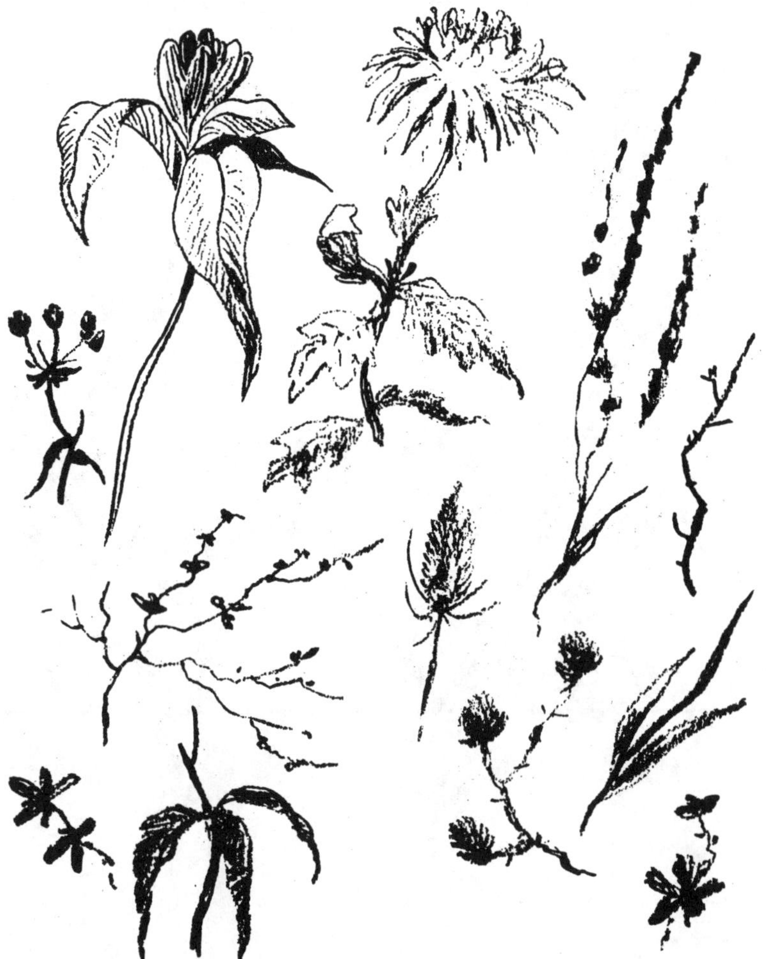

Fig. 2—Fragments of a Flower Treatment

lion, or a pansy is better to begin with than a rose, a peony or a chrysanthemum.

Any Weed Offers Good Practice.—Nothing is better than a twig with a leaf or two attached. When the natural flowers are not to be had, artificial ones can be made to fulfill the purpose.

The general lines of direction in a drawing should be indicated, and the general shapes of the detail also should be

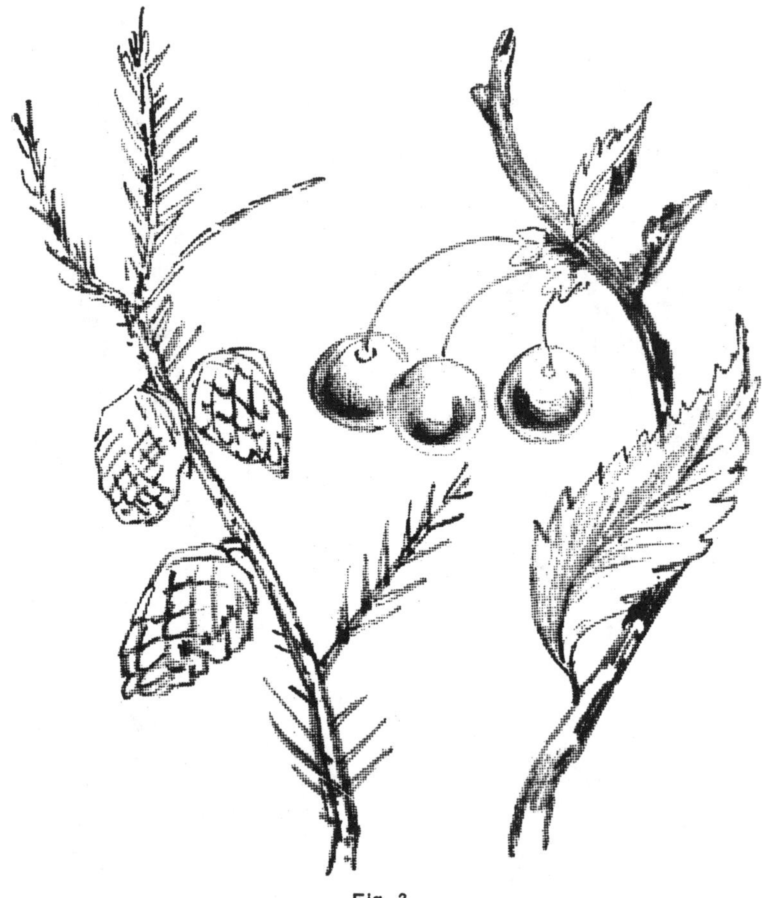

Fig. 3

shown by light lines before the finishing touches are attempted. By doing so, defects in the lightly drawn lines can be easily remedied; whereas, after the drawing is completed this is almost impossible without smudgy effects being produced. See Fig. 1.

In the sketches shown on page 114, the idea conveyed in the foregoing paragraph is illustrated, and three stages of progress shown.

Curved and Straight Lines.—One should become equally proficient in the use of curved and straight lines, both being useful for different purposes. For instance, in the example shown in Fig. 3, straight lines are most effective for drawing the pine cones, the twigs and needles; on the other hand, curved lines are best for rendering the cherries, etc., at the right.

In the earliest exercises, when drawing flowers or leaves from nature, the objects themselves should be rendered in simplified form. For instance, remove the leaves from the stem, leaving only a single flower. Again, remove the flower, leaving only one or two leaves. Increase complexity as ability develops.

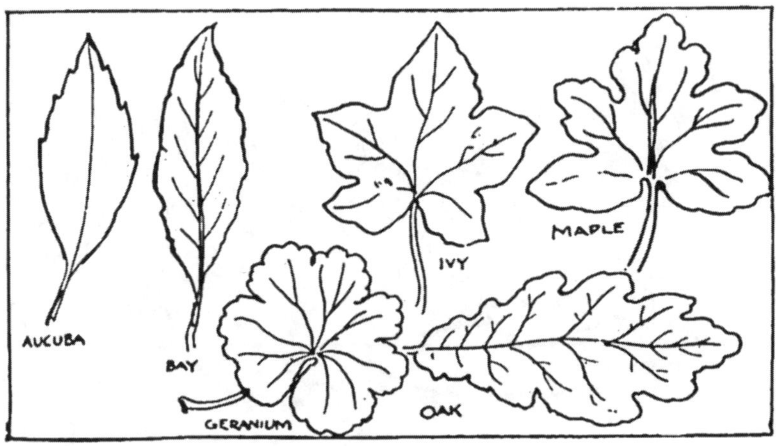

Fig. 4—A Few Leaf Forms

Notes.—Other forms will be found on pp. 105, 111, 113, 222, 238, 267, 274, 279.

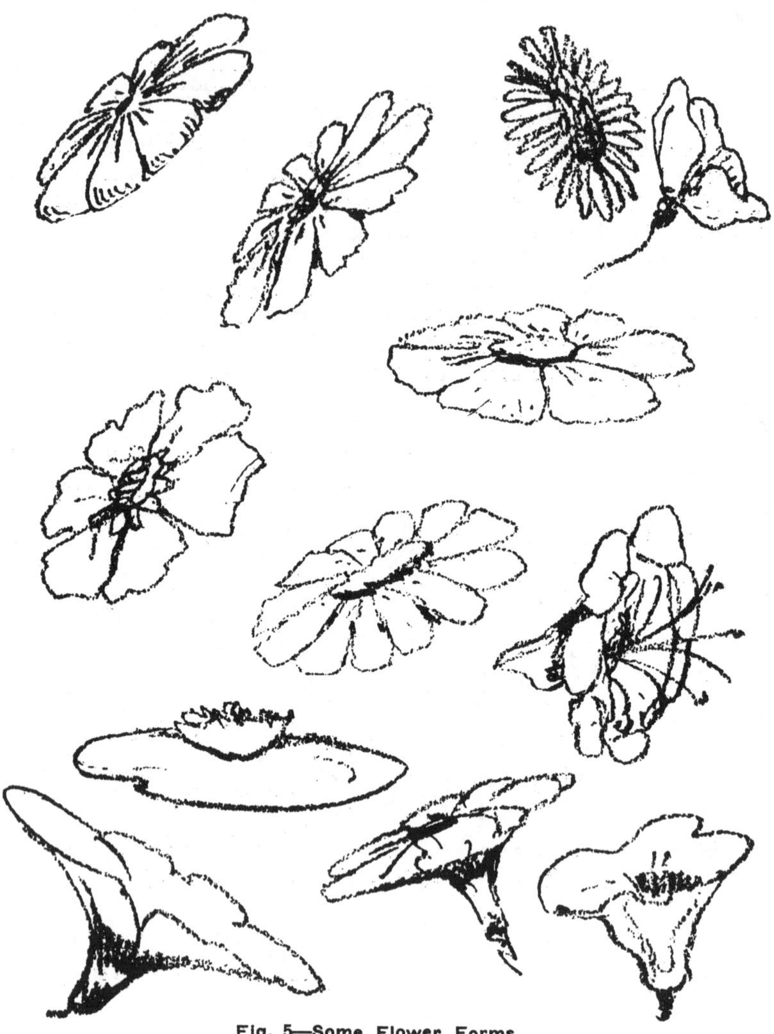

Fig. 5—Some Flower Forms

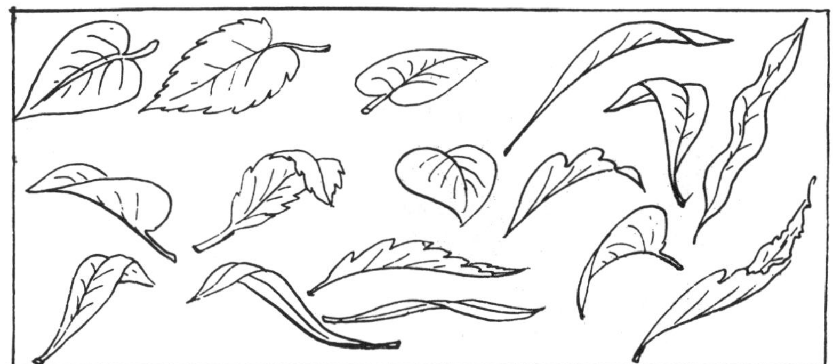

Fig. 6—Leaves Foreshortened. (See chapter on Foreshortening.)

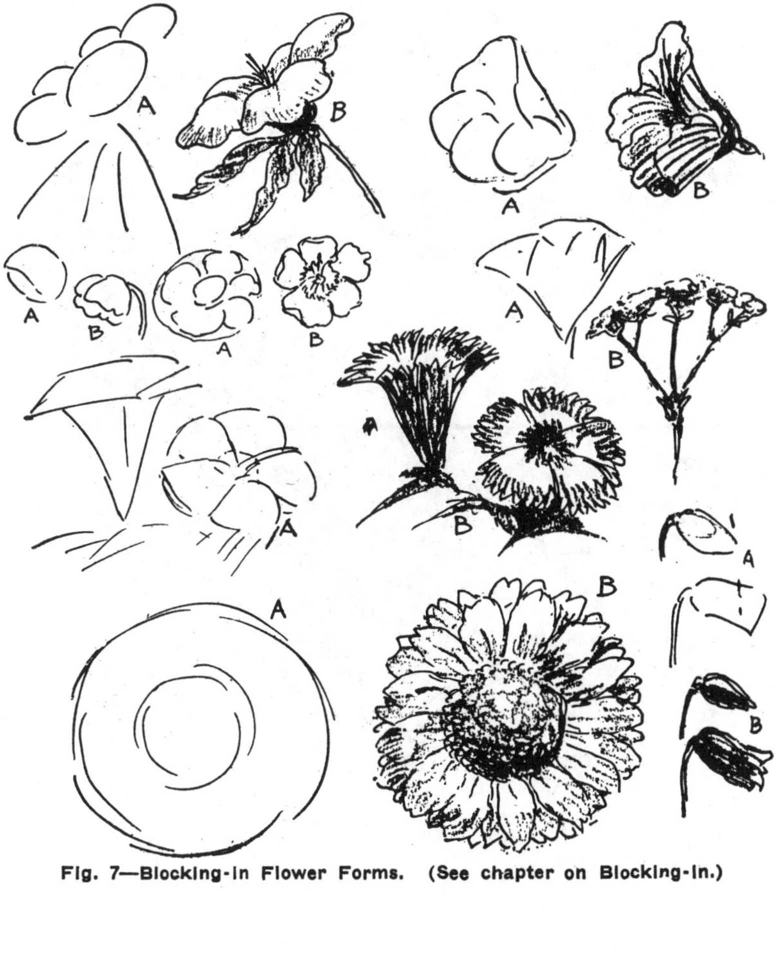

Fig. 7—Blocking-in Flower Forms. (See chapter on Blocking-in.)

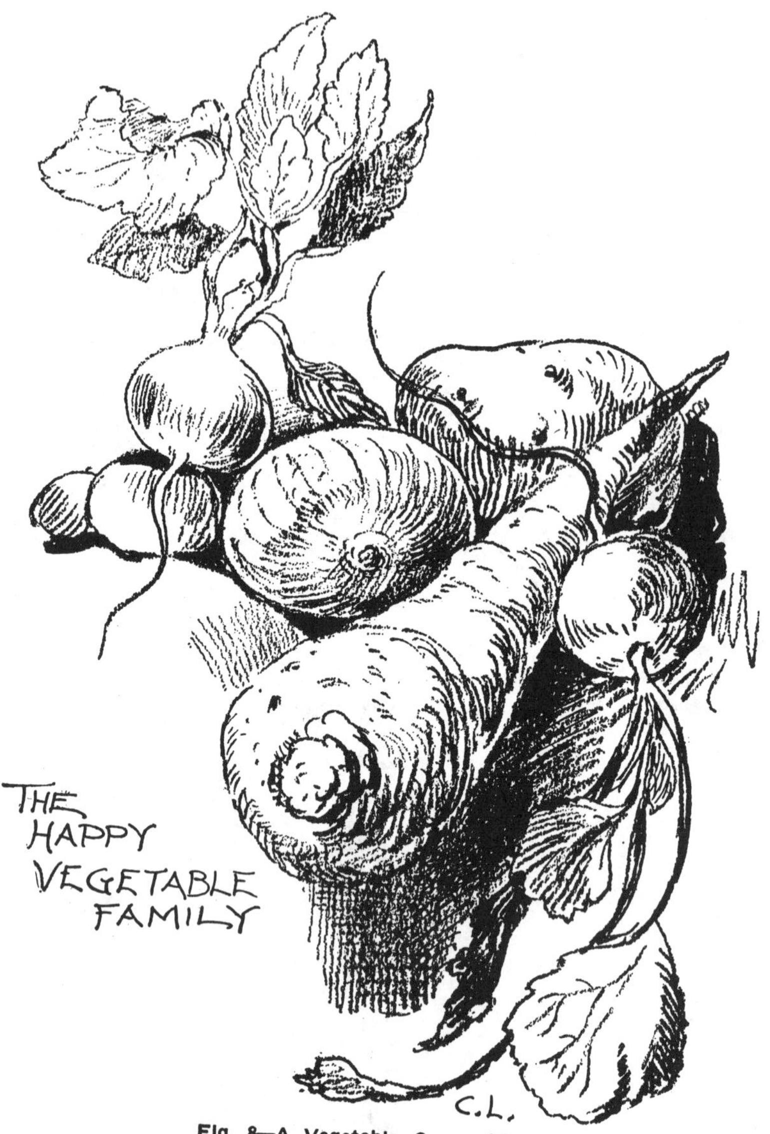

Fig. 8—A Vegetable Composition

CHAPTER XVIII

SOLID BLACK EFFECTS

Solid Blacks.—The placing of solid blacks should be done very carefully. Until you have had adequate practice it will be well to outline in pen and ink the spaces to be filled with solid black, before applying the brush. (See Fig. 1.) This process will prevent the abrupt or uneven edges frequently found in the brush work of the beginner. The brush should be used with just sufficient of the black pigment to produce denseness when the ink has dried. The best results are obtained by putting the blacks in after the pencil sketch, or guide lines, have been erased. Otherwise, the rubber eraser may remove part of the black surfaces, leaving them somewhat grayish.

Methodical Brush Handling.—The brush should be used methodically. It should not be splashed back and forth. (See Fig. 2.) A good way is to commence at the upper parts of the spaces to be covered and slowly work downward. (See Fig. 3.)

Things to Be Avoided.—To get so much ink on the brush that it will drip.

To get so little ink on the brush that the blacks are semi-transparent or streaky.

The advice given just above applies to brush work generally.

It will repay the effort to make several drawings of an experimental character showing how effective a picture can be that is made up of merely simple outlines fortified by solid black masses thrown in by means of a pliable pen or a small brush.

For practice, two drawings should be made as nearly alike as possible. On one of them, with pencil, the places intended for solid blacks should be outlined and then filled. The other should remain in outline.

The difference between the drawings respectively with and without the solid blacks are to be noted and their respective merits compared.

OUTLINED FIRST
NOT OUTLINED
OUTLINED FIRST
NOT OUTLINED
OUTLINED FIRST
NOT OUTLINED
OUTLINED FIRST
?
?

Fig. 1

BRUSH LINES, OR STROKES THAT SHOW PURPOSE.
BRUSHLINES THAT SHOW NO PURPOSE.

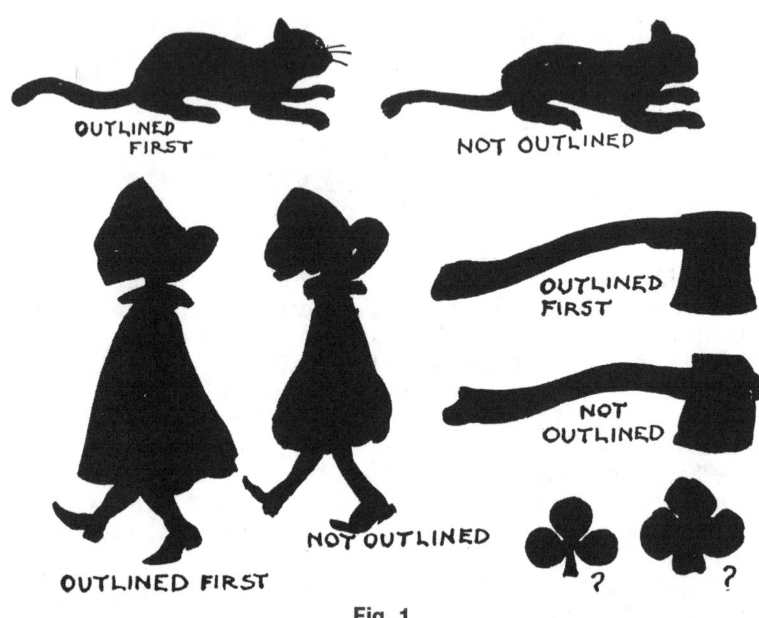

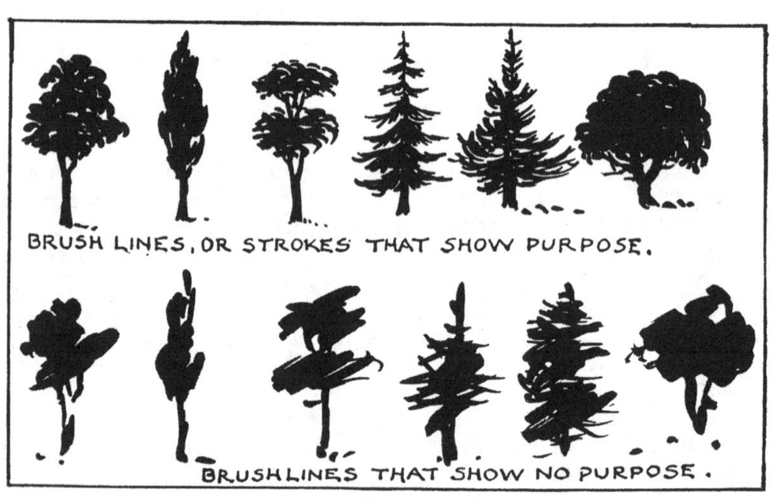

Fig. 2

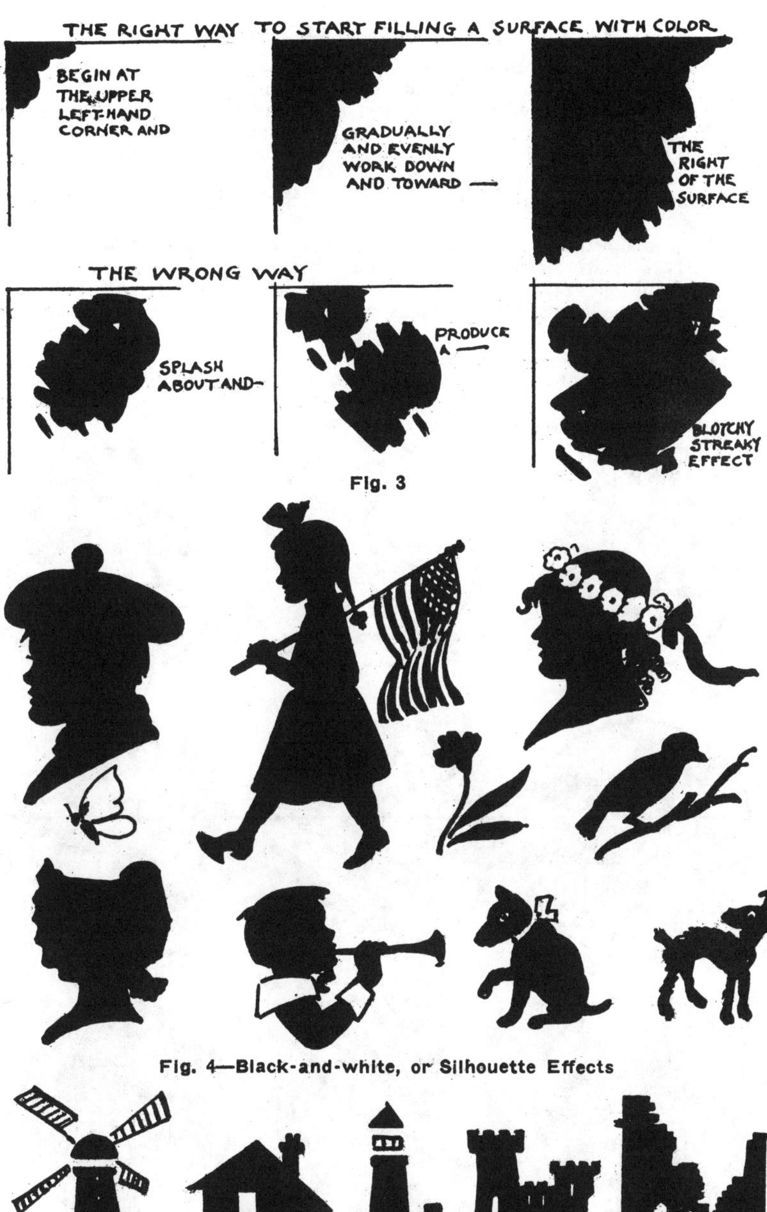

Fig. 3

Fig. 4—Black-and-white, or Silhouette Effects

Fig. 5

Black and White Exercises for Brush and Pen

The examples on this and the following pages (Figs. 6 and 7) are simple exercises in pen and ink and brush combined.

The circles are used to give a sort of frame to the little designs and to add a sense of regularity in the matter of shape.

Make the circles first in pen and ink, whether the outlines which they enclose are made with pencil guide lines or not.

A and B should be made with pen and ink without the aid of pencil outlines.

In C, make the horizon line in pencil before using pen or brush.

In D, indicate the mass of the foliage before using pen or brush.

E should have penciled outline for all details and pen-and-ink outlines should be made for the areas which are to be completed with the brush.

F—Outlines in pencil only.

G and H are exercises for brush only, without any guiding lines.

I—Pen outline for the moon and the *upper* outlines of the battlements of the castle and for its doors and windows.

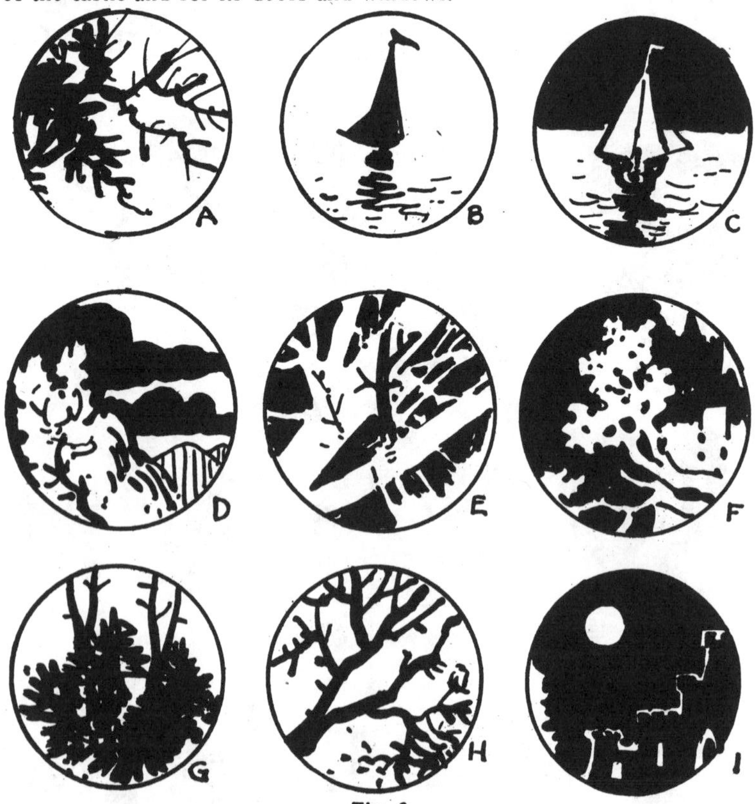

Fig. 6

J—Outlines in pencil for the branches only, which in turn may be made with strong pen lines; the leaves to be added free-hand with a brush.

K is to be outlined with pencil and completed entirely with brush.

L is to be outlined with pen only and completed with the brush.

M, N and O—Outline with pencil and complete with pen and brush.

P and Q—Outline with pencil and complete with a brush.

R—Outline with pen without pencil guides and complete with brush.

In each case, after the drawings are quite dry, erase the pencil lines.

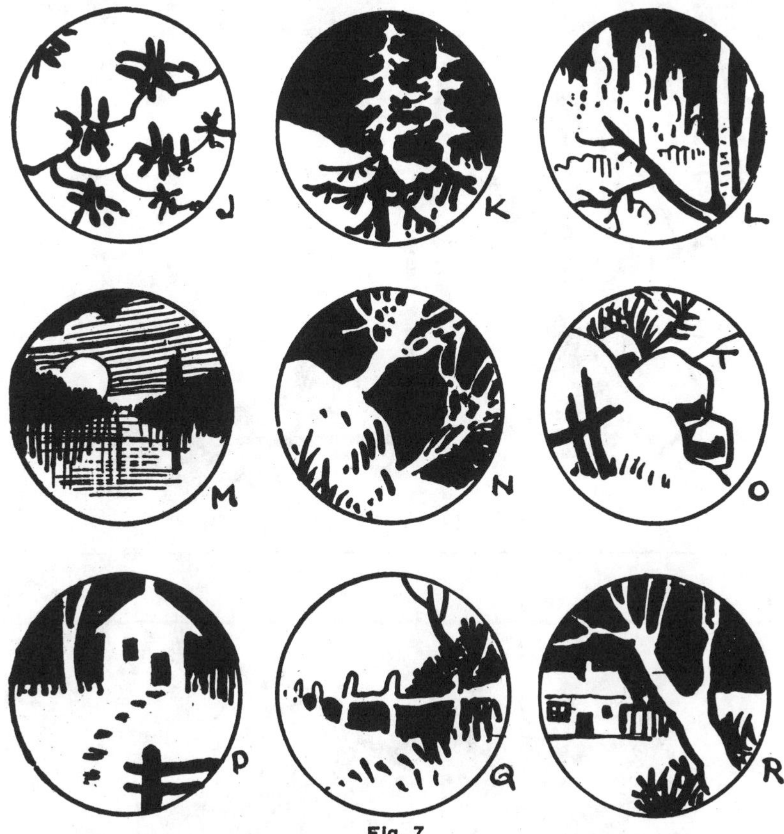

Fig. 7

Solid Blacks.—The solid black exercise previously described may be used in connection with pencil or pen effects by adding other details, either background or foreground, to the objects drawn in solid black. The best effects are secured by making these additions in a monotone, in order to secure a happy contrast between the two treatments. That is to say, no attempt need be made to blend the black subjects to the added detail.

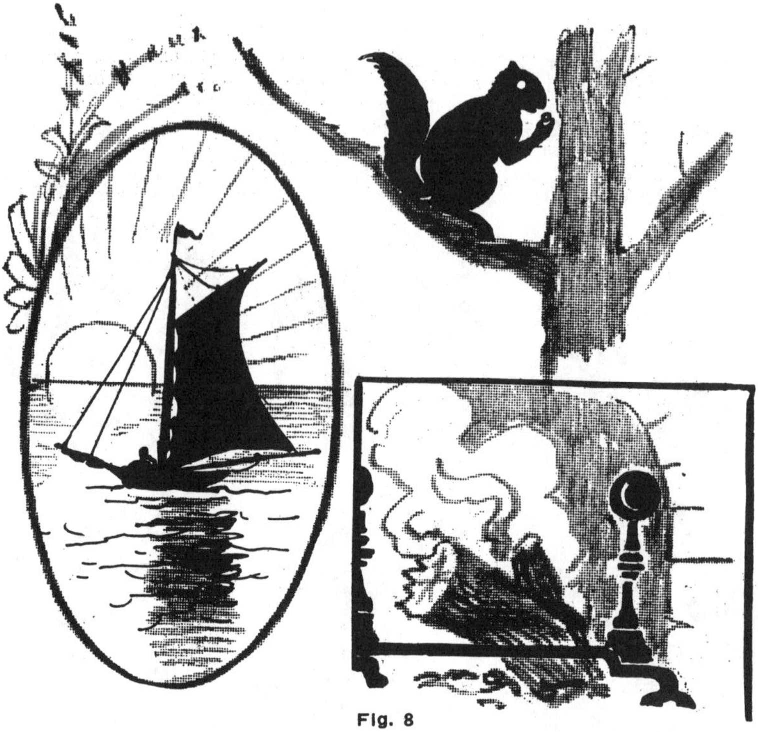

Fig. 8

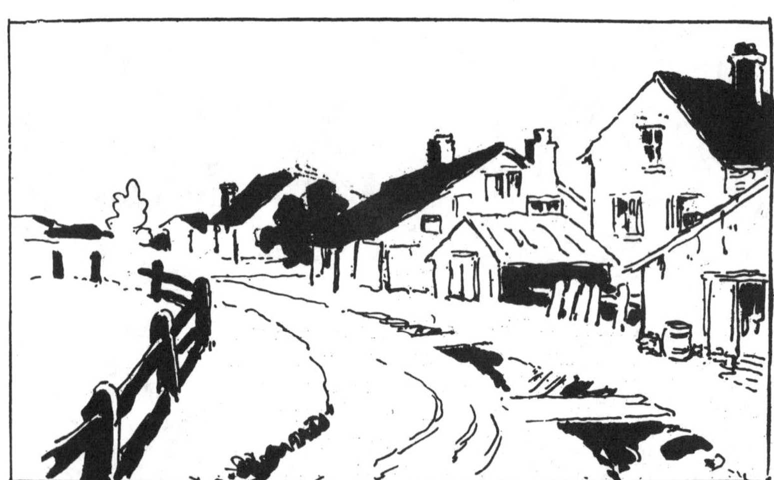

Fig. 9

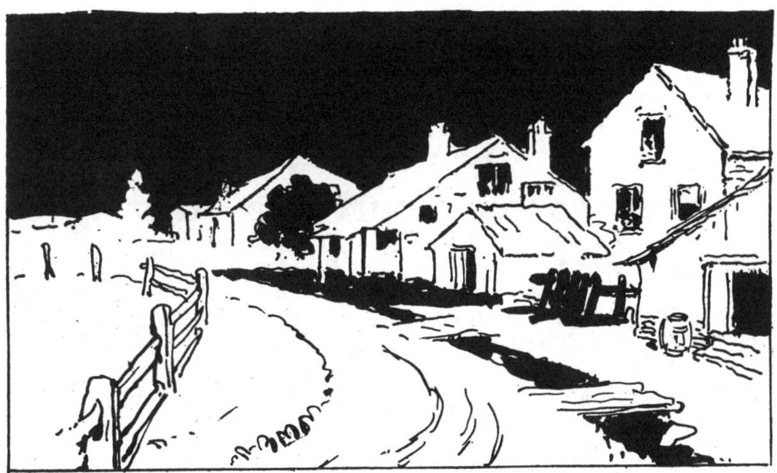

Fig. 10—Examples of Same Subjects Treated in Varying Effects by Means of Solid Black

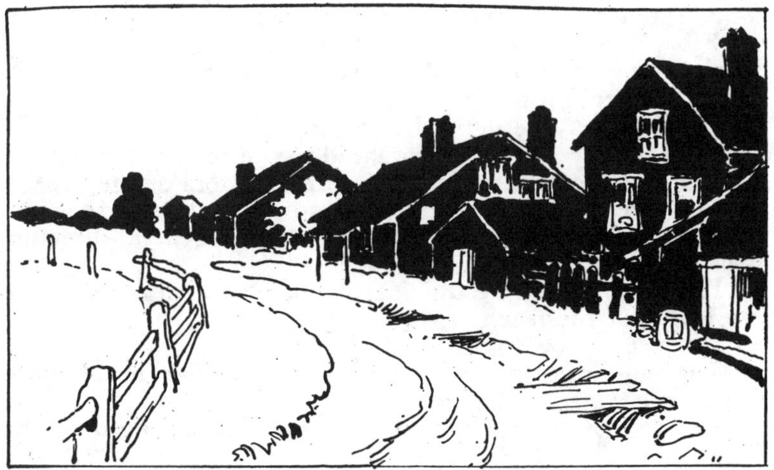

Fig. 11

Notes.—Other pages in which black effects are essential features are 52, 63, 66, 136 (Fig. 10), 147, 161, 176, 177, 178, 186, 192, 193, 194, 195, 196, 197, 253, 257, 290, 299, 300, 301.

CHAPTER XIX

DRAWING MEN, WOMEN AND CHILDREN

Proportions of the Human Figure.—The Greek statues have regulated and determined the standard of beauty in art. These proportions, however, vary in individual cases and individual tastes. They are, however, valuable as a foundation from which modifications may be made.

In the Greek statues, the height of a developed man was usually eight heads; that is, the head was one-eighth the length of the body.

The height of a woman, Greek standard, about seven heads.

The human figure may be divided into four parts of equal length, namely:

1. From the top of the head to the arm-pit.
2. From the arm-pit to the middle of the body.
3. From the middle of the body to the knees.
4. From the knees to the soles of the feet.

From finger-tip to finger-tip, when the arms are extended at right angles to the body equals the length of the entire figure from crown to toes.

The face may be divided into three parts:

1. From the top of the forehead to the root of the nose.
2. From the root of the nose to the bottom of the nose.
3. From the bottom of the nose to the bottom of the chin.

The ear is the length of the nose and its general direction is parallel to it.

From the top of the shoulder to the elbow measures twice the length of the face.

From the elbow to the wrist, one head.

The hand measures three-quarters of a head from the tip of the middle finger to the wrist.

The foot measures one-sixth of the whole length of the body.

These proportions are not exact or to be arbitrarily followed.

Drawing the Human Figure.—When drawing the head, whether in profile or three-quarter view, avoid making the facial line too upright. There can be no rigid rule regarding this or any other part of the human figure, on account of the variance of different persons. The degree of difference is even greater if we consider racial variances.

Making the features too small is a common error. Sometimes, however, the error is in the opposite direction, especially in respect to the eyes. They should not be made too large for the face. In drawing the normal eye, place the pupil slightly under the upper lid. Do not draw a line directly under the eyeball. If this is done, it is apt to give an impression of soreness to the eyes. Let the line indicating the upper line of the lower lid be a trifle distant from the eyeball. Eyelashes should be sparingly introduced. Eyebrows should not be too strongly demarked.

The ears should not be longer than the nose, and they should be level with it.

Things to Avoid.—Do not make the mouth too small.

Do not make the space from the eyebrows to the top of the head too narrow.

Do not make finger nails too distinct or prominent.

Do not make goose-necks on your women nor bull-necks on your men and children.

Do not make the arms too long, unless you are making a caricature and wish to produce an ape-like effect.

Guide Lines Again.—When intending to draw a draped or clothed figure, first draw, in faint lines, the figure itself through the clothes. Erase the faint lines, which are guide lines only. This method will be of special assistance in getting the feet in the right place and in the right direction. That is, first draw the feet without the shoes, putting the latter on afterwards.

Hands

The Left Hand as a Model.—Holding the left hand in any rigid position that is most convenient and using it as a model is fine exercise. The hands are among the most difficult objects to draw, but by continued practice and observation much of the difficulty is overcome. The blocking-in method is particularly required in drawing the hands and feet.

ADULT
1
2
3
4
5
6
7
8
THERE IS NO EXACT STANDARD.
THE ADULT FIGURE VARIES FROM FIVE TO EIGHT HEADS TO THE ENTIRE HEIGHT, THE CHILD'S FROM ABOUT FOUR TO FIVE HEADS TO THE BODY.
CHILD
1
2
3
4
5
CARI-CA-TURES
BABY
1
2
3
4
WEE BABY

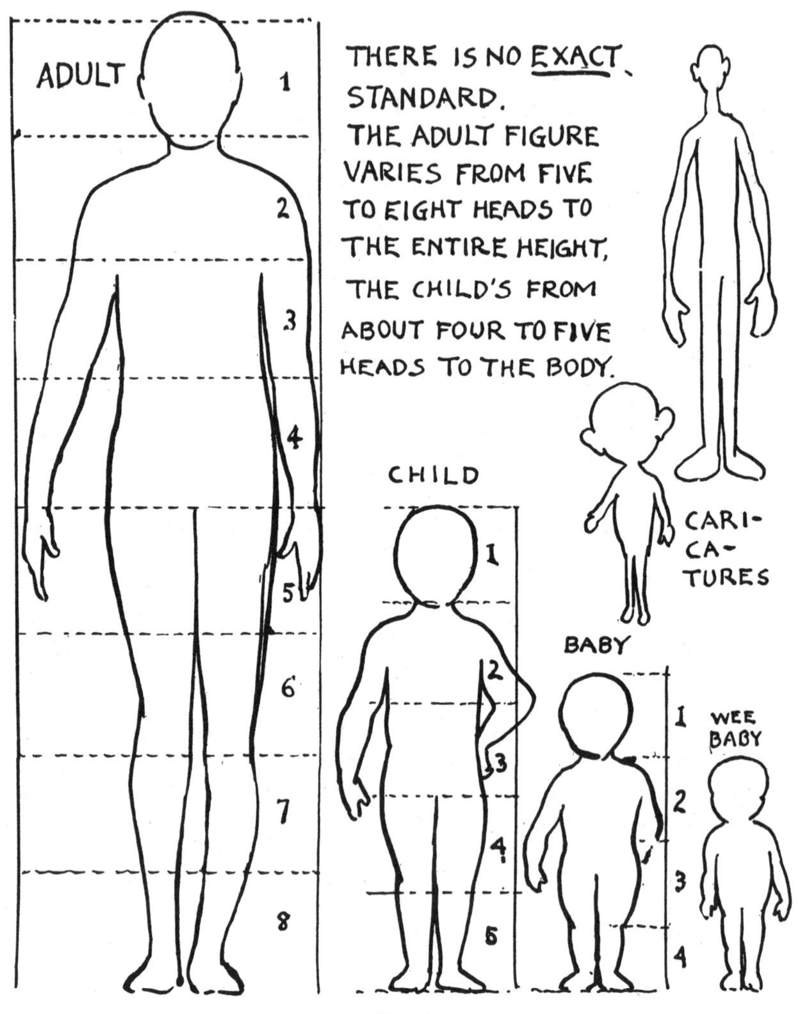

Fig. 1

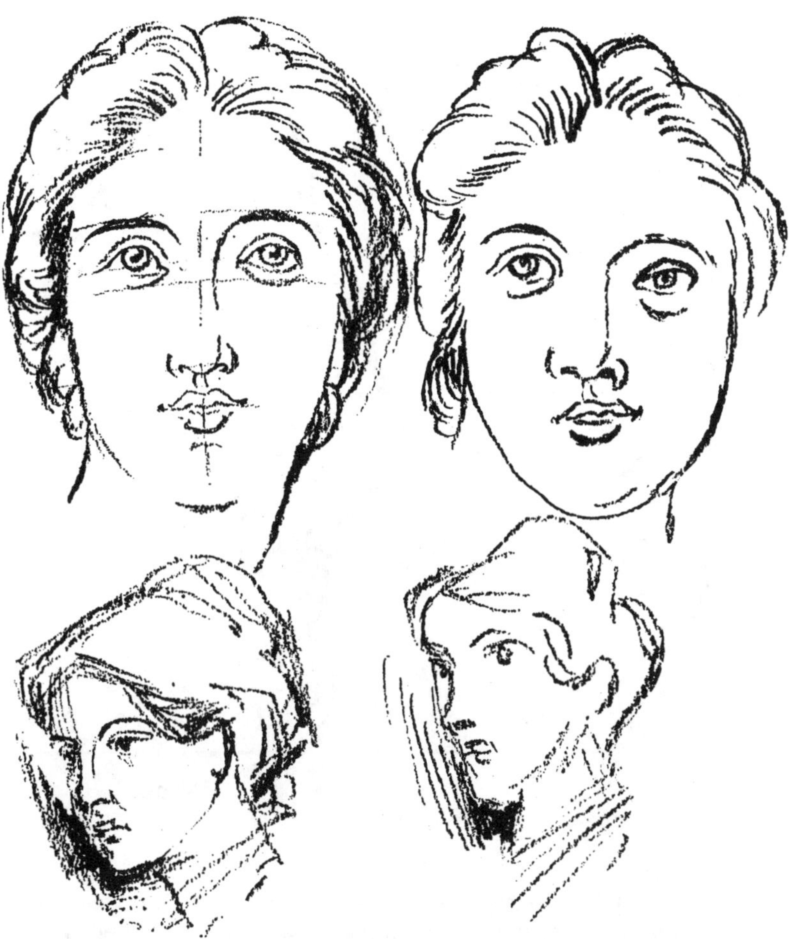

Fig. 2

Here is shown the effect of drawing faces by means of horizontal and vertical guide lines and by means of blocking-in lines, and also the effect of drawing without these aids. See how "out-of-drawing" the faces on the right appear!

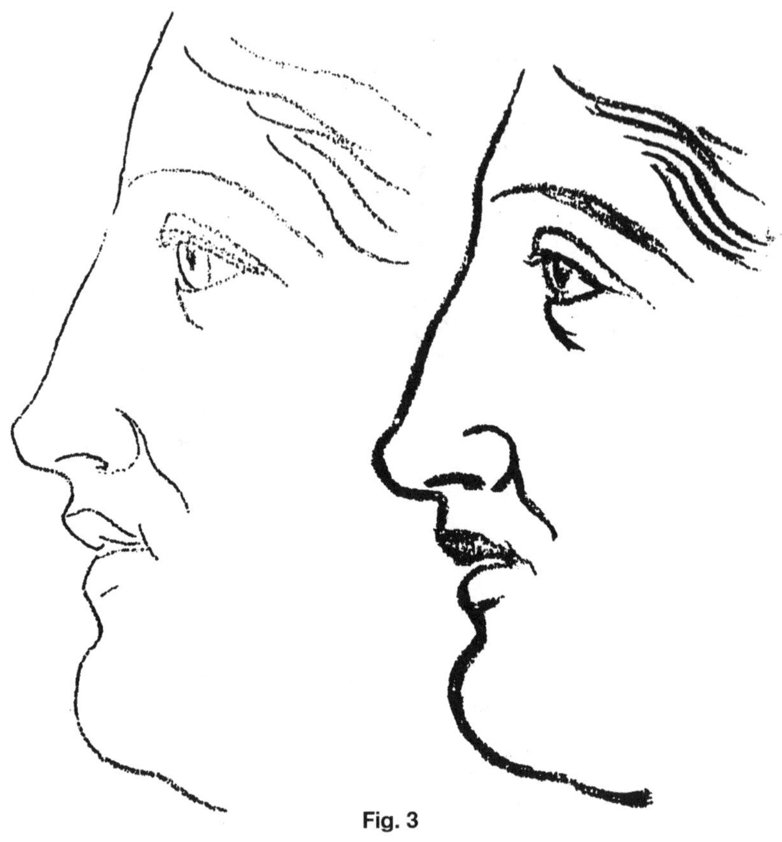

Fig. 3

Line Variations.—Fig. 3—Two big crayon faces. Choose a subject and make one drawing in which ordinary lines are used. Then treat the same subject with extremely heavy lines, using a broad-pointed pencil or crayon. The lines in the latter exercise should be made broad, with single, modulated strokes in order to make the lines sufficiently broad, instead of going over and over in order to obtain breadth.

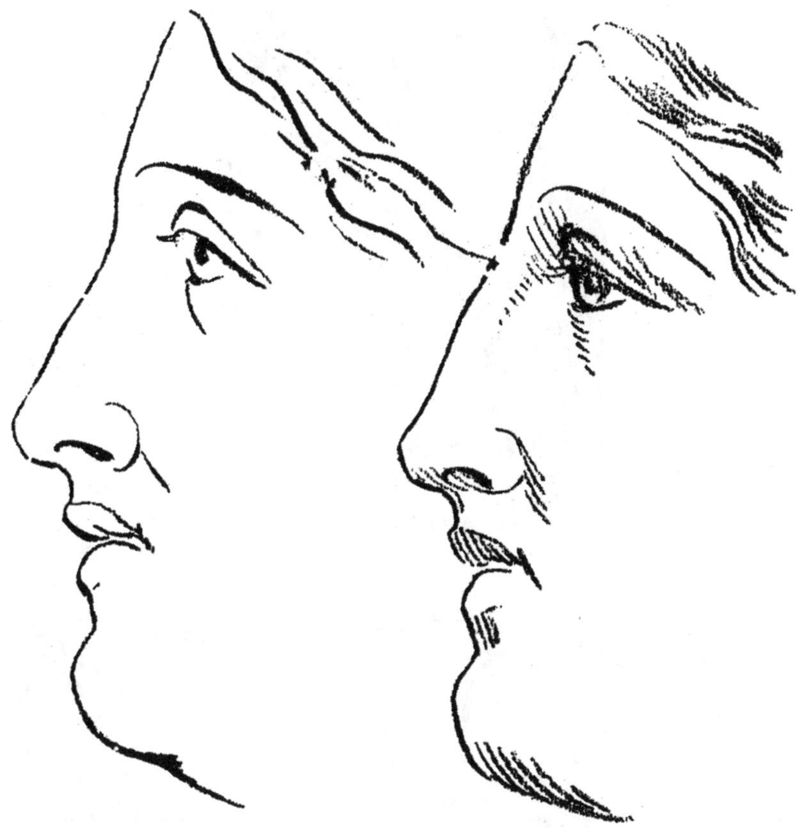

Fig. 4

The same subject may be treated with accentuated lines, and with shaded lines to give the impression of form.

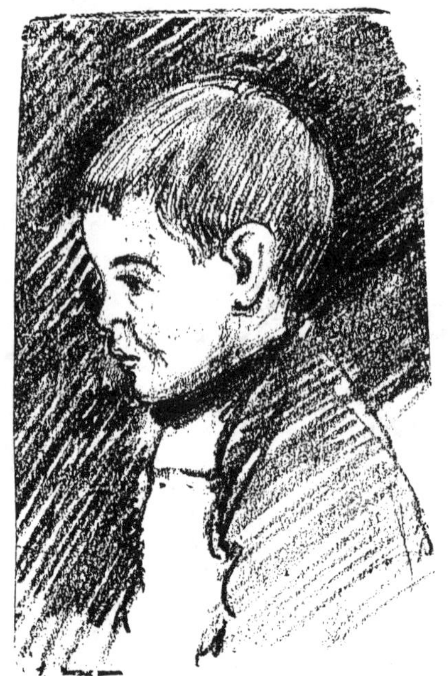

Fig. 5—A Colorado Lad. (Sketched from life.)

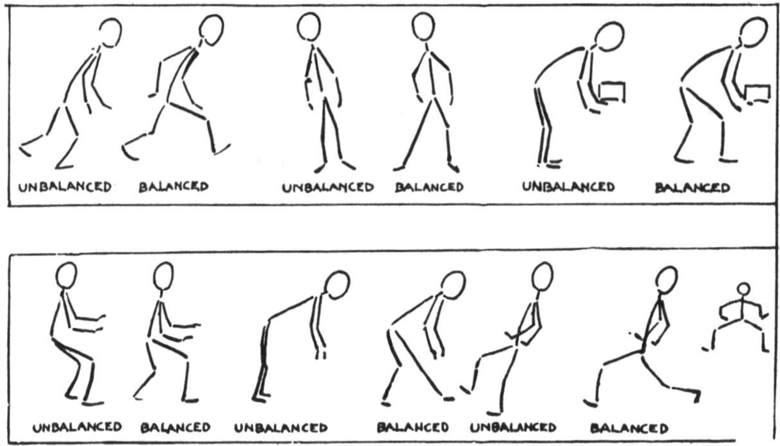

Fig. 6

Human Figures in Action.—In portraying figures in action, the principles of equilibrium may portray various forms of action other than falling, but a figure out of balance conveys to the eye the impression of falling. Thus:

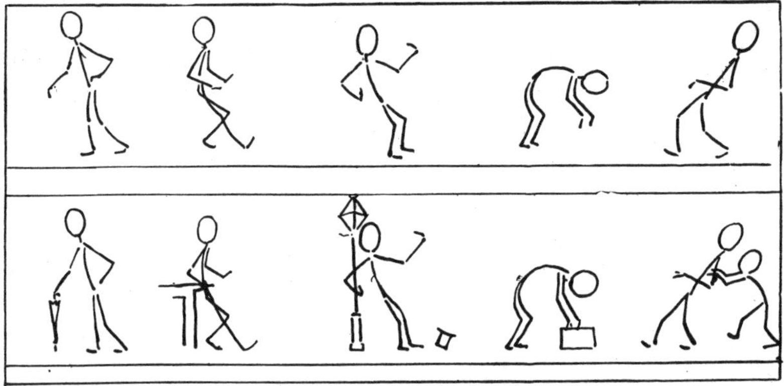

Fig. 7

In the upper drawing the figures have no "visible means of support." In the lower part the deficiency is supplied.

As a general rule, if a vertical line is drawn from the feet upward, and half of the figure lies on each side of the line, the figure will appear balanced.

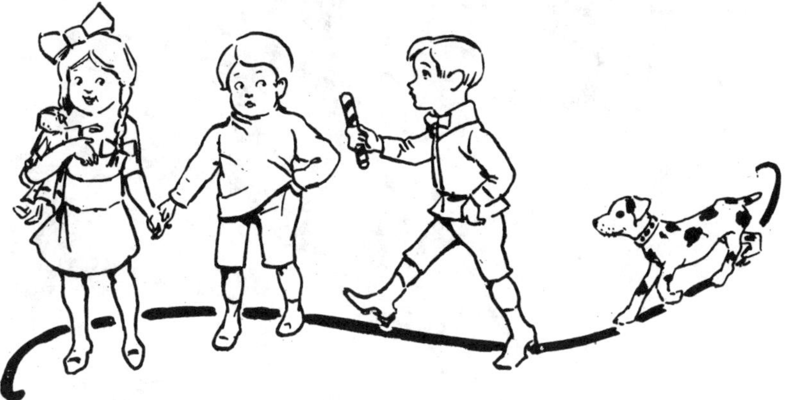

Fig. 8—Children in Simple Line Drawing

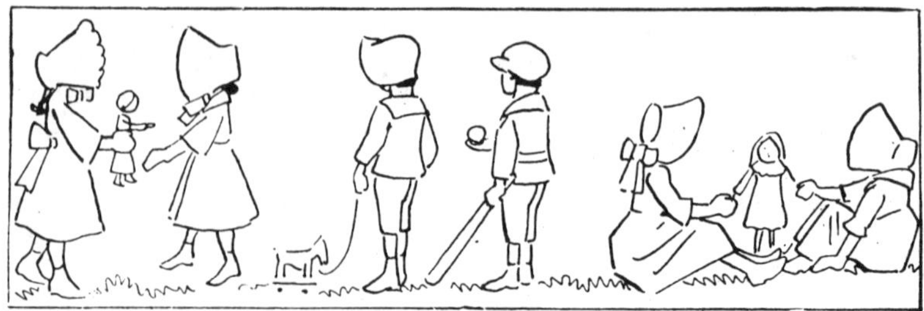

Fig. 9

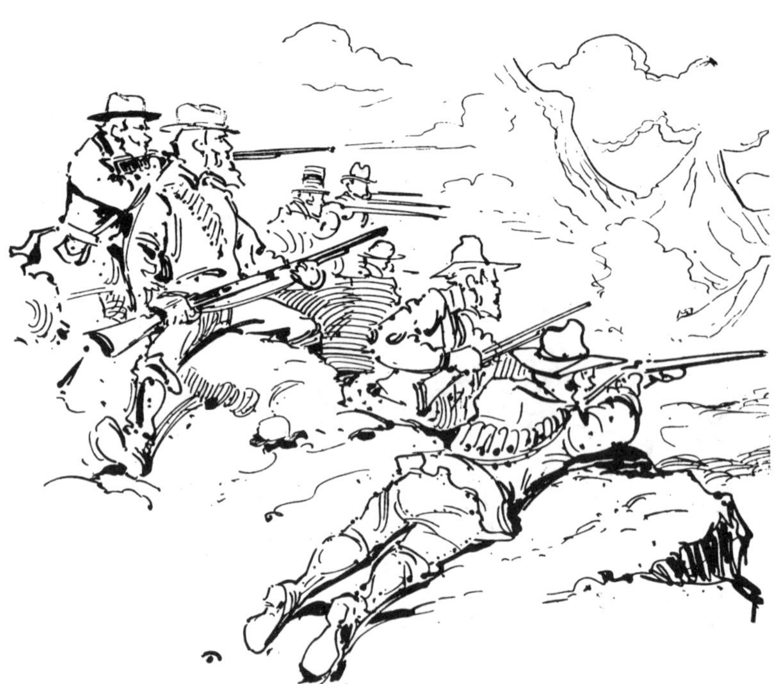

Fig. 10—Sketched During the Boer War

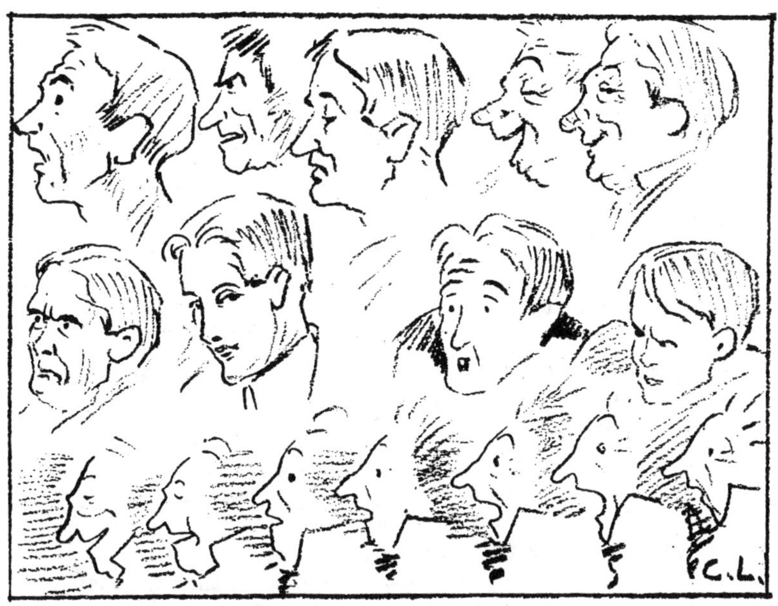

Fig. 11—Studies in Expression

Notes.—Other pages in which human figures in some form are introduced are 13, 14, 28, 29, 44, 48, 50, 51, 52, 53, 60, 63, 79, 84, 86, 87, 88, 89, 90, 92, 95, 96, 97, 99, 102, all of chapters XX and XXI, pp. 257, 258, 259, 260, 281, 286, 292, 295, 296, 299, 300 and 301.

CHAPTER XX

EXPRESSION AND EMOTION

When we do not go to nature for expression we adopt certain conventional representations of emotion. By the means of these we are enabled to convey by such lines and tones the visible signs which the face gives when mental agitation is taking place.

Indifference, joy, anger, all the emotions, in fact, serve a useful purpose to the student of art.

On succeeding pages (Figs. 3-6) are given slight hints for what may be termed the emotions arranged in such a way as to be easily understood. You may adopt, adapt, amend or exaggerate according to your own ideas and judgment and, of course, according to your advancement.

It should be understood that it is practically impossible to represent all the emotions with lifeless material. Many of the faces herewith shown might be unintelligible were it not for the text that accompanies them. How seldom it is that one can read the thoughts of even a real human being by means of the expression on his face merely. Nevertheless, some people can scarcely conceal their thoughts, although they speak not a word.

A man there was whose emotions were usually shown in his face. A bright young lady said to him: "You shouldn't think so people can see you." What a splendid model he would have made!

The actor can make quick facial changes indicating the emotions he imitates, whereas the artist is limited to immovable lines. The artist must take one expression or, perhaps, merely a phase of the expression, and then attempt to represent the emotion he desires to portray, fixing it immovably. unchanging. He can portray but one movement of many that in life go to tell the story or emotion without words.

Emotion Pictures.—In all ages workers with the brush and canvas, mallet and marble, have been practically unanimous in accepting certain representations of form to parallel, as well as they may, muscular and color changes caused by mental emotion—the telegraphic signals of the brain in action. Take, for instance, the facial diagram that portrays joy. In this the emotion is mostly expressed by the partly closed, but vivid eye, the mouth, with lips slightly apart, and the corners of the mouth slightly elevated.

The figures depicting sorrow show the muscles of the face relaxed. In application the head should be inclined forward, the inner ends of the eyebrows are raised toward the forehead, the eyelids droop, while the pupil of the eye is raised. The lips are parted, somewhat as in joy, but the corners of the mouth are lowered. The general tendency of this emotion, because of the laxity of the muscles, is to lengthen the face. When sorrow, pity, pain, dejection, or melancholy, hold sway, man's face is proverbially long.

Pain, anguish and despair can hardly be separated from the general term of sorrow; to an extent they are analogous, synonymous.

Next, take the figures denoting anger. The eyes blaze (usually shown in a black-and-white drawing by a very dark iris and strong high lights), the eyebrows are contracted, with the inner ends downward, and the outer ends inclining upward. The lips are compressed at the center, with a tendency to parting at the outer ends of the mouth. Approximately, the same lines are used to express revenge, hatred, rage and fury; different degrees of intensity and rigidity of lines being used to suit the ideas of the individual.

The study of expression is so full of interest that one is easily encouraged to go to nature in order to gather more than a slight smattering of knowledge on this subject.

The effect and force of nearly every drawing in which the human face appears depends very largely on the extent to which the artist knows how to give expression to the human features. The beholder of the picture can be guided only by the artist's interpretation; if it is false, the picture is misleading, therefore valueless.

The definitions that accompany these diagram-like outlines of the various emotions are conventional. They are not absolute, and are even interchangeable to some degree. They are offered as hints and suggestions to aid individual observation. For the real thing in the way of emotion no better aid can be had than a mirror. Survey yourself in that and sketch the changes in your own features. Make faces at yourself and then sketch them. You should try to keep the varying expressions in mind long enough to transfer to paper the principal lines by which they are formed.

Expression in the human face must be felt. It is difficult to teach it. There are so many minor points which go to make up the varied expressions that can be assumed by human features that detailed instruction is almost impossible.

Animation may be expressed by dark touches in the eyes and under the lids. The nose also has much to do with expression; especially the shape of the nostrils and the direction of the lines of the sides of the nose running down to the mouth. Nostrils that droop downward at the outer edge give a serious expression; on the contrary, if the line is elevated, the tendency is towards a bright and animated expression.

The mouth, of course, is of great importance, and influences the expression more than any other feature. When smiling, the corners are turned upward and the lines or dimples are curved in an outward direction. In a sad face, the corners of the mouth drop downward and the lines grow straight.

The student of expression must look for indications in many faces, for there he will find more suggestions of importance than in all the pages of written instruction. Without such knowledge, he may work on blindly, puzzling himself to find out where he is wrong, and why the expression is just the opposite of what it should be.

Expression Exercises for Beginners

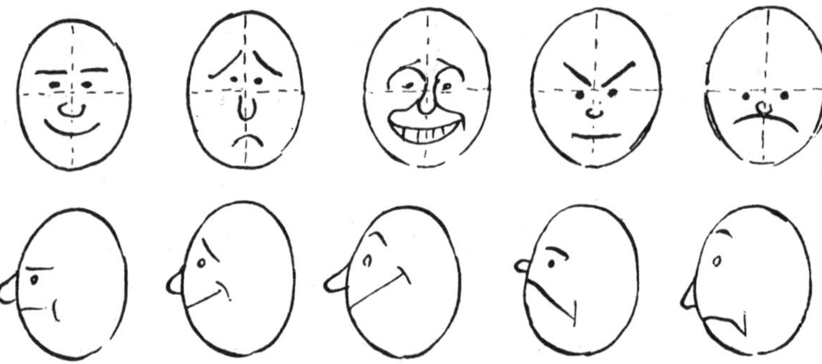

Fig. 1—Expression Exercises for Beginners

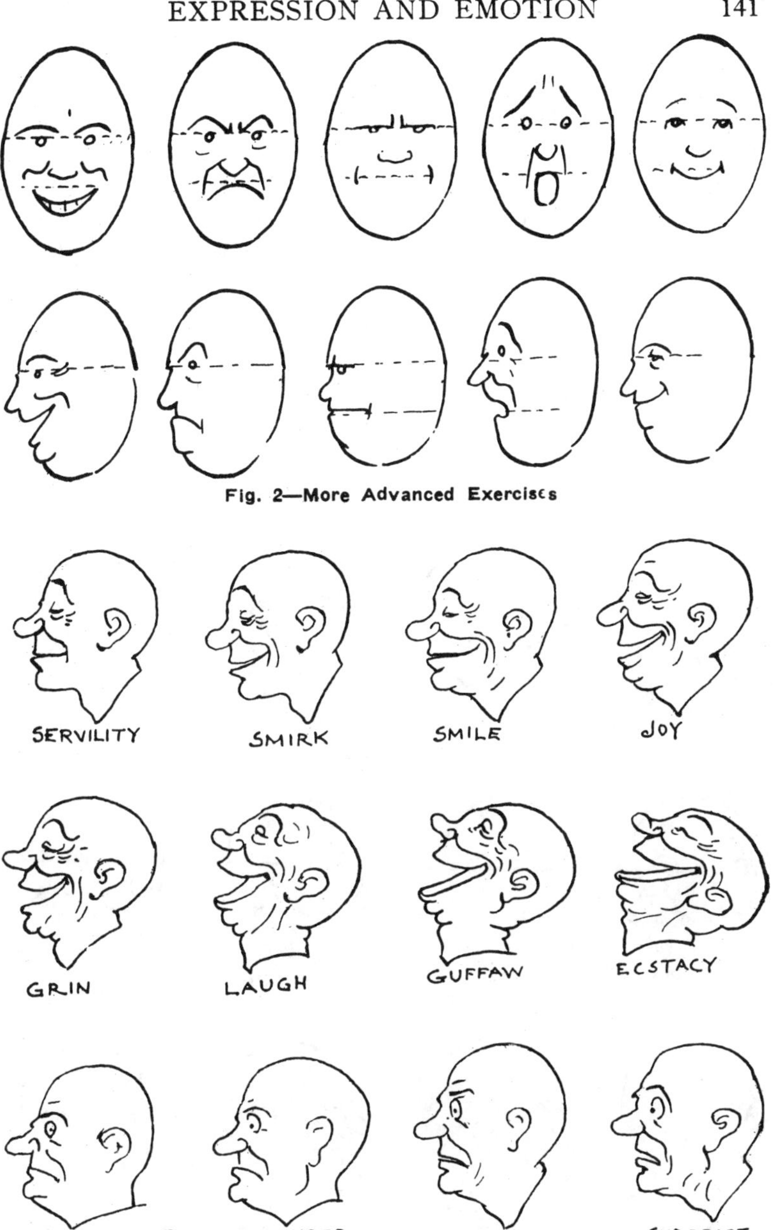

Fig. 2—More Advanced Exercises

Fig. 3—Expressions in Profile

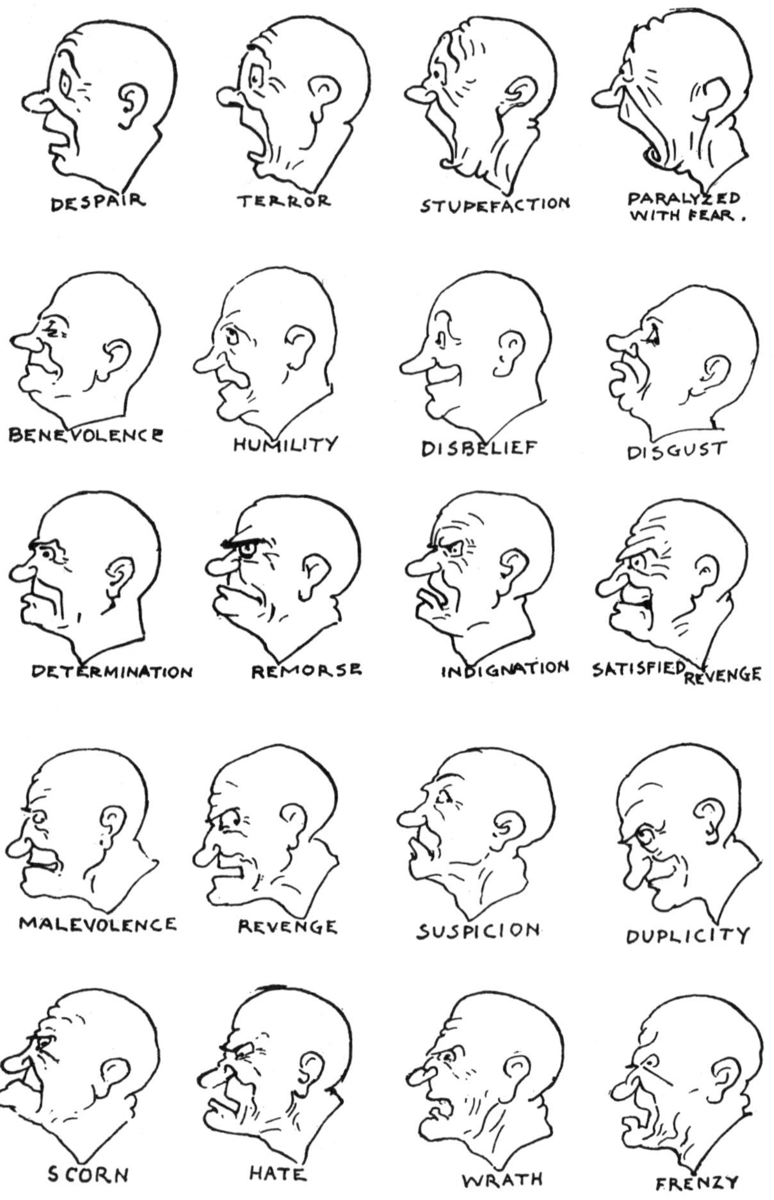

Fig. 4—Expressions in Profile

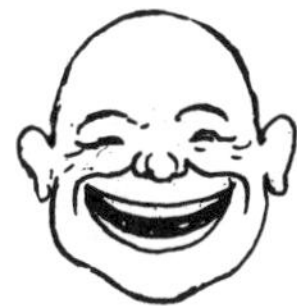
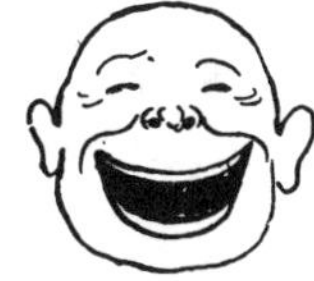
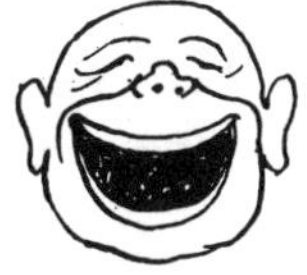
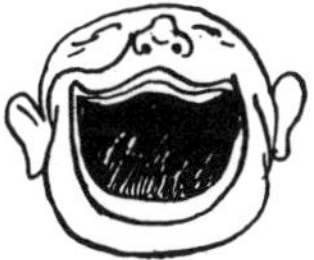

Fig. 5—Some of the Pleasant Emotions

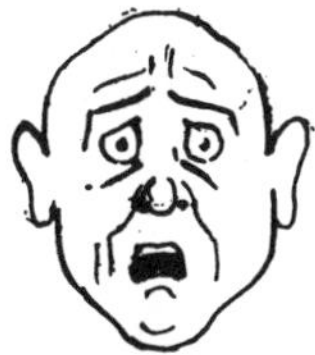
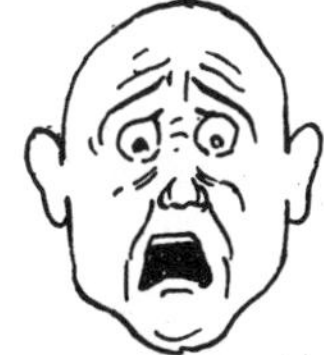
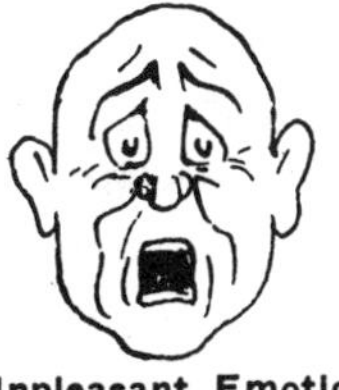
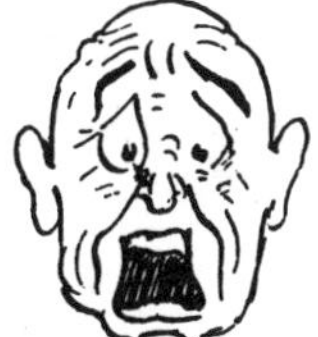

Fig. 6—Some of the Unpleasant Emotions

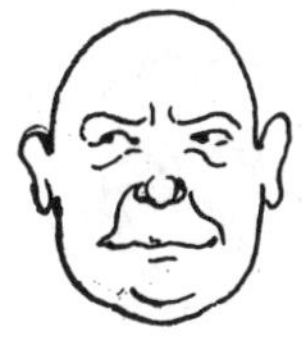
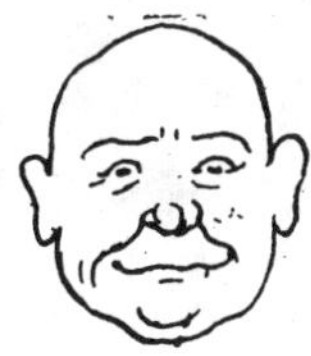
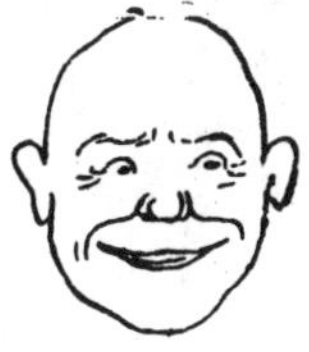
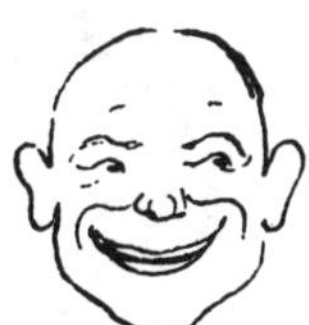
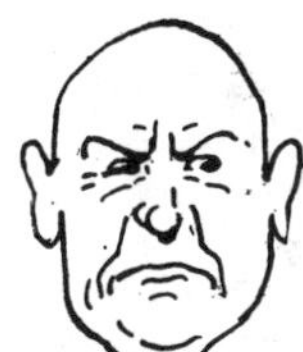
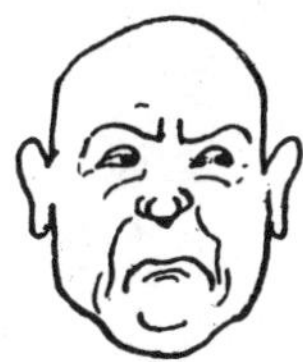
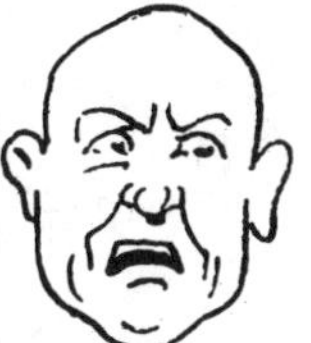
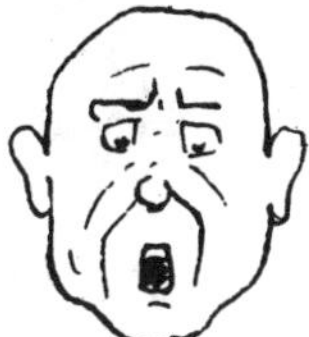

Fig. 7—What Emotions Do These Expressions Represent?

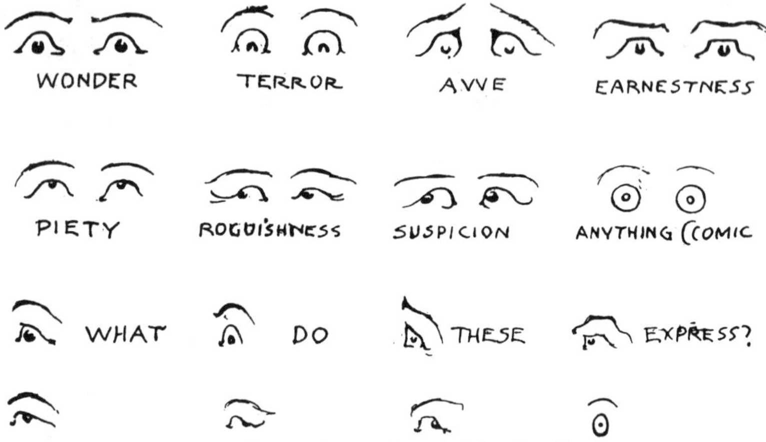

Fig. 8—Expression as Denoted by the Eyes

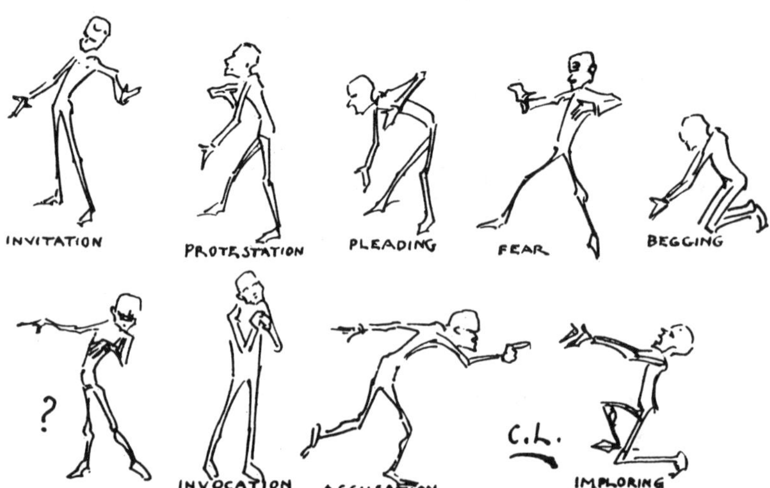

Fig. 9—Expression as Denoted by Gestures

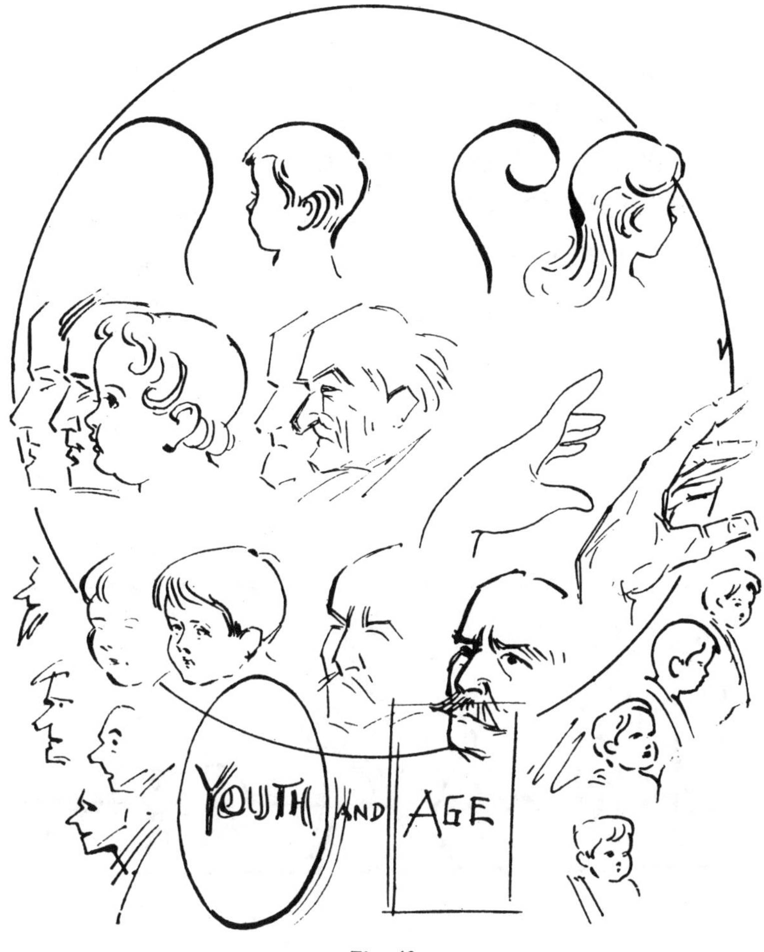

Fig. 10

Youth and Old Age.—Curved, graceful lines convey the impression of youth, while straight, angular lines are those mostly used to express age in various stages of advancement. In vegetable life, as may be noted (Fig. 11), the young have graceful lines, while in their old age angularity of lines is apparent.

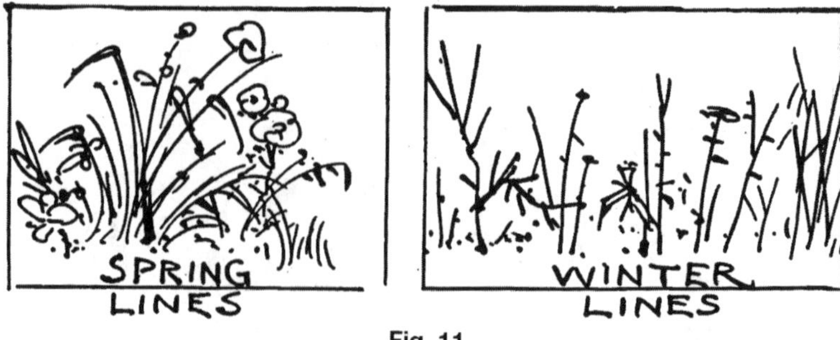

Fig. 11

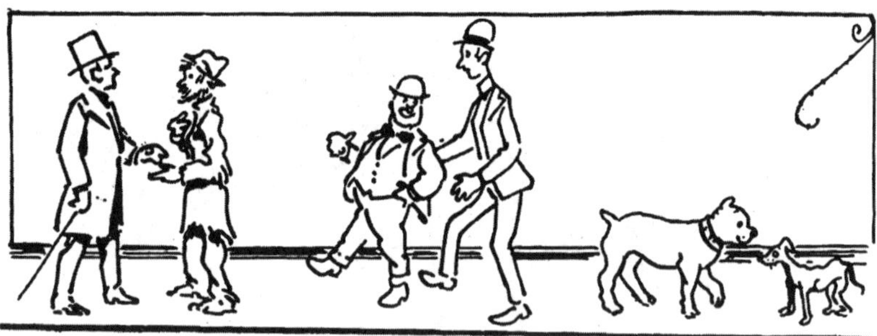

Fig. 12

Contrasts of some sort are generally considered necessary to every drawing. Contrasts are not invariably caused by strength of line or tone or areas of black against white; but they are frequently matters of character and costume. Thus, a poorly dressed man talking to a finely dressed man appears more tattered than if he were addressing a commonly clad person, or if he were in a group made up of similarily dressed people. A short, heavy man seems more obese if his companion in the picture is long and lean.

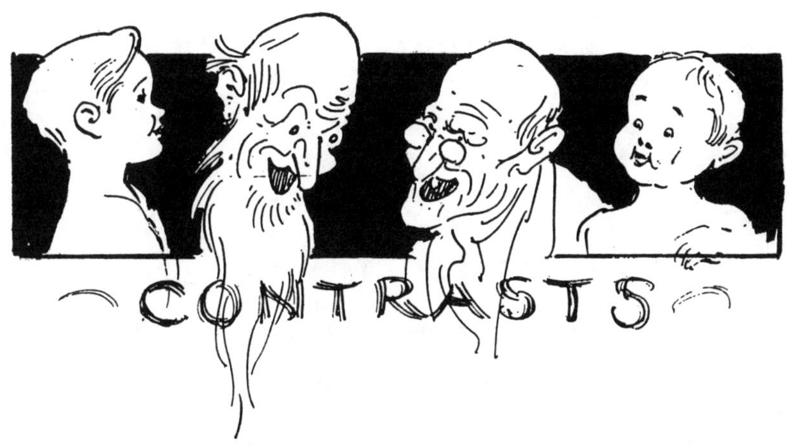

Notes.—Human expression or emotion is expressed in some form in illustrations on the following pages: 48, 87, 88, 95, 97, 135, 137, 150, 151, 152. 153, 154, 155, 286, 292.

CHAPTER XXI

CARTOONING

Comic Drawing.—It seems hardly necessary at this day to defend comic drawing. The comic artist has come to stay, and he is certainly one of the best paid of any profession. So, from a practical business standpoint, it may be seen that the tendency towards the ludicrous in art should not be discouraged. Therefore, it is not amiss to devote a small section of this manual to the study of the principles of comic drawing. These lines afford, at the same time, a backhanded apology for an occasional tendency toward humor in other parts of this work. Anyhow, pray bear in mind, that Americans naturally are a fun-loving people. Nearly every form of popular amusement proves this conclusively.

Cartoonists Should Be Able to Make Serious Drawings.—Comic drawing is a study that should not be taken up to the exclusion of any other branch of art work. One great trouble with many embryo "cartoonists" is that they seem to think that they do not need to know much about the general rules of drawing to make so-called cartoons. To the contrary the most successful cartoonists—for that seems to be the general term nowadays applied to all makers of humorous pictures—are those who are capable of making well-drawn serious drawings if required. It is as absurd to suppose that a comic artist needs only a limited knowledge of correct drawing as it would be for a writer of dialect stories to have only a slight command of properly spoken language. So the artist with a fund of humor need not fear that he will lose it if he keeps it under subjection and confihes his studies mostly to serious drawing.

To be able to draw graceful lines, to have an inkling of human anatomy, to know the fundamental laws of perspective, etc. will give him greater ability to draw side-splitting pictures later on. At the same time one's tendency to draw with humorous design should not be entirely diverted or at all discouraged. The ultimate outlet for mirth-provoking drawings is so great that the artist competent to do this work well may be assured of a profitable career when he enters the field of cartooning professionally.

Expression in Comic Drawings.—The goings-on of the human mind, the internal changes, are shown in the face. Gesture of limbs and pose of body follow as if further to define the emotion. Besides the actual expression the comic artist adds external indications. For instance, to intensify a glare, the artist projects a dotted line from the eye of the subject towards the object at which his character is glaring. The effects of a blow on the head or a heavy fall are given pictorial adjunct by means of various celestial and planetary bodies. That is to say the artist surrounds the victim with stars and comets so as to emphasize, explain and proclaim beyond the faintest shadow of a doubt that the subject is "seeing stars."

Take the emotion of fright. How often does one see a man so frightened that his hair "stands on end like quills on the fretful porcupine"? Hardly ever except in comic pictures.

Such means of forcing the effect may not mean art, even of a low order, but it saves the onlooker from wear and tear of the brain. The "cross-shows-the-spot" style of comic picture seems to have come to stay —for a while at least, and therefore is worthy of attention if not respectful consideration.

For exercise, block in some of the other figures according to the manner shown in Fig. 1, 2 and 3.

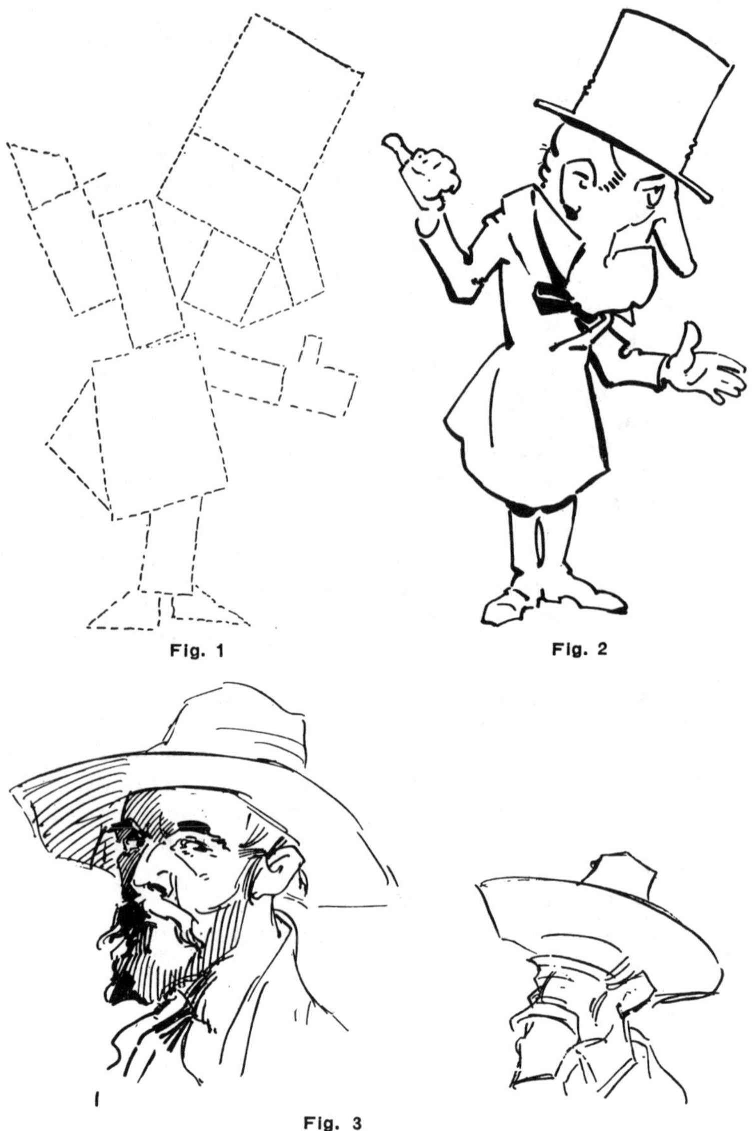

Fig. 1

Fig. 2

Fig. 3

Fig. 3 was drawn with blocking-in lines and Fig. 4 without them. Which looks the better?

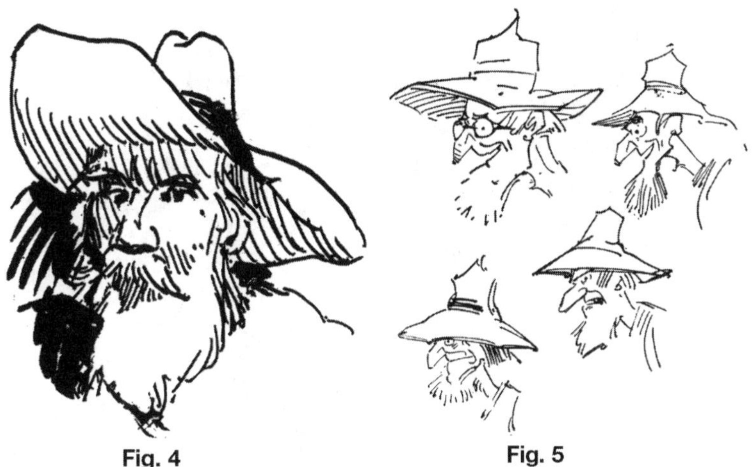

Fig. 4

Fig. 5

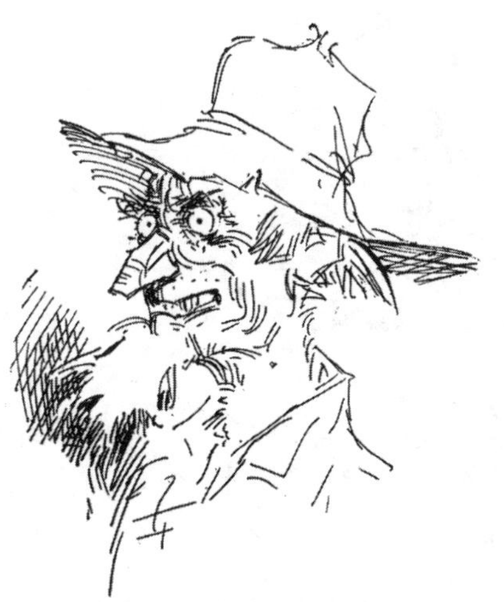

Fig. 6 – A Libelous Caricature

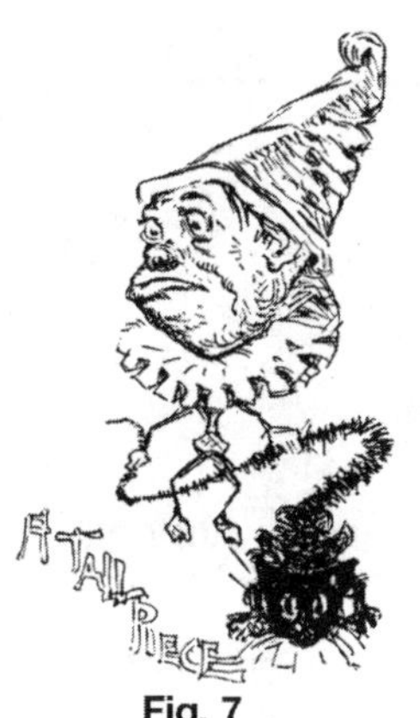

Fig. 7

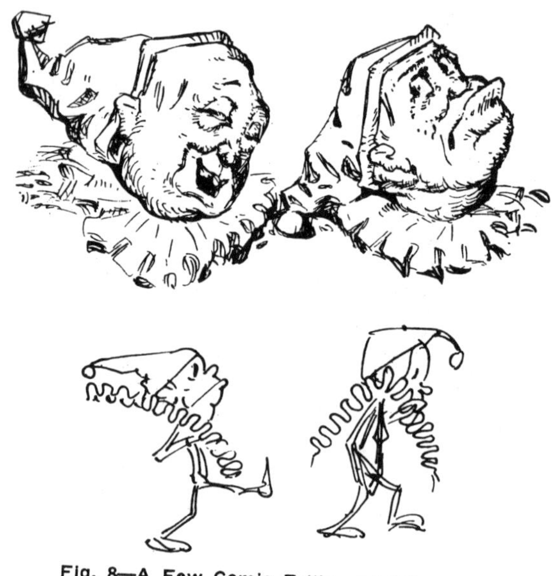

Fig. 8—A Few Comic Frills and Wiggles

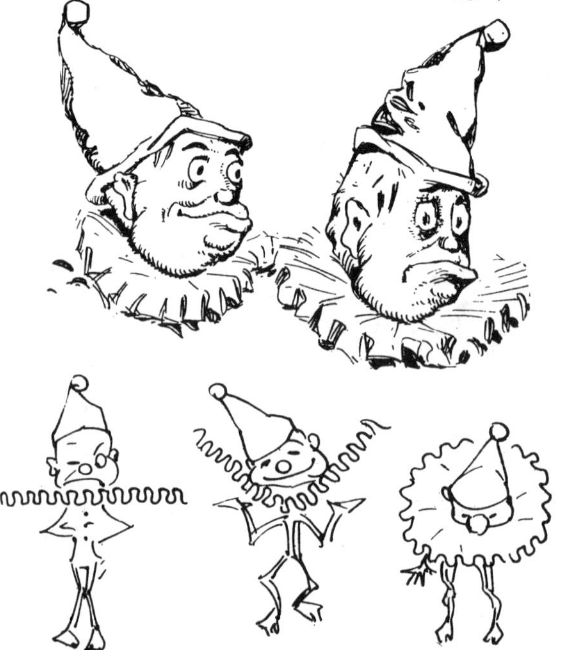

Fig. 9

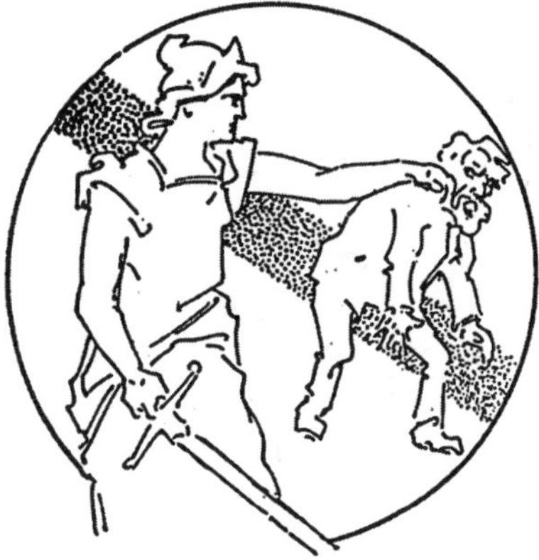

Fig. 10

Young Americans, on the average, take naturally to action and humor, rather than to mere form for form's sake. They are more apt to take to the practical side of things than the sentimental. It is hoped that the artist will gain *interest* in the subject, even though the ideal and the beautiful be subjected to temporary obscurity.

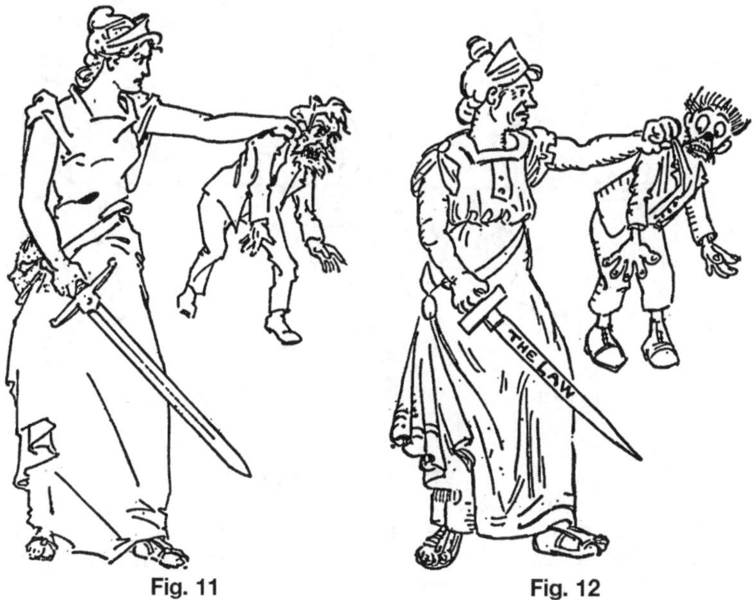

Fig. 11
A Refined Style and

Fig. 12
A Coarse Style of Cartooning

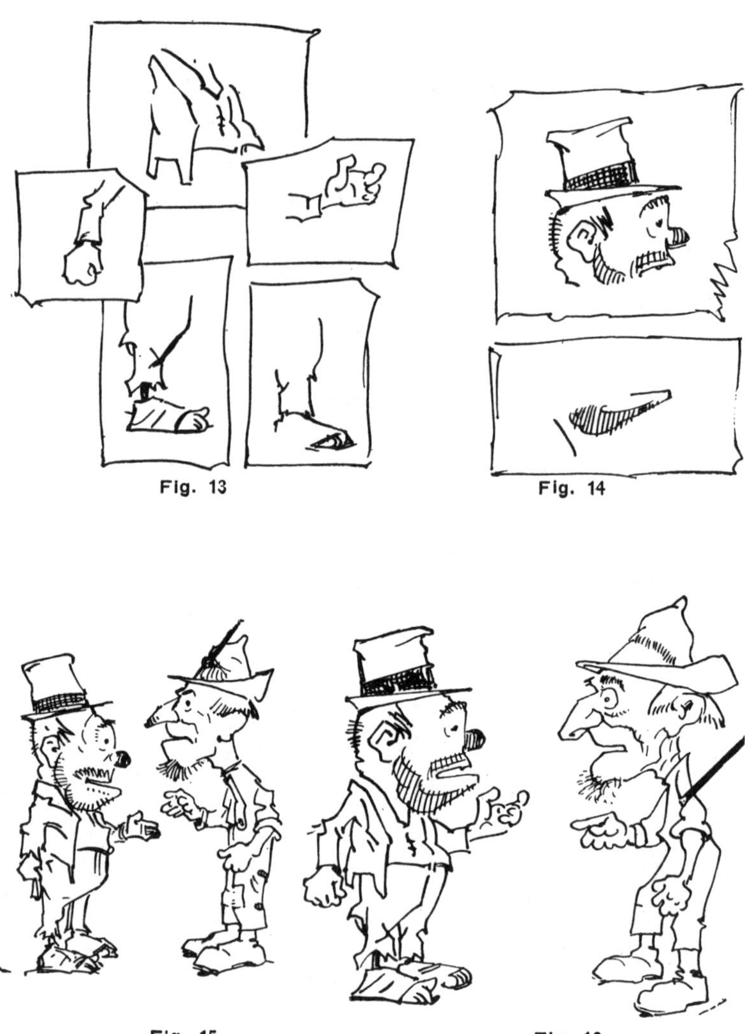

Fig. 13

Fig. 14

Fig. 15

Fig. 16

For exercise draw parts of the figures and arrange the figures in different poses.

Blocking-in is as necessary for comic drawing as any other. The upper right-hand head was drawn without blocking-in. Note the difference.

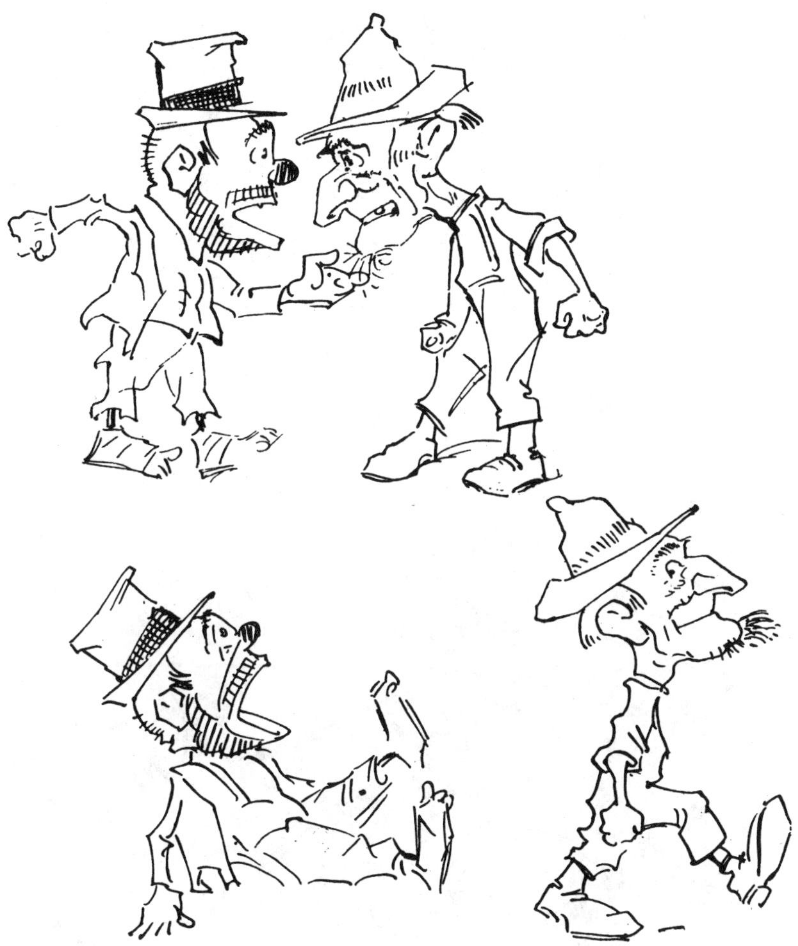

Fig. 17—Offended Dignity Avenged

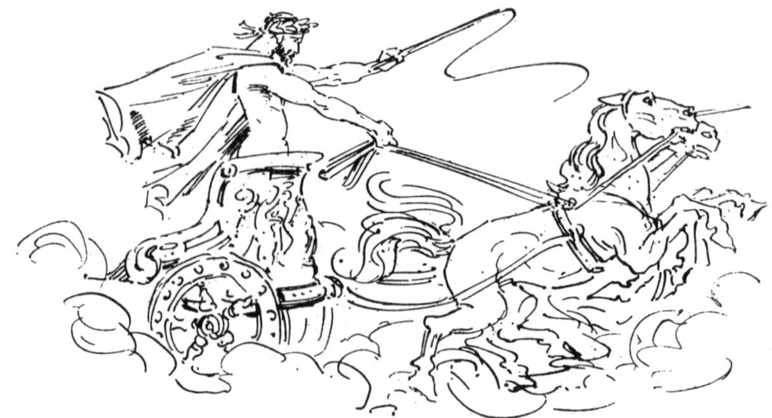

Fig. 18—An Artistic Cartoon Drawing

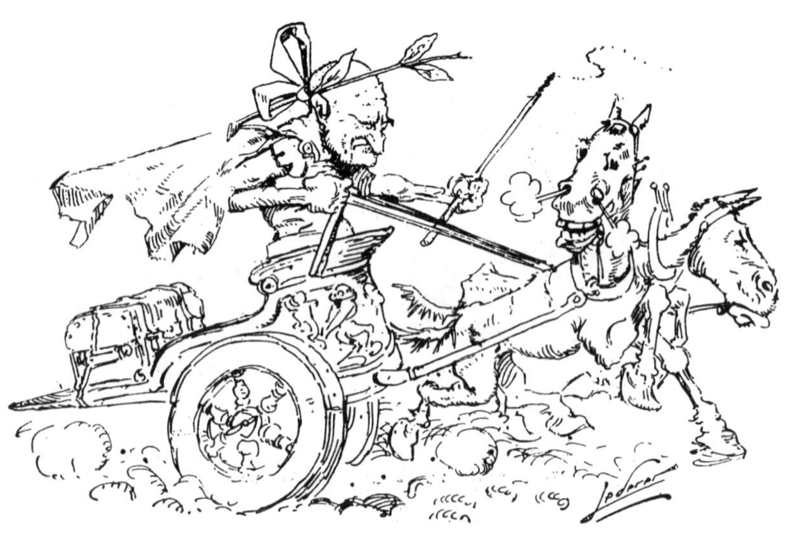

Fig. 19—A Humorous But Less Artistic Cartoon Drawing (Both Drawn by the Same Artist.)

The comic figure of the policeman (Fig. 20) is an instance of head and feet distortion. The body and hands are nearly normal in their proportions.

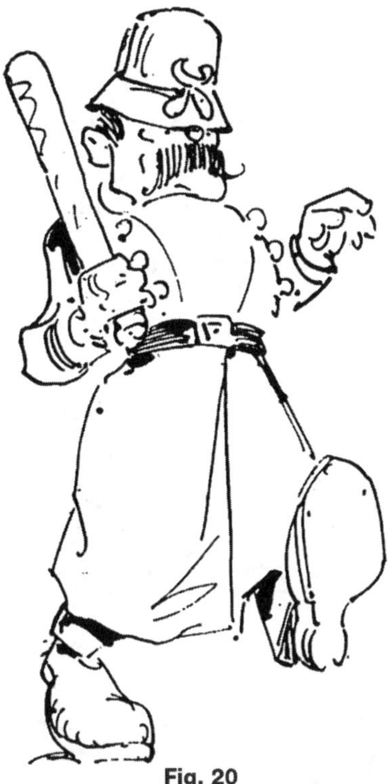

Fig. 20

The same sketch is shown on page 257, on Lettering, Initials and Book Covers, adapted to a comic book cover. And in the chapter on Elements of Perspective it appears repeatedly in connection with the subject of atmospheric perspective.

Indulge and stimulate to a sensible extent your own natural sense of humor. Allow yourself free reign to your imagination, but strive to define, direct and correct the images that you convey.

Note.—In chapters XIX and XX examples will be found that will-assist the young cartoonist.

CHAPTER XXII

DRAWING ANIMALS

Curved Lines are best adapted for representing the forms of animals of all kinds. It is next to impossible to find even an approximately rigid, straight line in the outline of any living animal. In fact, outside of the plumb-line sometimes formed by the spider and the horizontal line where land and sky apparently meet, Nature seldom employs a straight line.

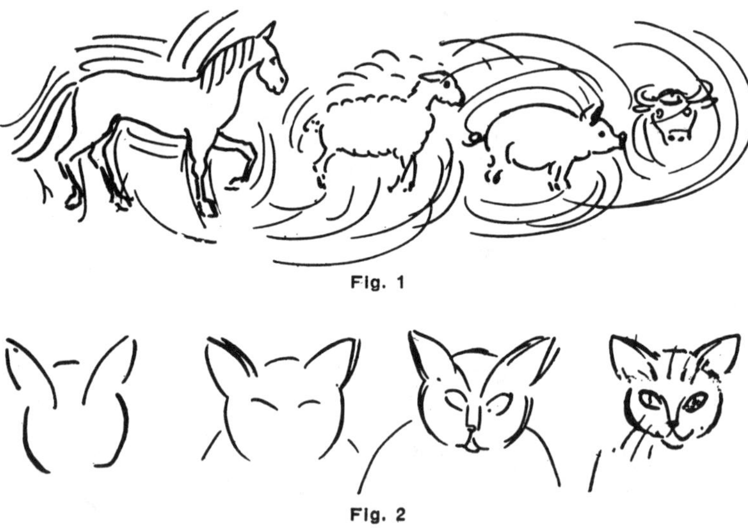

Fig. 1

Fig. 2

The Horse.—The body and legs of a horse viewed from the side will be found enclosed in a square space as seen in A, B, C, D, in the diagram. The added triangulation will assist in describing the proportions of the head; the length of the head being about three-fourths of one of the four squares formed in the main square A, B, C, D. Observe a horizontal line cutting the main square in equal portions will just touch the elbow of the near fore leg.

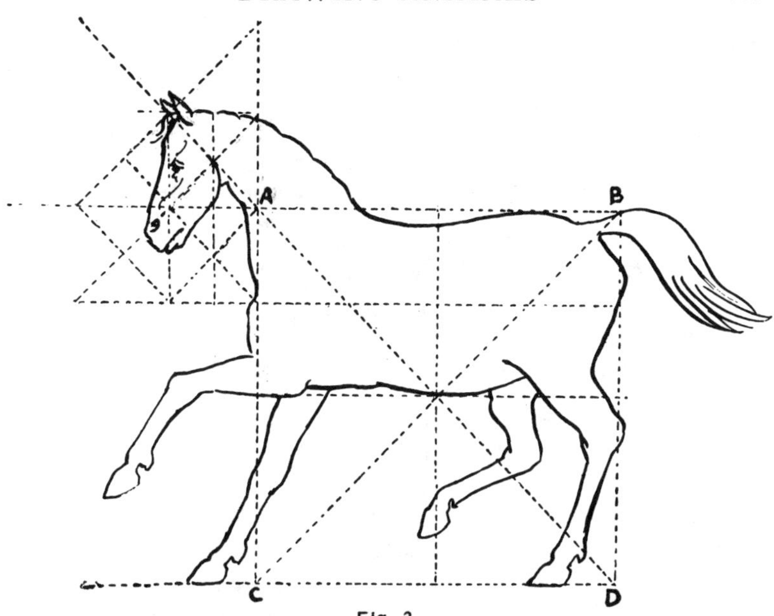

Fig. 3

The Cow.—A square the same height as the distance from the ground to the top of the head will be found to include the body and legs. About one-half added to its width will

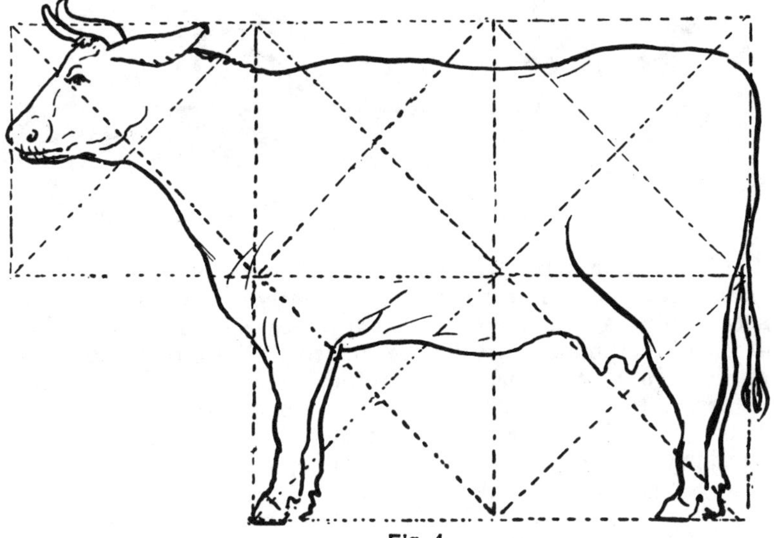
Fig. 4

give a parallelogram that will include the whole animal. The angles in the triangulated diagram will assist in making the drawing in correct proportions.

Dogs vary so much in breed, etc., that no exact proportions can be given. Examples will be found in the chapter on Pen Drawing that will serve as examples to copy.

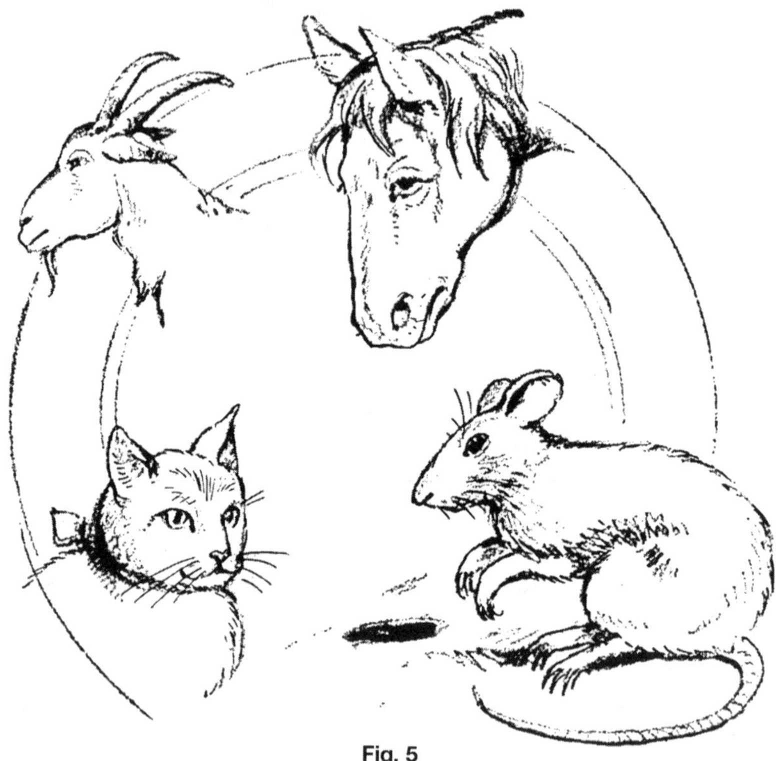

Fig. 5

Quite as much attention is necessary to draw animals as to draw the human figure properly. Animal drawing seems to be a gift by itself that few possess. For one thing, as a rule, animals do not pose quietly. They have no sense of duty in that respect. Therefore, it is usually necessary to resort to some sort of copy in order to draw them. A photograph, however, is not always obtainable and, for the beginner, is exceedingly difficult to copy from.

For this reason, you should take the initiative to copy freely

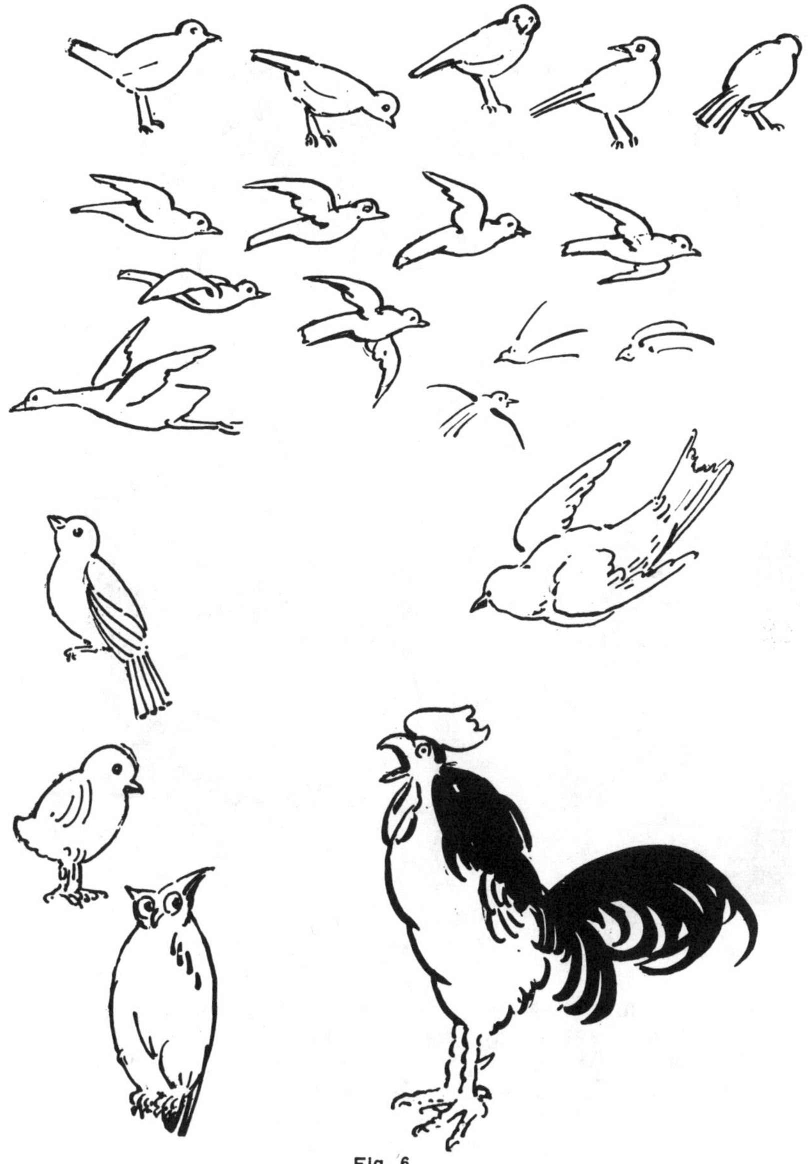

Fig. 6

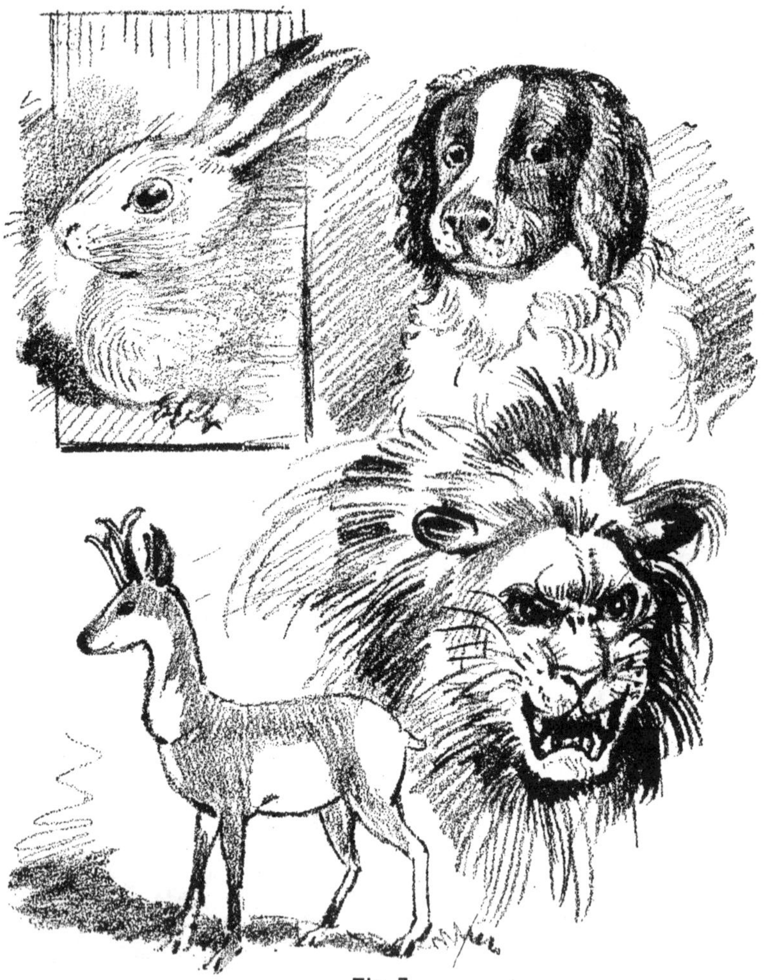

Fig. 7

from the examples in this chapter—a chapter, by the way, that does not pretend to be a natural history.

In Shading Animals represented by drawings use delicately placed lines. Curved lines, radiating rather than paralleling, produce the best effects. Edges of shadows should blend, rather than make harsh contrasts; in the case of a drawing of a lion, however, in order to cause the effect of fierceness, stronger gradations may be used.

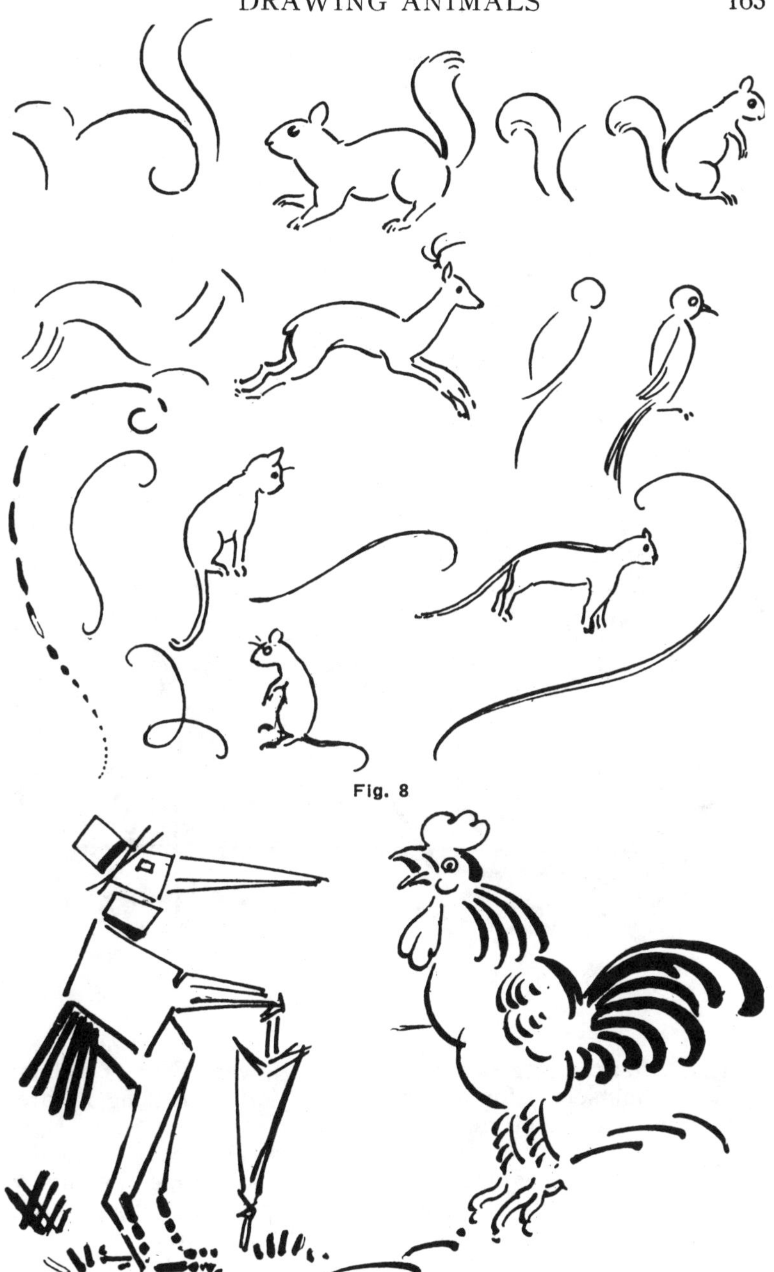

Fig. 8

Fig. 9

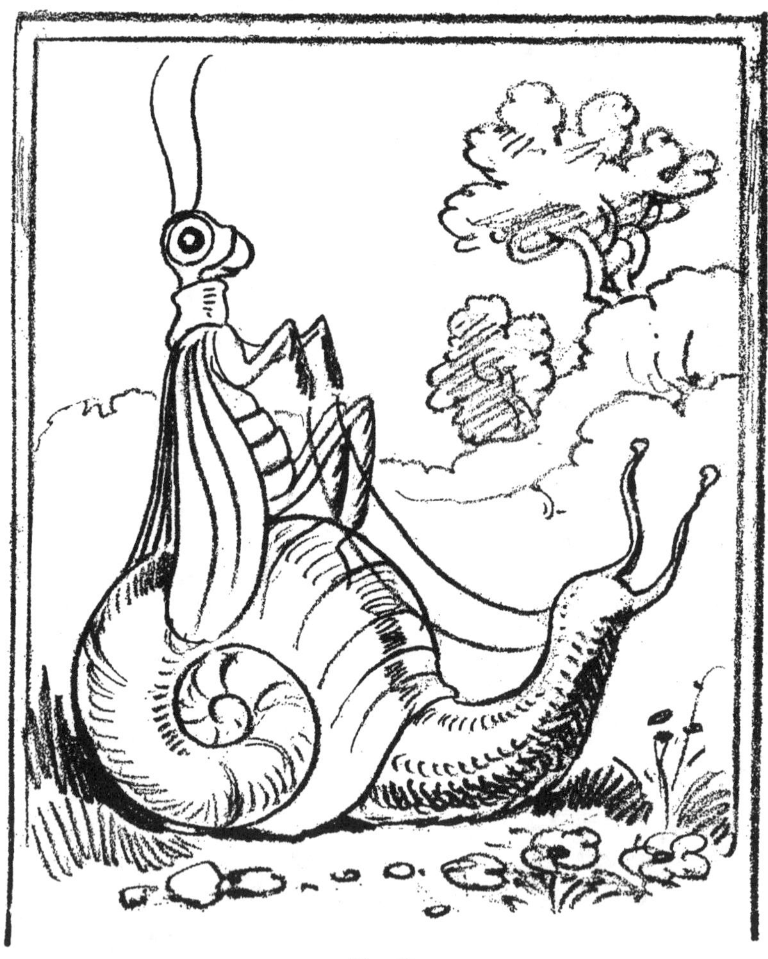

Fig. 10

Insects and other specimens of the lower order of animal life lend themselves for pictorial display of a pleasing nature. Grasshoppers sometimes remain quiet for a long time, especially when no longer alive and, therefore, are apt to be model models. The slow-going snail presents for inspection many graceful lines, and, like some other mollusks, offers a fine opportunity for the study of the spiral in form.

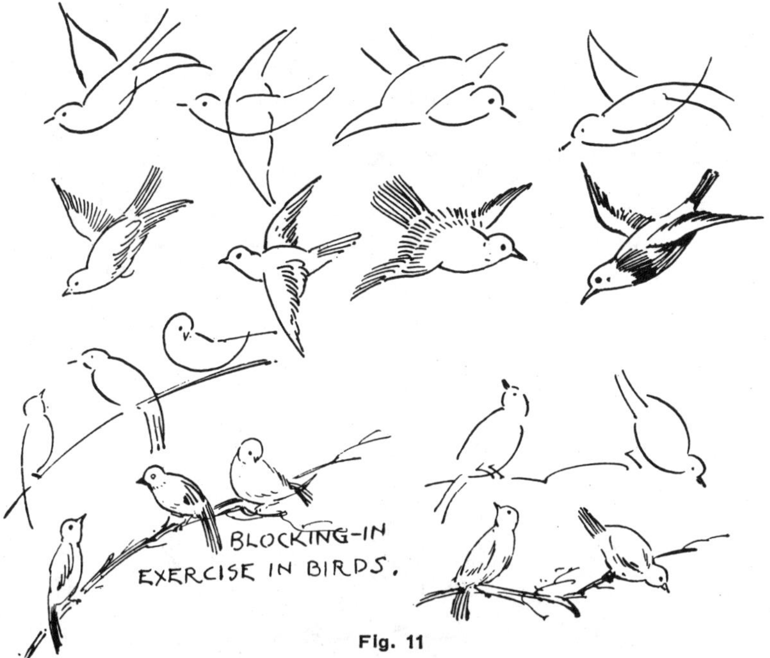

Fig. 11

An Easter Suggestion.—A good subject for an Easter card. Draw with very light pencil marks. Then color, and after-

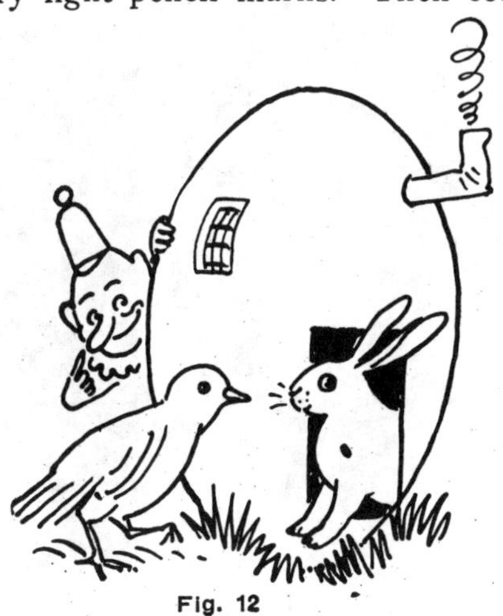

Fig. 12

wards outline again but with heavier lines than before. Suggested colors: the egg, white; the rabbit, yellow; the bird, red; the imp, green, except face (pink for that); the sky, blue, but blending into white at the outer edges. All colors should be light; merely tints.

Combinations in Curved and Angular Lines are often pleasing. The curved lines in the bird, contrasting with the angular lines in the old tree top intensify the bareness of the branches, thus producing strength by contrasting effects.

In the little scene below, the round lines in the moon offset the angular lines of the tower and the trees.

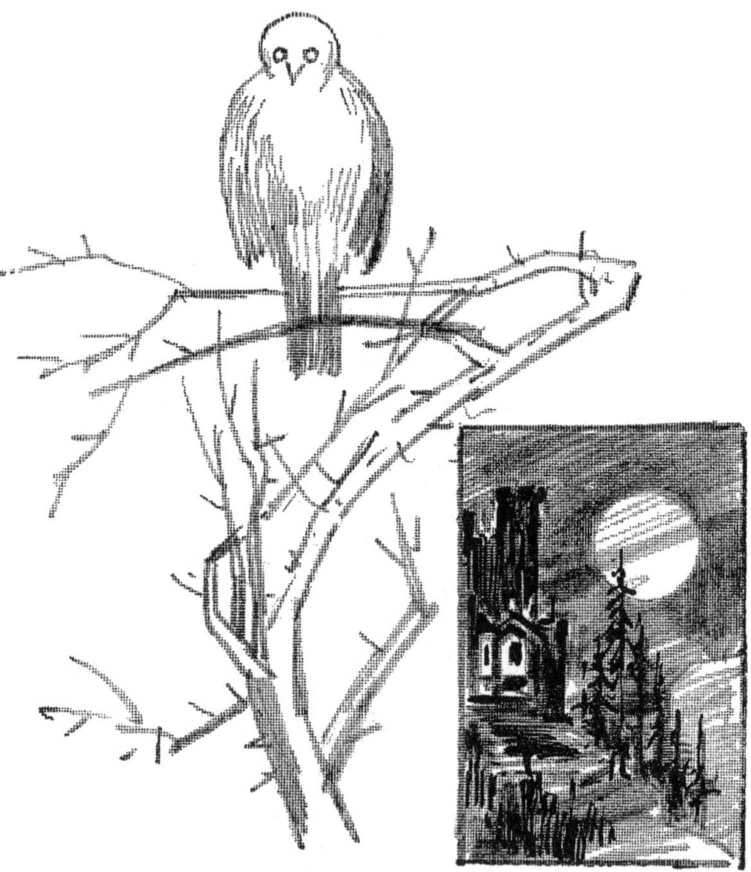

Fig. 13

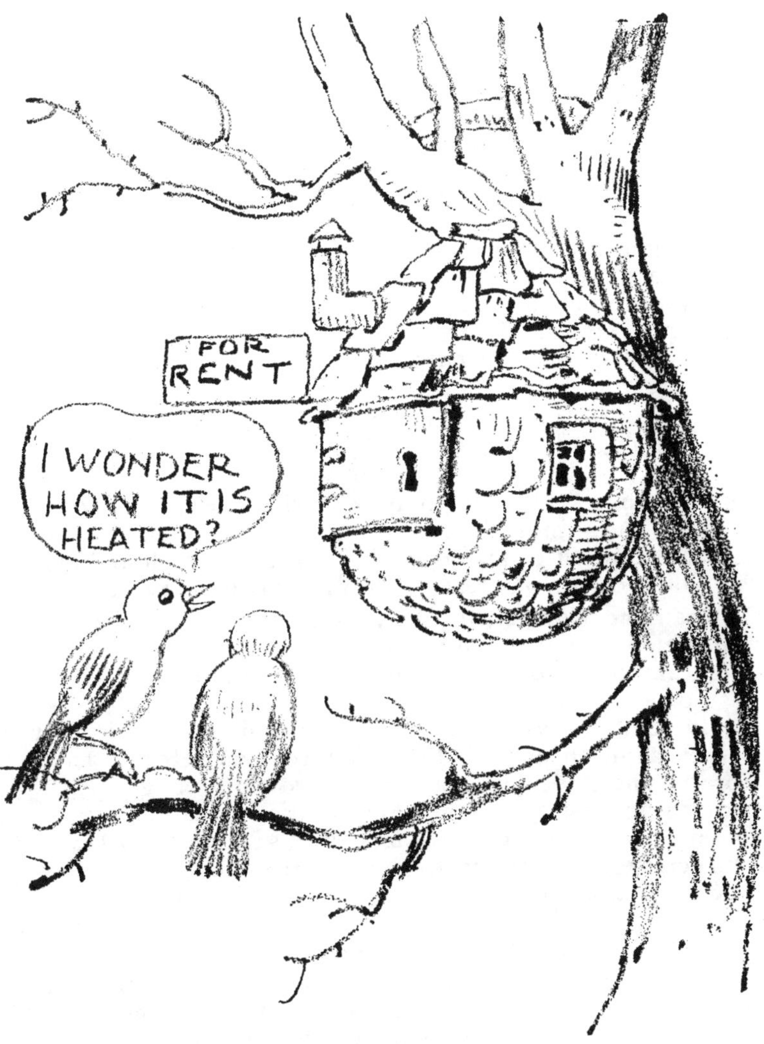

Fig. 14

Notes.—Other examples in which animal life in some form, (including birds, fishes, etc.) will be found on pp. 29, 48, 50, 51, 52, 73, 84, 85, 88, 93, 95, 97, 102, 111, 122, 126, 156, 238, 258, 259, 260, 283, 293, 294.

CHAPTER XXIII

PRINCIPLES OF COMPOSITION

The general arrangement of the characters and surroundings of a picture is implied in the word "composition." By a composition is meant an original grouping of the objects and the light-and-shade scheme comprising a picture. The simplest manner is generally the most harmonious and satisfactory.

Things to Avoid in a composition are too many isolated groups and too many spots of light and shade. Few absolute rules can be laid down for composing a picture. All dresses are not alike. One's own good taste, one's sense of proportion, one's individual judgment must prevail. No inflexible standard of arrangement to guide us is found among the works of the painters of old or of modern times.

Changing Component Parts.—In composition of pictures, that which is seen in nature is frequently displaced or altered by means of addition, subtraction, multiplication, and transposition.

By addition, we add objects that we do not see in nature, if such addition appears to add grace, symmetry or balance. For instance, we place a tree where no tree grew before, because another tree in the composition needs a companion to remedy its apparent loneliness, or to give that appearance of connectedness necessary to the general effect.

Subtraction—if something of nature obtrudes or we wish to erase it we subtract it from the picture.

Multiplication—if we find only a single fence post, in order to get the necessary line that imagination demands, we stretch a dozen fence posts towards the horizon, diminishing them in size as they approach the vanishing point.

Transpostion—We may transpose a mountain from one side to another in our picture as easily as we would a book from one shelf to another. This is true in sketching from nature, where adaptability and mobility are desired. It was Ruskin who said that it was the artist's privilege to move his objects around—be they mountains or pebbles—just as a chess player moves the figures on the chess board.

The Shapes of Drawings.—The rectangle is the least pleasing shape for a drawing. One twice as long as it is high (or the reverse) is more pleasing. But the proportions of two and three, for a drawing, is the best average proportion. That is to say, one dimension should be two-thirds of the other. Thus: A is not, while B and C are well proportioned. D and E are shapes adapted for pastel and water colors.

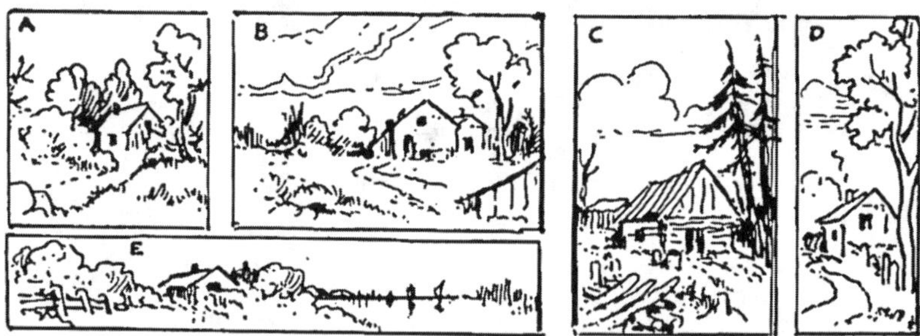

The impression and effect on the beholder are the principal objects to be sought for.

Morning, Noon and Night.— Figs. 1, 2 and 3 exemplify the manner in which nature's effects may be studied. The same scene is pictured, morning, noon and night. In the morning when the light comes from the back of the objects in the distance, the latter is silhouetted against the rising sun. The shadows are thrown towards the sketcher, while in the noon aspect, the light "eats up" the shadows, which are short and sharply defined. At night the light is thrown directly towards the far distant parts, and they stand out in strong relief against the dark cloud-settings. There is no attempt at definition, or minuteness of detail in these sketches the principles involved being merely indicated in a general way to assist you with the artistic truths that must be absorbed by self-observation, rather than by the strict letter of written instruction. If you can avail yourself of the time and opportunity to make a sketch of some similar scene and study Nature's scheme of contrasts at the most distinctive periods of the day's divisions, it will be of great help.

The spectator in the scenes depicted in Figs. 1, 2 and 3

is supposed to face the east. Fig. 1 is a morning scene and the sun is just rising. Fig. 2 shows the same scene at noon. Shadows now are barely perceptible. Fig. 3 is a sketch of the same place with the sun setting behind the sketcher.

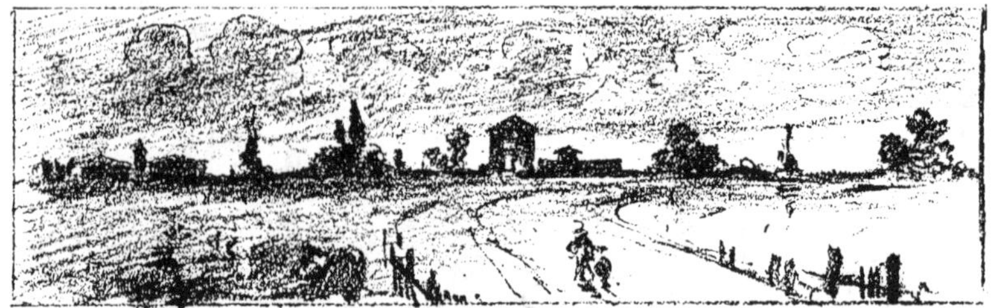

Fig. 1—Morning

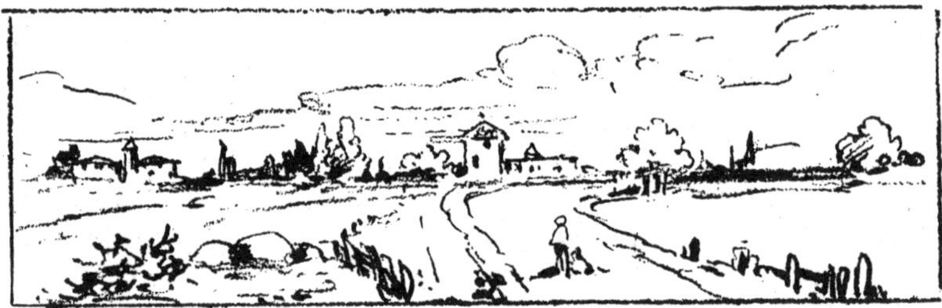

Fig. 2—Noon

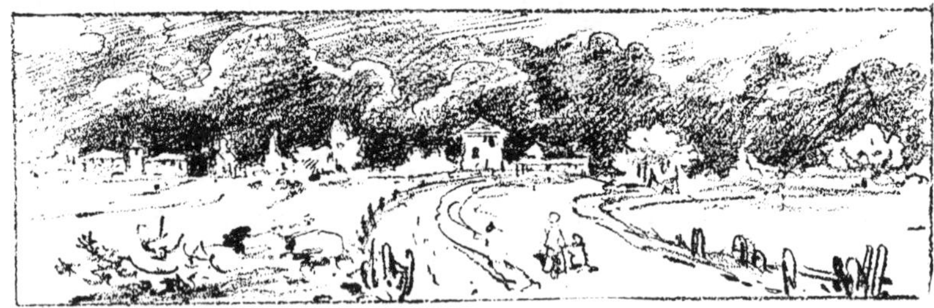

Fig. 3—Night

Avoid Monotony.—Living or inanimate objects that are intended to be the principal parts of a picture should not be overshadowed by their surroundings. Give the former more pronounced outlines and depth of shade or color, and use lighter, thinner lines and tones for the accessories—the fewer the better as a general thing.

First Impressions.—Be sure to develop your powers of composition and to make the best arrangement of all objects selected. All that you learn relating to blocking-in will help, for the blocking-in habit is a good one and tends to looking at things artistic as a whole rather than piecemeal. Good composition relies greatly on the general aspect, the first impression that is made on the eye of the beholder. And by the blocking-in method a good first impression is more easily obtained. The mass is of more importance than the detail. A tendency to make very heavy lines at the outset will retard success in the blocking-in process. The pencil should be held long and loosely for blocking-in or when composing a picture.

A shadow often determines the length and other dimensions of an object so forshortened or hidden that the eye has no apparent means of measurement.

Notes.—Further examples of composition, landscape, figures, etc., that will assist in the study of this subject will be found on pp. 13, 14, 42, 43, 45, 51, 52, 60, 62, 66, 81, 120, 126, 135, 136, 164, 166, 167, 168, 183, 186, 187, 188, 190, 192, 193, 195, 196, 197, 199, 280, 281, 282, 290, 302. 304.

CHAPTER XXIV

LIGHT AND SHADE

How and Where to Place light and shade in a drawing is an oft recurring source of perplexity to the beginner.

It is the more perplexing because often all light and shade

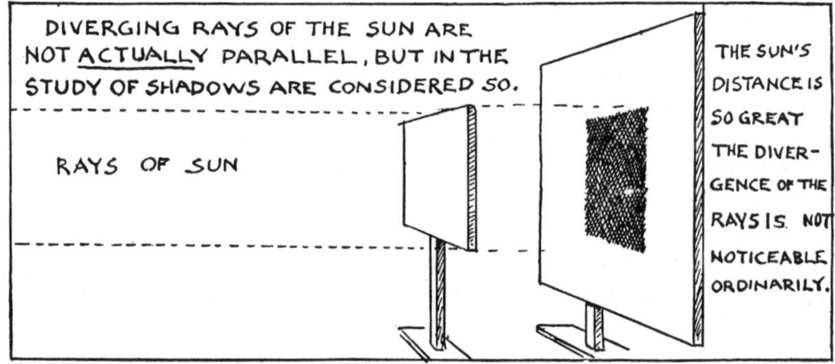

Fig. 1

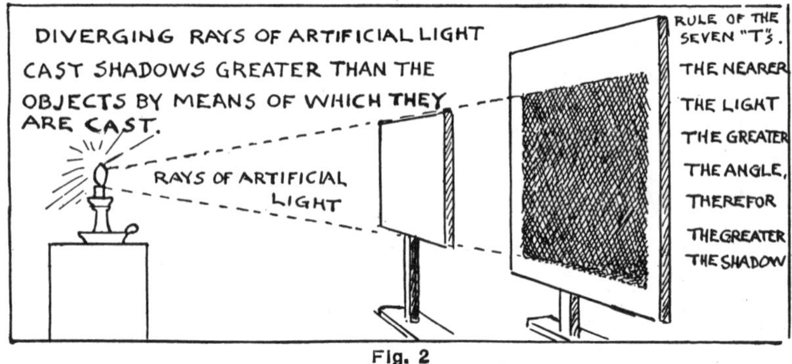

Fig. 2

in a one-color picture are merely substitutes for color as seen in nature. Light and shade values in a black and white drawing are merely relative in their attempt to imitate the pigments by which nature lets us discern form. In drawing, forms are represented by outlines, or by light and shade areas, or by a combination of both.

If light were to pervade a room evenly—the light not coming from any particular direction, as from the sun, or some fixed artificial light or lights—there would be no shadows.

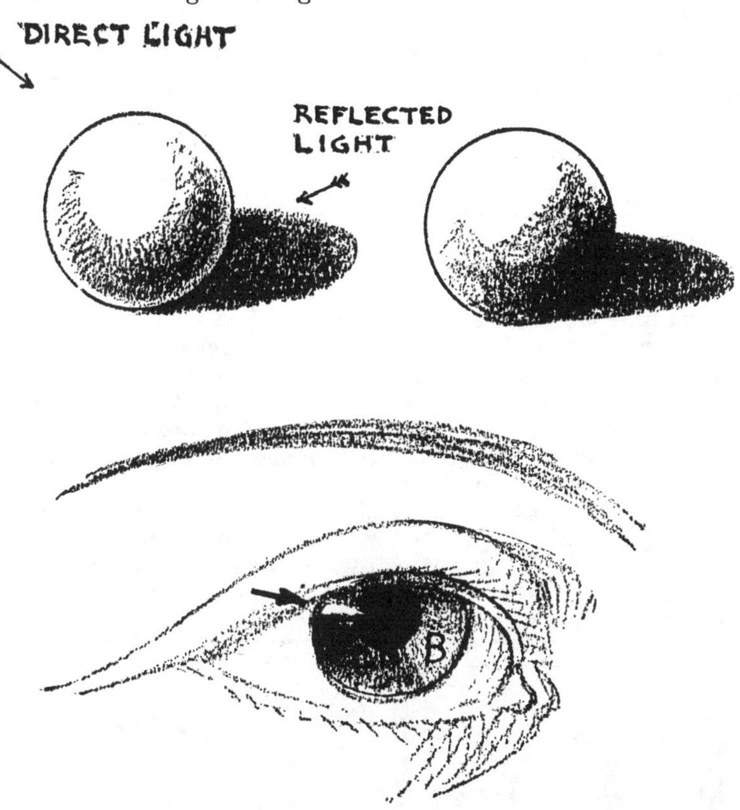

Fig. 3

We could then perceive such forms only as they were made visible by their different colors.

Every Curved Object Has Two Lights.—An even opaque object, if it is curved, has its brightest and its darkest side, and intermediate parts where light and shade seem to combine. The main part of brightness in an object is called the high light. The darkest part of an object is not necessarily the part most distant from the chief point of light, for the reflected lights play a part in lighting up just those portions that seem in most need of the borrowed lights—"borrowed lights" being the term frequently applied to certain forms of reflected light. (See Fig. 3.)

Reflected Lights Enable Us to Distinguish Forms.—The point of light indicated by the arrow at left of iris of the eye is a sharp, reflected light. The lighter portion of the iris at B is caused by diffused light—the effect of the light passing through the semi-transparent eyeball. The portion of the eyeball nearest the light is always darker than the other side. except that portion where the point of reflected light appears as shown by the arrow.

Cast Shadows Darkest.—The shadow cast by an object is usually darker than the object itself, because the part receiving the shadow is not apt to be the recipient of the reflected lights. The shadow follows the shape of an object to the extent that the surface, by its angles and variation of form and shape, will permit it. (See Fig. 5.) In order to draw shadows with absolute correctness, certain rules should be followed that are to be obtained only by a study of the most advanced rules in perspective. To attempt here to explain these rules would take more space than is allotted to the subject, and, besides. could not be made plain or interesting.

The Course of Shadows.—Shadows follow or are broken by the shapes of the objects on which they are cast. Note that the shadows in Fig. 4 are thrown in (diffused) straight lines on the wall, while in Fig. 5 the shadow of the stick is broken by the steps on which the shadow is cast.

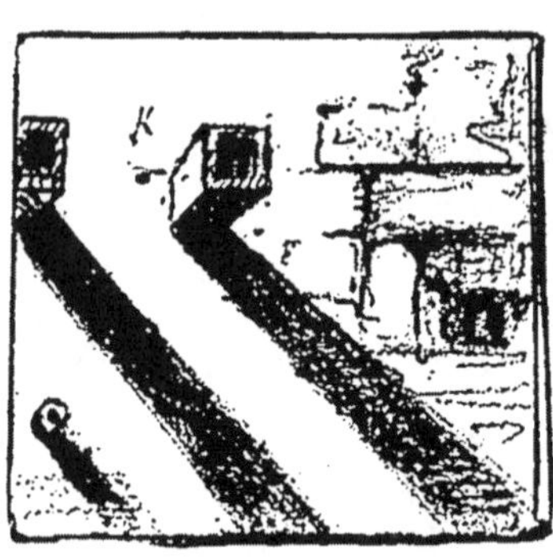

Fig. 4

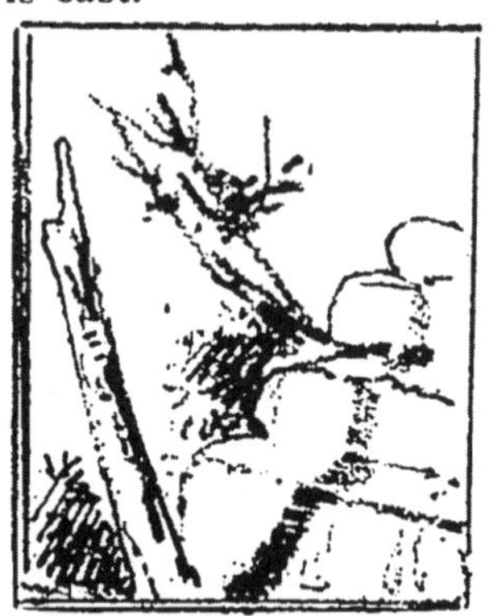

Fig. 5

Shadows from the Point of Projection.—Shadows broaden if there are reflected lights that may cause multiplication of the shadows; thus, in Fig. 4 the shadows broaden as they leave the spouts. This is owing to the presence of reflected light. Reflected lights are those which are thrown from one object to another, each object in turn reflecting light which, coming in contact with still another object, causes the latter to throw a shadow.

It will be enough to lay down a few condensed rules for ordinary use in the study of light and shade.

Intercepted rays of light cause shadows. (See Figs. 1 and 2.)

The light may be direct from the sun, candle, lamp or any glowing substance. These throw strongly defined shadows. (See Figs. 1 and 2.)

Or the light may be caused by diffused or reflected rays. Diffused lights are such as are given by a north window without the presence of sunshine, by the lights we receive on a cloudy or misty day. These lights cast soft and more or less undefined shadows.

Reflected Light.—A reflected light is cast into a room by an outside wall opposite a window, and is usually a subdued light. The reflected light cast by a mirror should not strictly be considered as a reflected light, for the rays are almost as strong as the source itself. The side of a cloud in the east will, at sunset, cast a reflected light on the earth. In the same manner will the side of a piece of chalk facing the window cast a reflected light on an object facing opposite the window light, but so placed as to be within the rays of the bit of chalk. The general effect is the same, be the scale great or small.

Shadows Have no Substance.—An object seen through a shadow, but beyond its area, is seen as plainly as if the shadow were not there. A shadow is not a dark object in itself. If an object comes within the scope of a shadow thrown by another object it will receive that shadow, but if it is beyond the shadow, although within the direct line cast by the shadow it will not be affected.

Shadows are invisible unless they have some plane or object upon which to fall.

In landscape work one is apt to forget the direction from which the light comes. (See Figs. 10, 11 and 12.)

Density of Atmosphere Renders Distant Objects Less Distinct.—For that reason the objects nearest to the eye should be drawn with strong lines and tones to indicate their nearness. Therefore, subdue the distant tints and intensify those appearing in the foreground.

Direction of Outlines.—As a general rule, any object with a decided form should have shading to correspond with the direction of outlines or to the general shape of the object itself; thus, curved objects may be drawn with curved lines, the sweep of the curve corresponding somewhat closely to the form of the object. When these curved lines cannot be conveniently formed with one stroke the adjoined or overlapping should be as imperceptible as possible.

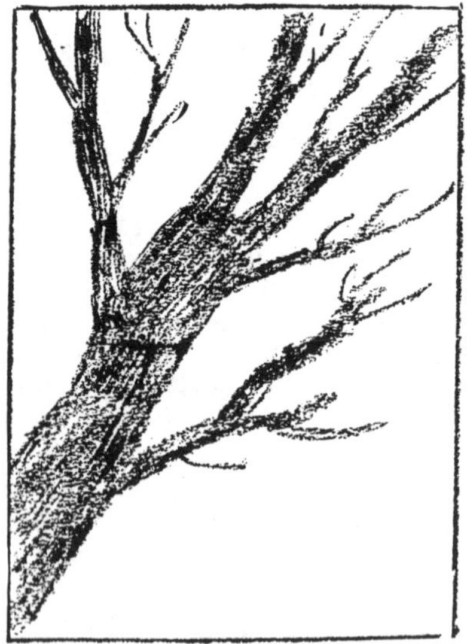

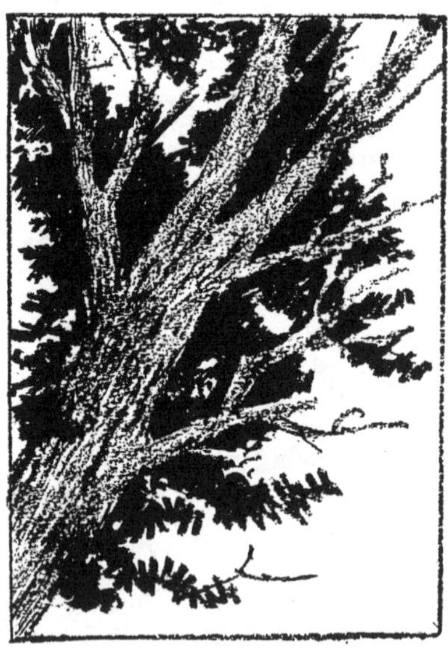

Fig. 6

Tints Relatively Light or Dark.—Fig. 6 illustrates the fact that tints are only relatively light or dark. In the first illustration, all of the branches seem quite dark because they are projected against a white background. In the illustration at the right, a mass of darker foliage is introduced; the result is that, by comparison, the boughs and twigs, though in the same tone, or shade, seem light in color, except where there is a projection beyond the area of the foliage. This is a matter that should be kept in mind, for nearly as much depends on the scale and key in drawing as in music.

Shadows Should Not Be Confused With Reflection.—There can be reflected darks as well as lights. Thus, we are apt to speak of shadows in the water when we really refer to reflections. There can, of course, be shadows thrown into any body of water. Reflections are cast only on the surface of the water, and the surface is generally what we see. In fact, the less clear the light and water the more clear are the reflections. And in this case a shadow would hardly be seen. Because it is customary, we say, "Reflections in the water." Reflections, however, are on the water. Reflections are not affected in shape by any changes except by those on the surface of the water, such as ripples or waves. Reflections have the same perspective as the object causing them except that the former are inverted.

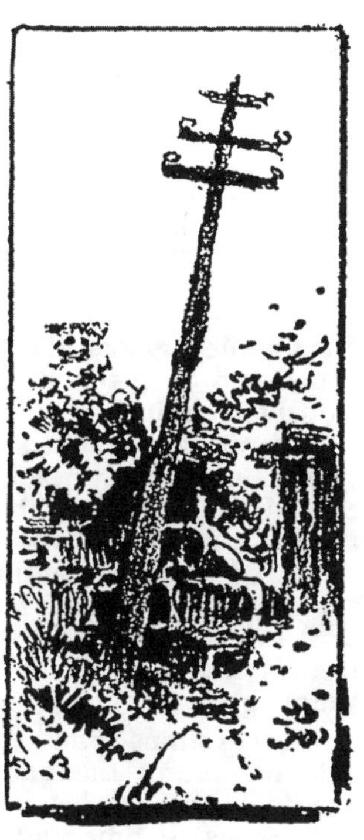

Fig. 7

Shadows Not Considered as Lines.—In putting in shadows and tones, lines should not be considered as lines, but simply as part of the surface by which we endeavor to represent or render something in nature or as a result of imagination. The lines placed more or less evenly and close together are components of some unit or part of a whole. By such means we try to imitate nature.

Where to Avoid Placing Lights.—Every object under the influence of a single light receives it only on that surface which is exposed to its direct rays. Therefore, avoid strong lights on the shaded side of an object.

The Comparative Values of Different Tones should be noted as frequently as possible. Fig. 7 is a pencil exercise in which the contrasting effect of a single tone is again shown by means of contrasting effects. Note that the prevailing tone on the telegraph post is the same throughout.

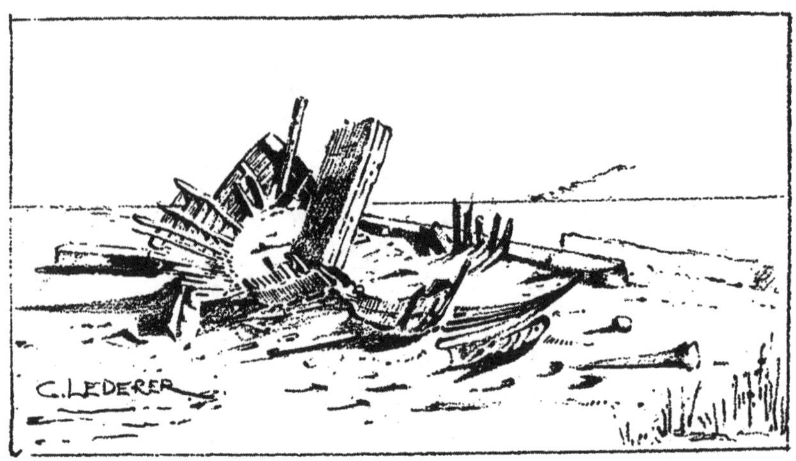

Fig. 8

Yet, while against the sky, it appears as a dark mass, as, contrasted with the still darker tones of the wall, it is comparatively light.

The drawing of the skeleton of the wreck of a small sailing vessel on a sandy beach (Fig. 8) shows the brilliant effects caused by a strong, direct sunlight on a light surface. The shadows are crisp and rather sharply defined, with small, clustered blacks accentuating the high lights. The shadows are concentrated and scarcely weakened by reflected lights. This drawing is not a "studio" composition, but made directly from a sketch made on the shore of Lake Michigan several years ago.

Foregrounds and Backgrounds.—There is no absolute rule regulating the question as to whether the foreground should be darker in tone than the background; for circumstances, as to time and place, must be taken into consideration. Generally speaking, however, the foreground and middle ground should be the parts of the picture in which appears the greatest display of color or tone; where the darkest effects are shown.

Suitable Contrast.—It is, however, more a question of

suitable contrast than anything else. In pictures where a single human figure or a group occupies the foreground, the background should be light and merely suggestive in the way of details. The contrast is more generally produced by having the objects in the foreground dark and those in the background light. The lines in the background should, in certain instances, be much finer than those in the foreground, and with very slight, if any, accentuations.

Avoid Flatness.—The keynote of attractiveness in a picture is frequently a matter of contrasts. Flatness is an almost unpardonable fault. By introducing strong contrasts, flatness is avoided. By playing heavy lines against light ones, strong tones against weak ones, contrasts are produced.

Practice Outline.—The outline is of the greatest importance, frequently being complete in itself as a means of representation of form. To copy slavishly the outlines found in copies or nature is not altogether necessary if the general forms are preserved.

Mass Drawing.—In drawing, a knowledge of the masses will aid greatly in giving the general impression and in indicating the position and form of the various details. These masses should be shaded in the drawing to reproduce the tones as they appear to the eye. A soft pencil is best adapted for this purpose. A very limited range of tones is required to produce excellent results. It is best to draw masses not with the point of the pencil, but by holding it at an angle and drawing with the side of the lead. This is to relieve the mind of the impression of lines and to allow the mind to concern itself simply with the shape and density of the various tones of light and dark. It is a good plan to outline the various masses before filling them in, as this will enable you to adhere more closely to the true shapes and edges of the masses.

Easy Examples in Light and Shade.—The examples in Fig. 9 show how, by simple means, the direction of the light may be indicated. In 1 may be seen the light coming from the right side; 2 shows the light coming from above, and in 3 the light on the walnut is from below.

The heavy lines in an outline or slightly shaded drawing should be made to indicate those parts which are against the light; the light lines the parts nearest to the light. In the drawings of the tree trunks, light and shade effects are shown by opposite instances. In 4 the light comes from the right, in 5 from the left. Draw other objects from nature or imagination, such as a cup, a stone, an ink-bottle or top, and note the light and shade effects.

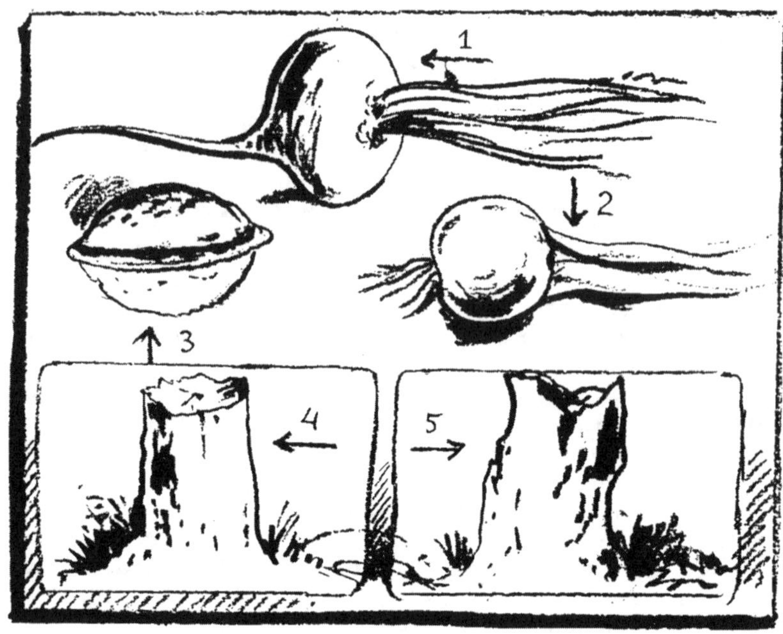

Fig. 9

Accentuation in Outline Drawings.—In outline drawings, this general rule may well be adopted, subject to exceptions dependable largely on common sense: The strongest accents and broadest lines should represent the nearest or most important lines of the subject.

Lines representing portions of the background or unimportant detail should be drawn with lighter and less accented strokes.

Accented lines can be taught profitably at the outset almost. Their use produces facility and strength in handling. The invariable use of unaccented lines is more or less offending, even to the uneducated eye.

In the upper drawing the lines are even, monotonous. In the lower one accentuation is evident. Which is the more pleasing to the eye?

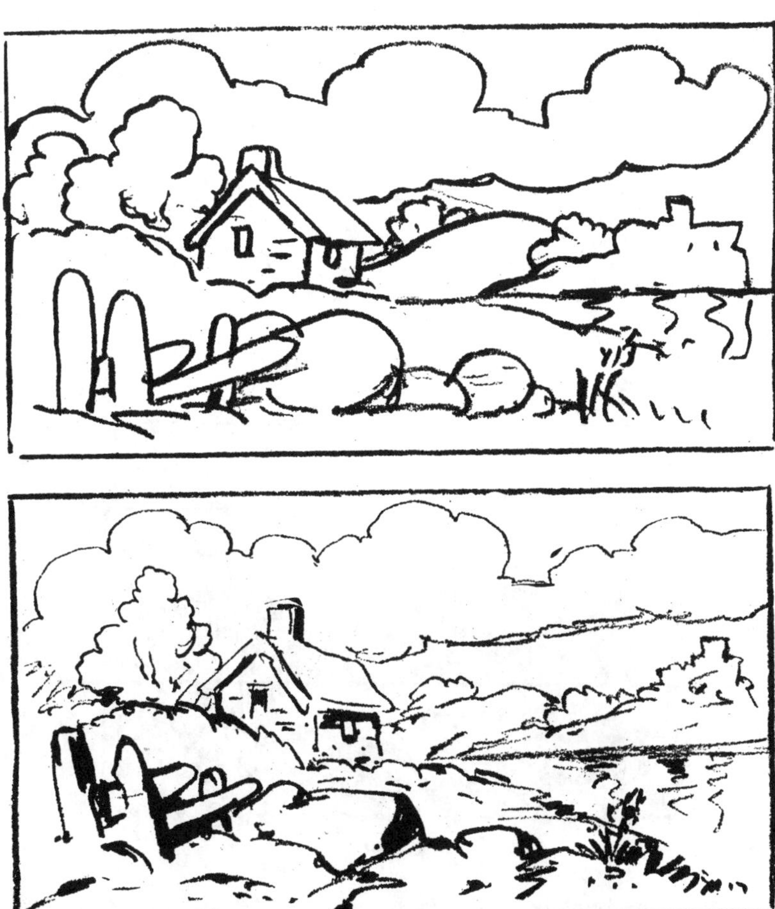

Fig. 10

Figs. 11, 12, 13. and 14. Fig. 11 is the beginning of the finished sketch, Fig. 12; while Fig. 13 is the beginning of the finished sketch, Fig. 14. When drawing Fig. I2, the student finished the foreground first, which looked strong at the time. Nevertheless, when the background was put in, with its tones similar to the foreground, the latter appeared weak. Fig. 13 shows the beginning of the other sketch, Fig. 14. In this

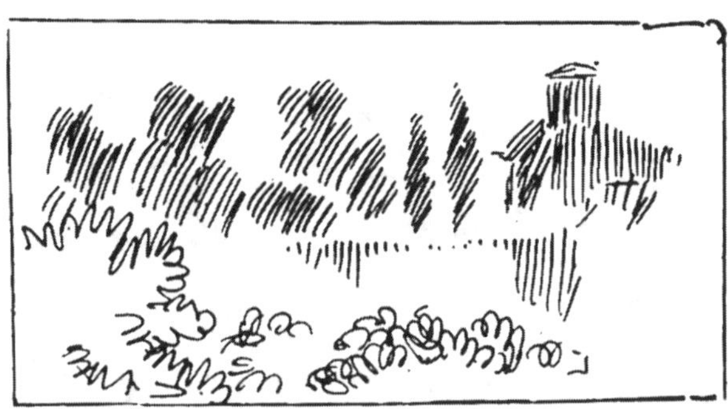

Fig. 11

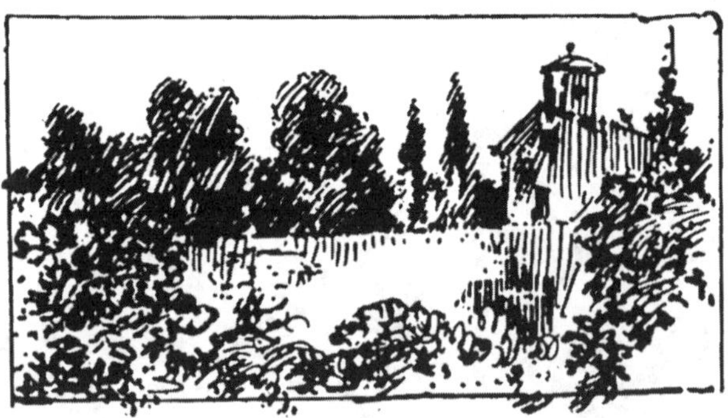

Fig. 12

drawing the background was finished first and the foreground last. As a result, the foreground stands out strongly in contrast to the background. Whenever the background is put in first the impulse is to place strength in the foreground. By doing so an arrangement of strongly contrasting light and dark tones is more apt to be produced, giving to the sketch the ever desired effect of power and value.

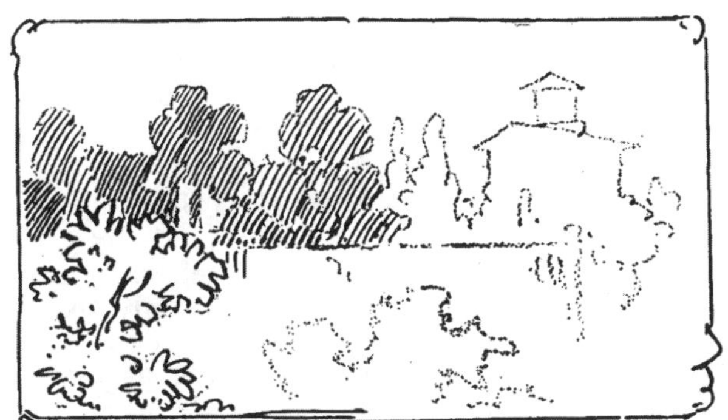

Fig. 13

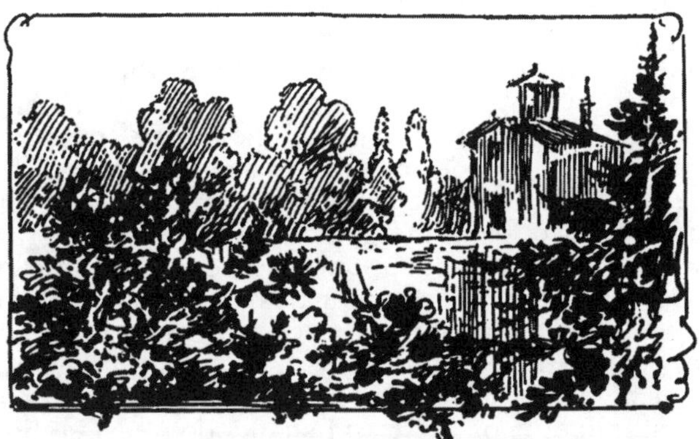

Fig. 14

Notes.—Other examples relating to the subject of this chapter will be found on pp. 39, 40, 42, 43, 44, 79, 114, 115, 116, 119, 120, 127, 133, 134, 136, 162, 164, 166, 167, 170, 186, 188, 190, 192, 193, 194, 196, 197, 198, 278, 288, 289, 290, 292, 295, 303, 304.

CHAPTER XXV

DRAWING FROM NATURE

In drawing from nature we should refrain from drawing that which is *known* to be present. Draw only that which is *seen.* Our vision should now be the guide, not our imagination.

Distant Detail Appears Dim.—Looking at a tree in the distance, we do not see the individual leaves on each bough. Or, if in town, in looking at a distant brick building we do not see each individual brick. But we know they are there. Nature provides that distant detail should appear dim to the human eye. Hence, such minor detail should not appear in the sketch. *Knowing* that they are there, there is a natural inclination to supply from memory the apparent deficiencies of the vision. Such inclinations should be resisted. The same principles apply to the detail in the foreground, for, even here, the moment the vision takes in the whole, multiplicity and detail are lost; only the general masses being grasped by the eye. Therefore, no attempt should be made to put in many minute objects. Let all those parts of the picture that are accessory to the main objects have little more than the impression that will be given by a momentary view. The absence of detail is still more to be desired when considered from the standpoint of light and shade alone. The lights and darks of the trees in the immediate foreground contain much diversity of light and shade; in the foliage of the middle distance, less will be noted; while further away from the eye there is still less, and the objects there seem almost flat in their sameness. This is a phenomenon to be observed in all nature sketching, for details vanish as they recede from the eye.

Tendency to Put in Detail because one's experience or memory tells that it is there, is so great that it is well to keep in mind always this axiom: The greater the distance of an object, the less detail is to be seen.

Even the *forms* of objects become more and more indistinct as they recede from the eye. This is a law of atmospheric perspective. If this law be broken there will be disturbance, including encroachment and trespass, and these, as every one knows, are serious offenses; for distance will encroach on the middle distance and the latter, in turn, will trespass on the immediate foreground.

Distant objects should, if placed against the sky, be well relieved against the latter, but not harshly; on the contrary, their outlines or outer tints may melt softly into the sky.

When Finish Is Unnecessary.—In sketching from nature, avoid, as far as may be, any tendency to work over and over. Study the effects, as far as can be, in advance, and, as far as possible, make the drawing with single operations. Otherwise, distance and atmospheric perspective are lost and the effect is one of flatness devoid of air and expression. In sketching from nature it is by no means necessary to make a finished drawing, but it is quite needful to indicate the character of the masses in outline and tone sufficiently to guide one in the more finished drawing or colored sketch to be made afterward. In sketching from nature one should strive not merely to make a pretty picture but to make lines and tones that will, to an extent, approximate those seen in nature, the model. In a composition to be made later, one may arrange the component parts of the picture to suit the individual taste.

Cloud Forms.—Give much attention to cloud forms. With rare exceptions, outlines should be defined, but not harshly. To take out the high lights in a pencil sketch use the sharp corners of the rubber eraser or use the paper masks as described in the chapter on Pastel-Stencils. One may use the "stump" in the main tones of the clouds or similar objects. Sharply defined objects projecting against the sky should be put in last. The lines in the distance may be partially obscured, but the sharply defined outlines in the foreground and middle distance should not be smudged or obliterated by the "stump" or anything else.

In shading a landscape, a clear sky may be represented by drawing horizontal lines so that they will join or blend together, but the joining should not be perceptible. Masses of foliage may be shaded in a similar manner, except that the strokes forming them are less elongated and the pencil may have a more blunt point.

Curved Lines for Clouds.—In shading clouds, slightly curved, parallel lines may be used to advantage, and, where deeper accents of the shadows are to be indicated, these curved lines may be crossed by a second series of parallel lines.

While there is no set rule or rules relating to the direction of tone or shade lines, a very good line of practice is to shade an entire drawing with nearly all lines running in the same direction. (See Fig. 5.)

Lines that Indicate Distance.—In drawings made with closely drawn lines, parallel or otherwise—to convey the impression of tints or tones—the following may be considered as almost a rule, namely; the greater the distance of the object, the lighter the lines that represent it. Reversely, the nearer the object the heavier the lines by which it is represented. As an example, Fig. 1 represents the rule. The clouds, being considered the most distant, were drawn with light lines—much lighter than they appear in the printed reproduction

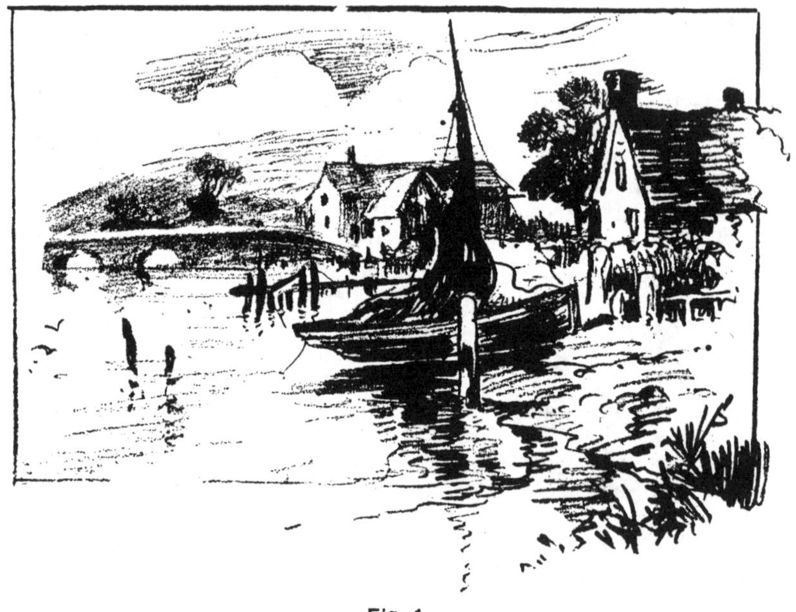

Fig. 1

The mountains being somewhat less distant, were drawn with slightly less weakness of line. The bridge, the trees just beyond, and the houses all in the middle distance, were lined with more broad lines than in the cloud or mountain. Nearer, in the approaching foreground, the tree and house at the left, the lines are seen to be coarser still and aid in giving a sense of nearness. The detail of the sailboat, even its reflection, everything, in fact, in the immediate foreground was drawn with strong, vigorous treatment.

Fig. 1 is an example that is a little more ambitious in its character than those preceding it, and may tax the ability of those who have not made considerable progress. The central point of interest is the sailboat, which has been treated with considerable strength in the way of intensely black lines, which are supplemented by the dark reflections in the water. The background is treated in light, close lines that contrast purposely with the freedom and boldness of the lines in the foreground.

Finder for Nature Drawing.—Cut out the center from an oblong of cardboard as shown in Fig. 2. Hold it either vertically or horizontally as a picture frame at arm's length and select what to draw by moving the frame from side to side or up and down. Then draw what appears within.

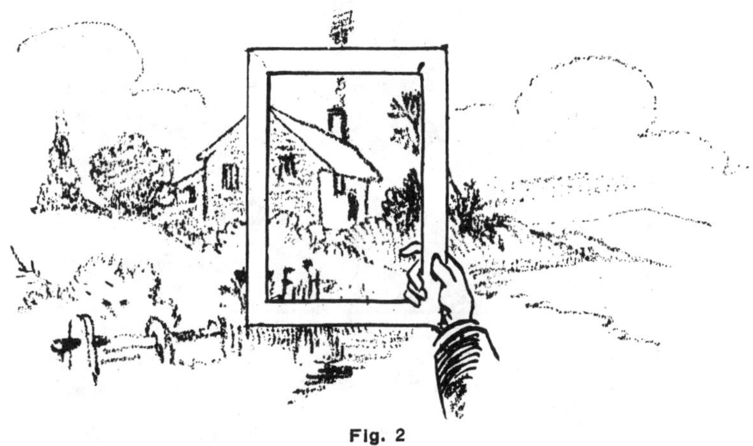

Fig. 2

Notes.—Further reference to nature drawing may be found in chapters XVII, XIX, XX, XXII, XXIII, and XXIV.

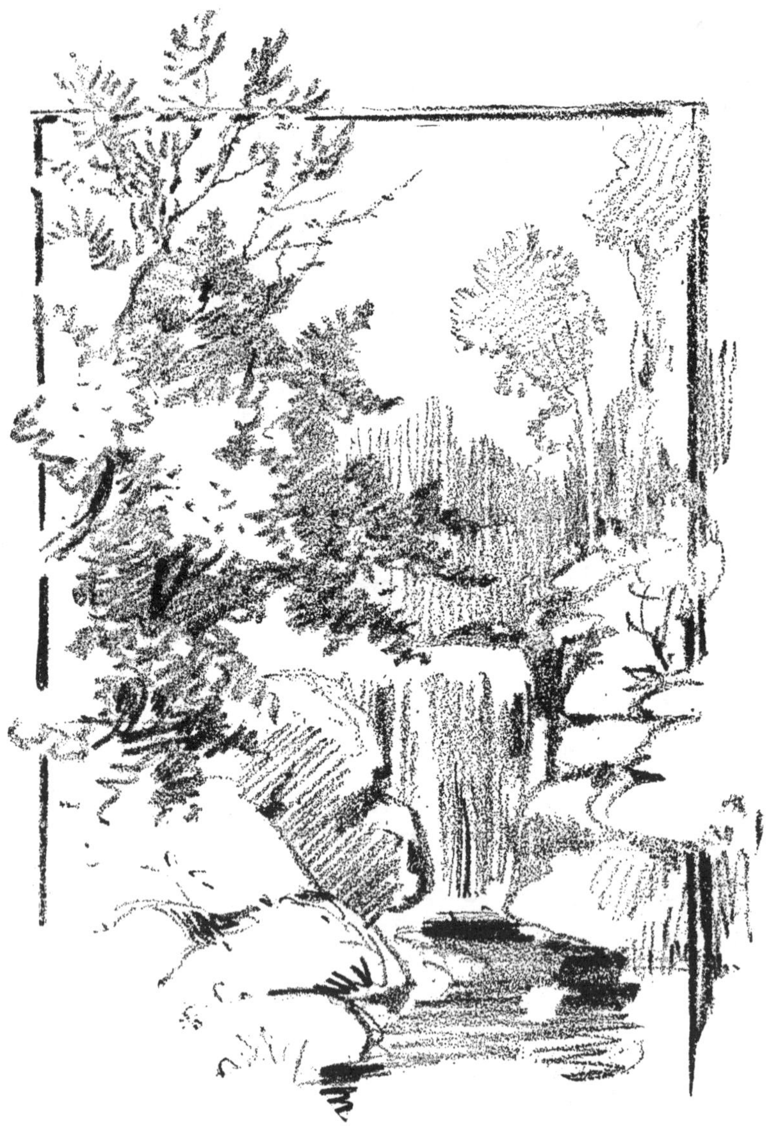

Fig. 3—A Nature Sketch

In drawing both figures and trees, it is well to begin with the simplest forms; the figures without the adornment of clothes or even flesh, the trees without foliage.

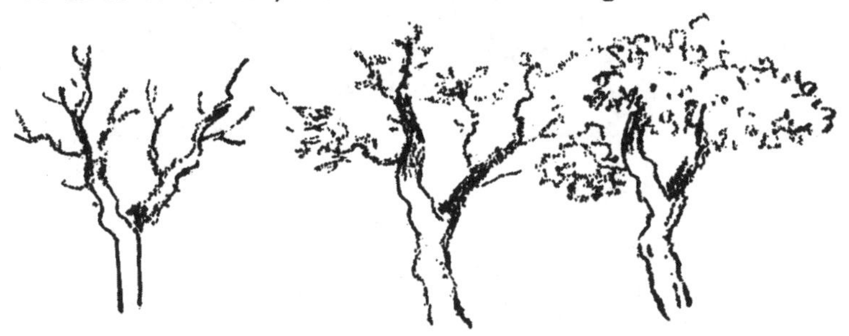

Fig. 4 – Winter Spring Summer

Contrast and Values

"Value" as understood in the terms of art expresses the comparative relations of tones to each other, whether of shade or color.

In making a drawing of a landscape, we would look at the tone of the trees against the sky and observe which is darker. If the sky be heavy and stormy and the light comes from behind the spectator, the trees may seem light by comparison, while the sky is darker in value.

On the contrary, under ordinary circumstances, trees with dark, rich foliage would stand out in strong relief against the sky, the latter being this time lighter in value than the trees.

The Keynote of a Picture.—Similarly, we compare the rocks with the water, the fence to the road, the bough of the tree with the foliage, and so on, according to the different objects that come within the draftsman's vision. In the production of a drawing containing light and shade as it appears to the eye, in order to obtain the best results, it is necessary to establish at once the darkest value in the whole. This, the deepest spot of shadow in the picture, becomes the keynote with which all other tones of light or dark may be compared.

Only by studying and observing the comparative variety of tones do we arrive at correct values.

As an important quality in art, this cannot be overestimated, for the quality of a picture is apt to depend on a just appreciation of the values that it contains.

Exercises in Single Line Direction.—The exercises in Fig. 5 require careful attention. They are adaptable for any medium except the brush. Their significance lies in the fact that the principal lines in each scene are made with strokes in the same general direction. This does not apply, of course, to the details. In the upper sketch, the prevailing lines are vertical; in the middle scene, the lines are horizontal, while in the botton scene, most of the lines are oblique.

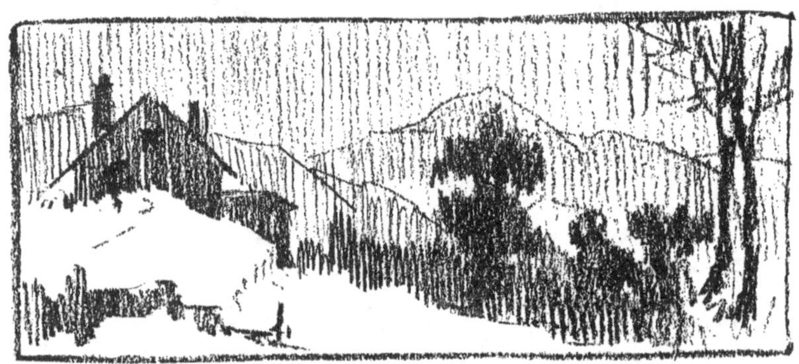

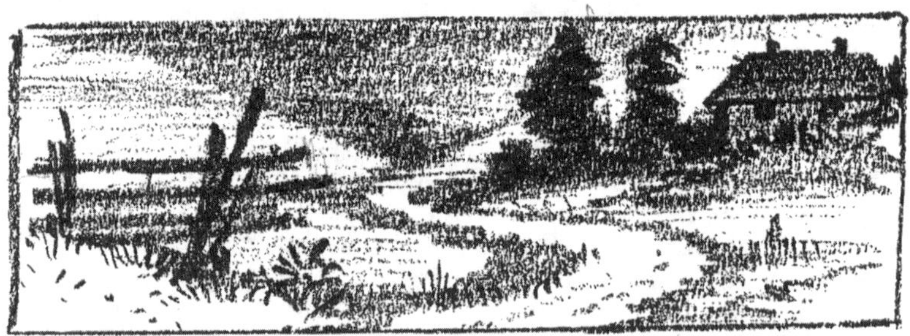

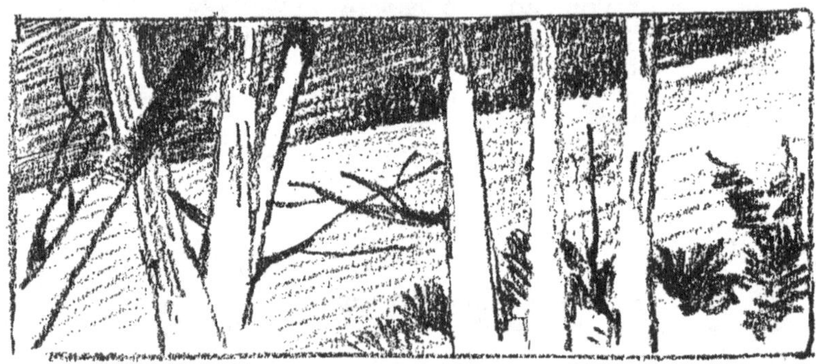

Fig. 5

CHAPTER XXVI

DRAWING IN CHARCOAL AND CRAYON

Charcoal is a material that can be used with striking effect and on a large scale. It is also adapted to the most careful work, where a high degree of finish is required. Charcoal is especially valuable as a medium, for the reason that it can be so easily erased. Charcoal is used in the principal art schools of the world for drawing from the cast and from the human figure. It is well adapted to sketching from nature. By its use, the most charming landscapes and marine effects may be obtained. For monochrome, moonlight effects, it is not to be surpassed. On pages 192-3-4-5 several examples of moonlight scenes are given which may be used for exercise in charcoal, crayon or pencil.

Two Methods of Drawing in Charcoal Prevail.—First, that in which the charcoal point is used alone, the shading being put in with lines which are not blended, without the use of the stump or rubbing of any kind.

Second, that in which the charcoal is blended with the stump or a soft rag, no lines being visible in the modeling. This manner of drawing is most popular in schools, and with reason, for it is susceptible of higher finish than the first method described. It is by this means that charcoal and crayon portraits are drawn.

Paper for Charcoal and Crayon Drawing.—For general purposes, the rough charcoal paper, made especially for the purpose, is the best.

Crayon.—Black crayon comes in several numbers or degrees of hardness and is to be had in two forms. First, the wooden pencils, and also in the shape of short sticks. The latter should be fastened in a crayon holder while using. For most purposes, crayon No. 2 is sufficient.

In addition to this, a fine, black, powdered crayon, called "sauce crayon," may be used. It comes in handy when large masses of dark are necessary and is rubbed on with a stump.

Stumps are made of leather, chamois skin and paper. For our purposes, paper stumps will be all that need be used. The stumps come in two forms, one made in various sizes of rough paper, measuring from one-fourth to an inch or more in diameter.

The other form of paper stump is known as the tortillon, and is made of strips of paper rolled to a point, like spills. It is used in detail work, where the other form of stump would be too coarse.

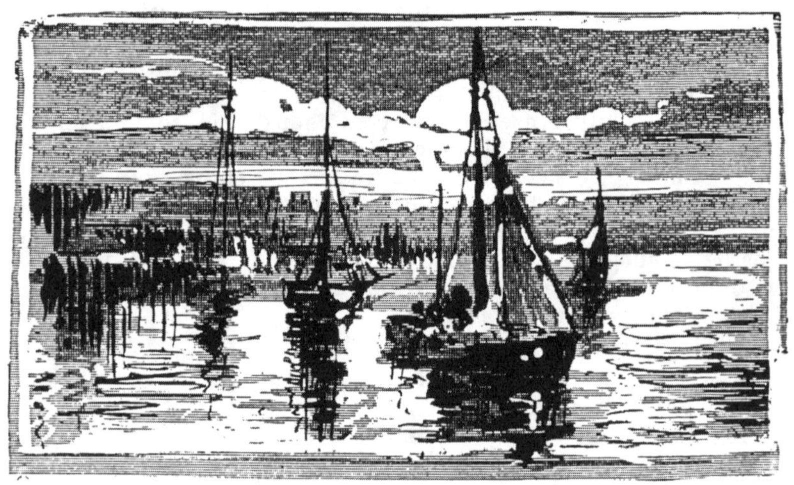

Fig. 1 – Example of Strong Effects with Charcoal

Ordinary bread, at least a day old, that is free from butter, lard or milk in its making, is used for rubbing out charcoal or crayon, erasing mistakes, and taking out lights from a mass of dark. In order to correct a line or erase the charcoal by means of the bread, take a small piece between the fingers, roll it into a ball and shape it to a point, use it as you would a rubber eraser only more slowly.

A fine, soft, cotton rag is a necessary adjunct to work with charcoal or crayon. It is used sometimes to dust the charcoal from the paper, and if the charcoal has not been very heavily used, the rag is often sufficient to make an erasure without the use of bread or rubber. A rag is useful also when too much charcoal or crayon has been rubbed on a tone. If a shadow appears too black, a soft rag may be passed gently over the surface, when the superfluous charcoal or crayon will come off, leaving behind a tone more soft and light in quality. This tone can be worked over in any manner desired. The rag, too, may be used in sketching landscapes to spread a soft, flat mass, such as a sky. In many cases, it is preferable to use the stump for this purpose. In lieu of the "sauce," charcoal may be powdered and used in the same manner as the "sauce."

To "Fix" Drawings.—Unprotected, a charcoal drawing will become smeared and defaced. Hence it is necessary to "fix"

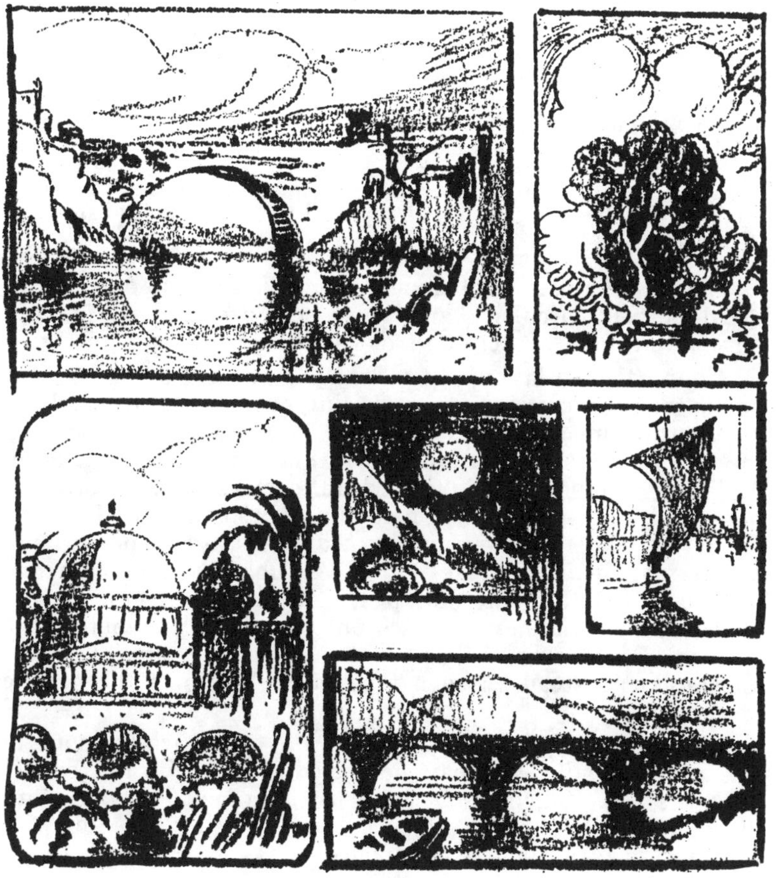

Fig. 2

the drawing by the application of some varnish-like preparation. To use a brush for this purpose would be obviously wrong. A fixative may be made by using four ounces of alcohol, in which has been dissolved a few grains of white shellac. Fixative also comes ready prepared in bottles.

The fixative is applied to the surface of the drawing by spreading it by means of an atomizer. The atomizer used for medicinal and perfume spraying is not applicable to this purpose; the shellac in the fixative soon clogs the tubes. The cheapest, and as good as any, consists of two small tubes of tin. These are connected and fastened by a small hinge or pivot. One end is placed in the fixative and the other end taken in the mouth, and the breath blown through it. This causes the liquid to mount in the lower tube and dissolve in a cloud of spray so light as not to dislodge the delicate particles of charcoal, and yet attach them so firmly to the paper that ordinary rubbing will not efface the drawing.

In blowing through an atomizer, care should be taken to make the breath steady, avoiding short unequal puffs. The atomizer must be held sufficiently far from the paper to avoid causing the fixative to run down in streams, to the ruination of the drawing. If held too far from the drawing it will vaporize too much and fail to "fix" the charcoal.

Simple exercises in charcoal. Fig. 2 is a group of sketches in which semi-circular shapes purposely prevail. By practicing curved lines, gracefulness of handling is acquired.

Charcoal.—In laying out a drawing, to be made by means of charcoal or crayon, make a faint outline of the shadows where they meet the light. After having done so, charcoal the mass of shadow within the outline, making a flat, even, dark tone. In order to do this with the charcoal, draw straight parallel lines, slightly oblique, almost touching each other, until the whole shadow is covered. A large paper stump, or the rag, is now used to unite these charcoal lines into one flat tone of dark. The stump is held in the fingers, so that about an inch of the point lies on the paper, not merely the tip end. With this, the charcoal is rubbed in until no lines appear, but instead an even tone of dark fills in the outline of the shadow.

Should too much charcoal get on the paper, while laying in a mass of shadow, it may be wiped off lightly and evenly with the rag. Then, if the tone has become too light, work on it again with the charcoal, as before, using the stump in the same way until it is satisfactory.

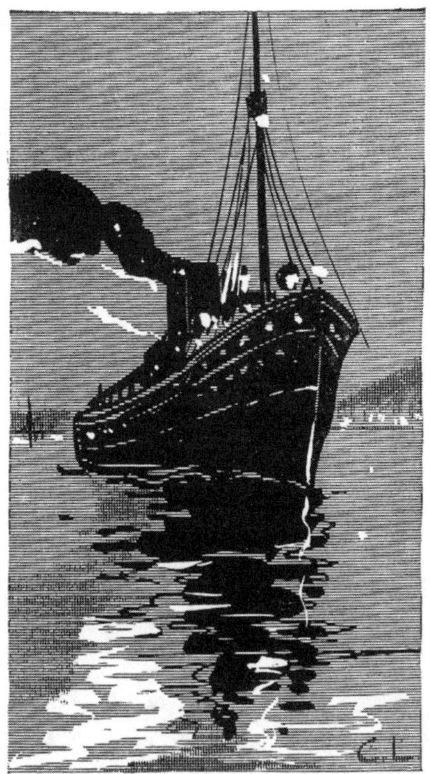

Fig. 3

In this exercise, cover the entire surface of the paper with a single dark tone. Add the blacks and take out the high lights with white crayon or chalk.

After all the shadows are put in and the proportions are found to be correct, further details may be added with the point of the charcoal or crayon.

Keep a clean stump always at hand for delicate half tints.

"Sauce" is sometimes used for putting in large masses of dark, such as shadows, drapery, etc. Sauce is a finely powdered crayon, but not used as such.

The "sauce" should be rubbed off on a small piece of charcoal paper, and tacked on one side of the drawing for convenience. It is used for especially delicate tones.

The charcoal or crayon point is always used in finishing up a drawing, with the darkest accents being put in last.

The high lights are taken out with the bread rolled to a point, and should be made sharp and distinct.

Keep Paper Covered.—In rubbing on charcoal, and before using the stump, be sure to cover the paper well, so that very little rubbing will spread the tone into an even mass. No matter how much charcoal is put on at first, the superfluity can be taken off with a rag. On the other hand, if there is not enough and one is tempted to rub the surface too hard, the paper becomes rotten and spoiled.

It is even more necessary than when using the pencil to avoid letting the hand rest directly on the paper; have a sheet of clean writing paper to place underneath the hand.

In blocking-in, or when drawing long, sweeping lines, the hand should not be steadied upon the paper as in writing, but one should try to acquire freedom of handling by practice, resting the hand upon the paper only when absolutely necessary, as in drawing fine details or when great precision is required.

Charcoal Sketch.—Use tinted paper in making this sketch (Fig. 4), a gray tint being preferable. If tinted paper is unobtainable, use the stump or cloth according to previous directions, covering the entire surface of the paper as evenly as possible with a medium dark tint of the charcoal. Outline the details and put in the sky and sky reflections in the water. Next put in the heavy masses, such as the house at the left,

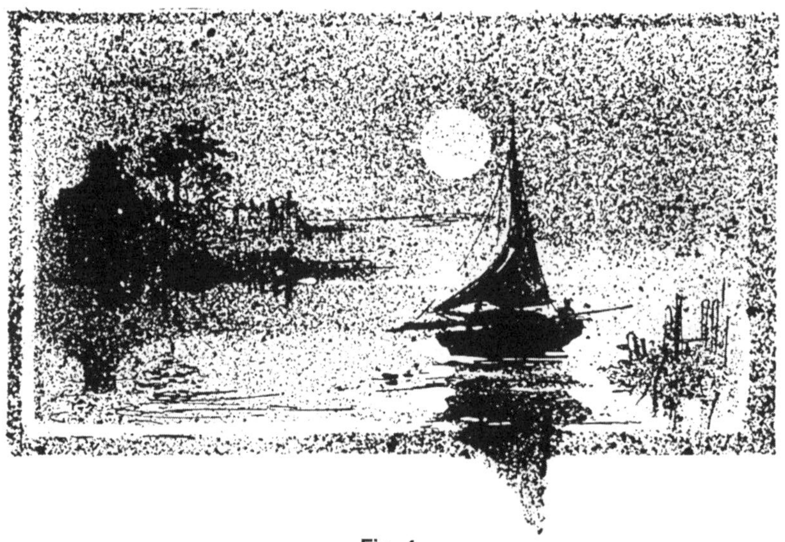

Fig. 4

and a boat with its reflection. Then the solid black and sharp details, such as the windows of the house, the spars of the boat, etc. If tinted paper is used, make the high lights, including the moon, by means of white chalk. If white paper is used, take out the high lights with a pointed rubber or bread.

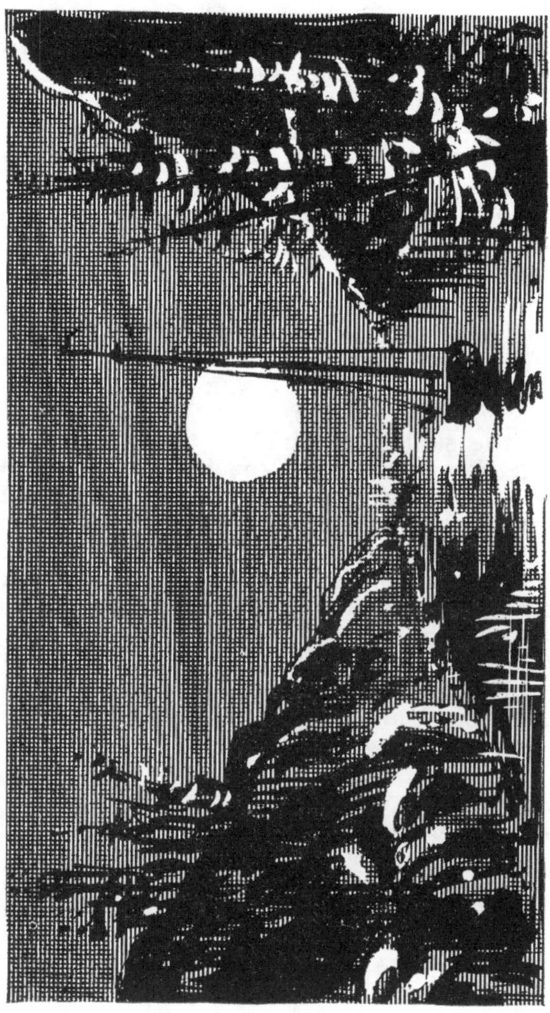

Fig. 5

The moon is especially adapted as a leading motif in charcoal drawing, and for this reason so many moonlight scenes are introduced into the exercises in this chapter.

Pastel Painting

Pastel painting is akin to working with colored chalks or crayons. Pastels are soft enough to be powdered under the finger and graduated and blended by means of stumps. The latter is applied to cigar-shaped rolls of leather or paper, especially made for the purpose. Pastels lend themselves readily to the painter who desires to produce quick effect. They require no elaborate preparation and, unlike water-color work, may be interrupted and resumed at will.

Pastels Produce Pretty Effects.—Applied to paper or cardboard, the pastel produces soft opaque shadows that have not the depth of oil painting, neither do they create the transparent effect of water-color painting. But the colors show freshly. Flesh tints may be produced with tenderness and brilliancy, while in landscape work, it appeals strongly to one desiring to produce sky effects, especially those of sunrise and sunset. Little skill is required in the blending of colors, but crisp detail and vigorous touches are generally found wanting in pastel painting. Very pretty effects may be had by cutting out stencils and instead of a brush using a soft cloth or piece of chamois, as described in the chapter devoted to Pastel-Stenciling. The pastels may then be rubbed on the cloth and by gently rubbing transferred to the paper. Different portions of the subject may be treated with various tints and the details afterward put in with a crayon. The examples in Figs. 6 and 7 were made by this means, although here shown in black and white. By making a single unit of ornament and repeating it, various designs, such as borders, etc., may be made.

Notes.—Other subjects suitable for exercise in charcoal, crayon or pastel will be found on pp. 42, 43, 45, 79, 91, 92, 93, 97, 105, 131, 132, 133, 134, 160, 162, 164, 166, 167, 170, 173, 174, 176, 177, 178, 186, 188, 190, 232, 243, 276, 277, 278, 292, 294, 295, 296, 303.

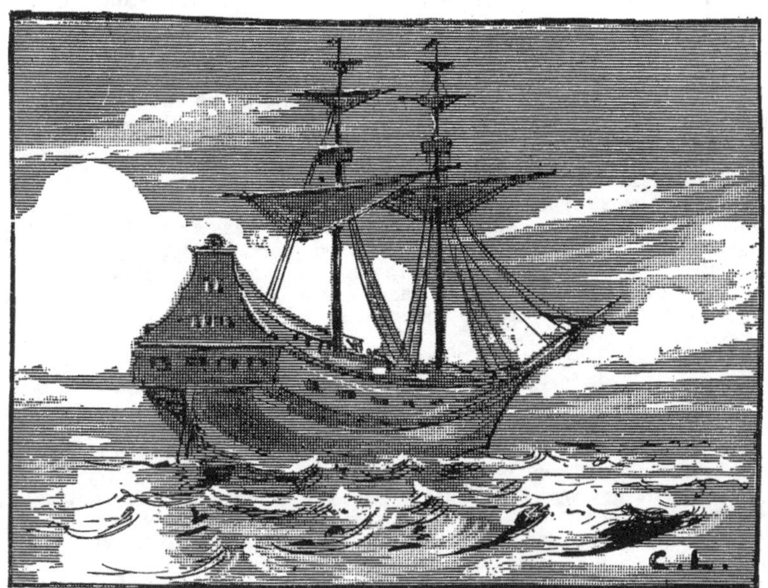

Fig. 6

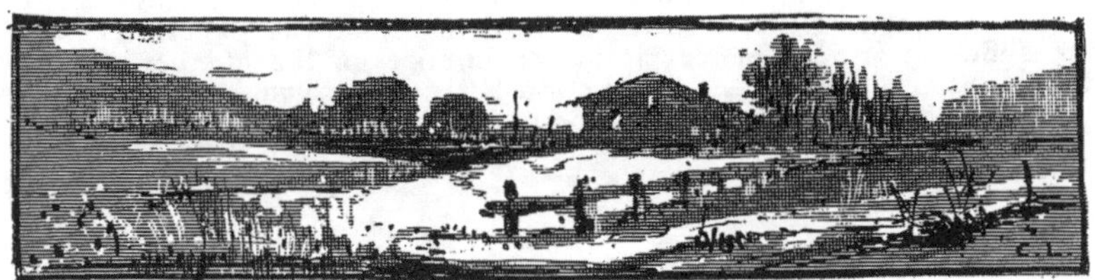

Fig. 7

While a drawing may sometimes be improved if the pencil or crayon lines are gently rubbed with the finger tip, rubber or paper stump or soft rag, such devices should be avoided in early practice work. This method of softening is too temptingly easy and its use is apt to make one careless in the matter of producing of soft effects with the point alone. "Stumping" must be done with considerable care or it will give the shading and outlines a dulled or rubbed appearance, not readily restored by retouching.

In shading with pencil, crayon, etc., it is well to keep a piece of glazed or blotting paper under the hand to prevent rubbing. This will also prevent the paper from becoming warped through the warmth of the hand. Another precautionary measure against smudging, when shading, is to work downward from the upper part of the drawing. In a very important drawing the precaution may be taken to cover the entire drawing surface with a sheet of thin paper which may be torn away, piece by piece, as the finishing of the drawing progresses.

A FEW NEVER, NEVERS.

Never "rub off" a pen drawing until the ink is quite dry. If there are large wet spots of ink that simply won't dry, dab them very slowly but gently with the corners of a blotting paper. Do not press the blotter flat as you would in blotting a letter. Do not try to get the ink quite dry with the blotter. Let the final moisure dry naturally so as to leave a smooth surface of ink.

Never make a very long tapering point to the lead pencil, unless there is some very fine detail to be worked up.

Never leave your ink bottle unstopped when not in use unless you want the ink to get thick, not to mention possibilities in the way of spilling.

Never dip your brush *into* the ink bottle, unless you are very careful not to touch the neck of the bottle with the brush. If the brush strikes the neck of the bottle while *inserting* it, the hairs will become separated and likely remain so. Of course there is no danger of doing so when withdrawing it from the bottle—in that case the brush can be wiped off on the inside of the neck of the bottle. The best plan is to pour out a few drops of ink on a saucer or ink slab. By so doing one can more easily regulate the supply of ink taken up by the brush.

Never leave less than a half inch margin of plain paper around your drawing, more will be better. Never try to see how many drawings you can get on one paper.

Never have two or more drawings facing different ways on a piece of paper. Do not draw on both sides of the paper. If you are suffering from a paper famine economize on the number of pictures. Keep down on the production but don't crowd.

Never use light greyish ink, or in fact any except very black ink.

CHAPTER XXVII

ELEMENTARY PERSPECTIVE

The study of perspective is usually considered premature in the early stages of the study of drawing. This is true in its general sense; nevertheless, it is well at the outset in drawing from imagination or nature to learn a few of the rudiments of that branch of the art. It becomes necessary to study perspective in order to avoid distortion when drawing interior views, buildings, etc.

Importance of Perspective.—Many are impressed with the belief that Perspective is the most dry and least interesting of any subject taught along the lines of illustrative art. This is a mistake. After having mastered the *rudiments* of perspective, further study becomes not alone interesting but easier with each step in the program.

However, to secure anything more than a superficial knowledge of perspective would entail the study of many volumes, and require knowledge of an apparently interminable array of rules and diagrams, the latter covered with perplexing tangles of dotted lines, projections and angles. Many of the so-called simple hand-books on perspective confuse the beginner with their complexity of detail.

Throughout this chapter the endeavor has been made to avoid complexity and to bring the lessons within the mental grasp of the ordinary student.

A knowledge of the principles of perspective is indispensable to everyone who intends to go to nature for his subjects. One may no more be able to make a good picture without some knowledge of perspective than to write a story without a smattering of the rudiments of grammar.

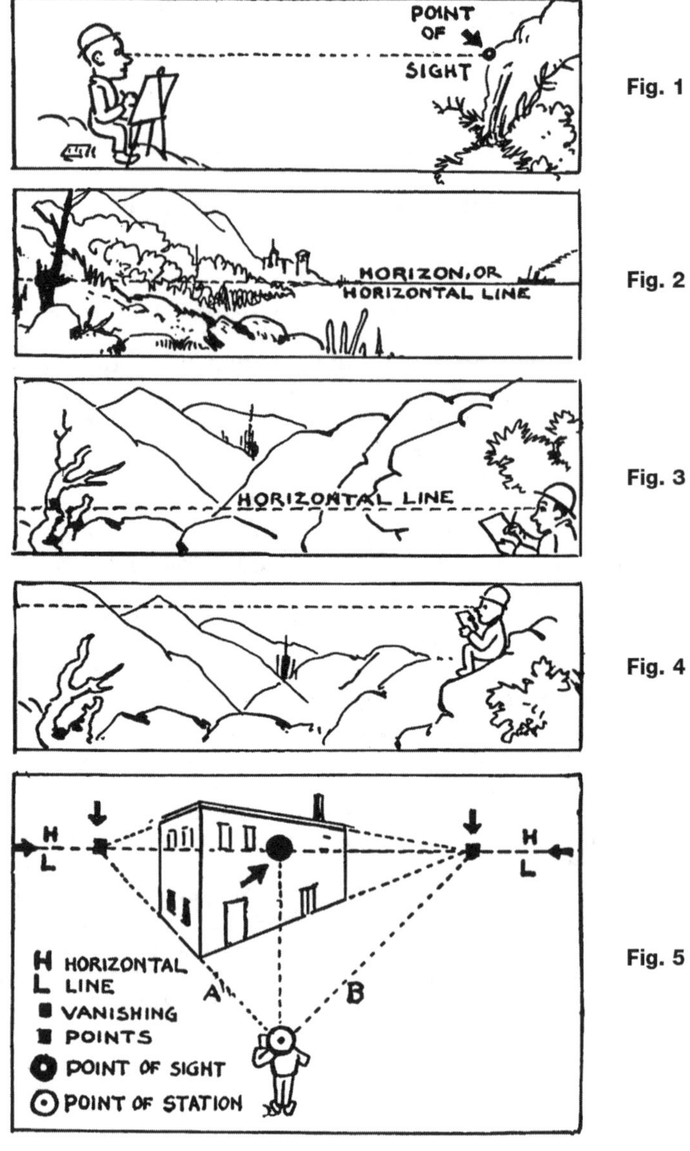

Fig. 1

Fig. 2

Fig. 3

Fig. 4

Fig. 5

Perspective for Beginners Illustrated

The explanatory illustrations are not intended as actual representations, but as aids to the study of the simplest rules in perspective.

Fig. 1.—The Point of Sight is that point to which the eye of the spectator is supposed to be directed when he looks straight before him.

Fig. 2—The Horizon (or Horizontal Line) resembles that horizon or boundary line that seems to part the sea from the sky, forming this apparent line of conjunction.

Fig. 3.—The Horizon Line in a picture is determined by the elevation or depression of the point of sight. The point of sight is determined by the real or supposed position of the spectator. (See Fig. 1.)

Fig. 4.—If the position of the spectator, or artist, is low, as in Fig. 3, the point of sight and horizon line will be correspondingly low. On the other hand, if the artist ascends, the point of sight and horizon line ascend with him.

Fig. 5.—Shows the four principal points and lines in perspective. The human figure is emblematical, and not to be considered as part of the picture any more than are the dotted lines.

Note that the lines A and B from the point of station to the horizon line and vanishing points are at right angles. The angles of such lines should *always* be right angles, or 90 degrees, in their relations with the vanishing points on the horizon line.

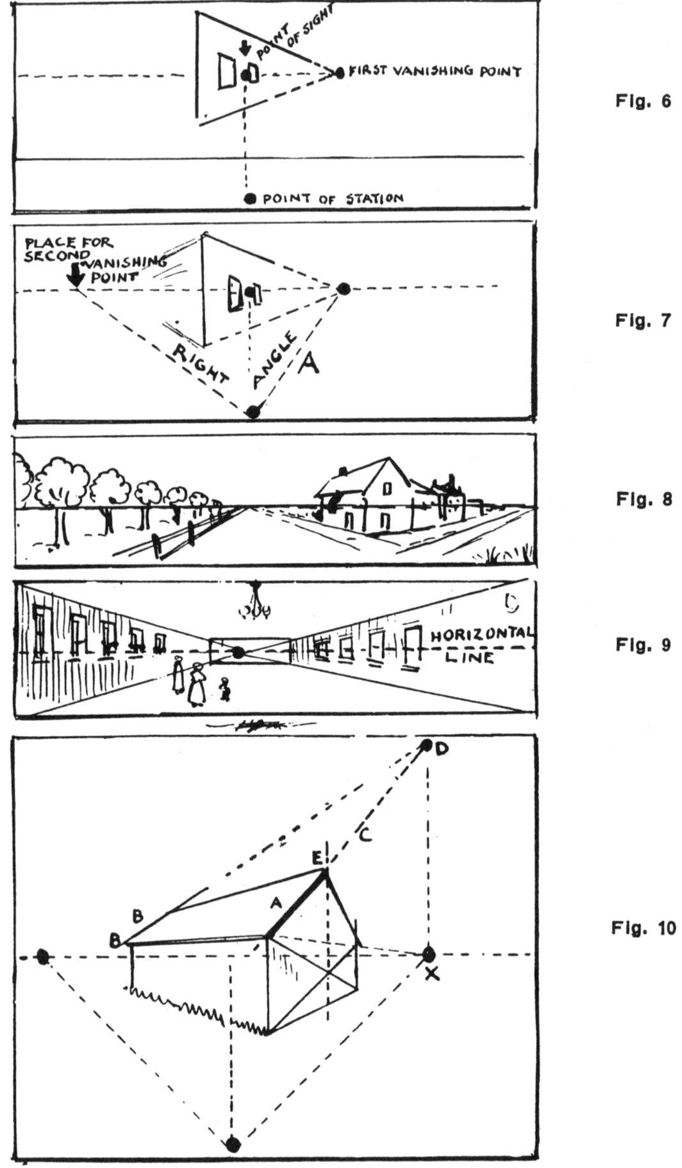

Fig. 6

Fig. 7

Fig. 8

Fig. 9

Fig. 10

Fig. 6.—The horizon line, one vanishing point, the point of sight and the point of station having been determined, the other vanishing point is found by proceeding according to the diagram—Fig. 7.

Fig. 7.—Project a line at right angles to the line A (connecting line between determined vanishing point [see Fig. 6] and point of station), and where it intersects the horizon line is the second vanishing point. By similar means the point of station can be found by having determined the point of sight and the vanishing points.

Fig. 8.—All lines above the horizon line that are not parallel with the picture descend to the horizon line. All lines below the horizon line not parallel with the picture rise to the horizon line.

Fig. 9.—A correct drawing of the sides, ceiling and floor of a hall or other enclosed room should have only one vanishing point, namely, the point of sight.

Fig. 10.—Having established the pitch of the roof at A, the angle at B is found by projecting a line vertically at right angles with the vanishing point at X, namely, D. A line carried to B from D will give the proper pitch. The apex of the roof E is determined by projecting a line through the crossed oblique lines on the right hand side of the house.

The following rules which are few and simple will tend greatly to overcome many of the most obvious defects in drawings made by pupils.

Primary Rules in Perspective

Rule 1.—Lines and figures in planes parallel to the picture planes, that is, facing you, retain their original relations and forms; thus, parallel lines will be presented parallel; a square will remain a square; a circle, a circle, etc.

Rule 2.—Parallel lines not parallel to the picture plane appear to converge or come together; in terms of perspective, they are said to vanish. The point at which they would meet if sufficiently projected is called their vanishing point. Whatever the number of lines, if parallel to each other, they will all converge to the same vanishing point.

Rule 3.—Horizontal parallel lines will converge to a point on the horizontal line. If above the eye, they will come down to the horizon (or horizontal) line; if below the eye, they will rise toward it.

Rule 4.—Vertical lines will always be represented vertical.

A Point Illustrated

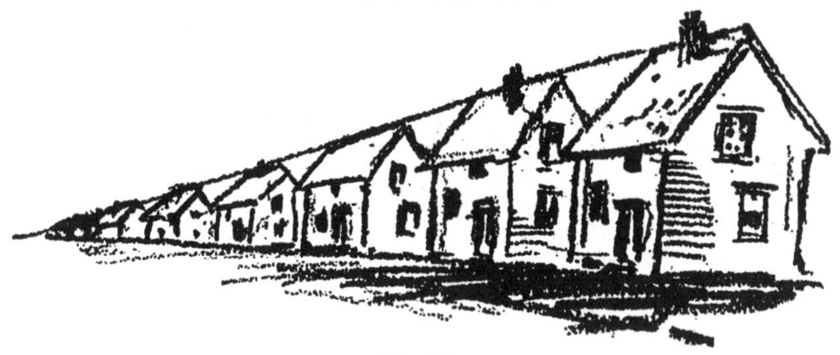

Fig. 11

If one stands looking down a long, straight, level street, the houses appear to meet in the distance—the vanishing point. (See Fig. 11.) If you look down a long, straight railroad track, the rails and telegraph poles appear to meet at the vanishing point. If you are looking at a long procession of men, marching in a straight line (or nearly so) with the line of your point of sight, the last man is almost indistinguishable. He is at the vanishing point, for our intent and purposes. (See Fig. 36.)

A in Fig 12 shows an example of a drawing that lacks perspective, while B explains wherein the drawing is incorrect, showing the manner of finding the proper vanishing point and horizon line. If the point of station, etc., seems too complicated, think in terms of the lines of the sides of the building receding as shown in B.

When drawing the houses in Fig. 15 it is easier than in Fig. 12 to establish the point of sight and vanishing point, because they are the same. The lines in the houses that recede from the beholder converge to those points. The side of the houses, as at C, being parallel to the horizon line, have no vanishing point.

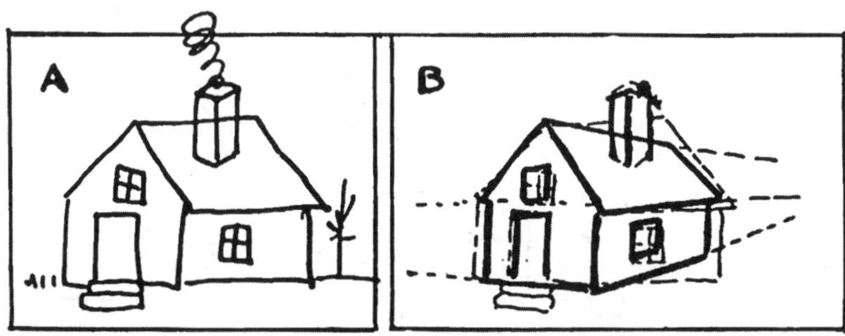

Fig. 12

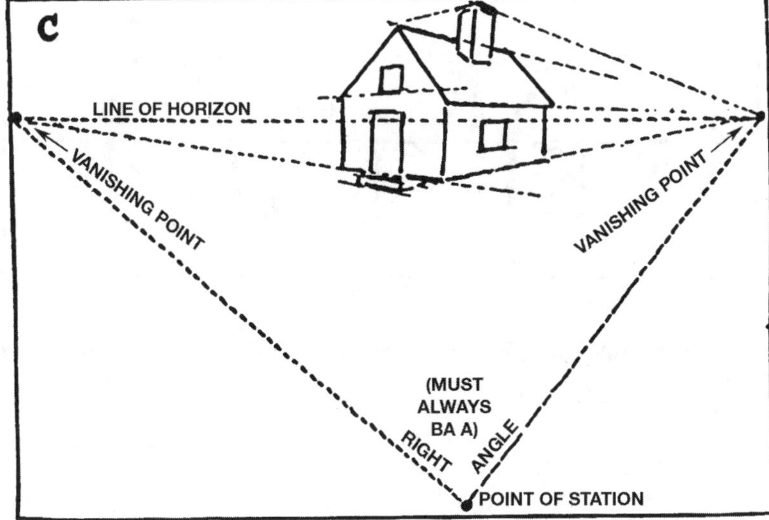

Fig. 13

Mistakes in Perspective Corrected.—In Fig. 12 is represented a crude drawing of a house made by a boy who lacked knowledge of perspective. In B the dark and dotted lines show how the house should have been drawn, the light lines being those of the original and the dashed lines those of perspective. Fig. 13 shows how the correct drawing was made.

The same boy drew the four houses shown in Fig. 14. In Fig. 15 the houses are drawn according to the simple rules of perspective shown in this chapter.

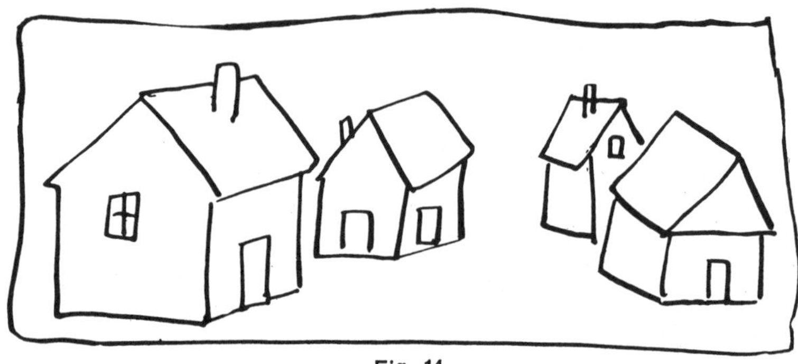

Fig. 14

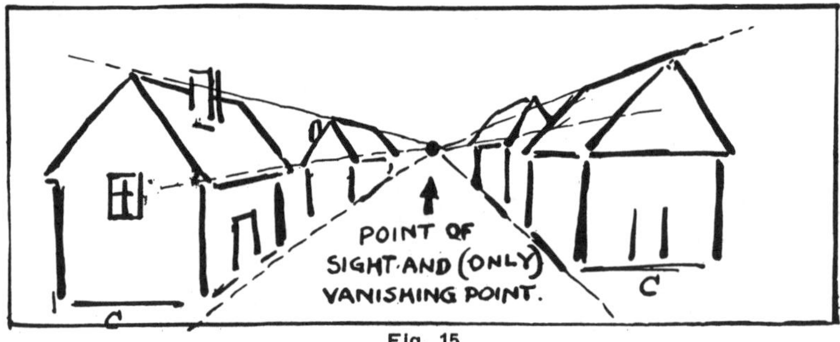

Fig. 15

Four Important Points in Perspective.—First, the point of sight; second, the horizon line; third, the vanishing point; fourth, the point of station.

The Point of Sight is that spot which the spectator sees when he looks straight before him.

The Horizon Line is a line parallel with the top and bottom of the picture drawn through the point of sight. The distance between the top and bottom of the picture, at which the horizon line is drawn is determined by the point of sight. If the point of sight is high, the horizon line will be correspondingly high. All actual horizontal lines (not parallel from right to left) above the horizon line are inclined toward it. Every receding line of the same kind that is below will run up to the horizon line. The vanishing points, with few exceptions, lie on the horizon line and are independent of the point of sight.

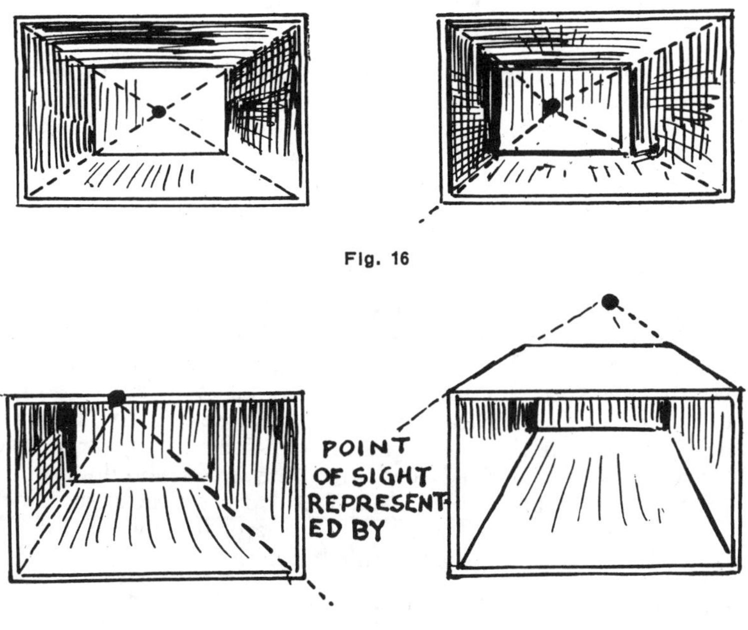

Fig. 16

Fig. 17

The Point of Sight Becomes a Vanishing Point for all lines (to the right and left of the spectator) that are at right angles to the upper and lower borders of the parallelogram containing the picture.

A large box, open at one end, has its front and back lines in parallel perspective if the opening is parallel with the body of the draftsman as he faces it, while the lines of the sides, top and bottom, recede directly from him. In this case, the point of sight becomes the vanishing point, because all the straight lines receding from the sight converge on this point.

On the contrary, the nearest and furthest lines of the top and bottom of the box being, both in reality and in the drawing, parallel, must be so drawn. These lines, however far they may be extended, would never meet. Whereas, all lines that recede from the spectator would meet if continued sufficiently. (See Figs. 16 and 17. Also see Fig. 4, chapter on Foreshortening.)

The box should now be turned around so one edge is toward the draftsman; thus two sides will be seen, each of which will require its own vanishing point.

In a Picture, There Is But One Point of Sight.—There can be several vanishing points. A picture should never contain more than that which can be seen without moving the head. This area is comprised generally within an angle of sixty degrees, or one-sixth of everything the artist could see if he turned completely around as he would in order to sketch a panoramic view, which, however, does not come within the scope of these lessons.

Each Vanishing Point Determined by Point of Station.—The point of station is somewhere in front of the landscape or picture, and is, in fact, the eye of the spectator. The distance of the spectator should be at a distance *less* than the front dimensions of the scene to be enclosed in the picture. That is to say, if the front line of the scene to appear in the picture was one hundred feet wide, the artist should not be stationed *more* than one hundred feet from the nearest object that appears in the picture. He may, and in most instances should, however, be stationed much nearer.

Locating the Point of Station.—The point of station may be determined by having located both of the vanishing points. Or one vanishing point may be determined, which, together with the point of station, will determine the other vanishing point.

Two lines drawn from each of the vanishing points to the point of station should invariably form a right angle.

In the study of perspective it will be helpful to keep the following definitions and rules in mind. Even those already versed in art, through disuse, are prone to forget some of the simplest definitions.

Additional Elementary Rules

A right line is a perfectly straight line in a position or direction. Parallel lines are lines which are the same distance from each other throughout their length, whether straight or curved.

A horizontal line is one which is parallel to the earth's surface or the sea level.

A vertical line is a perfectly upright one, pointing to the vertex or zenith and to the center of the earth.

A perpendicular line is a line at right angles to any other straight line, but is not necessarily vertical.

A plane is a perfectly level surface, which may be either horizontal, vertical, or inclined in any direction.

A straight rod applied to any such surface would touch it throughout its length and breadth. A line is said to be in a certain plane when throughout its length it touches the plane, or coincides with it. In perspective, the picture plane is the surface, paper, canvas or whatever it may be upon which the drawing is made. This is always supposed to be at right angles to the direction in which the spectator is looking. If we are standing erect, and looking straight in front of us, the picture plane will be vertical; for instance, if the picture were placed close to an ordinary wall, the picture plane would be vertical. A point on the picture plane exactly opposite the eye is called the center of vision. The horizontal line indicates on the paper the position of the natural horizon. It will be higher or lower, according to the position of the spectator. If the latter stands on a hill, the horizon line would be high. If he stands on a level with the sea beach, the horizon line will be low.

The three principal methods of representing objects are orthographic, isometrical and perspective projection. Linear perspective is the only one with which we deal.

An Illustrated Summary

One may successfully copy a picture without a knowledge of perspective, just as a carpenter may, if he has plans before him, erect an intricately constructed building without a knowledge of architecture; but no one could properly prepare such plans without any acquaintance whatever with the rudiments of the laws of architecture. One cannot paint well without some knowledge of drawing. One cannot draw more than the simplest picture without some knowledge of perspective.

The horizon of perspective, the horizon line, is more readily understood if you will imagine yourself standing at the sea shore gazing out upon the water. Where the sky apparently meets the water, is the horizon. Seen in a picture, from the level of a low beach, the line appears low down, under the middle of the picture. Now, go upon some promontory, and the horizon seems to go up with you, and in a picture would appear above the middle of the picture.

Imagine a large number of high poles placed upright in

the sea, each pole twenty feet above the water's level, extending at right angles to the shore far out at sea. (Fig. 18.) Now, if the line of poles comes within the range of your vision, each one that is more distant from you than the other will, in turn, seem to get smaller and smaller until the last one seems to disappear, as in Fig. 18. Row out on the sea until the poles are at right angles with the line of vision and the poles will appear as in Fig. 19. Now row back to shore.

We will suppose that another line of posts has been placed at right angles to the first mentioned. Their arrangement is shown in the plane diagram in Fig. 20. If you stand a little to the left of the nearest pole they will appear as seen in Fig. 21.

We will now suppose that the second row of posts has been taken up again and transplanted parallel with the first row, but a hundred feet away. Stand half way between them, but crouch close to the ground, and they will appear as in Fig. 22. The horizon will seem to have been lowered with you. Now stand on an elevation and look again. The horizon will seem to have risen with you. (Fig. 23.) Return to the place where you first stood, a rod or so to the left, and gaze again; the poles will appear as in Fig. 24.

Note: The horizon line in each of the figures is indicated by an A.

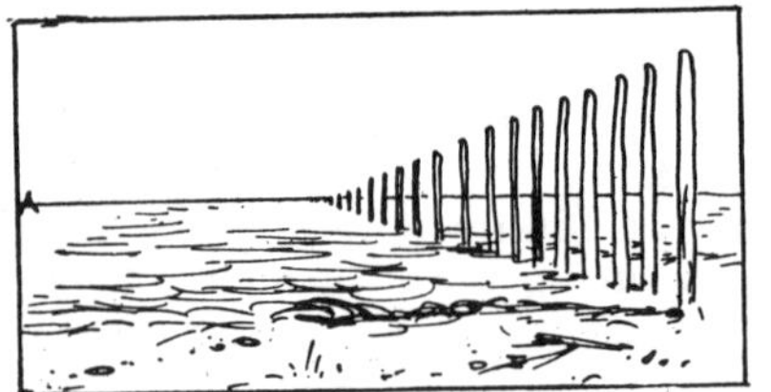

Fig. 18

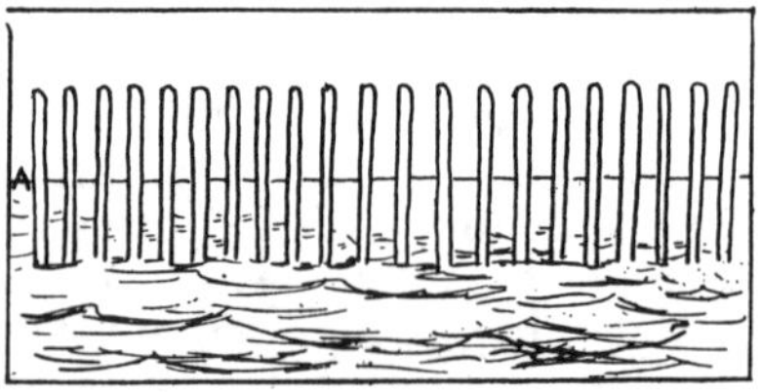

Fig. 19

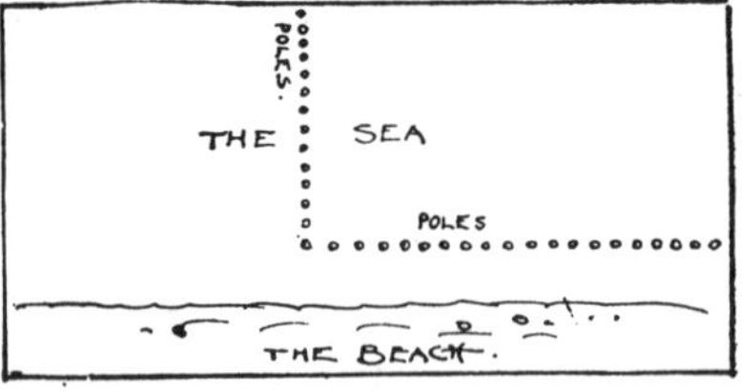

Fig. 20

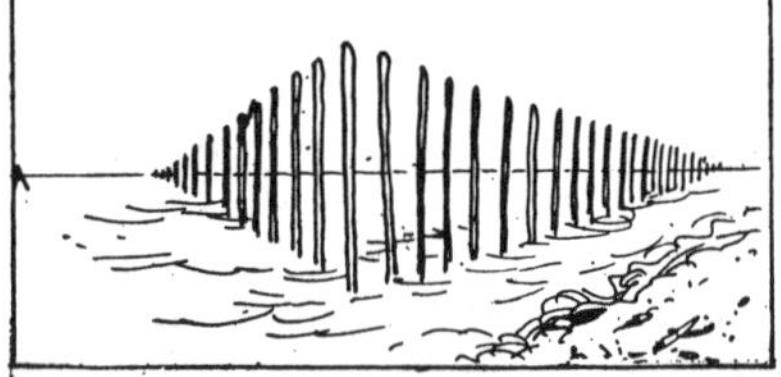

Fig. 21

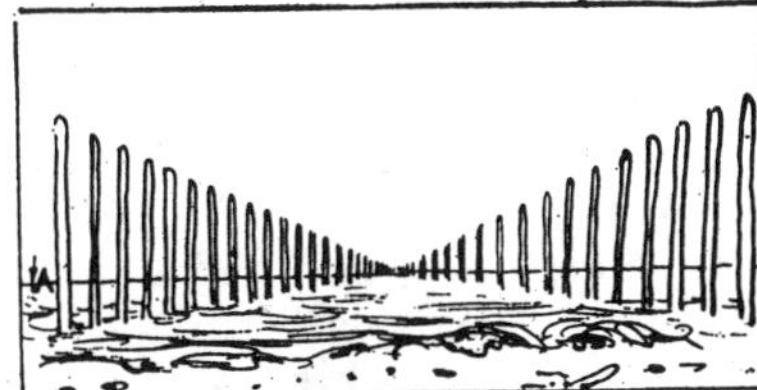

Fig. 22

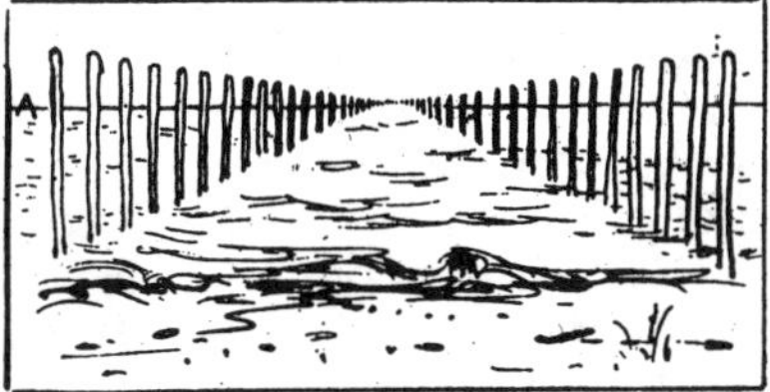

Fig. 23

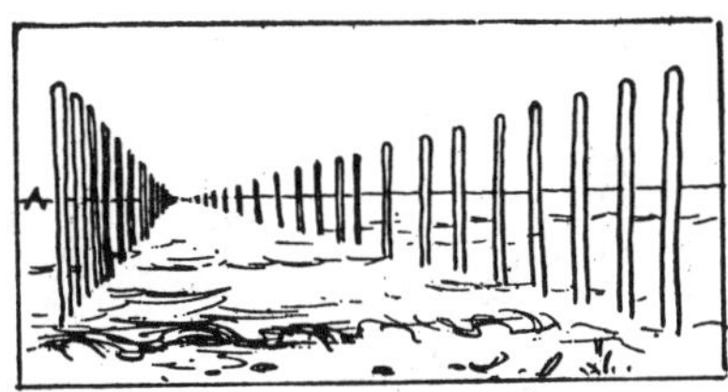

Fig. 24

Practically Illustrated

Perspective.—We know now that lines receding from the eye appear to meet at the horizon, the lines above the point of sight going down to the horizon, those below rising to it. This appearance is in line with the rule of perspective which says: A level line below the eye when not parallel to it, must be drawn upward from its nearest point, and, inversely, similar lines above the eye must be drawn downward. To illustrate the matter practically, one has only to step into the middle of the street. Look along the lines of the curbstone, the lower lines of the houses, the windows and the lines of the roofs. Then, by holding a pencil parallel to one's eyes, but about a foot away from them, it will be found that the lines which are above the eye run down to some point on a line level with the eye and that the lines below run up, but meet or tend to meet at the same point.

For further purposes of illustration, let us return to our beach by the sea. Let us suppose that there are three little huts there, a few feet apart and nearly on a line with each other. (Fig. 25.) Stand in front of one of them and you will see nothing of its sides. The sides of the others will be visible, but with the lines of the boards converging to a vanishing point, which is also the point of sight, in the center of the middle hut. Now walk away to the left of the huts and you may observe that all the lines of the sides that faced you before recede to a vanishing point within the picture. On the other hand, the sides that before receded from your line of vision now are almost facing you. (Fig. 26.)

Let us suppose that the tide has come and gone and taken the little huts a few feet out to sea. The plane diagram (Fig. 27) shows where they were carried. Looking at them now they appear as in Fig. 28. They are no longer parallel, but they are on a common level; therefore, they have the

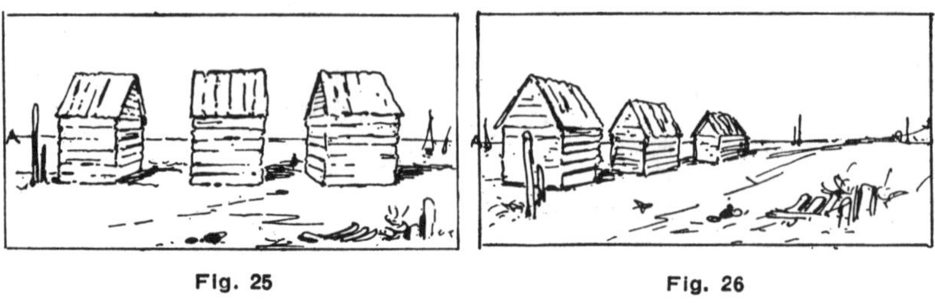

Fig. 25 Fig. 26

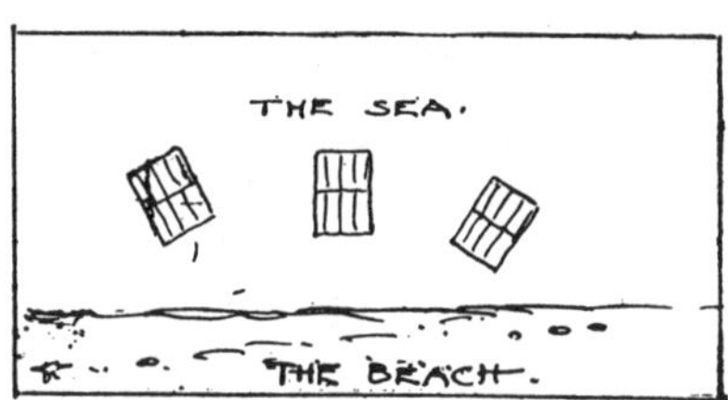

Fig. 27

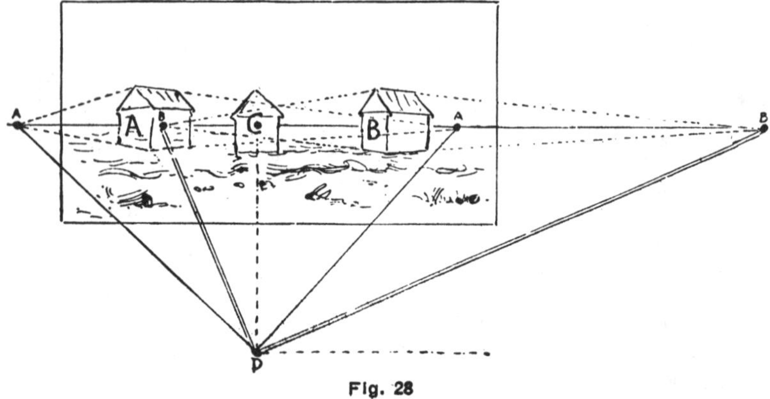

Fig. 28

same horizon line; the line of vision is the same for each, but each has its individual vanishing point. The two huts at the right and the left each have different vanishing points.

The drawings of the three huts clearly explain that, although each one has its own vanishing point, C having the point of sight as its only vanishing point, nevertheless, lines described from each pair of points to D, the point of station, form a right angle. The lines referred to are drawn in varying styles in order to show the angles more plainly. The hut on the left with single lines, the hut in the middle with dotted lines, and the hut on the right with double lines.

When the Point of Station Is Shifted

As you advance in the study of perspective, have this rule firmly impressed on your mind: The lines drawn from the point of station to the two vanishing points should always form a right angle (90°). (See Fig. 29.) However

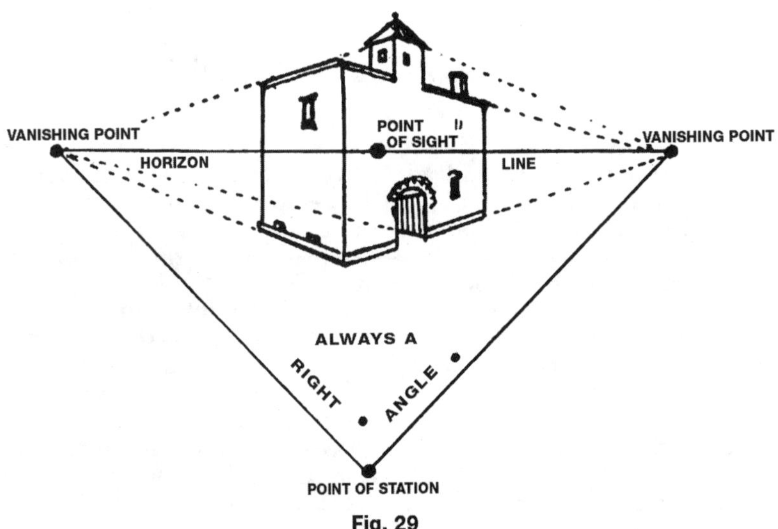

Fig. 29

the point of station is shifted, the angle remains the same. Thus, in Fig. 30, the point of station is moved to the left, but the angle referred to remains the same. For this reason, if the point of station is established and also one of the vanishing points, the other vanishing point will be at a point on the horizon touched by a line at right angles from a line drawn between the first two points mentioned. Thus, in Fig. 30, A is one vanishing point, and B the point of station; now, a line drawn at right angles from A to B touches the horizon line at C, and is therefore the proper spot for the second vanishing point.

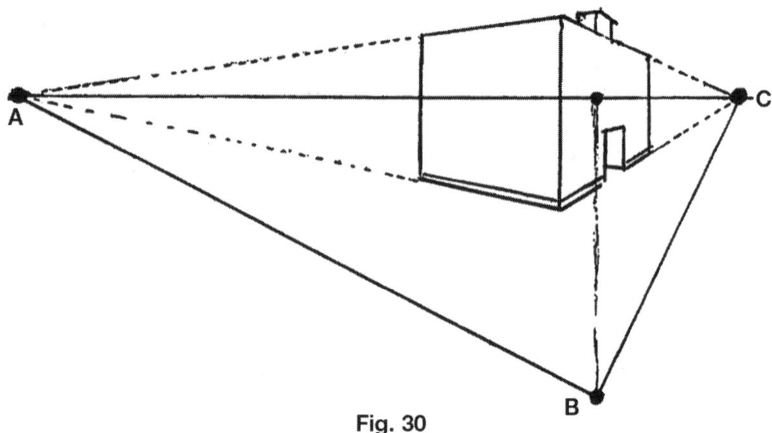

Fig. 30

Posts, Etc., in Relative Distances Apart.—We determine the relative distances and widths of a series of houses, posts, windows, tiles or other objects in perspective in this manner. We will suppose that instead of one house, as seen in Fig. 30, we wish to draw five houses—four added to the left of the house mentioned. Proceed thus: First copy Fig. 30, then describe a vertical line from the vanishing point at the left to a point where it meets a line drawn horizontally to the left from the point of station. From this meeting point, describe a line to the corner of the house at A. Where this line intersects the base line at B is the place to project an upright line—the left side of the second house. A line from C in a similar manner gives the side for the third house at D; E to F, the fourth house, and G to H the fifth and last.

Perspective of a Mosaic Floor.—Fig. 32 shows how a mosaic floor may easily be put into perspective with sufficient accuracy for illustrative purposes. The lines marked A are first extended to the vanishing point B; next, the line C is described. Lines D are now carried through wherever line C

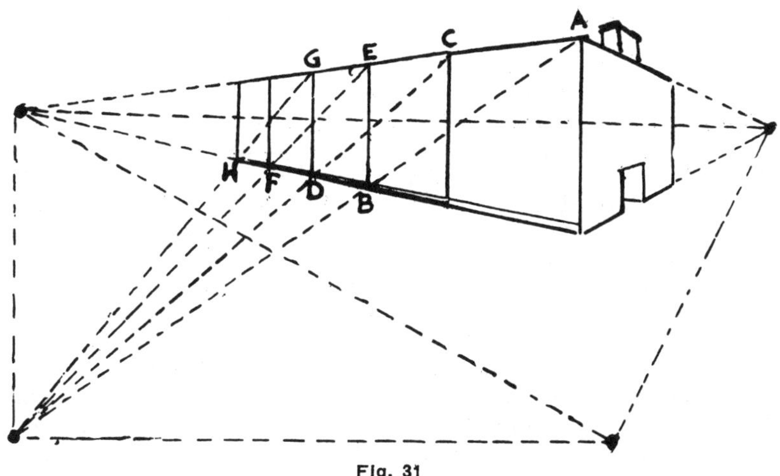

Fig. 31

intersects lines A. The spaces thus formed may be again further divided as here suggested or in accordance with any other arrangement or design.

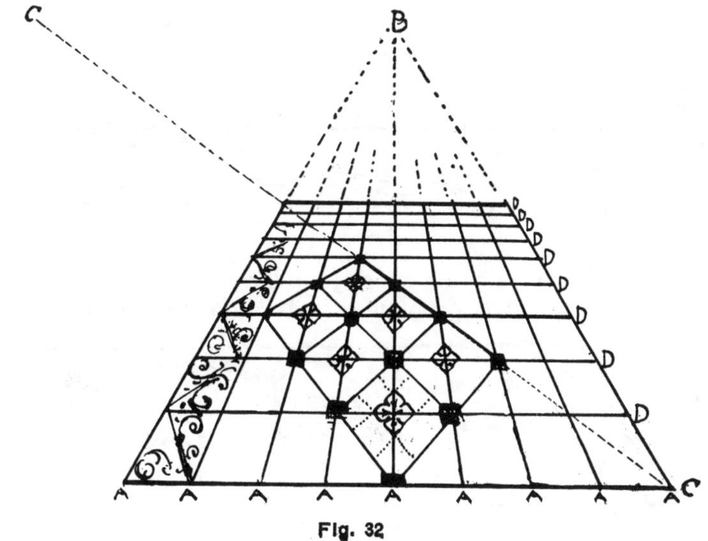

Fig. 32

The "Horizon" the Most Important Line

The word "horizon" is used to denote where the earth apparently meets the sky. This is not to be taken literally, for one might be making a drawing in a cellar, or even in a coal mine, where, not alone would the sky be unseen, but be far above the level of the beholder. In such cases, the "horizon" would be the line level and opposite the artist's station point; that is to say, at a line and level with the eye of the artist, no matter where he happened to be. If he were sitting down, instead of standing, his particular "horizon" would be lower than if he were making the drawing in a standing position.

Above all rules in perspective, the one to be ineradicably recorded on the mind more than all others is this: All receding lines *above* the horizon *descend,* and all lines *below* the horizon *ascend* to it.

In landscape drawing, to retain proportions in human figures that appear in the background, block out a figure in the near foreground and then project lines to the proper vanishing points from that figure. The figure in the first place must be made in proper proportions by comparison with some other object in the foreground. Then place the background figure in the space so projected.

Simple Problems in Perspective

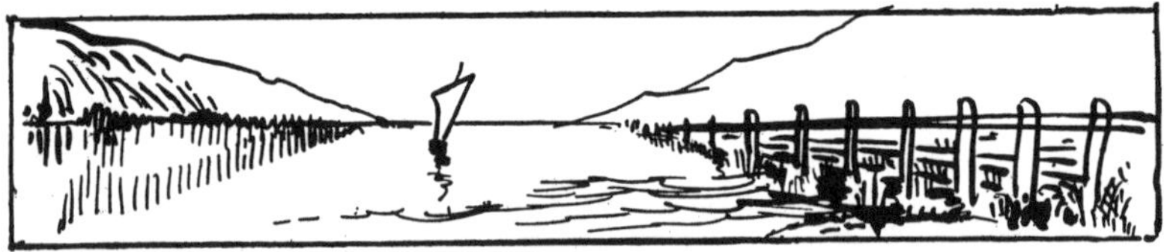

Fig. 33

Fig. 33, Exercise in Perspective.—Draw a picture in which the main perspective problem involved is the horizon line.

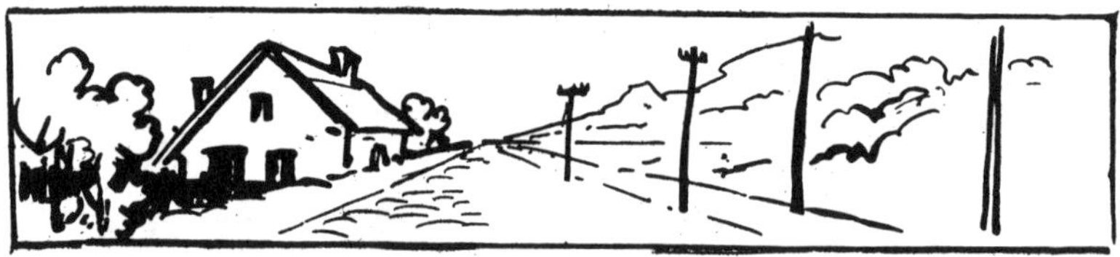

Fig. 34

Fig. 34, Exercise in Perspective.—Draw a picture in which the main perspective problem involved is the point of sight.

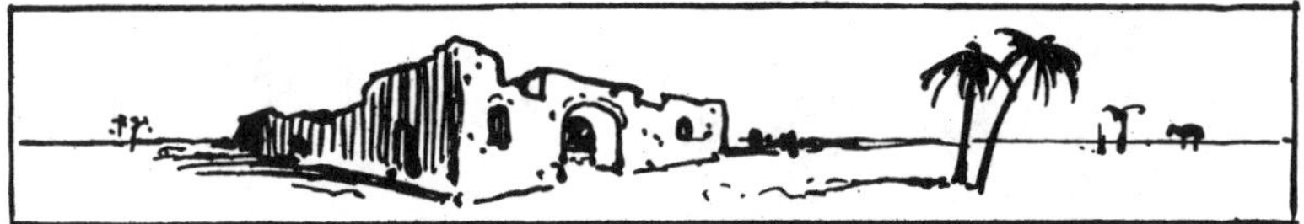

Fig. 35

Fig. 35, Exercise in Perspective.—Draw a picture in which the main perspective problem involved consists of the horizon line and two vanishing points.

Figures in Perspective—Atmospheric

The first object in a drawing such as a diminishing file of police (see Fig. 36) or a row of trees (see Fig. 37) should contain the most detail, the last, far distant, need be merely suggested. The eye is attracted by the first few figures and

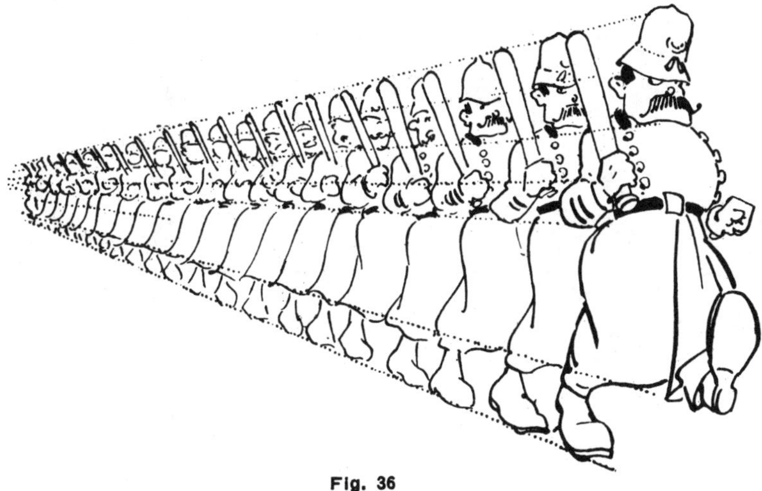

Fig. 36

does not by ordinary inspection of a picture detect the absence of minute details in the distance. Indeed, to draw each figure with the same care as given to the first would detract from the atmospheric perspective, that in a picture, by comparative size and quantity of detail, suggests distance.

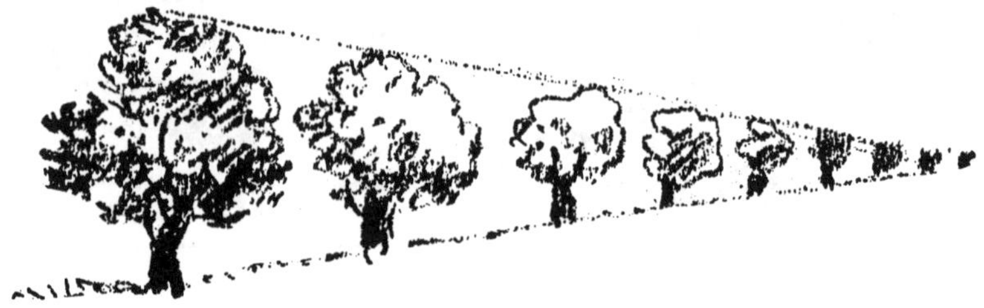

Fig. 37

Drawing Buildings

Before finishing a drawing containing architectural features, make sure that the upright lines of the buildings are plumb.

Note.—Additional instruction along the lines of perspective drawing will be found in the next chapter, namely, foreshortening.

CHAPTER XXVIII

FORESHORTENING

To teach how to foreshorten, entirely as a separate proposition, is difficult. Definitions of the word itself are somewhat vague. "Foreshorten—to represent figures as they appear to the eye when seen obliquely"; "to represent objects in accordance with the laws of perspective"; "the art of diminishing the entire length of an object when viewed obliquely."

"Foreshortening is to draw what we don't see," explained an exasperated art student on being examined as to his knowledge of certain rules of drawing. One can sympathize with him if not agree with his definition.

Knowledge of the rudiments of perspective gives one a better conception of the proper manner to foreshorten an object, animate or otherwise, than any amount of special instruction on the subject. Foreshortening is one branch of the study of the elementary laws of perspective.

Much of what we see in nature is foreshortened. With the exception of the lines at right angles with the line of vision, all dimensions appear foreshortened. Unless one were looking through a hole in the ceiling, the table and practically every article in a room would appear foreshortened.

Even the pictures on the wall, if above the level of the eye, are seen foreshortened. This will not be the case if they are tilted in such a way that their surfaces are at right angles to the line of vision.

One may be able to draw in perspective, according to instruction, a hemisphere and a cylinder lying on their sides and yet not realize that the same instruction applied to any object offering a round plane surface, as its principal problem for the moment, is of equal value—a lemon for instance.

Having drawn a hemisphere, a cylinder and a lemon, one may ask, "How do you draw the two wheels of: a cart?" The answer is: By the same rules as one draws the two planes of a cylinder lying on its side.

Having mastered these, one may inquire how to foreshorten a leaf.

Now, the best way to foreshorten a leaf is to get one, place it in the desired position and draw it from life. The experience thus gained will enable one subsequently to draw the leaf from memory.

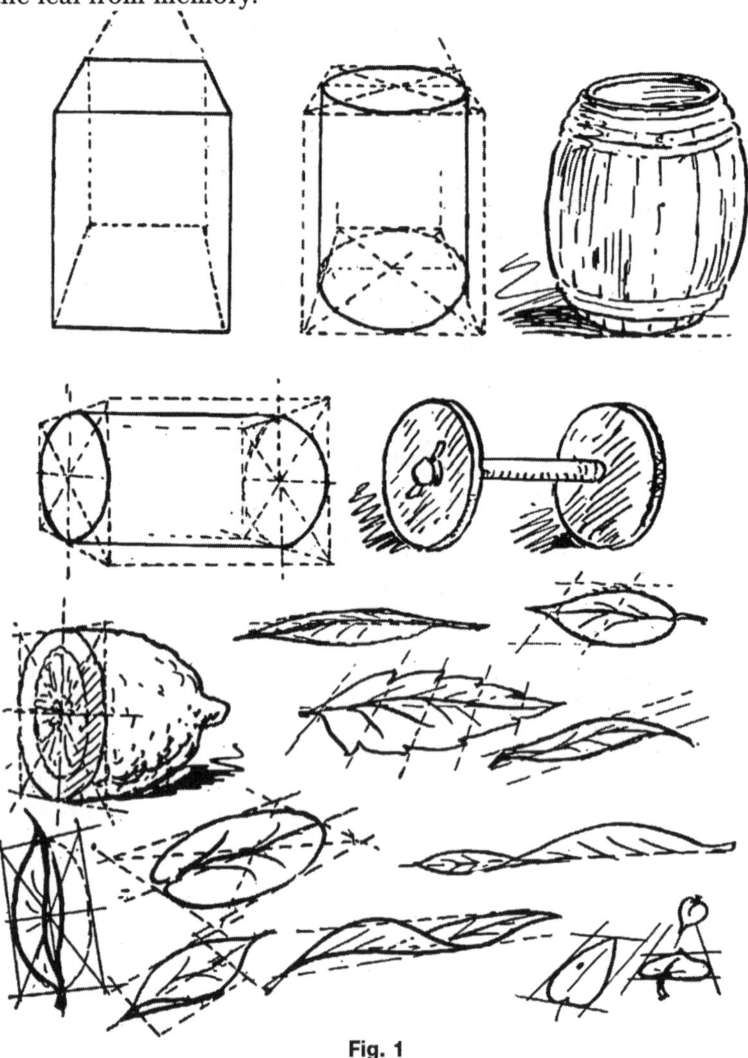

Fig. 1

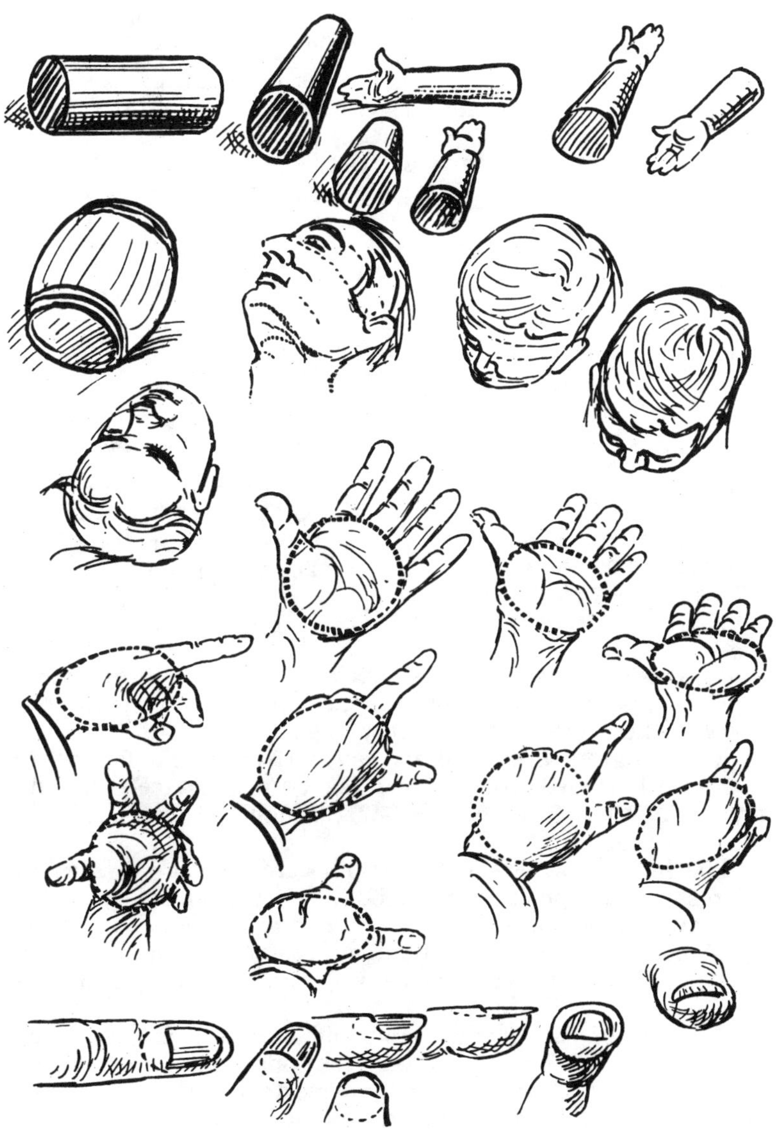

Fig. 2

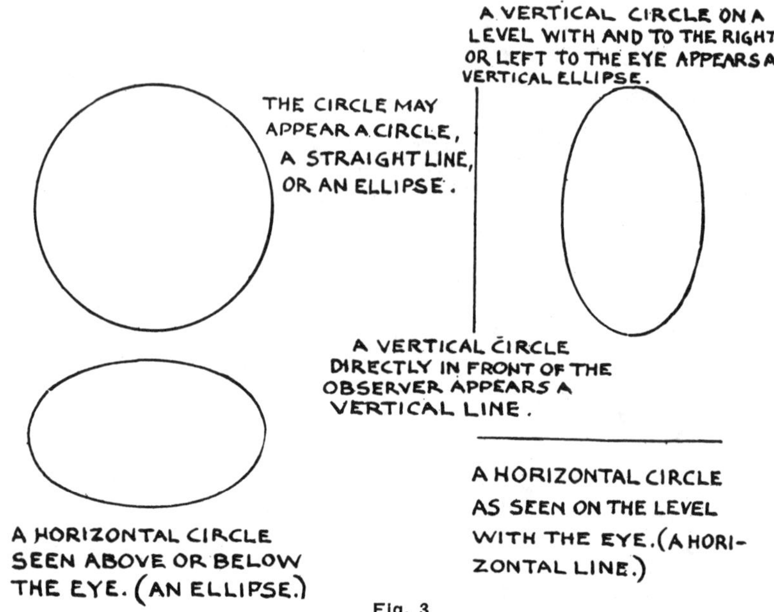

Fig. 3

All these objects are foreshortened. Practice foreshortening of leaves or other familiar objects from the objects themselves. These examples are only suggestions.

Knowledge of how to draw any part of the human figure in a foreshortened position can be gained scarcely in any other way than from nature—or through the experience of others, by copying.

The head of a person bowed forward or back is seen in a foreshortened position and should be considered as a circle drawn in perspective. The human arm even bears a resemblance to some geometrical figure, and when foreshortened must be considered as having some relative form geometrically.

Portions of the human hand and even the fingers when seen in foreshortened positions may be considered in the aspect of circles, ovals or cylinders drawn in perspective. The left hand as a model affords splendid exercise.

Take your left hand as a model. Draw the foreshortened views of it as suggested in Fig. 2. See how the rule shown in Fig. 3, regarding horizontal circles, is carried out in nature.

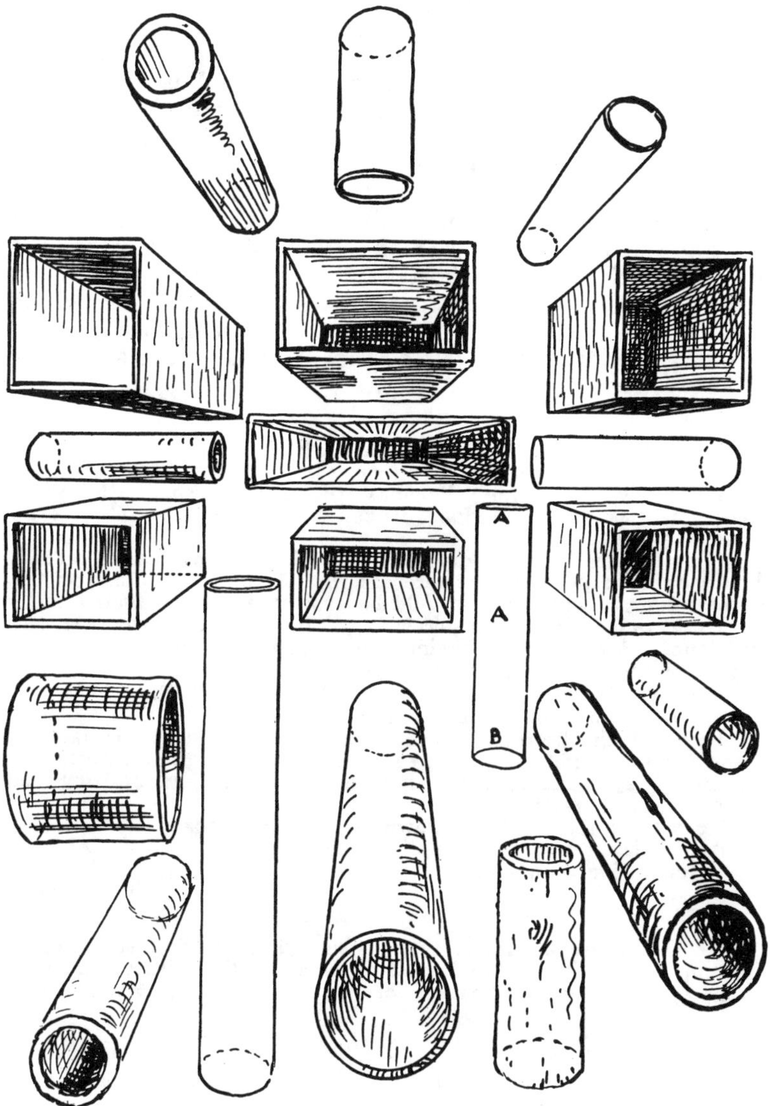

Fig 4—Exercises in Foreshortening

Exercise in Cylinders and Boxes.—Make free-hand drawings of cylinders in various positions, especially one that will show the visible end of a cylinder appearing nearly as a straight line (as in A in the accompanying illustration) and the invisible end (B) appearing as an ellipse, the width depending upon the length of the cylinder—the longer the cylinder, the wider the ellipse.

Draw a box from the model. Place it directly in front of the eye, but above or below it. Measure the back edge of the top and compare it with the front edge. Note that the back edge will be much shorter. Note that the two side lines will converge to meet the shorter lines. Place the box to one side, so that one side will be seen. Note the apparent shortness of the further (vertical) edge of the side. (See also Figs. 16 and 17, chapter on Perspective.)

LEARN TO SEE.

That is the secret of nearly all success in art work. To see. To see accurately, the outline, the phase of light and shade, the quantities, qualities and gradations of color. That is all. It must be learned by degrees.

The frequently heard question, "Can I learn to draw pictures?" should unhesitatingly be answered in the affirmative. "Can you tell me how long it will take?" should be answered in the negative.

To learn to draw *well* means application, patience, courage and confidence. And it means having those qualities more than the possession of so-called talent or even genius.

Certain rules may be laid down but there is that which one must do oneself—see. The art of seeing, that's it.

Begin at the bottom. A very large proportion of the failures among drawing students is due to a tendency to slight the early exercises. They want to start right out with finished drawings of an ambitious character.

Keep to simple subjects drawn with simple lines.

Avoid elaboration and complication.

Practice line economy.

Note.—The seeker for further instruction on the subject of foreshortening is advised to study and become familiar with the laws of perspective, and to go to nature for the true aspects of visible form.

CHAPTER XXIX

GEOMETRICAL FORM

There are certain forms to which certain names are applied. They occur frequently in the simplest subjects. Therefore, while these forms are known under the formidable title of geometrical figures, nevertheless most of these shapes are so simple as to be easily recognized and with a little exercise of the memory can be called by name. The easiest way to form their acquaintance is to make and draw them. Their application will readily follow.

Cut from cardboard the following geometrical forms:

The Square.

The Rectangle.

The Triangles (right, acute, obtuse and equilateral triangles).

The Circle.

The Oval.

Explain Simple Pictures.—In matters connected with the study of lines and form by means of simple illustrations, one may not, for instance, understand the meaning of parallel lines. See the picture of a ladder below, showing that no matter how far extended the lines would never meet. Then see the picture of a half-closed umbrella, and think of the meaning of converging and diverging lines, as shown in Fig. 1. The lines 1, 2 and 3 are converging lines, as they approach toward the ferrule of the umbrella—that converging lines tend to get close together.

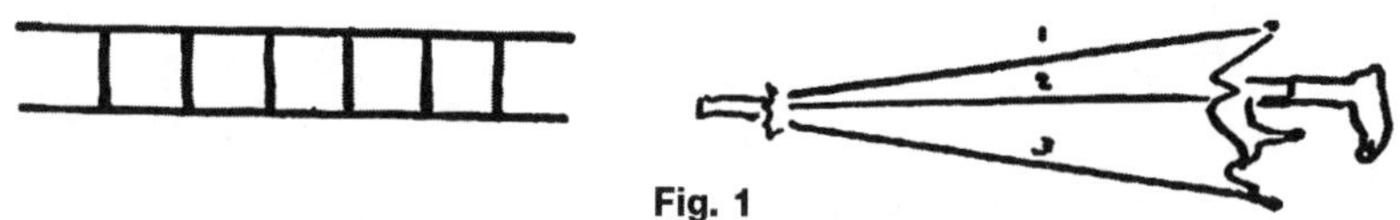

Fig. 1

On the other hand, as the lines mentioned approach the handle they diverge because they tend to get farther and farther apart.

Aids to Memory.—The trapezium, trapezoid, rhomboid and rhombus are terms difficult to remember. Therefore, these little wiggles are added. Memorize the trapezium by drawing it with the addition of the boy and the kite. And so on with the other forms. By combining the forms with other objects than here suggested, interest will be aroused and the memorizing will be helped.

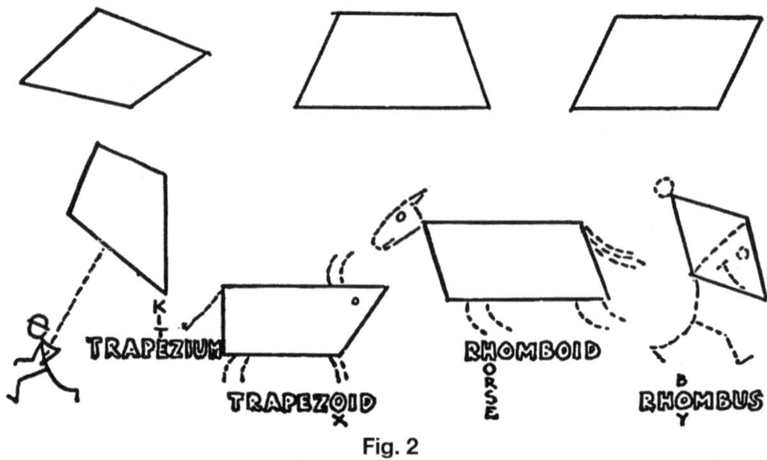

Fig. 2

Many people memorize forms more quickly if their meaning is combined with adjectives describing the kind of forms. Thus:

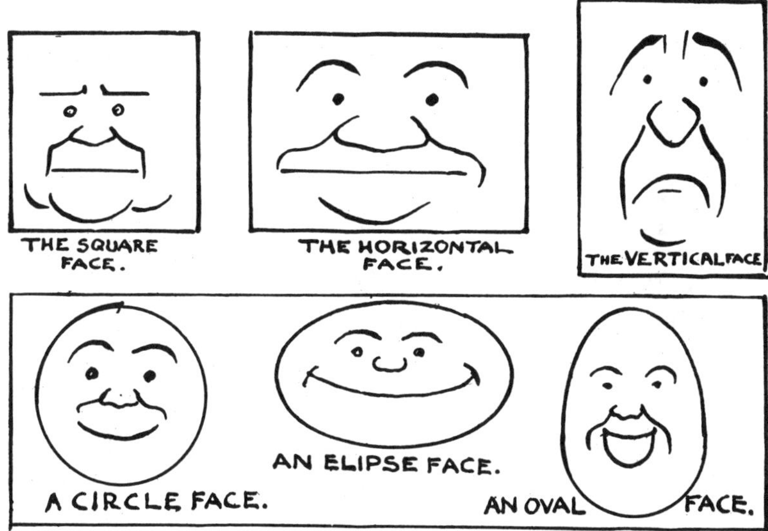

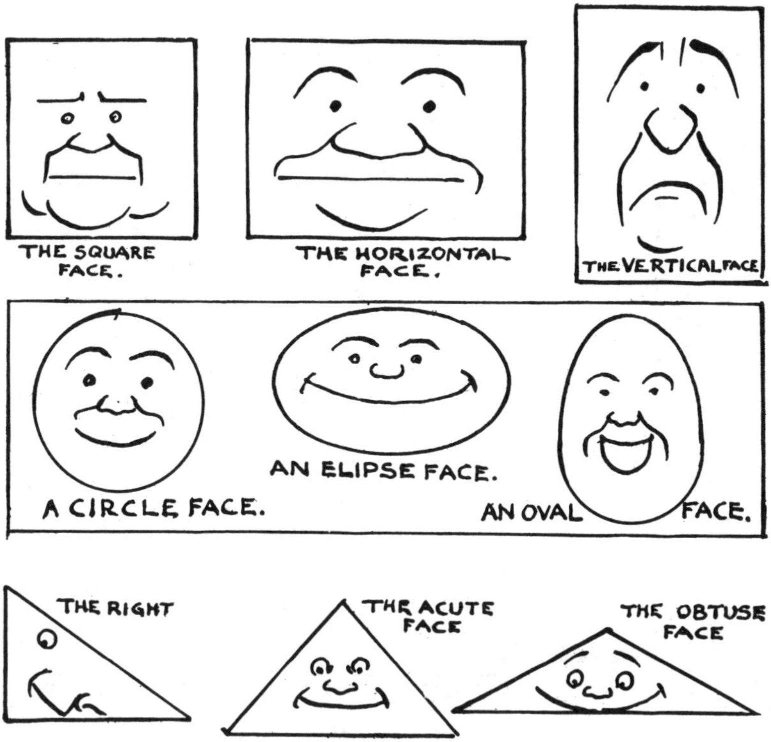

THE RIGHT

THE ACUTE FACE

THE OBTUSE FACE

Fig. 3

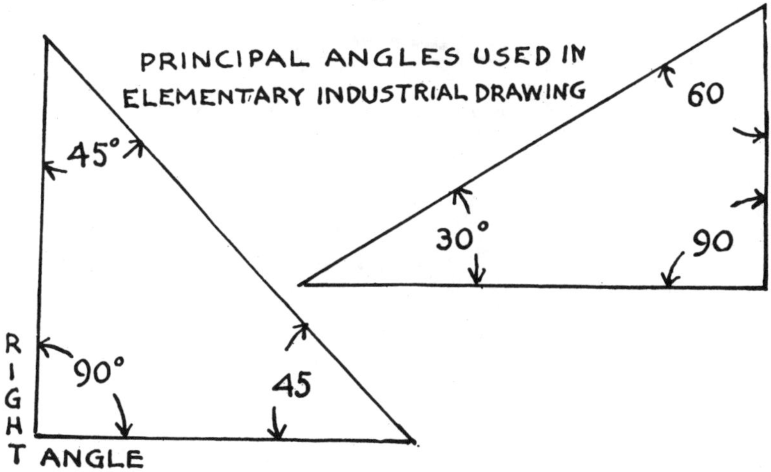

PRINCIPAL ANGLES USED IN ELEMENTARY INDUSTRIAL DRAWING

45°

90°

45

RIGHT ANGLE

60

30°

90

Fig. 4

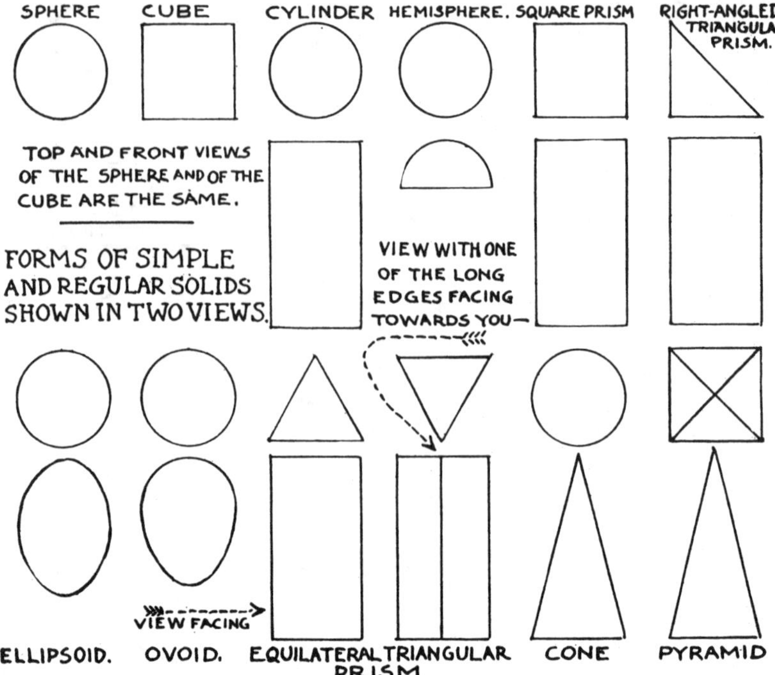

Fig. 5—Self Explanatory Diagrams

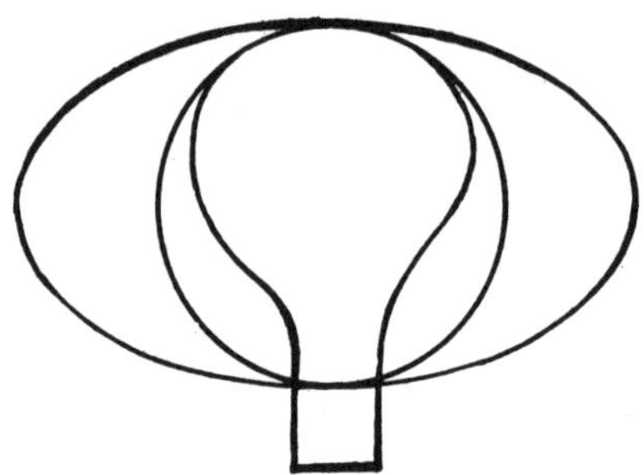

Four in One

Lines Used in Drawing.—Fig. 6 shows the lines used in drawing. Their forms and definitions should be thoroughly memorized. In Fig. 7 their application is shown singly, by combination and by repetition.

Parts of this exercise may prove too difficult for many beginners. In such cases, the exercises may be omitted for the time being, to be taken up later in the studies. The lines are made heavy in the examples merely to indicate their position. The letters A, B, C, etc., are repeated in the upper and lower diagrams as an additional aid in this respect.

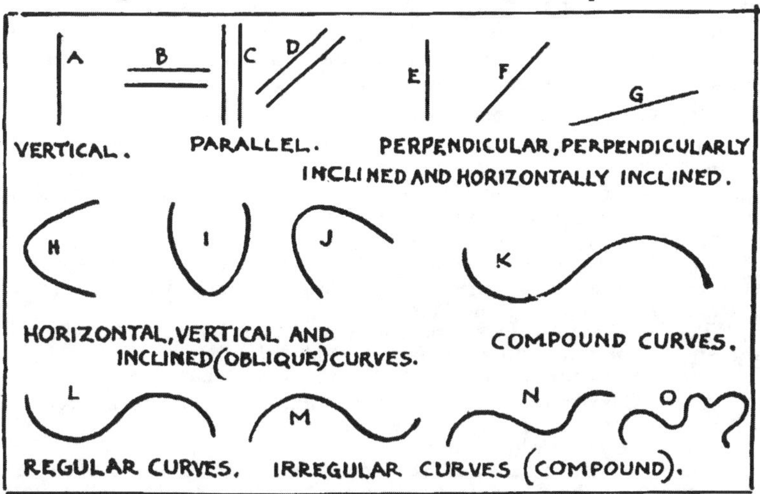

Fig. 6

Fig. 7

Form Study

The sphere, the cube, the cylinder, the square prism, the hemisphere and the right-angled triangulared prism. These may be considered in the following order:

1. The surfaces and faces.
2. The edges.
3. The corners.

The surface is the outside of any object. In the case of the cube, for instance, we find the surface limited and broken up by edges and faces. The *face* is a limited part of a surface. An edge is formed by the meeting of two faces.

When passing the fingers over the surface of one of the solids, you discover decided differences. You may note a plain or flat surface, a curved surface and a round surface. You will find that all are not the same shape.

Edges may be curved or straight.

Corners will be noted, as well as the difference in shape when studied. Having familiarized yourself by a study of each, it is well for you to take the sphere and cube together in order that you may observe their resemblances and their differences. Carefully study the meaning of dimension.

Dimension is an extent in one direction.

Considered as to surfaces, their differences are notable. The surface of the sphere is curved equally in all its parts, while the cube's surface has six equal plane faces.

Two of these six faces coming in contact form an edge, which is the subject of a second topic in the study of solids.

While the cube has twelve edges, the sphere has none.

As to Corners.—The sphere has none; there can be no corners where there are no edges.

The cube has eight corners.

Three or more faces must come in contact to form a corner. The angles of the plane faces of a cube are right angles, therefore on each cube twenty-four right angles are found.

Cylinder and Square Prism.—Considered as a whole, the points of resemblance are these: The dimensions are the same in each.

As to Surface and Faces.—The cylinder has both curved and plane surfaces; a square prism has only plane surfaces.

Considered as to their edges, the cylinder has curved edges; the square prism, straight edges. Considered as to corners, the square prism has the same number of corners as the cube; the cylinder has no corners.

Two cubes will make one square prism.

Faces are parallel to each other when they extend in the same direction.

Faces are perpendicular when they are at right angles to each other. A square corner would be formed by the intersection of three.

Faces are oblique to each other when they form angles other than right angles.

The **solids** are considered, first, as "wholes"; second, as "to surfaces and faces," and, third, "as to edges."

An edge is formed by the meeting of two faces.

Edges may be curved or straight.

The surface of the sphere is curved equally in all parts, while the surface of the cube is composed of six equal plane faces. When any two of these faces come in contact an edge is formed.

A profile limits the part that we see of any round or curved surface. Profiles and edges limit and give visible shape to the faces and parts of faces.

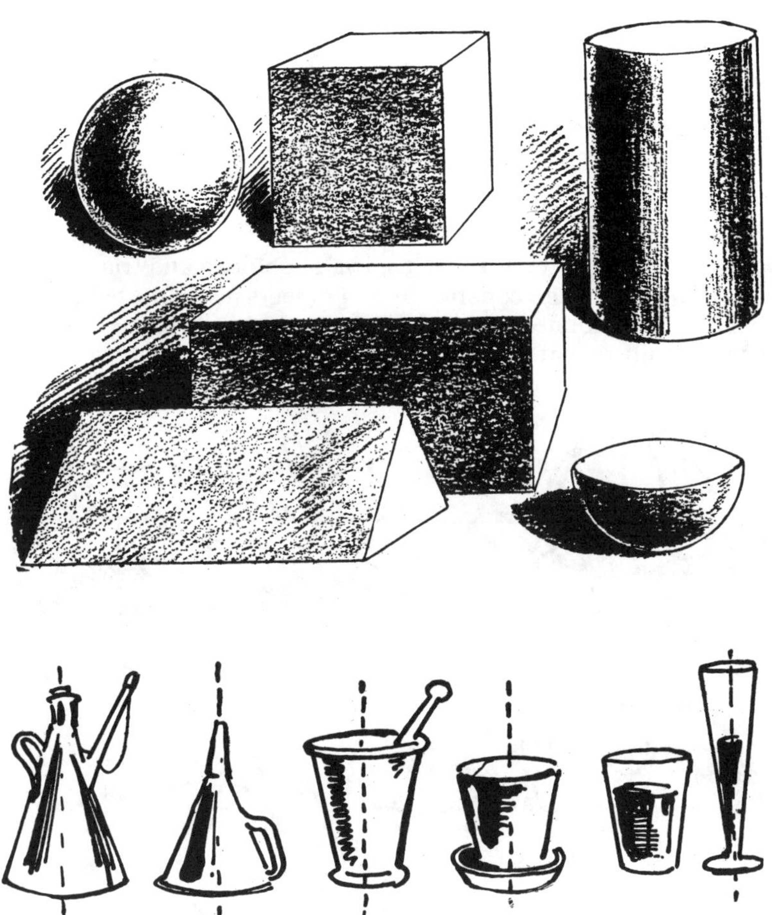

Adapting Geometrical Forms to Familiar Objects

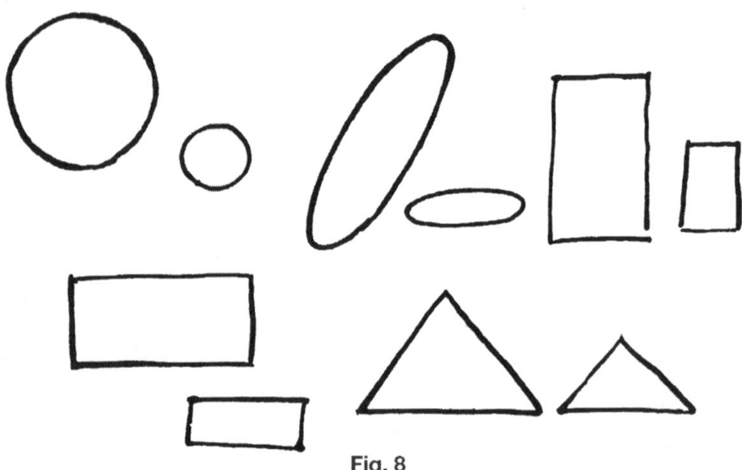

Fig. 8

Begin by drawing the circles, ovals, oblongs and triangles in Fig. 8. Now base the construction of objects along these lines as in Fig. 9. It is not necessary to adhere very closely to the outlines as originally demarked.

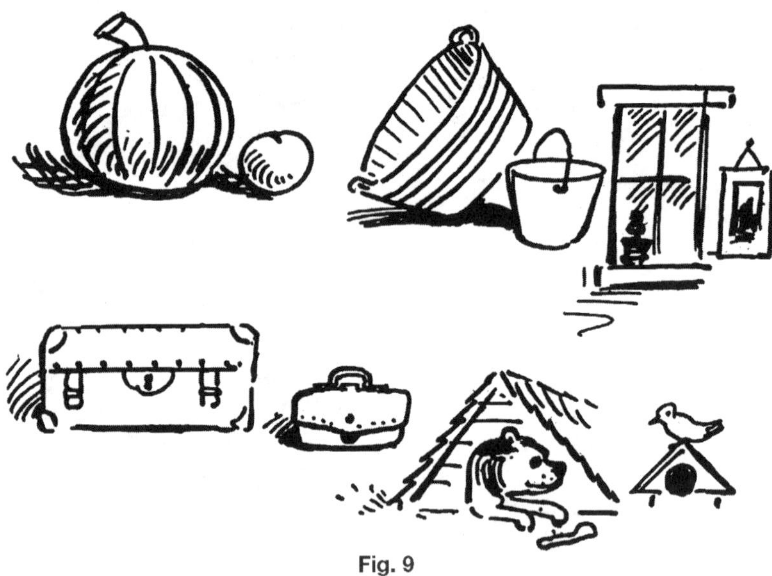

Fig. 9

In Fig. 11 the circle, oval, square, oblong and triangle in Fig. 10 are all introduced into a single picture. Make another drawing in which these forms are indicated. The oblong may indicate the body of a cart; the circle, one of the wheels; the square, a box on the cart; the oval, a bag of flour on the box. The triangle may show the angle of the roof of the house.

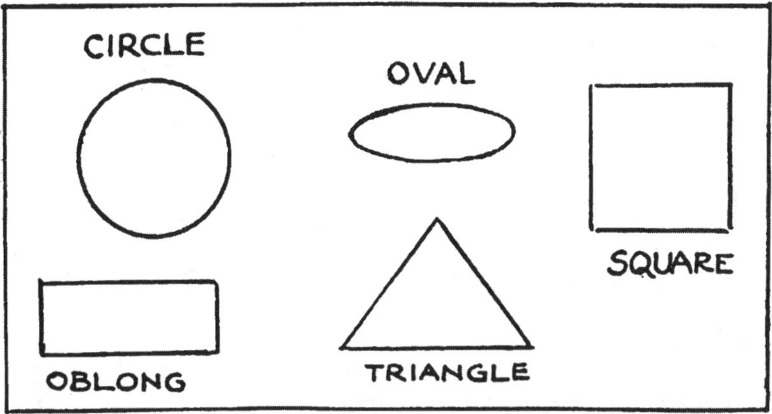

Fig. 10

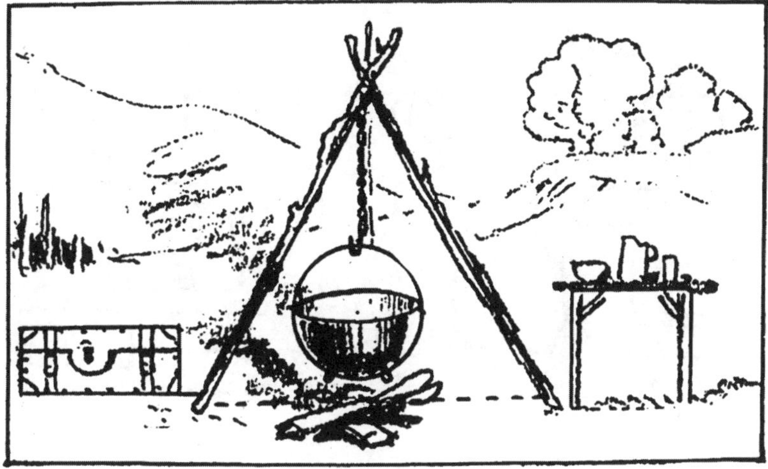

Fig. 11

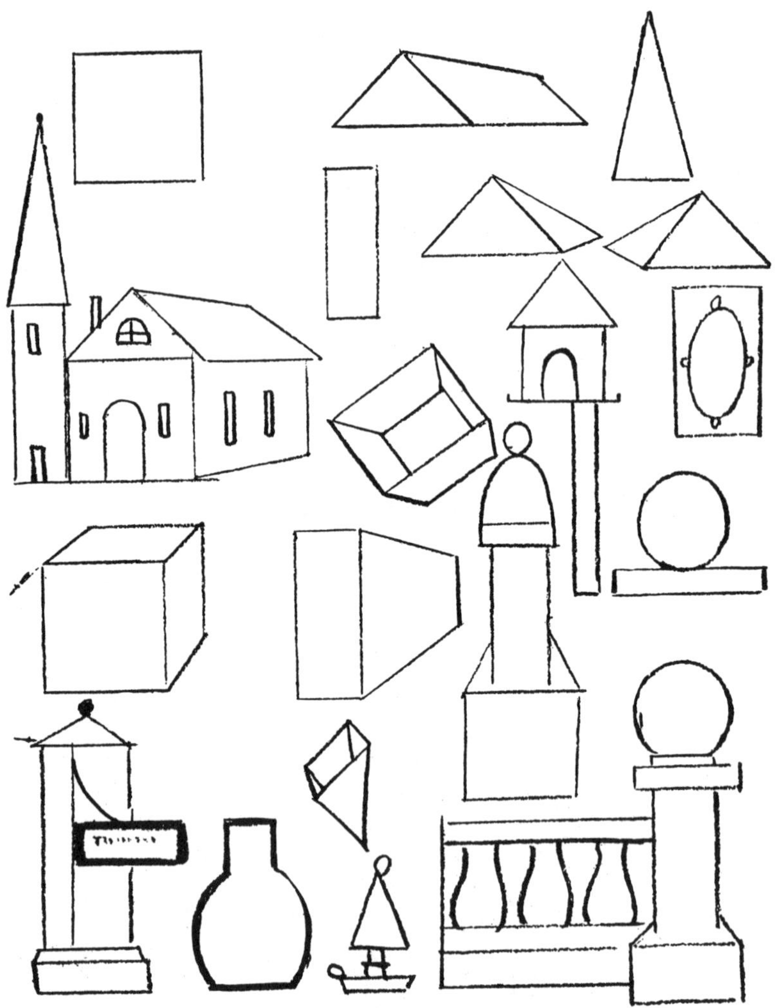

Fig. 12—Exercises in Various Forms Applied Constructively

Triangulation in Design and Composition

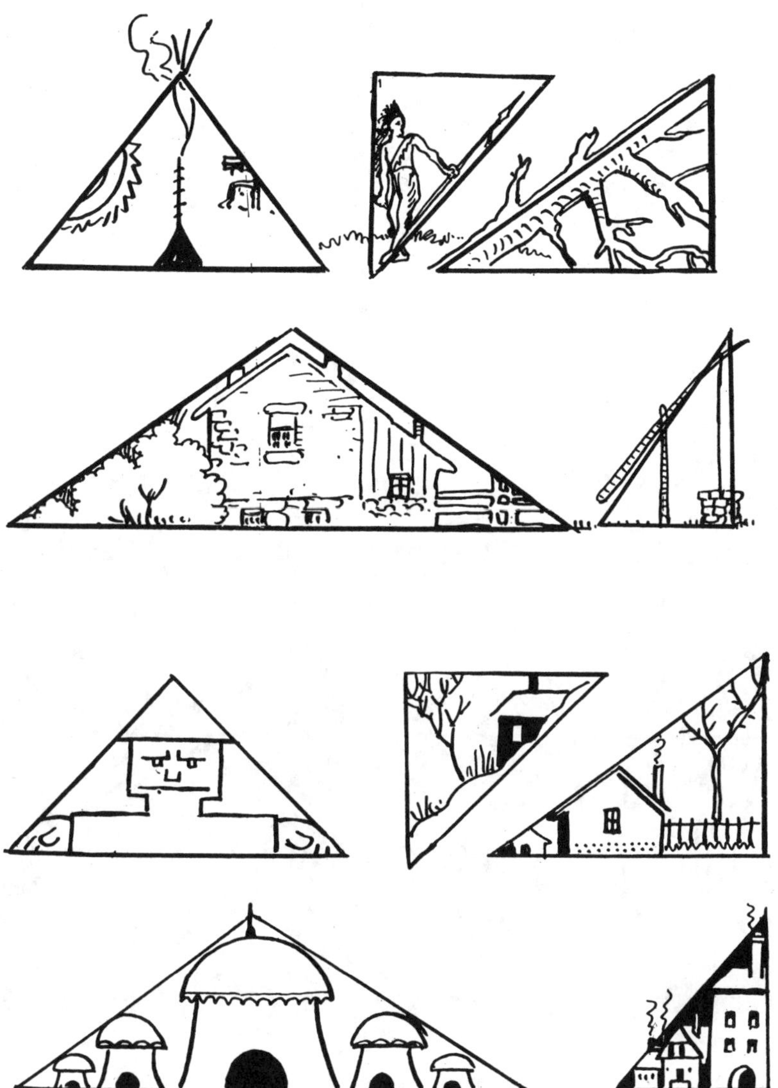

Fig. 13

The examples in Fig. 13 show the application of triangles as guides to the drawing of various objects.

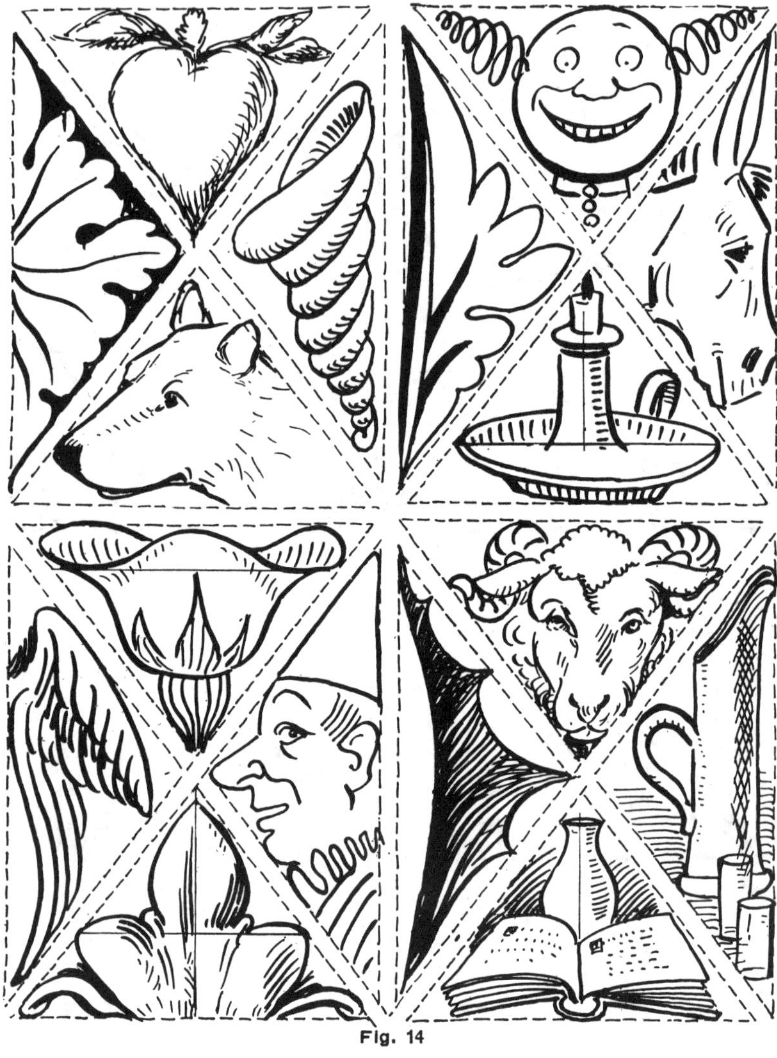

Fig. 14

In Fig. 14 are given varied examples of the application of triangulation in design and composition. The designs do not need to adhere closely to the outlines of the triangles.

How to Draw Triangles, Squares, Pentagons, Hexagons and Other Multi-Faced and Multi-Pointed Forms

Equilateral Triangle.—To make an equilateral triangle within a circle. Describe a circle, Fig. A. Without changing the radius place the point of the compass at each of the black dots, starting at the dot Y (at top of circle) and intersect the circle. The formation of the triangle is shown by the dotted lines.

Fig. B shows a simpler manner of making an equilateral triangle. Start at any of the dots, say, dot A, and describe a segment of a circle. At any point, as at dot B, with the compass at the same radius, intersect the first segment. At intersection C place point of compass and intersect the other curves as at B and A. Lines drawn from A to B, B to C, and C to A, as shown in dotted lines, will form the triangle.

Fig. C. To make a hexagon or six-pointed star. Describe a circle. From the point A at the circumference, with a compass (radius remaining the same) intersect the circumference at B. Repeat with C, D, and so forth, until the point A is intersected.

Lines drawn as shown in dotted lines from A to B and B to C, if continued to D, E, and so forth, will make a hexagon.

For a six-pointed star draw lines as in dotted lines G, H and I.

For dividing the hexagon into sections, as for rosettes, etc., divide the circumference as for the hexagon or star and project

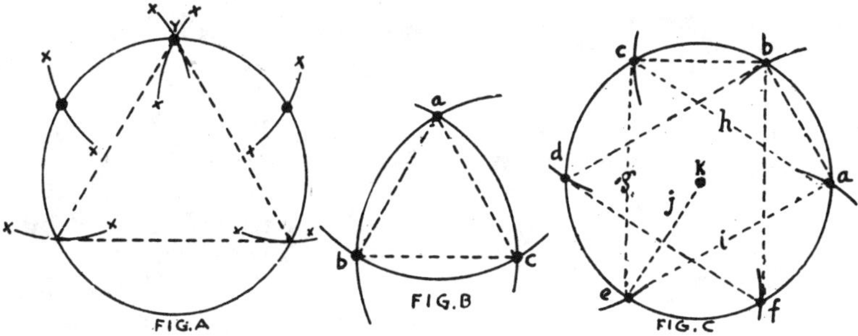

lines as shown in the sample dotted line from E to K. Proceed thus to make the six divisions of the drawing.

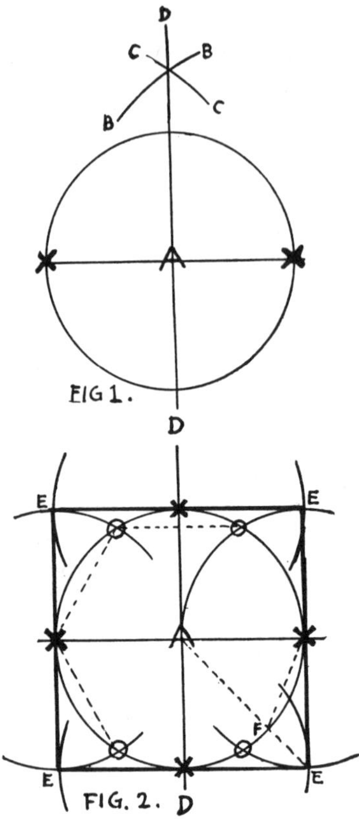

To Draw a Square.—To make an absolutely accurate quadrangle proceed as follows: Describe a circle as in Fig. 1. Bisect it through its center at A to XX. Make a segment of an arc, CC, by placing the point of the compass at X at the left. The line BB is made the same way from X at the right. A vertical line prolonged through the circle from the intersection of the lines BB and CC and intersecting the horizontal line at A, and continued to the base of the circle, completes four right angles.

On the same drawing (Figs. 1 and 2 being in reality a single drawing, but, for the sake of plainness, is made in two diagrams) describe arcs of circles of the same size or circumference, by placing the point of the compass at each X. The segments meet or intersect at EEEE. They also meet the circumference of the original circle at OOOO, but this has nothing to do with making the quadrangle or square. Now extend four lines from each E to the other and they will touch the circle at each X. A perfect square is formed by these four lines.

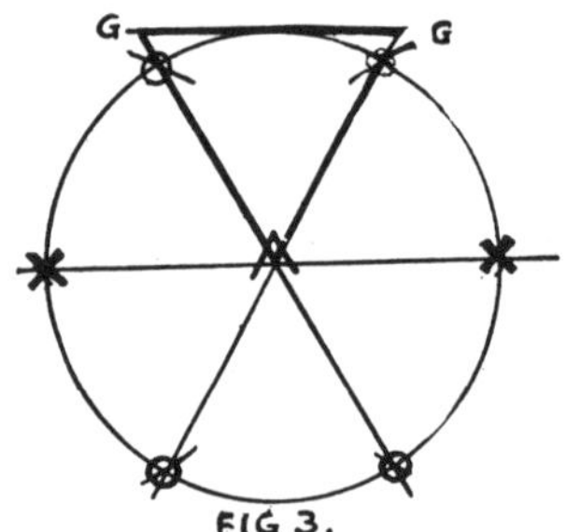

Other Forms Produced by This Operation

To Make a Hexagon.—Draw lines as shown at the left of the diagram (Fig. 2) (starting from below) from O, X, O, O, in the dotted lines, proceeding of course all the way around.

To Make an Octagon.—Extend the lines from each E to the center at A (Fig. 2). Now make eight lines as shown by the dotted line X to F, which gives one section of an octagon.

To Make an Equilateral Triangle.—A triangle having all sides of an equal length—draw a line GG parallel to XX at the top of the circle. Extend lines from the center A through the OO's (as produced in Fig. 2) to the line GG, and an equilateral is shown in the heavy lines as a result.

Pentagon.—To construct a pentagon, draw parts of three circles as A A, B B and C C, as in Fig. 1. Next draw the

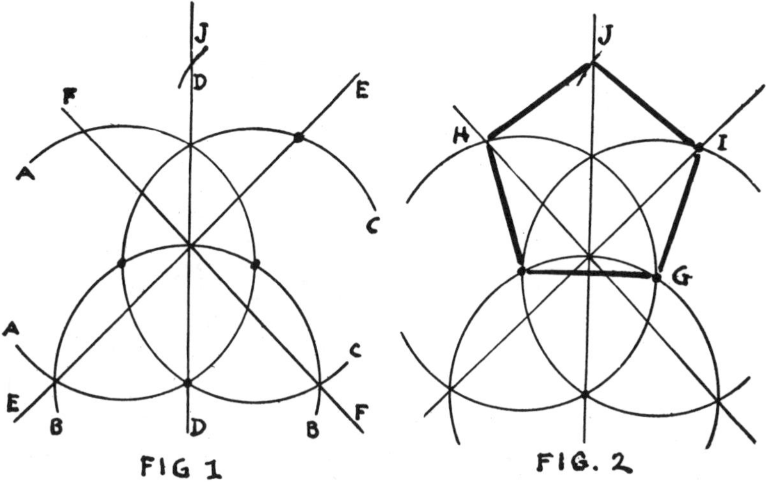

FIG 1 FIG. 2

vertical line D D. Then the oblique lines E E and F F. From the intersection of line E E at upper part of circular line C C describe segment of circle J. On the same drawing (as in Fig. 2) now construct the pentagon as shown by the heavy lines G, H, I and J.

Another Pentagon.—Method of drawing a pentagon by first locating the points required to make a decagon: Describe a circle as at A. Then half a circle as shown by dotted lines (same radius as large circle). Then the vertical line; next the dotted horizontal line. Now describe small circle; now the lower horizontal line. Extend a line from the intersection of the vertical line and the top of the small circle, thence to its intersection with the dotted horizontal line. Now describe a segment of a circle, starting at intersection of oblique line and lower horizontal line, and touching the small circle. The black dots on the oblique line indicate a distance that is the tenth part of a decagon, as shown in C and B. Use alternate spaces to form a pentagon, as at B, or five-pointed star at C. This exercise is not so wearisome as it looks.

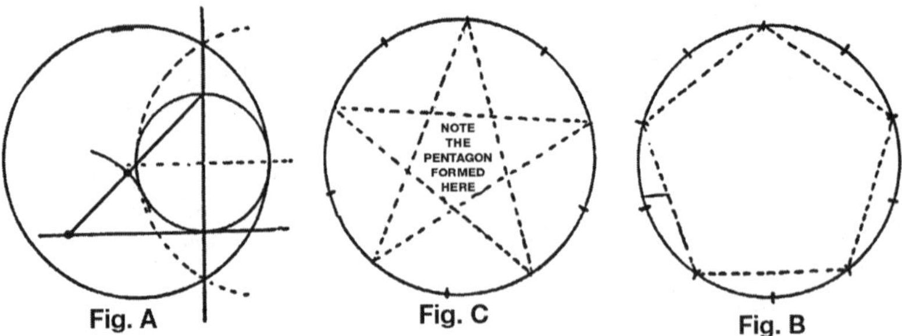

Fig. A Fig. C Fig. B

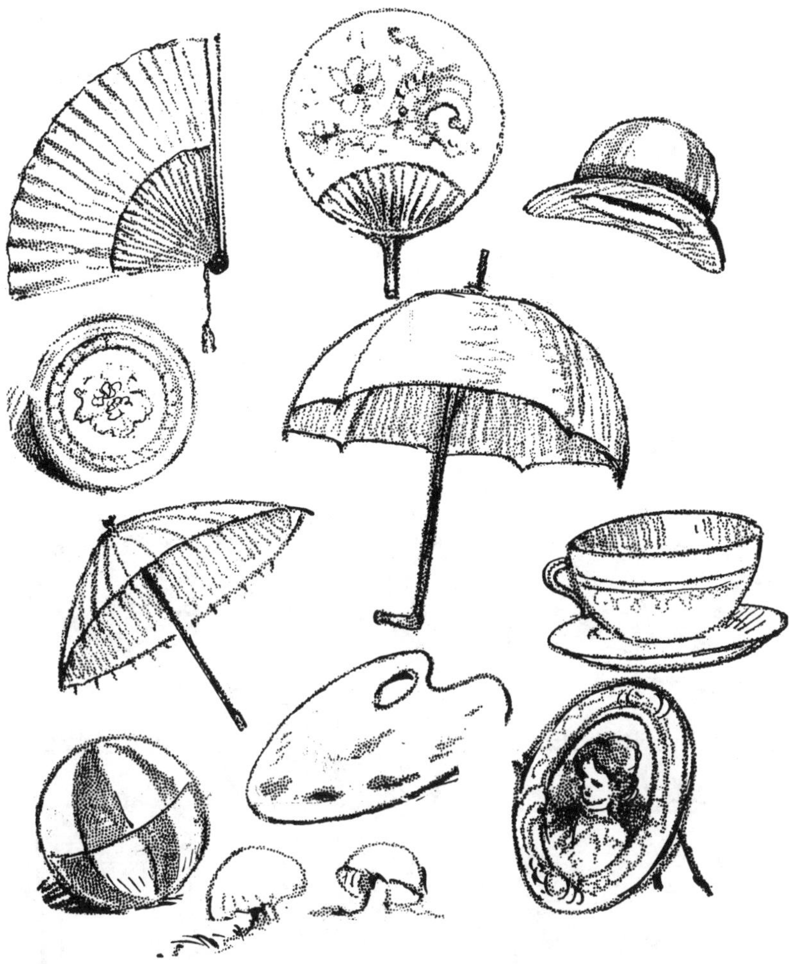

Mechanical Forms Applied Pictorially

Logs as Cylinder Models.—Small logs or branches of trees cut into suitable lengths make excellent models. The length of each piece may vary from one to two times the diameter. Saw out sections as shown in Fig. 2; that is, cut away one-eighth, one-quarter, one-third or one-half of four logs, as in A, B, C, D. Fig. 1 is made to show that the same methods are used for drawing cubes, prisms and other square-shaped objects as for curved ones. The perspective principle is the same for all.

The logs may be drawn in various positions, as vertical, horizontal, receding and right and left receding cylinders.

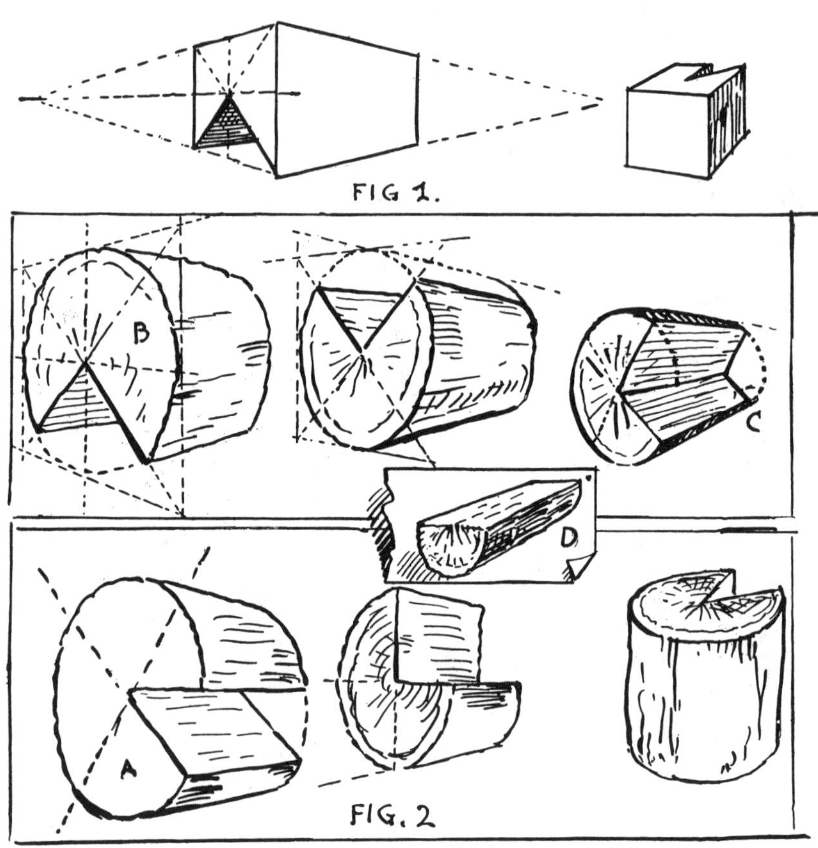

Dividing Square and Cylinder Forms

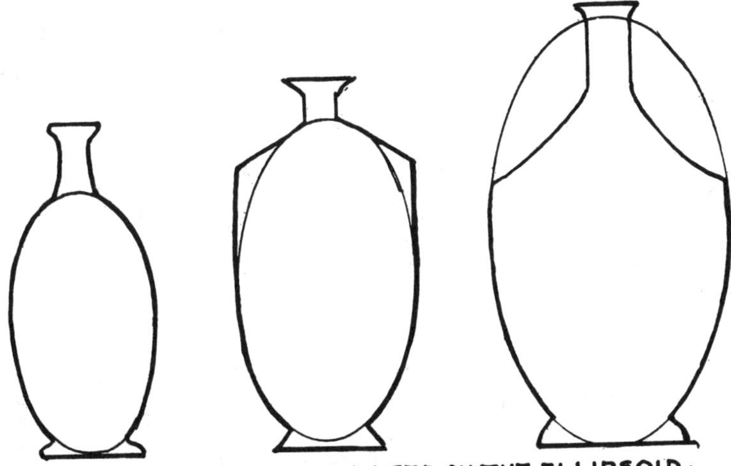

SIMPLE VASE FORMS BASED ON THE ELLIPSOID.
(FOR CONSTRUCTIVE WORK.)

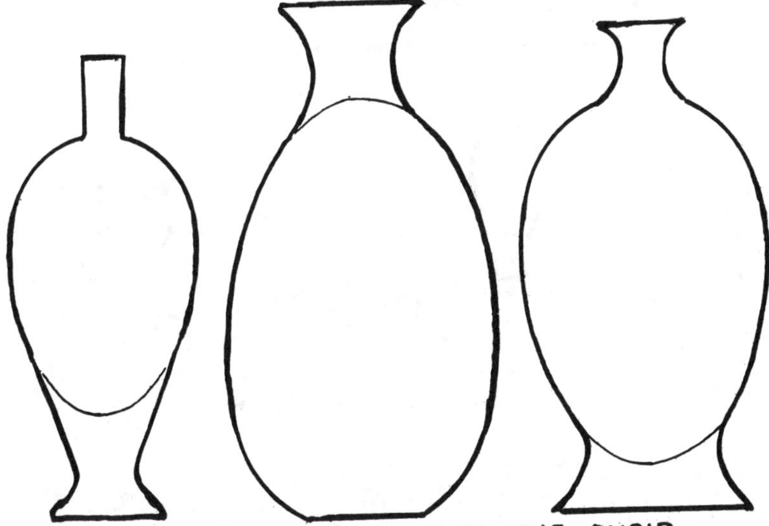

SIMPLE VASE FORMS BASED ON THE OVOID.
(FOR CONSTRUCTIVE WORK.)

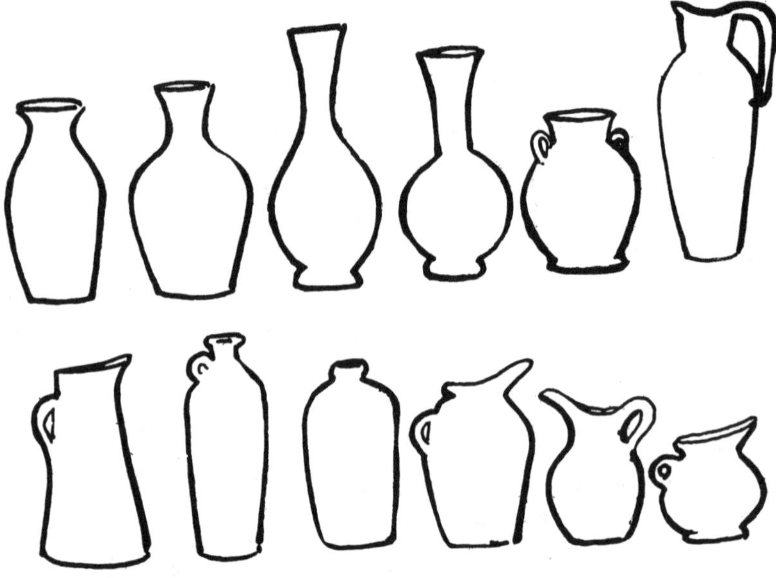

Freehand Exercises in Vase Forms

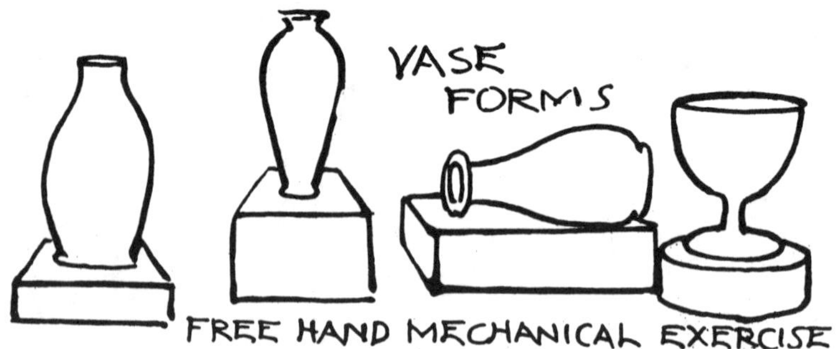

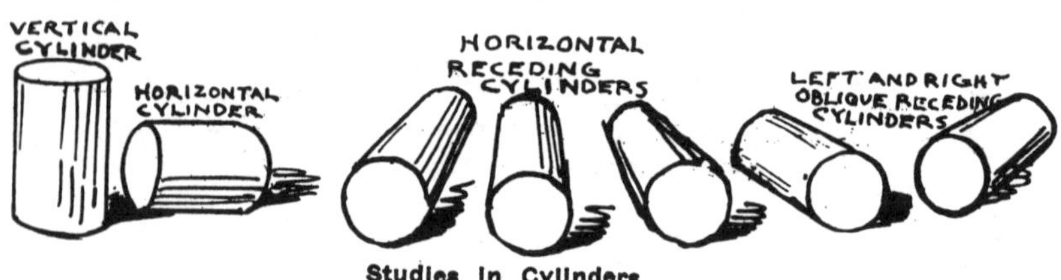

Studies in Cylinders

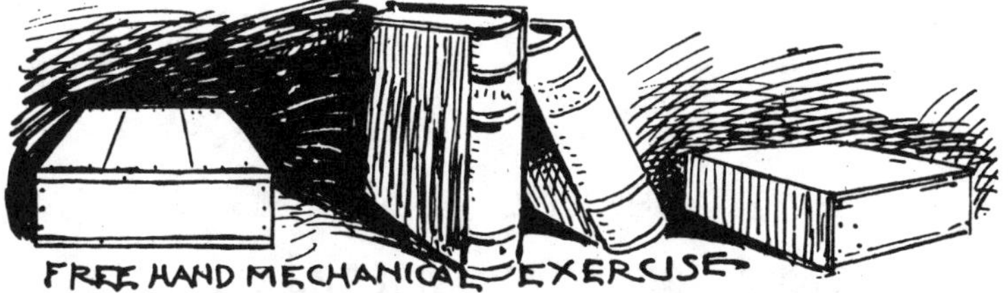

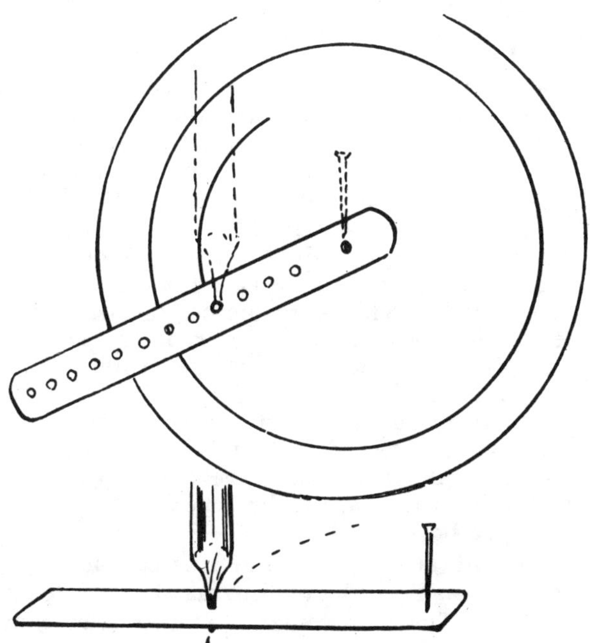

Substitute for Pencil Compass

Take a strip of cardboard about 1 x 4 inches in size. Prick holes at intervals of ¼ inch along the middle of its length. Stick pin through cardboard and drawing paper into the drawing board. Place point of pencil through any of the holes and circles are easily made. The diagram explains its construction and use.

Notes.—Additional instruction in Geometrical Forms will be found on pp. 55, 56, 57.

CHAPTER XXX

TRACING AND TRANSFERRING

Offset Sheets.—Necessity frequently arises for transferring outlines, etc., from one surface to another, as, for instance, from a pencil drawing on absorbent paper to a less absorbent paper suitable for pen drawings. For such a purpose, a thin sheet of firm paper with a surface that is not too smooth should be provided. This sheet can be made into fairly permanent transfer-paper by spreading over one side with any dry pigment, such as powdered indigo, red chalk, or the scrapings from the point of a pencil.

Another way is by a rubbing movement of the side of a soft pencil of any color. The entire surface of the paper should be covered. Whichever method is used, the surface should be blended by "stumping" or rubbing gently with the finger or a soft rag. Place this prepared paper with the colored side down on the blank paper that is to receive the copy. Over the former place the drawings from which the lines are to be transferred. Next take a stylus or sharp-pointed hard pencil—if a pencil, the harder the better—and trace over the lines that are to be repeated or transferred on the white paper below.

The result will be a faint outline that can be touched up if required with a pencil, or the picture may be completed at once with pen and ink. The "offset sheet," as it is called, may be preserved for frequent future use. Tracing paper treated in the same way may be used. Tracing paper is useful in many ways, but its general use is not to be recommended for the beginner. There are times, however, when tracing paper is a great help.

Pencil Transfers.—When a pencil drawing has been made that one wishes to preserve and also to reproduce practically line for line, in pen and ink, the use of tracing paper is advisable in order to transfer the outlines of the pencil drawing onto the paper on which the pen drawing is to be made. To do this proceed as follows:

Take a piece of tracing paper (in lieu of the regular kind, any thin, firm, transparent paper that is not oily will answer the purpose). With a finely-pointed rather soft pencil trace the outlines of the pencil drawing.

Then lay the tracing paper on another sheet of white paper, with the pencil lines of the tracing paper on the under side. Then again draw the lines on the tracing paper, but on the side opposite to those made before. The lines are now drawn on both sides of the tracing paper. Now place it on the paper on which the pen drawing is to be made with the lines that were last drawn underneath; that is, they should be in contact with the pen drawing paper. The tracing paper should now be briskly rubbed on the upper surface with the side of a stylus or stiff, flat-surfaced ivory or bone paper cutter. The thumb nail is sometimes used for this purpose, but its use should be discouraged, as it wears away the nail very quickly.

Tracing Transferred.—The tracing will now be found to be more or less faintly transferred to the pen-paper. If necessary, the transferred tracing may be touched up here and there, where a greater definition seems necessary to guide the pen.

Preserve Tracings.—The tracing paper after use need not be discarded, for it may be used several times, although after each transfer the "offset" will become more and more dim. Greater pressure is required then, and the lines on the tracing paper may have to be strengthened. By preserving tracings, subsequent impressions are available in case the first drawing in pen-and-ink is unsatisfactory, or in case one desires to work up the same theme in a different style of treatment.

Transfer from Opaque Paper.—Whenever necessary to make a transfer from a piece of paper that is not transparent, the reverse drawing (the lines which make the offset) can be made by placing the paper against a window pane, which will cause the paper to appear transparent, when the lines may be traced.

Interesting and Practical Experiment.—When it is necessary to make the transfer in contact with any certain part of the drawing this can be accomplished by placing the paper near the desired place and then rapidly lifting and lowering the transfer until the part on the transfer and the part on the drawing underneath appear as one. The phenomenon is similar to the principle on which moving pictures are based.

To illustrate the experiment make the drawing A in Fig. 1. Then another drawing B, which place over A. Then move up and down very quickly, as indicated in Fig. 2, in the directions as shown by the arrows E and F. Bring C towards you from D sufficiently far that the eye may see A as well as B. If moved with sufficient speed, A and B will appear as they do at the left of Fig. 3.

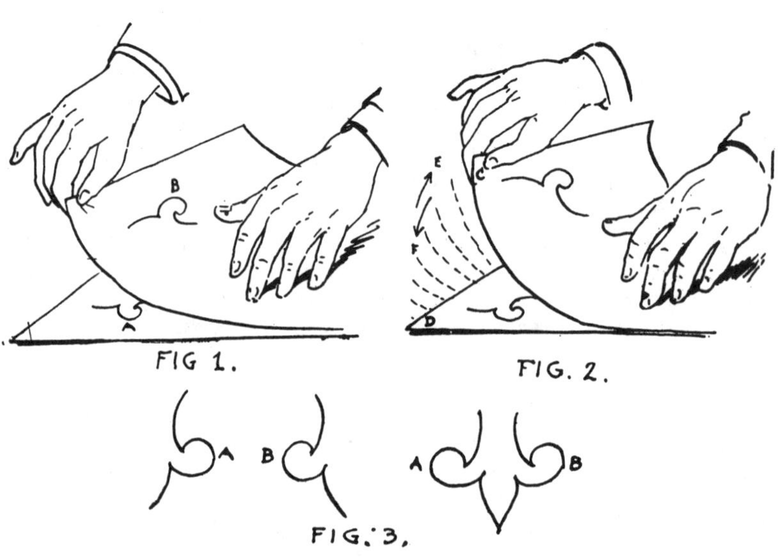

FIG 1.

FIG. 2.

FIG. 3.

REVERSING DESIGNS

For the purpose of making both halves of a design precisely alike fold a thin piece of paper and on one side draw half of the design. Then fold again and by rubbing briskly on the back of the paper with any hard substance, the design will even appear sufficiently legible to be penciled over. It can then in turn be transferred to paper that is not creased. The method is shown in Fig. 8. The heavy lines represent the half first drawn, while the dotted lines show the folds and transfer. If the subject is a wreath an initial may be added. In the upper right-hand corner is shown half of a "B" started in this manner.

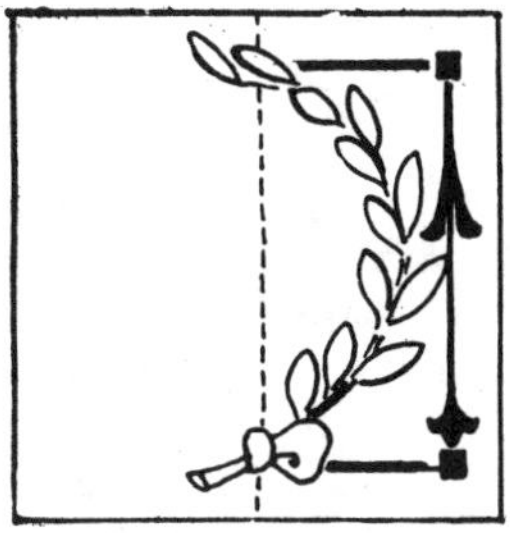

Fig. 4 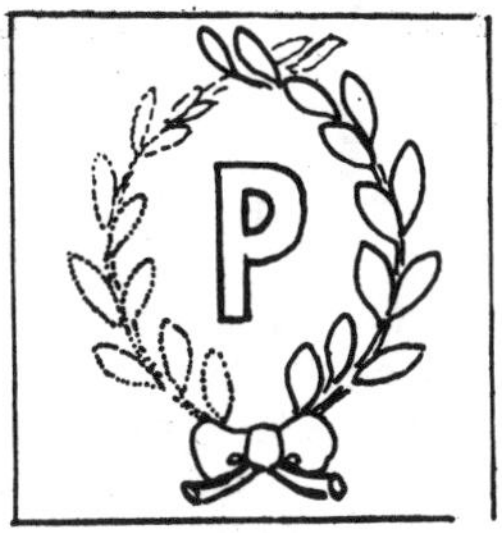 Fig. 6 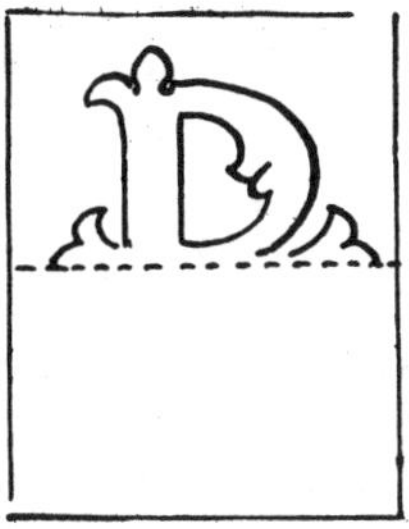 Fig. 5

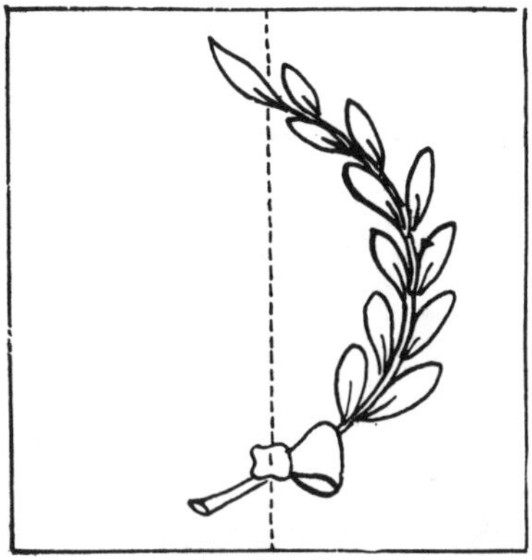

Fig. 7 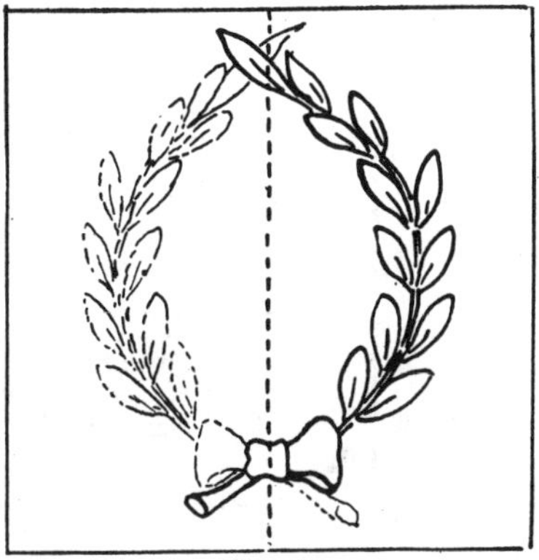 Fig. 8

Fold a piece of paper in the middle (Fig. 9). Draw half a butterfly on one side of the fold; transfer it. Pencil the trans-

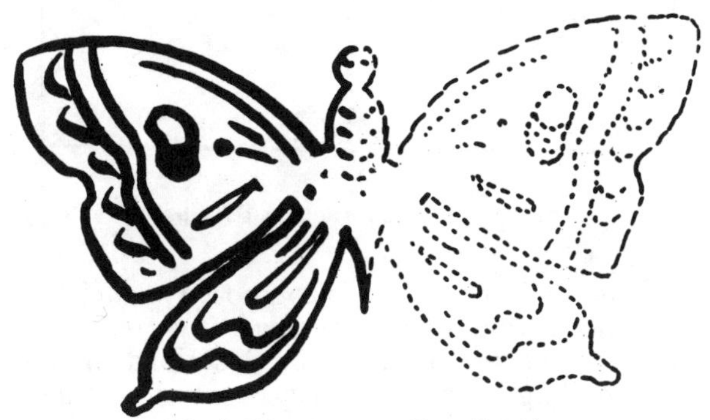

Fig. 9—Tracing and Transferring

fer. A very pretty and interesting variation of this exercise consists in using colored chalks instead of pencil, and then intensifying the transfer.

Take a piece of drawing paper about four inches square and fold it four times, according to the straight dotted lines in Fig. 10. Fold towards you, and open the paper after each folding. In one of the spaces, as at A, draw a design similar to the one shown. Crease and make a transfer, as at B. Pencil the transferred line. Fold at CC. Transfer the quarter design to the space E. Pencil as before, fold at DD and transfer to FFFF. Then pencil the transfer. Medallions can be drawn in a like manner by making the outside of the design follow an eighth of a circle, as at G.

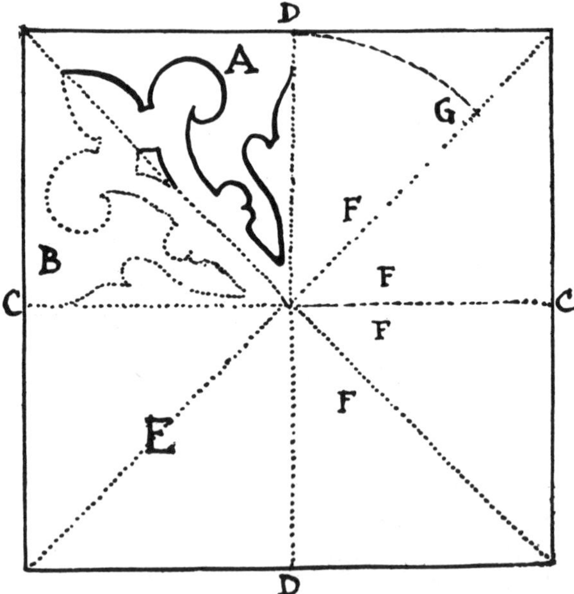

Fig. 10—Tracing and Transferring

The designs "e" and "f" are composed principally of the units a, b, c and d transferred, reversed, inverted and repeated somewhat according to the methods described in the chapter on Pastel-Stenciling. For exercise draw the same units or others, and construct other designs in a similar manner.

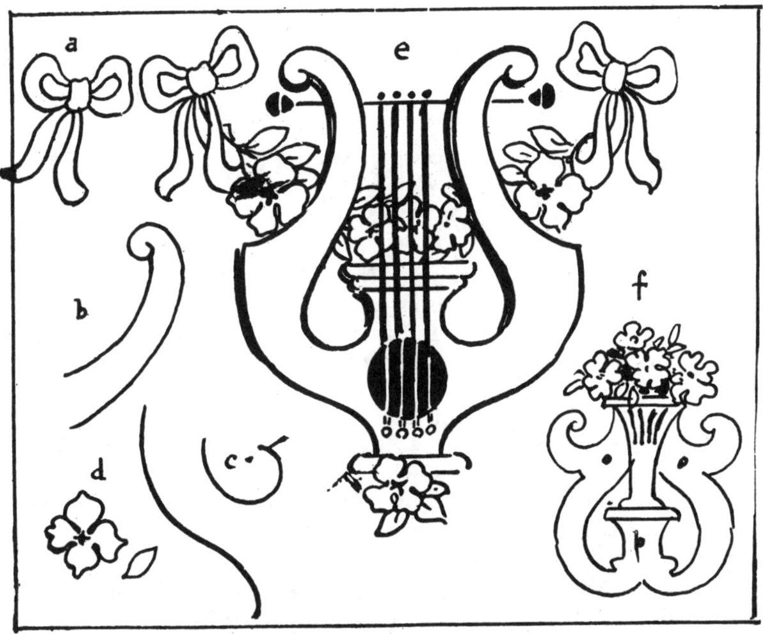

Design Made by Means of Transferred Tracings

It is advisable to make tracings of both front and back of each unit. If the face of a tracing is rubbed for the purpose of transferring lines that are on the other side, the lines on the face will no longer transfer.

For general use as a tracing point or stylus, the 6H pencil is very good.

Notes.—Additional forms adapted to purposes of duplication by means of tracing and transferring will be found on pp. 59, 60, 61, 62, 77, 78, 84, 87, 88, 89, 99, 102, 105, 106, 107, 108, 110, 111, 112, 113, 230, 233, 234, 238, 245, 257, 264, 265, 269, 271, 272, 273, 274, 275, 279, 280, 283, 292, 293, 294, 295, 296, 297, 298, 299, 300, 301.

CHAPTER XXXI

LETTERING

Ruled Lines for Lettering.—In making Roman letters, one should be guided by ruled lines just as in making script. Possibly there will come a time, as in writing, when the use of guide lines for lettering may be discontinued, but in the meantime it would be just as absurd for a child to learn to write without ruled lines as to draw without their aid.

Guide Lines Necessary.—For the purpose of making guide lines for lettering the use of the straight edge should be freely permitted. The straight edge may be a ruler, a pencil, a piece of cardboard or anything that may be used for the purpose.

Ruling short, straight lines for pencil or ink, by means of the simple contrivance described in Fig. 1 will be found useful. Take a new round pencil—the thicker the better—and around each end roll narrow strips of pasted paper about three-eighths of an inch in width and about 10 inches in length, the latter depending on the thickness of the paper used. The result should be about a thirty-second of an inch in thickness—just enough to keep the body of the pencil away from the paper on which it is used.

Roll it Along.—When rolled along gently on the surface of the paper to be used for the drawing, the pencil will be propelled in a straight direction instead of sliding from side

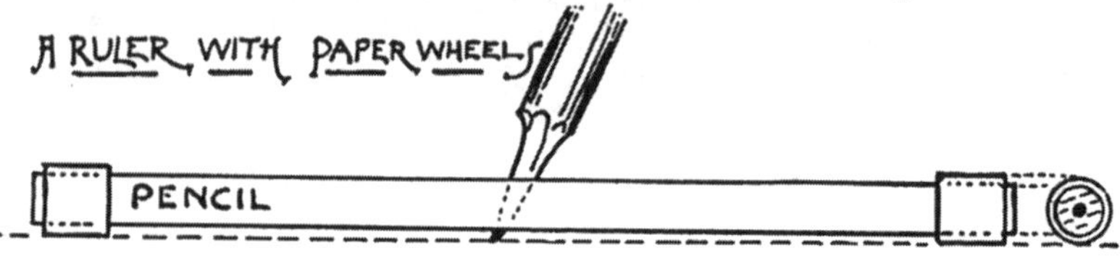

Fig. 1

to side, as is usually the case when a pencil is used as a straight edge and the endeavor is to make parallel lines.

The Gothic alphabet drawn by aid of guide lines. Note the vertical lines as guides to symmetry in forming some of the curved letters. Note that the upper divisions of letters are smaller than the lower. They are made so as to prevent their having a top-heavy appearance. Hold the alphabet upside down. Look at the letters B, E, H, K and S and see how top-heavy they appear when thus seen.

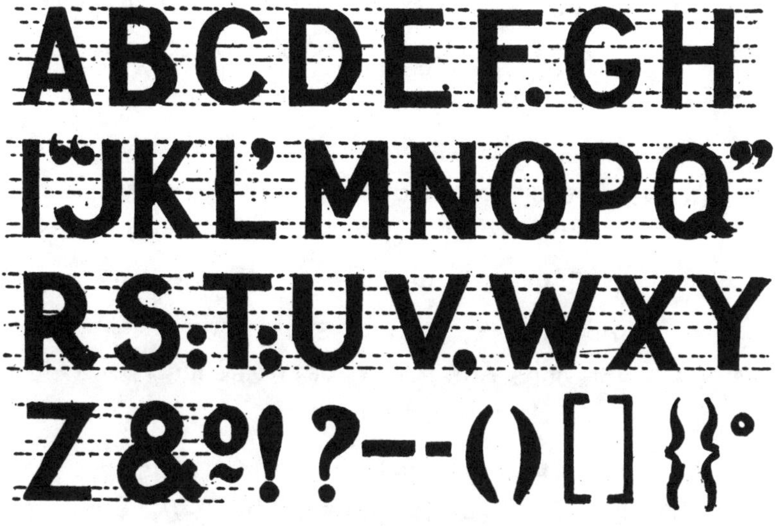

ABCDE.F.GH

I“JKL’MNOPQ”

RS:T;UV,WXY

Z&º!?—-()[]{}°

Fig. 2

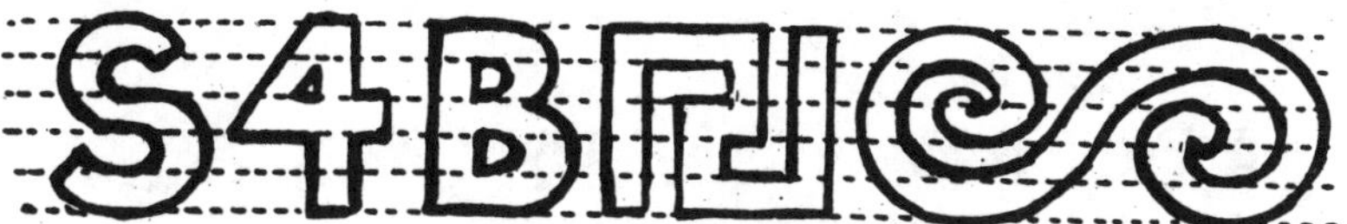

Fig. 3—Practicing Other Forms With Guide Lines in Connection With Lettering

Too much stress cannot be laid on the value of guidelines. Their use should be repeated at intervals throughout the entire course of study. The author of this work has never ceased their use.

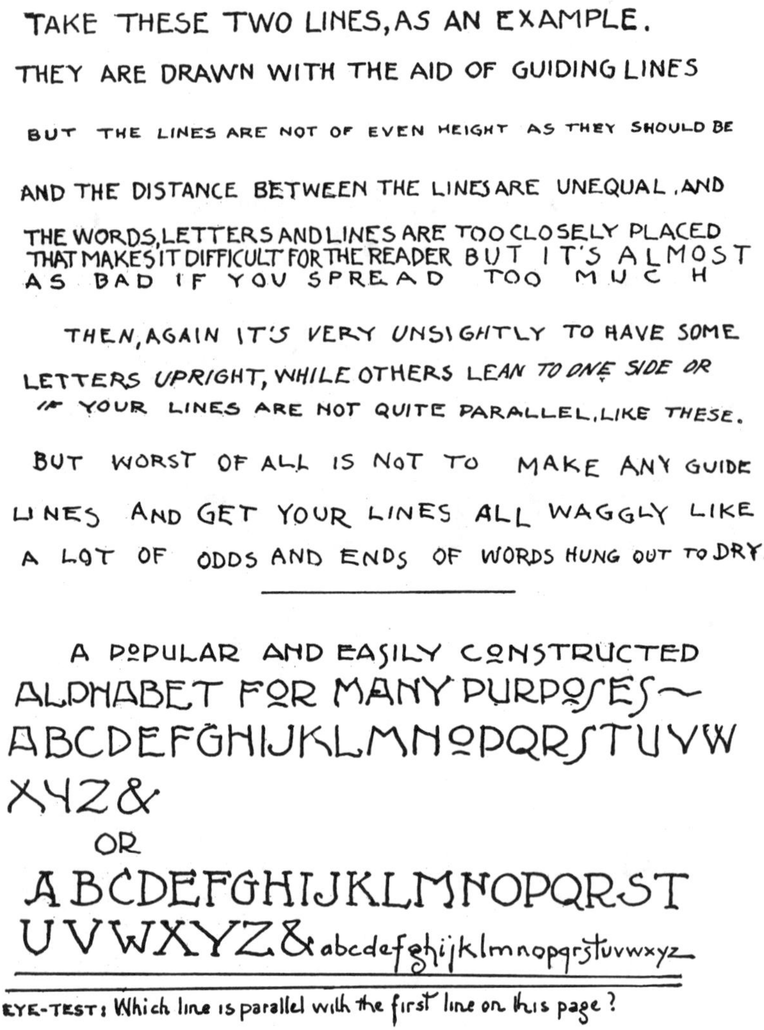

TAKE THESE TWO LINES, AS AN EXAMPLE.
THEY ARE DRAWN WITH THE AID OF GUIDING LINES

BUT THE LINES ARE NOT OF EVEN HEIGHT AS THEY SHOULD BE

AND THE DISTANCE BETWEEN THE LINES ARE UNEQUAL, AND

THE WORDS, LETTERS AND LINES ARE TOO CLOSELY PLACED
THAT MAKES IT DIFFICULT FOR THE READER BUT IT'S ALMOST
AS BAD IF YOU SPREAD TOO MUCH

THEN, AGAIN IT'S VERY UNSIGHTLY TO HAVE SOME
LETTERS UPRIGHT, WHILE OTHERS LEAN TO ONE SIDE OR
IF YOUR LINES ARE NOT QUITE PARALLEL, LIKE THESE.

BUT WORST OF ALL IS NOT TO MAKE ANY GUIDE
LINES AND GET YOUR LINES ALL WAGGLY LIKE
A LOT OF ODDS AND ENDS OF WORDS HUNG OUT TO DRY.

A POPULAR AND EASILY CONSTRUCTED
ALPHABET FOR MANY PURPOSES—
ABCDEFGHIJKLMNOPQRSTUVW
XYZ&
OR
ABCDEFGHIJKLMNOPQRST
UVWXYZ& abcdefghijklmnopqrstuvwxyz

EYE-TEST: Which line is parallel with the first line on this page?

Fig. 4—Sketchy Lettering

An easy way to enhance the appearance
of a line is to connect the letters with hair
lines, putting them in after the letters are made
It gives an odd effect

Fig. 5—Just a Trifling Suggestion

Adaptation of Comic Figures. — Many ordinary-looking things, by repetition and reversing, become good subjects for ornamental design. For instance, the comic policeman in the chapter on comic drawing is well adapted for a design for the cover of some book of humor.

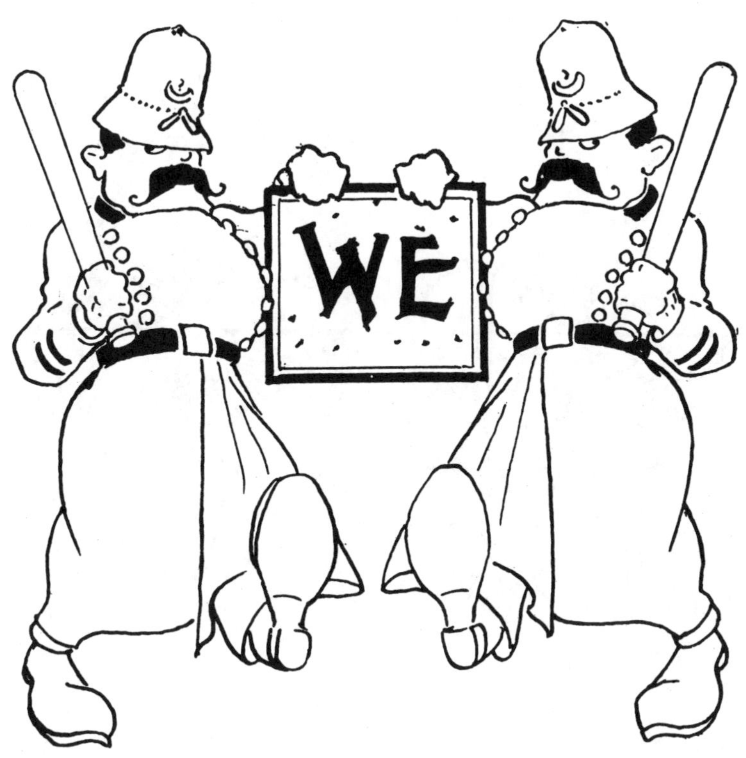

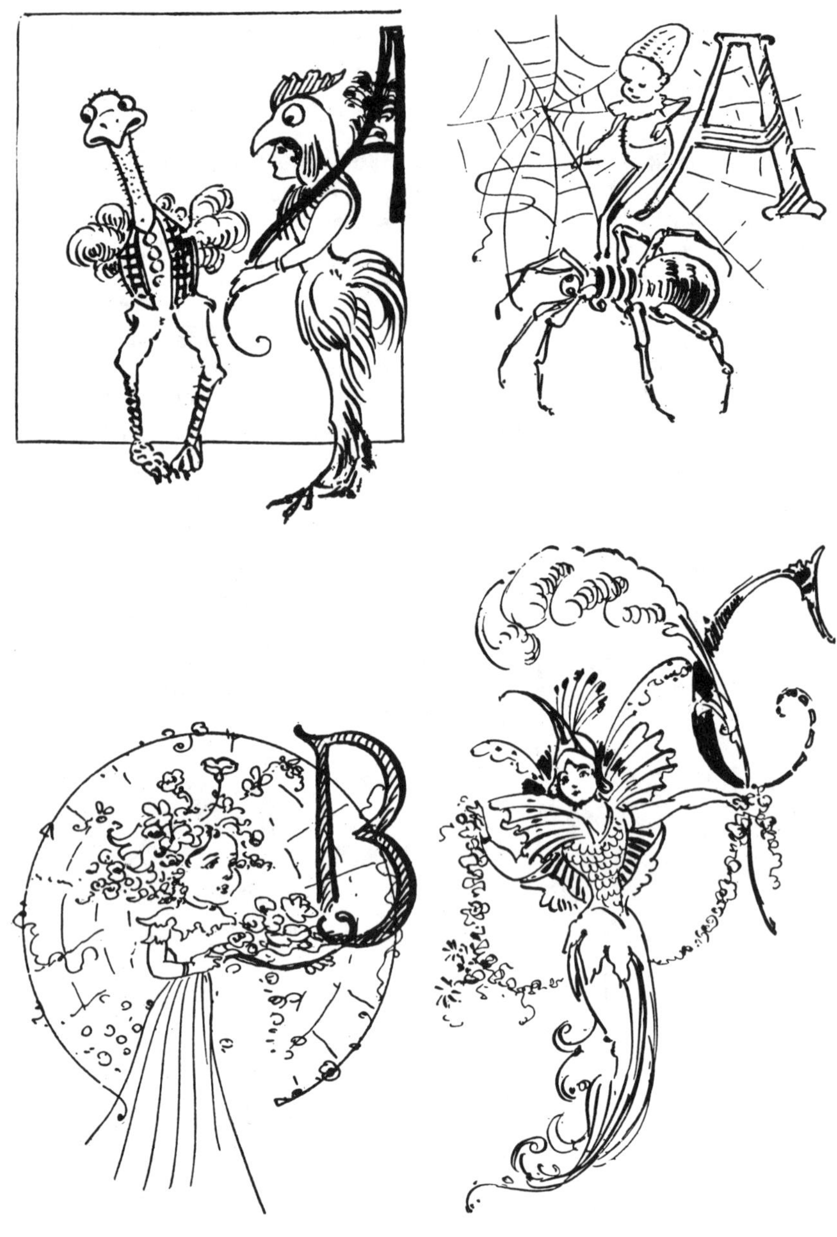

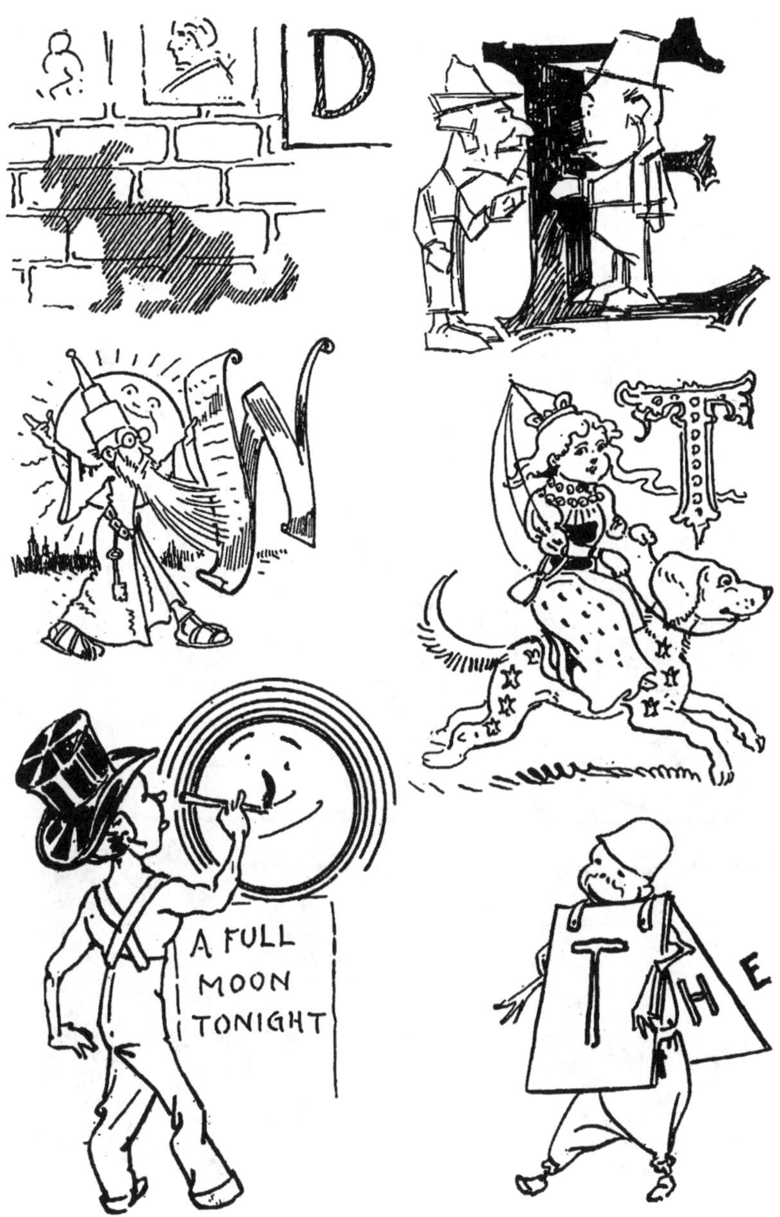
D
E
W
T
A FULL
MOON
TONIGHT
T
H
E

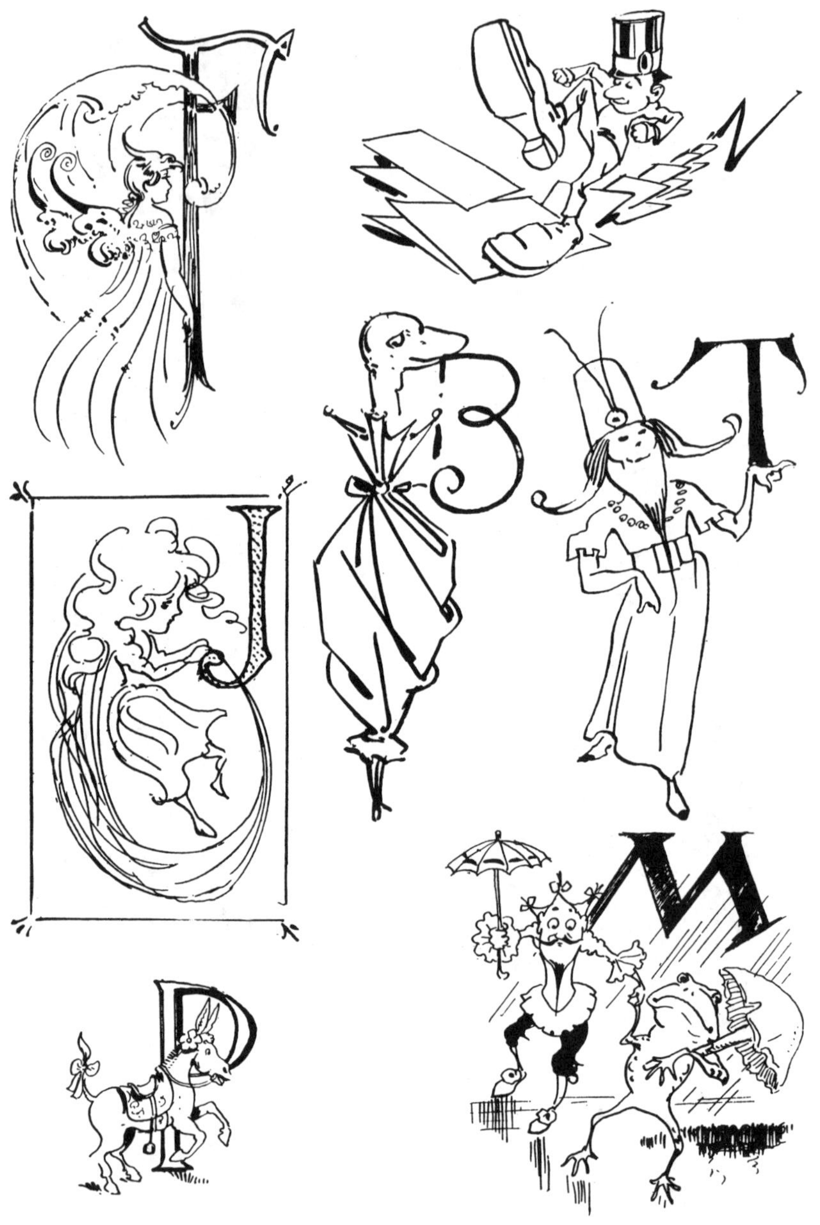

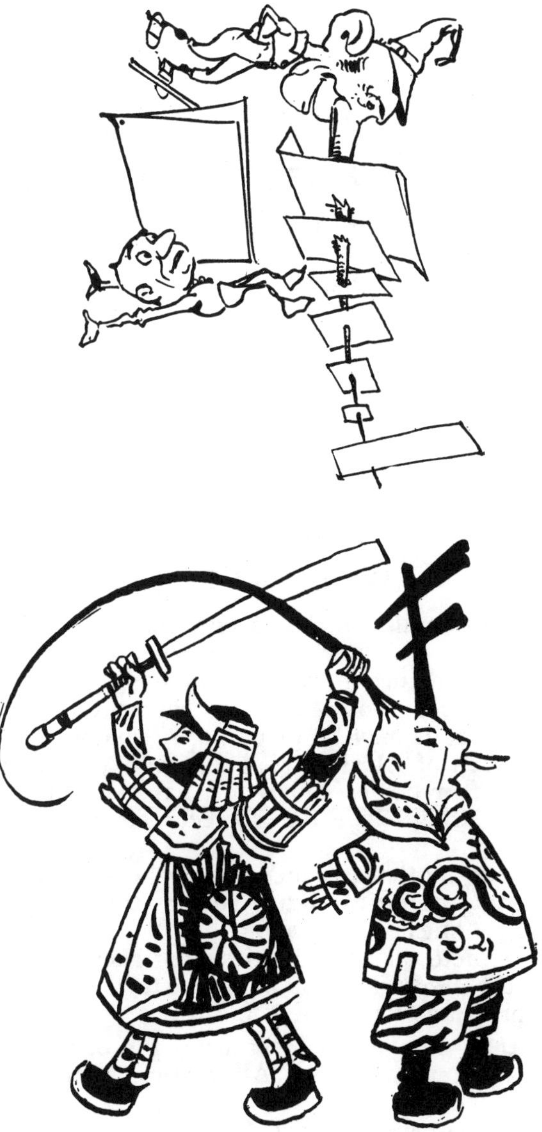

Note.—For other examples of lettering see book-covers on pages 281 and 282.

CHAPTER XXXII

DECORATIVE OR ORNAMENTAL ART

Decoration relates to the production of beauty in art, in which the first principle to be considered is symmetry—the equal balance of two halves. The second principle is repetition.

Repetition may be considered as Simple, when the same unit is used repeatedly.

As Alternate, when two units are used alternately.

As Combined, when several units (each one different) are used.

Simple repetition, Alternate repetition and Combined repetition are seen in Fig. 2. Further complication appears in Fig. 3.

Conventional Design

To conventionalize means to represent by symbol of some exact preconceived outline, rather than by an attempt to duplicate resemblance to a natural object. To conventionalize, for instance, is to produce an ornamental design of such a character that it may be made up of several different integral parts, each of which is copied from some natural object, such as a leaf or flower, but which has been formalized into the typical rather than the correct representation of the original.

Or, to give another instance, it may be a leaf made to conform to some geometrical figure, such as the maple leaf drawn within the confines of a hexagon.

Even in pictorial art, liberties are taken with nature to overcome the limitations of human efforts to make certain visible impressions by pictorial means.

Ornament.—In the ornamental designs of the Greeks and the Romans, Repetition and Alternation were the chief resources.

Modern ornamenters added Intersection, which means relieving Repetition and Alternation at intervals with additional forms or group of forms, and then continuing as before.

Complication also has been added. In decorative design, Complication is a term which differs somewhat from the ordinary meaning. It is here used to distinguish the results produced from the contact, interlacing of the various forms comprising the whole.

Confusion is the term of another element that has a valued place in modern decoration. Confusion, usually the synonym of disorder, when applied to decorative art is used in giving contrast and even harmony to the general composition. The ornamentist in employing Confusion gains the aid of every possible object, whose curves or symmetrical lines appeal to his eye. He will thus group in one design the most incongruous figures, all of which give zest and life to an otherwise purely mechanical design.

Confusion in designing ornament is the artist's license. The sculptor requires Confusion's aid, when he fills his pedestals, niches, etc., with ornaments imitated, at random it would almost seem, from the vegetable and animal world.

Cardboard Curves

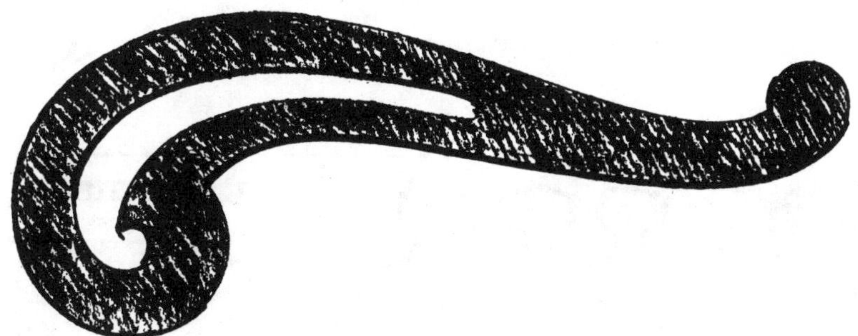

Cut out of cardboard or oil stencil board curved shapes similar to that herewith shown. They are useful in making designs where there is frequent repetition of simple curved lines. The complicated looking design on page 298 is an example of what can be done with a curve such as the one on this page.

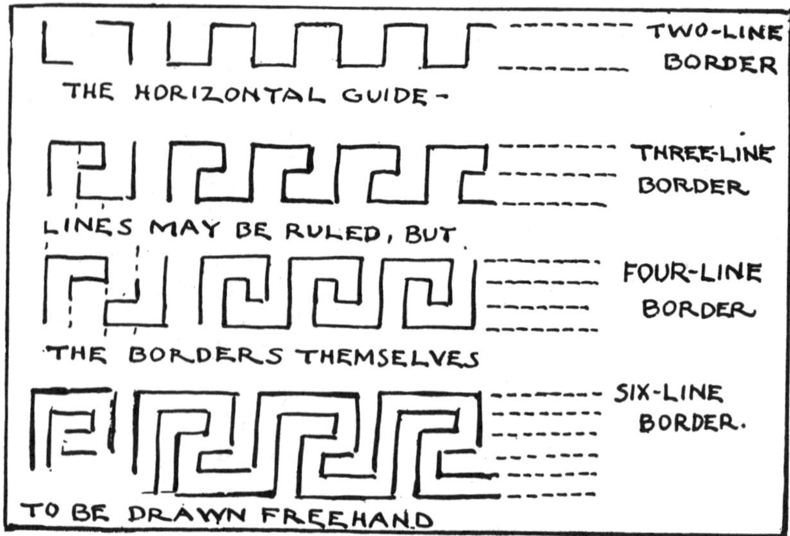

Fig. 1—Two, Three, Four and Five Guide Line Exercises

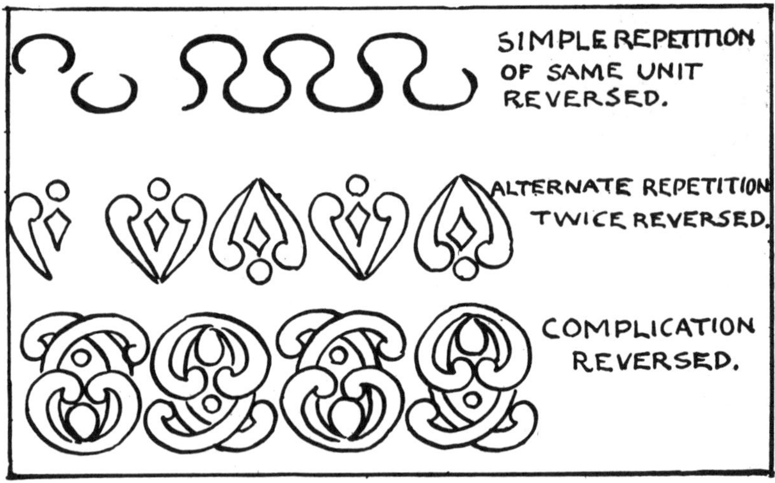

Fig. 2—Reverse Exercises in Units

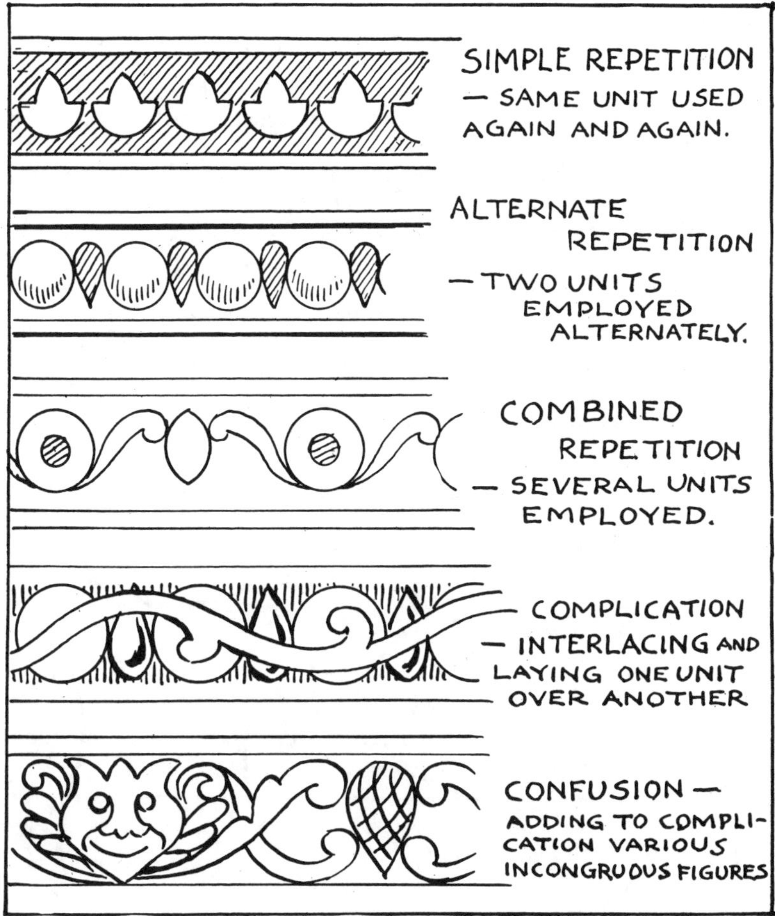

Fig. 3—Elements of Ornamental Design

Equilibrium and stability, commonplace in their aspects though they may seem, play important parts in the science of ornamental design. Solidity is a principle of art; strength does not exclude elegance.

Duplication of Design.—When making a design in which the details are frequently duplicated, draw each minor detail and then make a tracing with a sharp-pointed soft pencil; redraw the lines on the other side of the tracing paper, and with a stylus or whatever hard substance is used to make the offset rub briskly on the side opposite the last traced design.

To duplicate the design wherever it is to be placed repeat each part of the design as often as necessary to produce the entire plan of ornament.

In making a frame-like design make corner-pieces first and join to whatever border may be selected.

Retracing Necessary.—When each "repeat" is to be made frequently, it will be necessary to retrace (over the same lines) several times, because a portion of the graphite, of which the pencil lead is composed, is transferred to the paper beneath at each offset. After three or four offsets, the transfers thus made will become too dim to act as guides. The plan for transferring as described in the chapter on Tracing and Transferring can be used in these exercises.

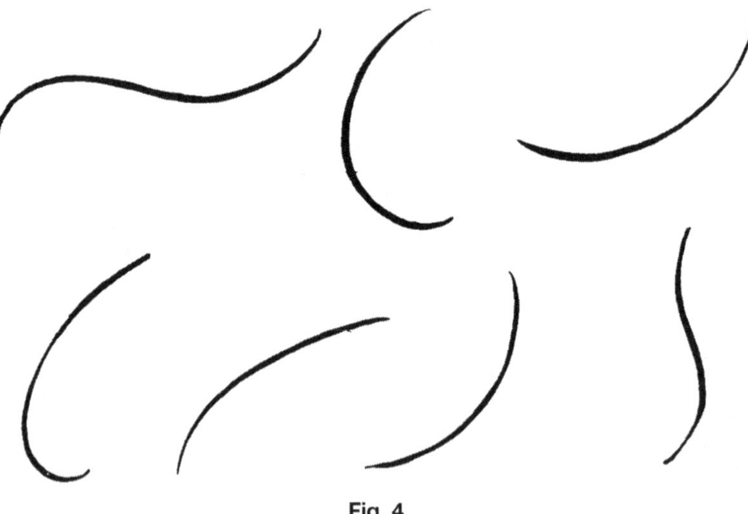

Fig. 4

Aids for Imagination.—Draw curves similar to the above and add floral and decorative forms as suggested below. The intention of this exercise is to arouse the inventive faculties. The curves should be all drawn separately and the decorations added afterward.

Fig. 5

EXERCISES IN FIGS. 6 AND 7

Permit Use of Guide Lines.—Among the first exercises in drawing, practically the same principles may be applied that are applicable to penmanship. Guide lines should be permitted; that is, simple lines constructed along the horizontal and oblique sides. The exercises indicated at the beginning of each row of figures should be made the subject of a single lesson. The lines indicated at the right of each row should be added as you advance; for instance, draw, say, a hundred straight, oblique lines, until you have become proficient in their use. Follow with the reverse and duplicated lines in the top row. After that draw the simple curves at the left of the second row a great many times before progressing to the added and duplicated, triplicated and quadrupled curves at the right.

Next draw repeatedly the compound curves at the left in the third and fourth rows, before proceeding to the more complex additions at the right.

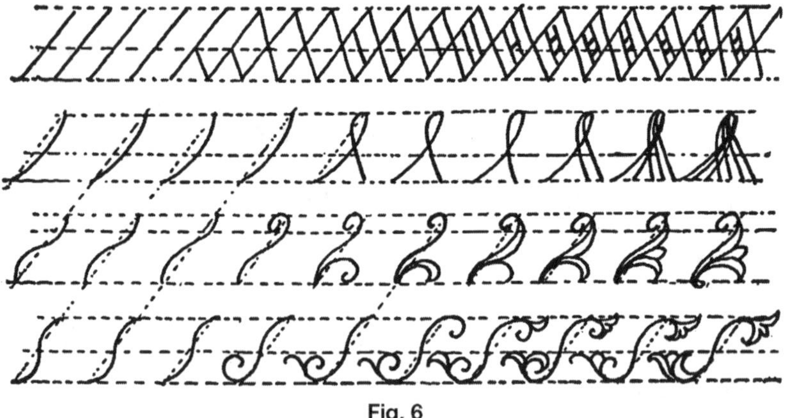

Fig. 6

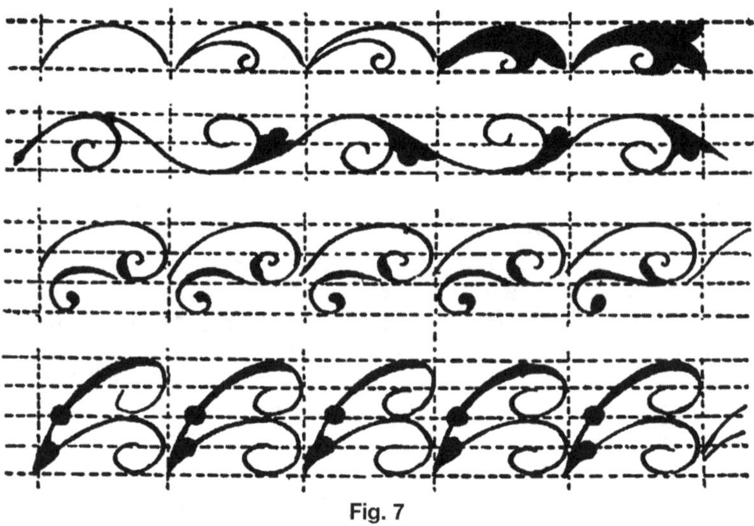

Fig. 7

After becoming proficient with the exercises in Fig. 6, draw the curves and ornamental devices in Fig. 7.

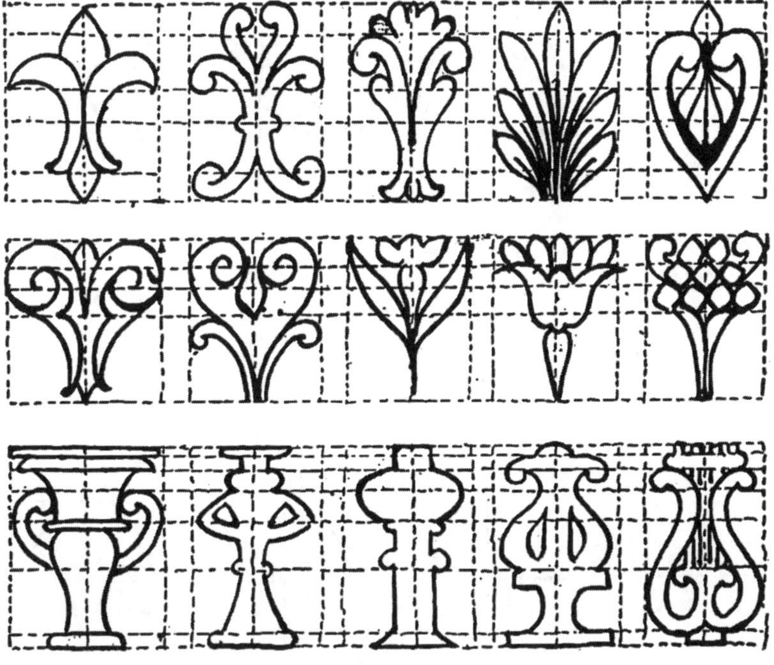

Fig. 8

Each of the designs in Fig. 8 is enclosed in a rectangle of the same dimensions. There are three sets of horizontal lines, in turn bisected by vertical lines. Three sets of five totally different designs are based on these lines. Let them serve as an exercise by which they are copied as herewith given. When you have made further progress, make variations from these, using the same kind of guide lines, but with the endeavor to make new and original designs.

Snow Crystals.—Fig. 9 shows four snow crystals greatly enlarged. They are formed by hexagons, or two equilateral triangles with apexes in opposition. To draw them by means of the latter proceed as in Fig. 10. Draw the horizontal line a. Bisect it as at b. Each oblique line in c equals the horizontal line a. Describe another triangle inverted as at d. Then proceed to construct the crystals on the lines of the triangles as shown in Fig. 11.

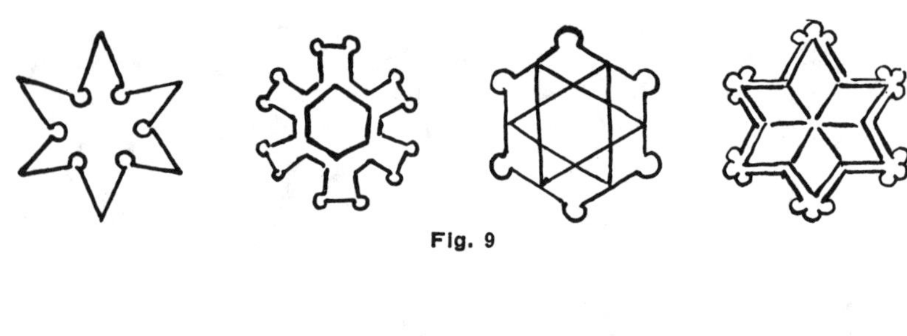

Fig. 9

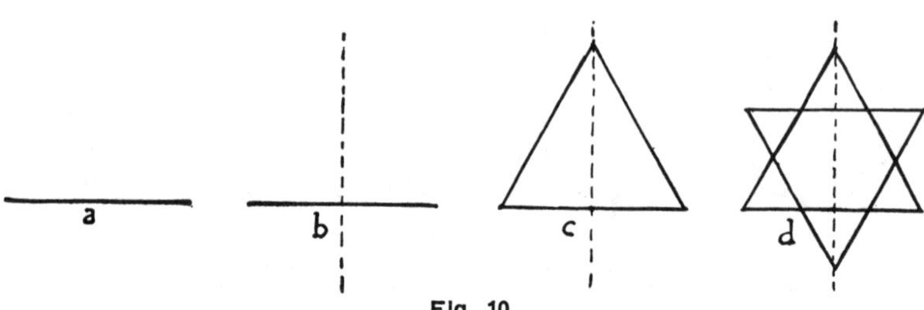

Fig. 10

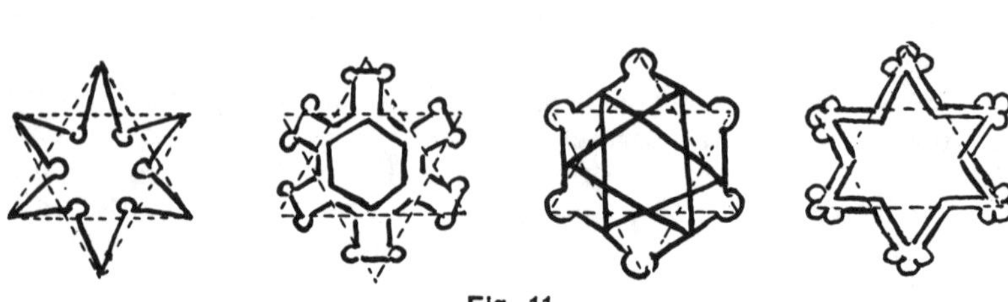

Fig. 11

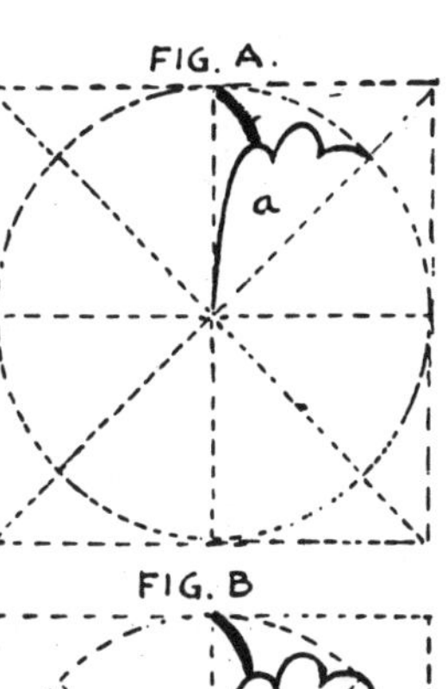

Rosettes

To make a rosette or medallion with four or eight units or sections, as shown in Fig. D. Draw one-eighth of the entire design, as shown in Fig. A at a. Reverse a, add b, in Fig. B, forming one-fourth of the rosette. Reverse this quarter, as shown in Fig. C, thus forming half of the design. Reverse this once more and the design is completed, as shown in Fig. D.

If an eight-point rosette is desired add points as shown in heavy lines in Fig. D.

The reversing of the sections may be done by any of the following three methods:

1. Free-hand.

2. By folding according to the horizontal, vertical and oblique dotted lines in Fig. A. Directions for this will be found in the chapter on Paper Cutting and Folding.

3. By means of tracings of the obverse and the reverse (Fig. B), repeated with the aid of the stylus or other means of offsetting, as described in the chapter on Tracing and Transferring.

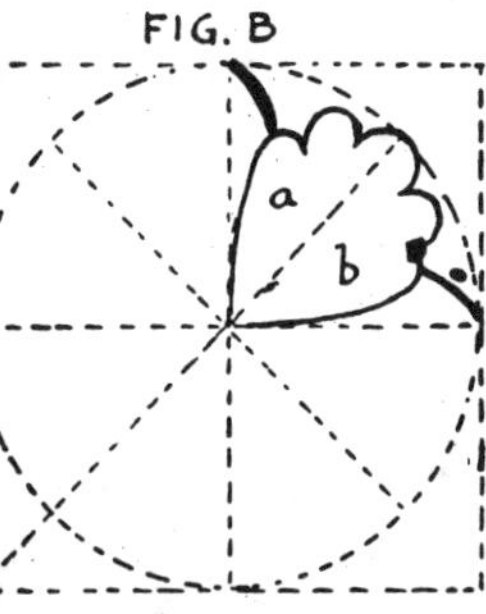

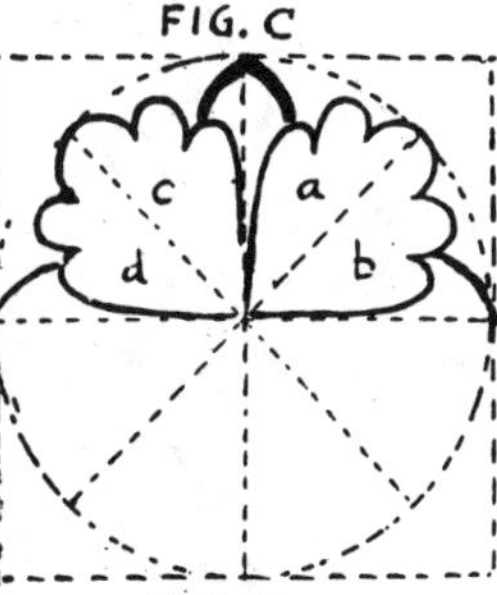

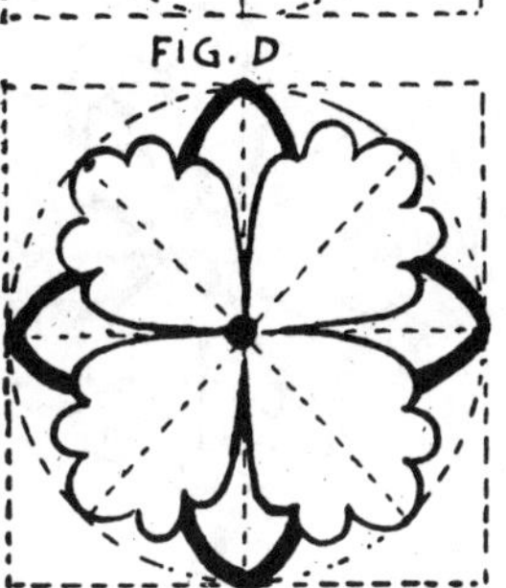

Fig. 12

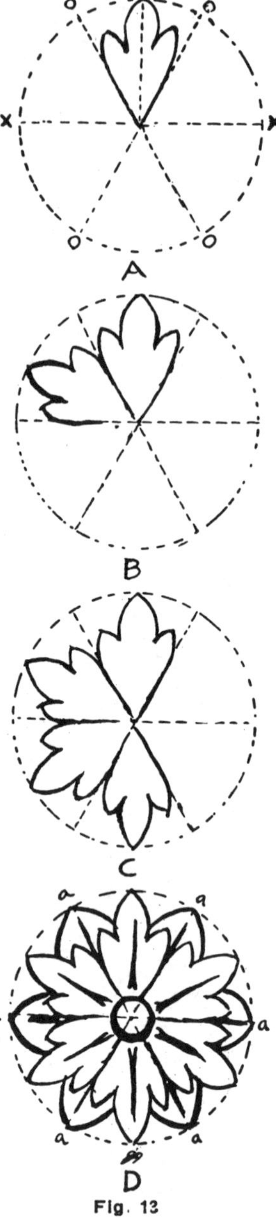

Fig. 13

To Make a six or twelve-pointed rosette or medallion follow the rule for dividing the circle into six parts according to directions for making a hexagon in the chapter on Geometrical Forms.

Draw one unit of design and repeat according to directions for making the four or eight-pointed rosette. The four diagrams A, B, C and D in Fig. 13 are supposed to be one drawing, but are shown as separate drawings in order to illustrate the successive steps for developing the rosette, as shown in Fig. D. The added six points A, A, A, A, A, A, need be made only if a twelve-point rosette is desired.

XX, OOOO correspond to the letters in the diagram in the chapter on Geometrical Forms.

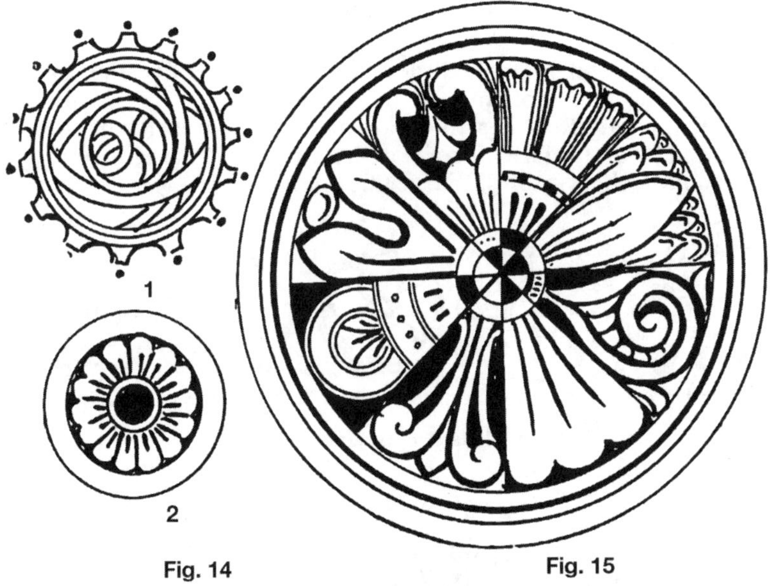

Fig. 14 Fig. 15

More Rosettes

Fig. 14-1.—A geometrical rosette or medallion, drawn with a compass, except the external cog-like projections.

Fig. 14-2.—A conventionalized daisy in medallion form. Draw the circles with compass; the rest free hand. If pen and ink, sketch details with very light pencil lines. For exercise draw a border containing four rosettes, alternated or separated by a circle about one-fourth the diameter of the rosette.

Fig. 15 is not intended as a copy for a single rosette, but for eight separate ones; each of the eight sections to be repeated eight times, when the circle will be filled. The units may be adopted also for border designs.

Historic Ornament

Individuality in ornament has been characteristic of most ancient and modern cultures. Each nation seems to have adopted some unit or series of units and adapted them so repeatedly that they have derived a claim to some specific form of ornament. When these designs have passed down the ages they have been accepted as the historical ornament appertaining to the respective nations.

The greatest historic styles of the ancients are the Egyptian, Greek and Roman.

Of the Middle Ages there are the Byzantine, Romanesque (founded on the later forms of the Roman ornament and approaching the Gothic), Saracenic and Gothic.

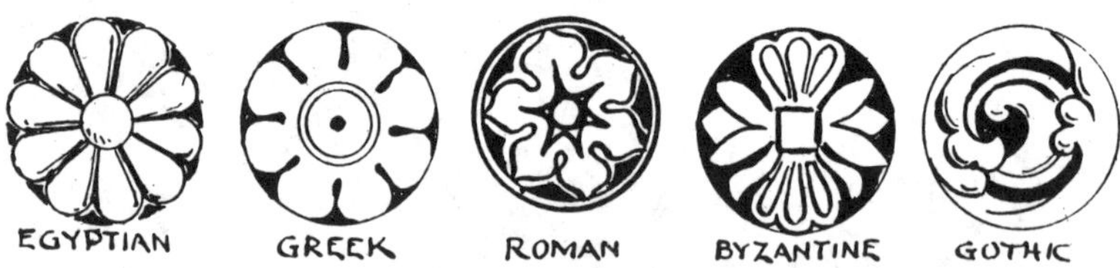

Fig. 16—Historic Ornament—Rosettes

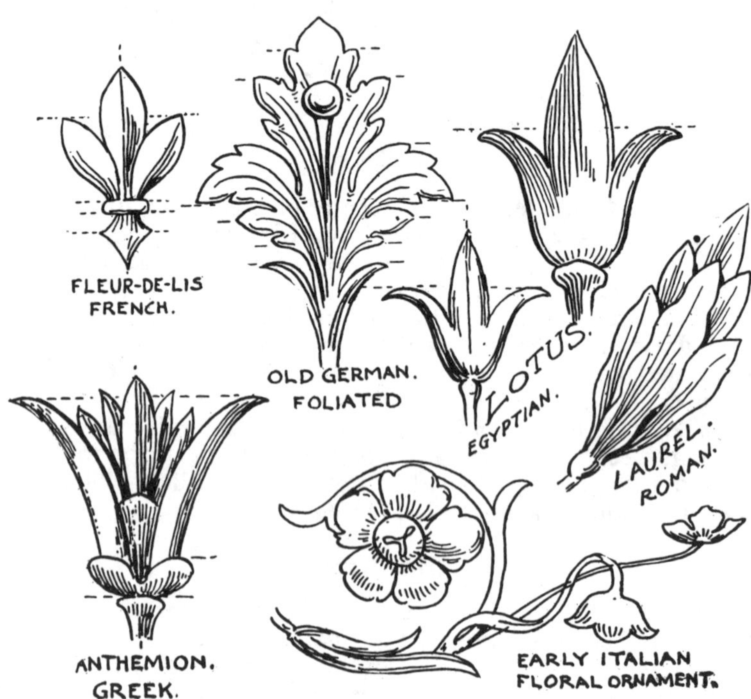

Fig. 17—Simple Examples of Historic Ornaments

The modern styles which, however, included those prevailing for several centuries past (since 15th century) are usually termed Renaissance, meaning literally, new birth, or the revival of anything which has been extinct or in decay. Previous to the Renaissance there had been a tendency to imitate in decoration the Byzantine and Gothic. The revival of Roman and Grecian art was called the Renaissance. Among the ancient styles are included, but as secondary, the Assyrian and Persian styles. There is today a tendency toward their revival.

The Oriental styles are the Persian, (East) Indian, Chinese and Japanese.

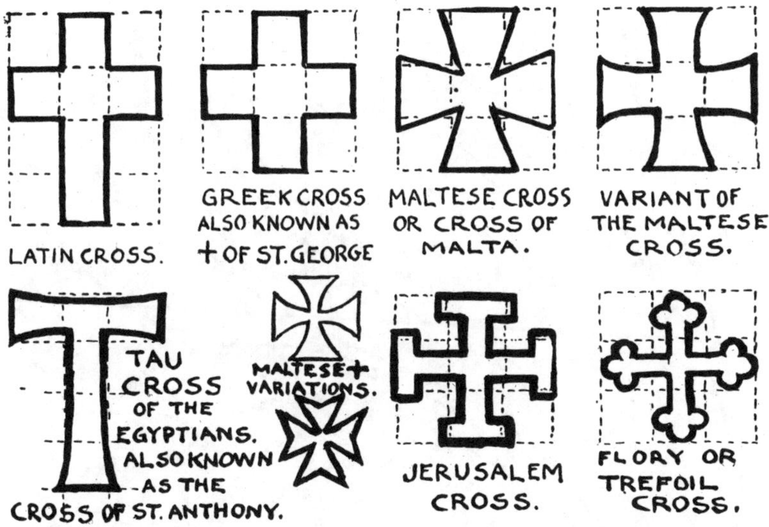

Fig. 18

Graceful lines running in the same general direction is all that is aimed at in Figs. 19, 20 and 21. The shading is to be added, with the same display of quick lines flowing along the same curves.

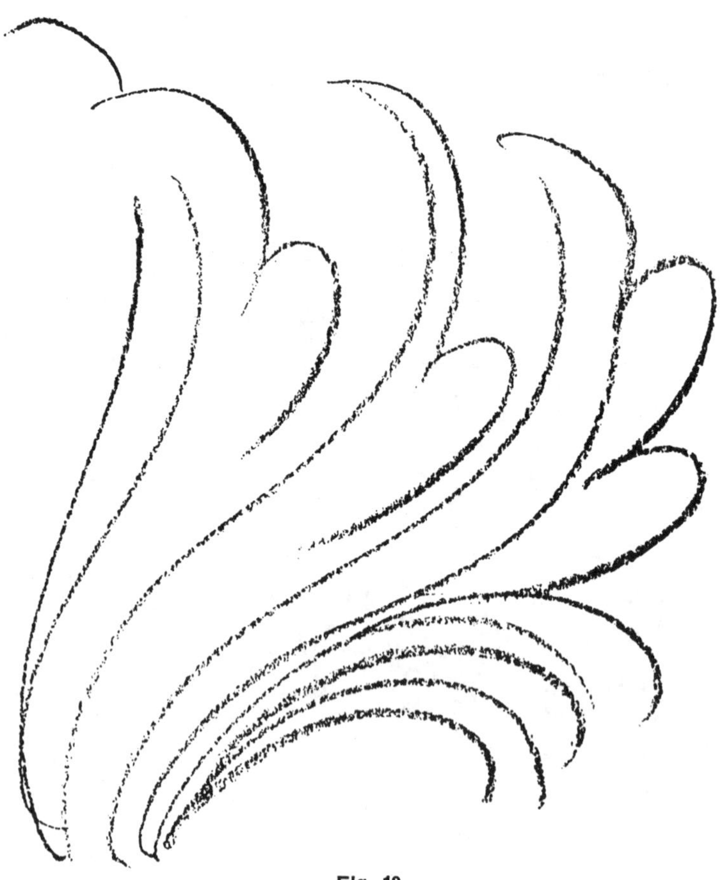

Fig. 19

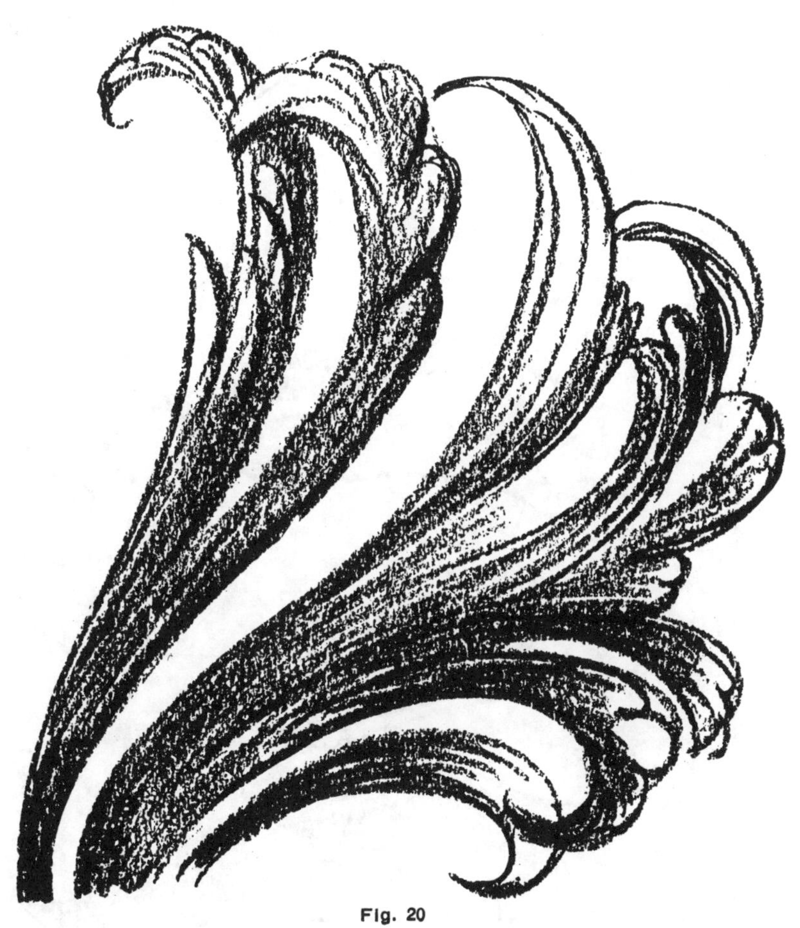

Fig. 20

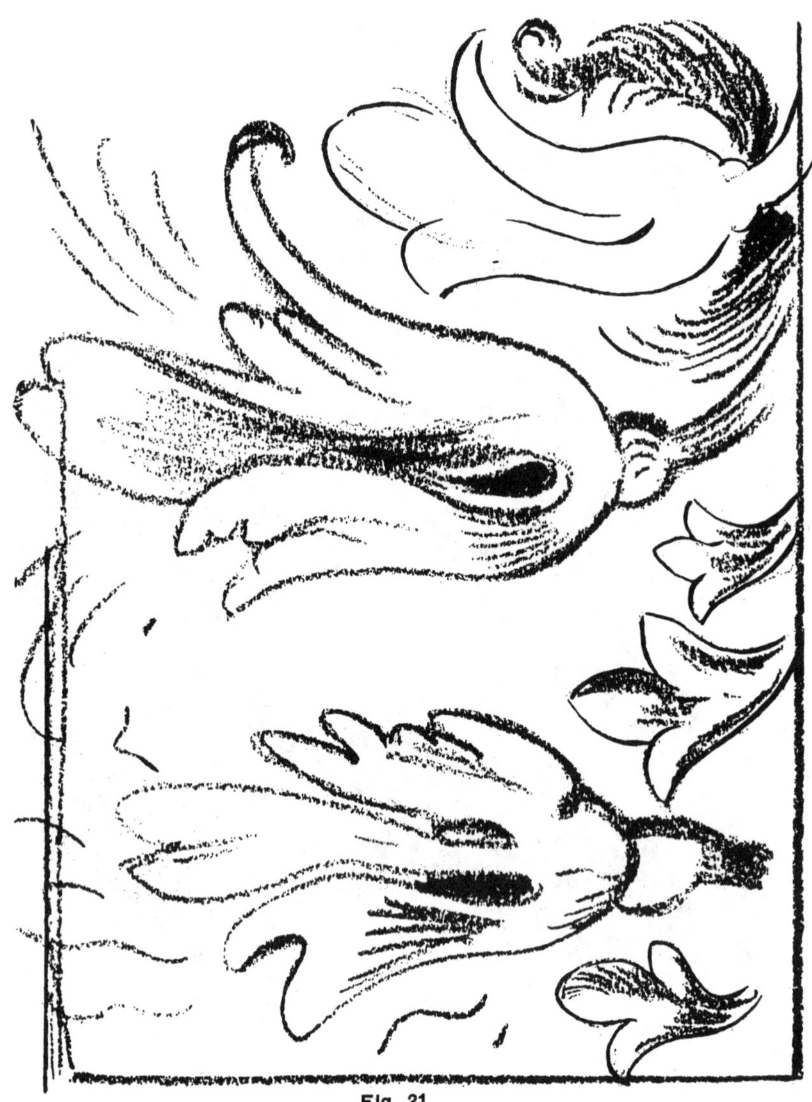

Fig. 21

Wall-Paper and Oil Cloth Designing

The principal requirement in a design for wall-paper or oil cloth is that the edges shall match each other; that is, when the ends and sides are connected the entire design must appear connected and continuous. Therefore, the design must be made so that if it is repeated side by side, and end for end, a continuous, harmonious pattern will be observed.

In the designs shown in Fig. 22 each unit is supposed to be the full width of a strip of wall-paper or oilcloth. They are drawn in conformity with the requirement noted. The height may be greater or less than the width, but the sides and ends must conform to the rule.

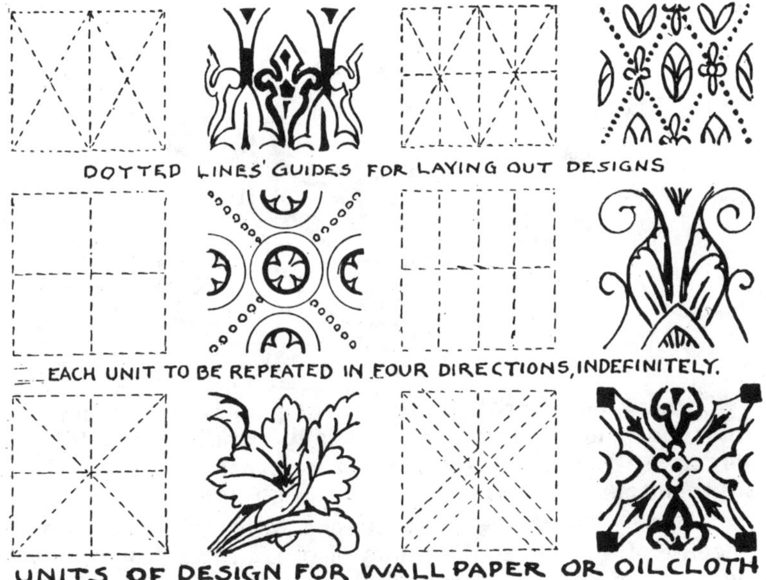

Fig. 22

A Wall-Paper Design

The casual observer would not be apt to guess that the design in Fig. 24 was based on the dotted line units in A, Fig. 23, placed in their regular order, aided by the oblique, horizontal and vertical lines of the diagram. Yet that is the manner in which the design is made. It will be interesting to see how readily the design B may be copied by resorting to the method of duplicating a drawing as shown in the chapter on Triangulation.

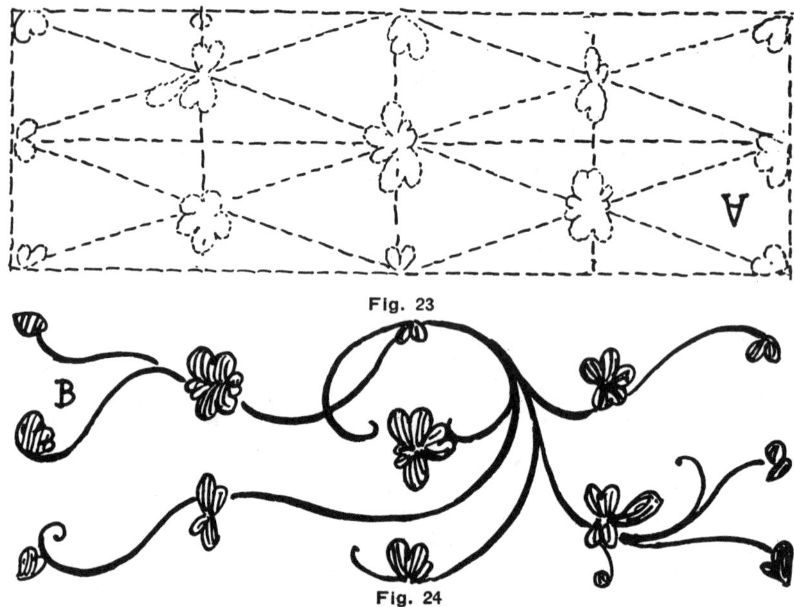

Fig. 23

Fig. 24

Corners and Borders.—In drawing corners and borders, guide lines must be made, especially parallel lines for the borders, so that the design will show evenly and straight, or in proper curves, according to the design used.

Weaving Units.—A good method for practice is to make tracings of various simple units of ornamental design, weaving them by repetition into various compositions, and varying the component parts according to the judgment of the student. These tracings should be preserved for future use in other designs.

Interspersing Units.—The various geometrical and ornamental figures shown may be broken, or separated, by interspersing flowers or units, such as leaves, or almost any of the conventional forms shown in this and other lessons.

Book Covers and Posters

Ornamental Lettering is often desirable, but it should not overshadow the main design of a book cover or poster. On the other hand, it is advisable to ornament the lettering in order to enrich the pictorial aspect of the design.

Posters may have much ornamental detail, and, as in the case of a book cover, the more gracefully the letters are drawn, the better becomes the general effect of the entire combination.

Simple Human Figures, harmoniously inclined, surrounded by a graceful and ornamental design may be added, usually make a pleasing cover. It is necessary, however, to guard against an extravagant use of ornament, which is a common fault.

Designs for Book Covers should at all times avoid complexity, and the style and quality of the embellishment should not detract from the legibility of the lettering or the promi-

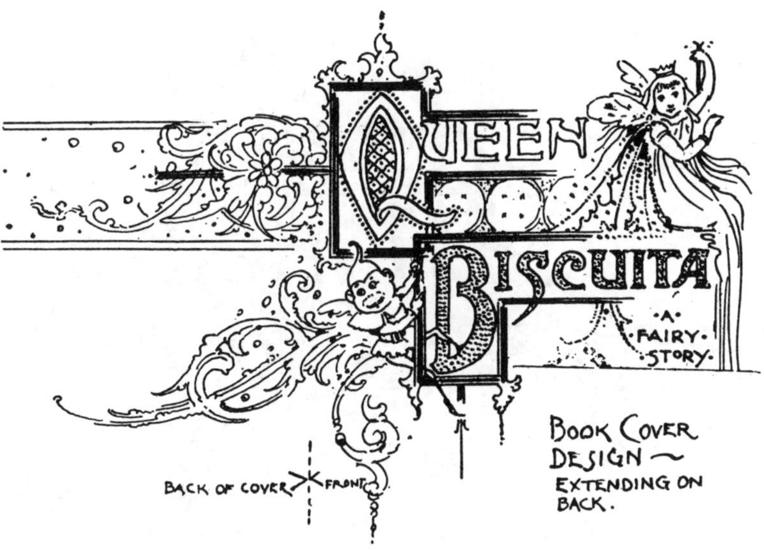

Fig. 25

nence of the main figure or scene introduced into the design, for if this occurs the result will be a bewildering confusion.

Heavy Lines.—In drawing a poster or book cover, especially in the case of the former, let the lines be heavier than in an ordinary drawing. The drawing, completed, should be held off for inspection at a distance greater than would be usual with an ordinary drawing. Little defects that would appear upon a close view will seem to disappear, whereas much that in an ordinary drawing would not appear complex would, in the latter case, seem blurred and inexpressive.

Simplicity is stronger at a distance; multiplicity of line and detail proportionately weaker.

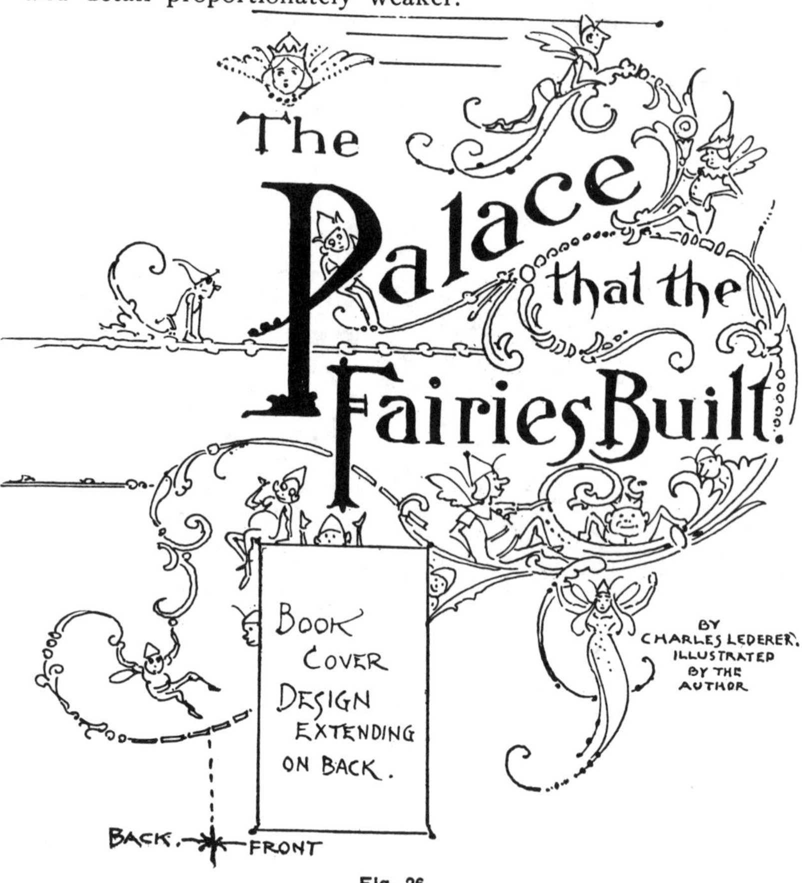

Fig. 26

The comic figures in Figs. 27 and 28 are given importance as a border design simply by being repeated.

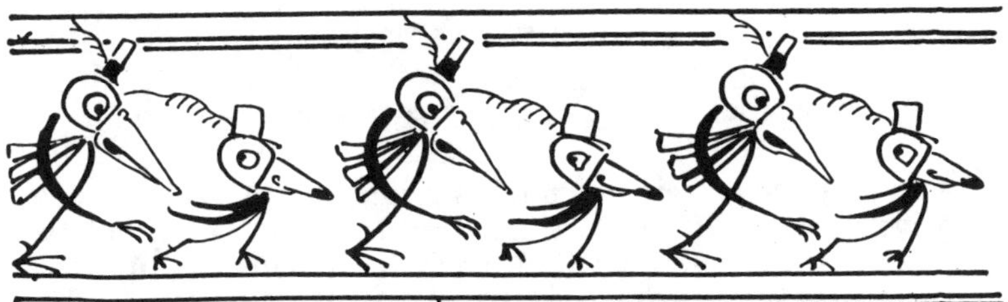

Fig. 27

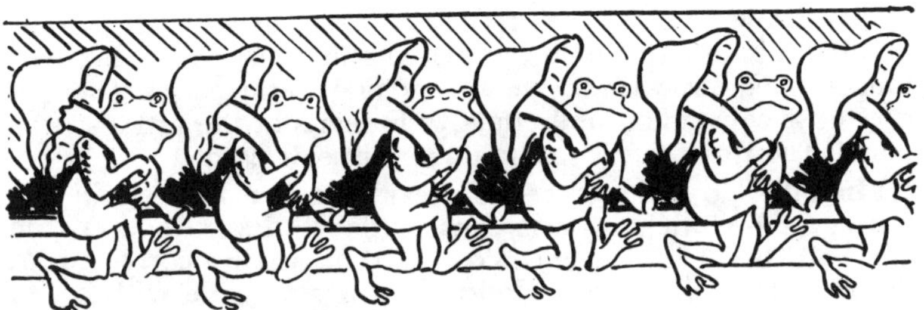

Fig. 28

CHAPTER XXXIII

PEN-AND-INK DRAWING

Pen-and-ink drawing is not, as might be imagined, a comparatively recent form of artistic work, for in the great galleries of Europe one may find many interesting specimens of pen work made by Angelo, Raphael, Durer, Titian and others of the great masters. The manner of handling and style of pen work has changed, however, with modern inventions in the way of reproductive methods. The very spirit of pen work has changed only within a comparatively few years.

Continue Pencil Drawing.—Even after pen-and-ink drawing is taken up, practice with the pencil should be continued. The longer one draws with the pencil and crayon the better. They are the most convenient and effective utensils at the artist's command. Their frequent use should never be discarded.

Inability to make corrections easily in inked lines will discourage the student who is conscientious. Pencil and crayon are valuable because mistakes can be easily corrected at the time they are made. Before a mistake made with a pen can be rectified the ink must be quite dry, and the erasures must be made carefully, especial pains being taken not to disturb or roughen the surface of the paper or cardboard. Erasure may be made with a sharp knife or ink eraser; or the misplaced lines may be hidden or obscured by the use of a glaze of Chinese white.

Outline First With Pencil.—Some teachers advocate drawing with pen-and-ink without the aid of a preliminary sketch with pencil. Writes one such teacher, "Practice drawing these (referring to certain subjects to be drawn) as rapidly as you can, without using the pencil in any way, using ink as a medium, you will be more apt to observe with care the exact character of each touch than if you employed the pencil, whose marks can be so easily erased. This will, in time, give you greater confidence and facility of hand than can be had with either pencil or crayon."

The quoted advice is wrong. The beginner should draw as slowly as possible. The writer is positive in these statements, and he is making them after many years of experience spent almost exclusively in making pen drawings for all sorts of practical purposes.

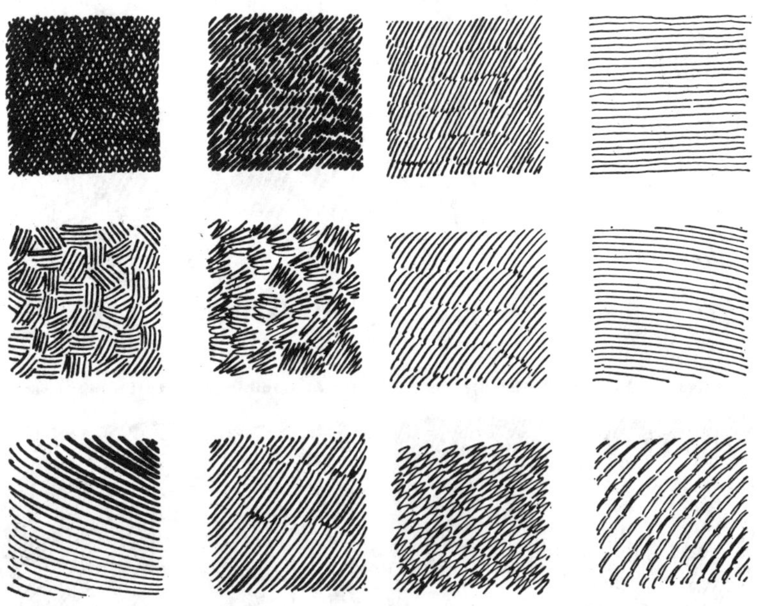

Fig. 1—Practice Lines for Pen-and-Ink **Fig. 2**

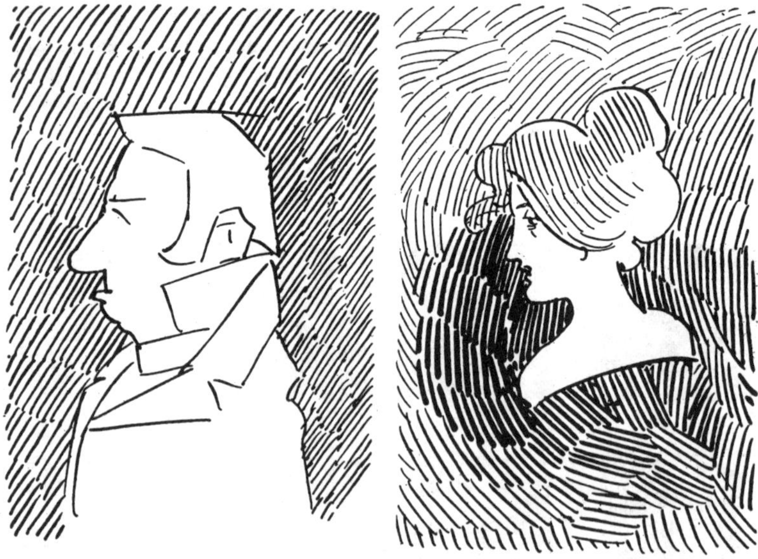

Fig. 3

Fig. 4

Exercises In Which the Elementary Lines Are Combined With Human Faces

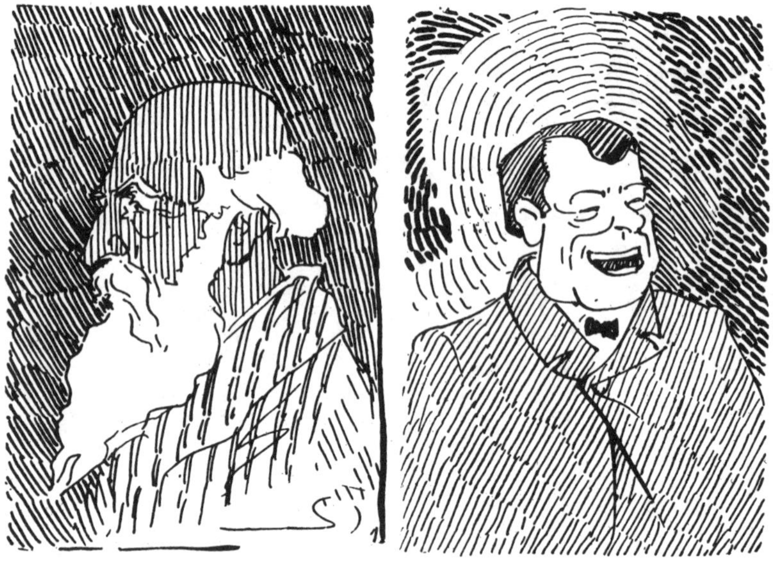

Fig. 5

Fig. 6

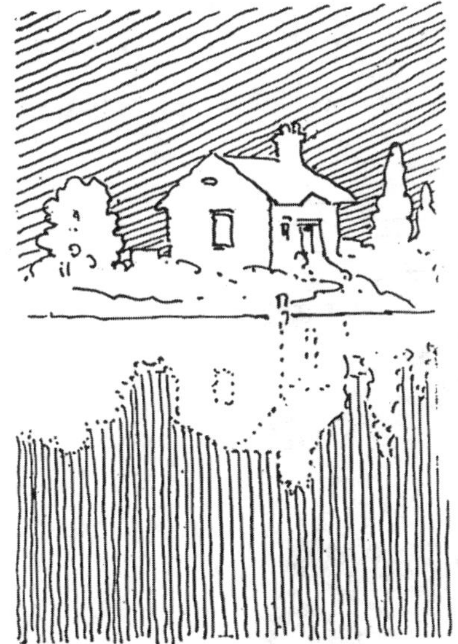

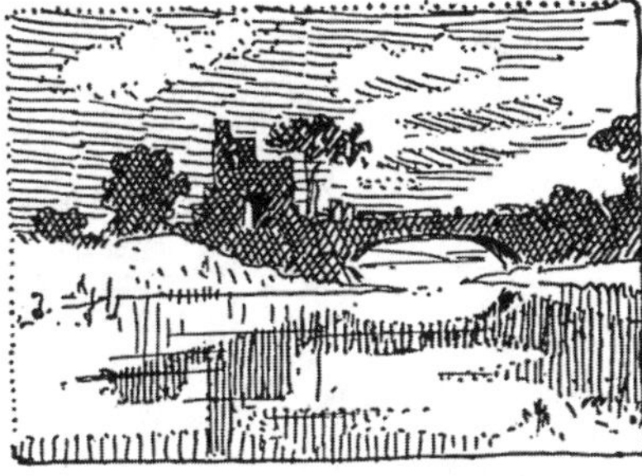

Fig. 8 – Introducing the Elementary Pen Lines Into Scenic Effects

Fig. 7

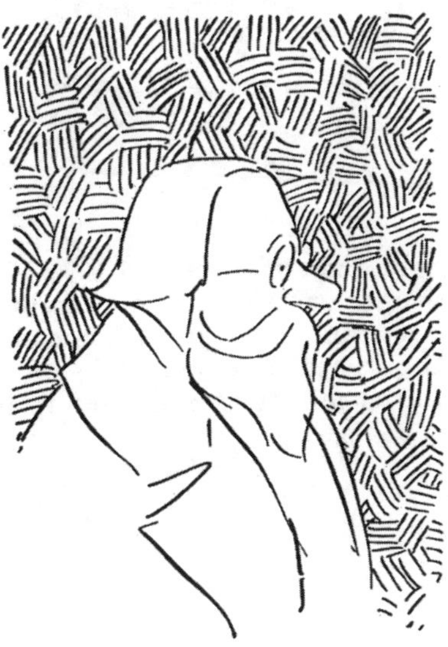

Elementary Line Exercises.—All lines should be drawn on double the scale shown in this work. Lack of space makes great reduction necessary.

Lines should be drawn as heavy as those immediately below.

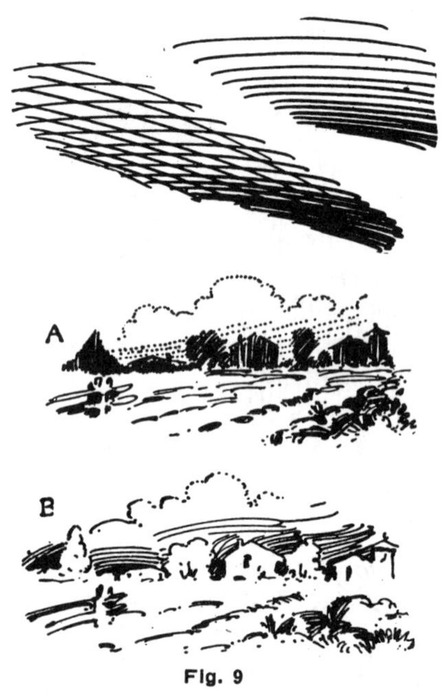

Fig. 9

Contrasting Light Exercise.—A and B in Fig. 9 are further examples of the contrast effected by varying directions of the light. In the former, the sun is somewhere behind the background; in the latter, the sun is behind the spectator. These examples are excellent as exercises in pen and ink.

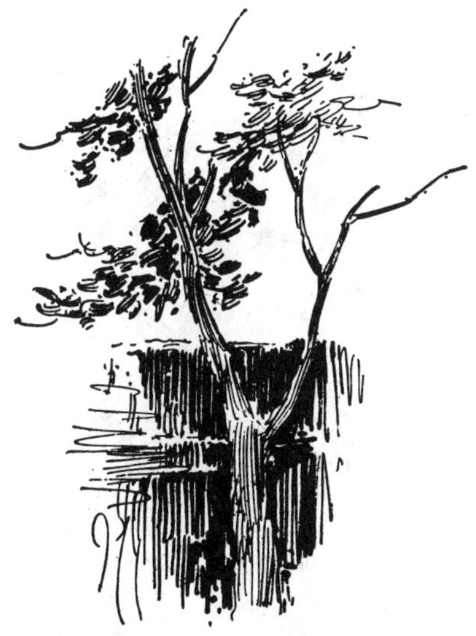

Fig. 10

Fig. 10 is another instance of light and shade contrast. It is intended as a pen exercise. Note the foliage drawn in groups of little parallel lines used to produce the effect of individual leaves. These should be drawn with quick lines.

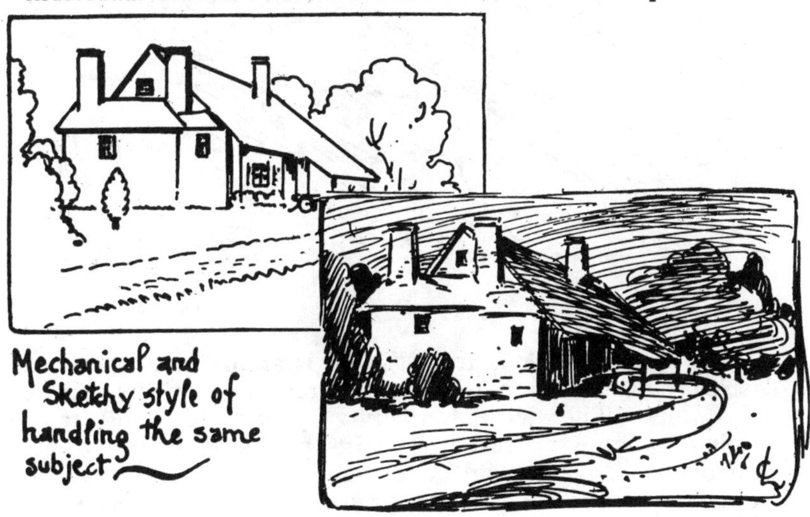

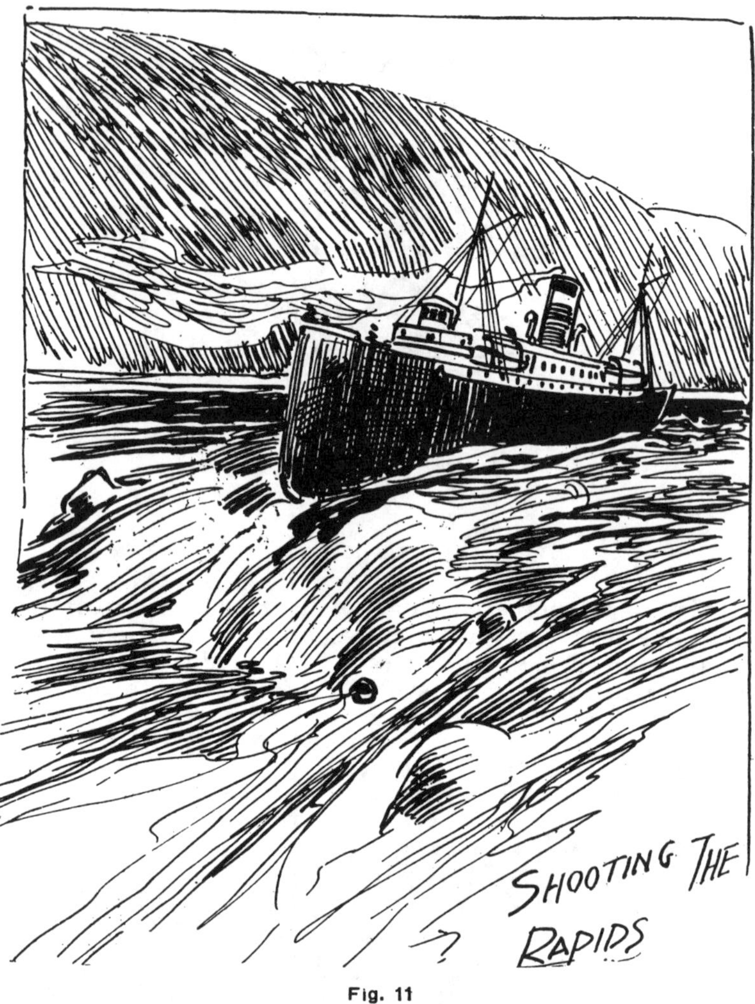

Fig. 11

Exercise in Quick Lines.—Fig. 11 is an instance where the desired effect could hardly be secured without the use of quick lines. The swirling, rushing appearance of the rapid flowing waters is produced by swift strokes of the pen firmly controlled. Make careful pencil sketch of this or something similar and see what you can produce in this effective style.

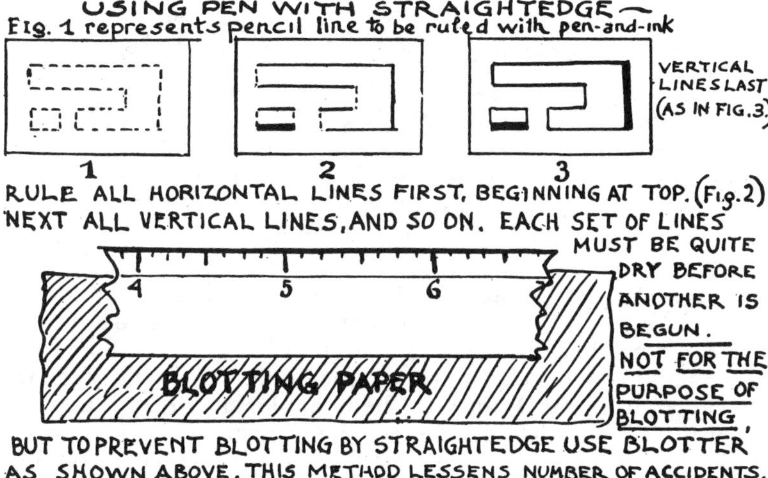

Fig. 12

Wavy Line Exercises.—Practice the pen lines in Figs. 13, 14 and 15; each exercise on paper about four inches square. The lower right-hand copy by means of a stub pen or one blunted by long use.

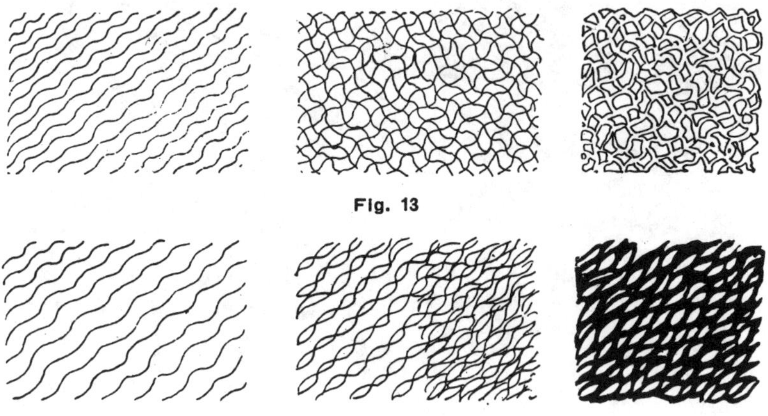

Fig. 13

Fig. 14

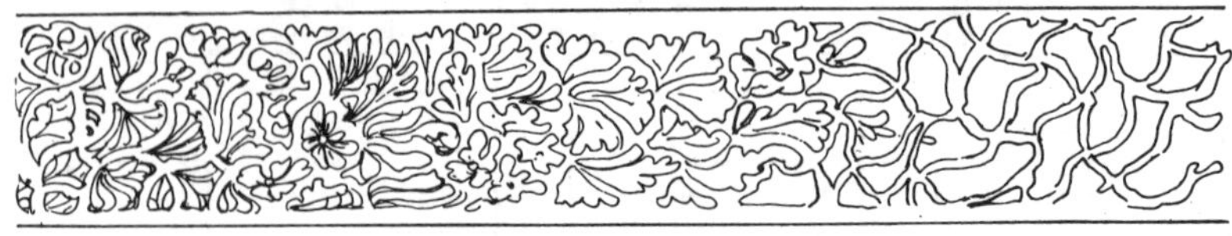

Fig. 15—Waving Line Exercises

Fig. 16 is a greatly reduced reproduction of a crayon sketch. Figs. 17 and 18 are pen drawings of the same subject copied from the original, Fig. 16. In Fig. 17, the head of the old man is treated in very simple style, while in Fig. 18, more detail is added, until in the final sketch, Fig. 19, there is even more light-and-shade effect than in the original drawing. Select a similar subject and make several faint pencil sketches of subject, and finish them with pen and ink, but each succeeding drawing with increasing intricacy.

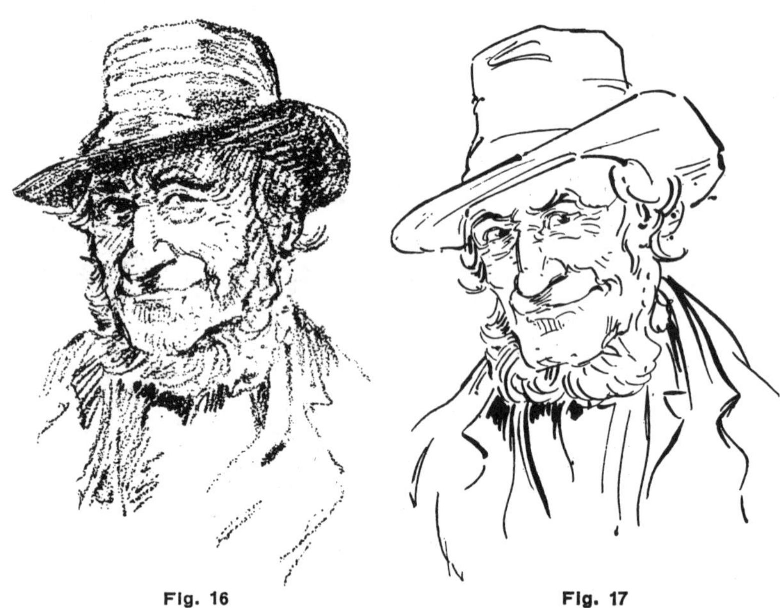

Fig. 16 Fig. 17

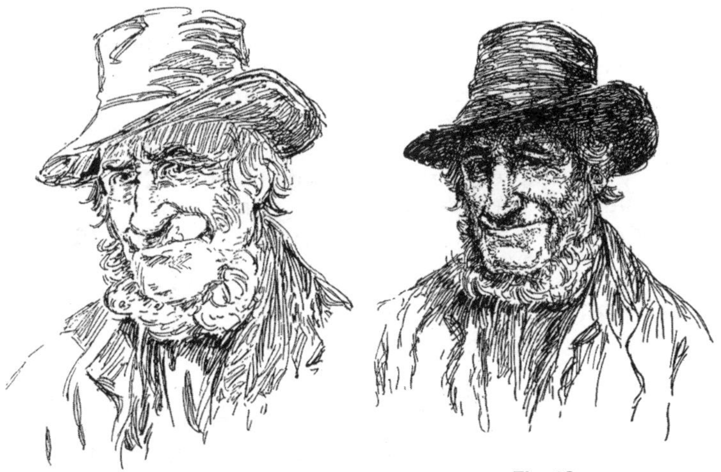

Fig. 18 Fig. 19

Imitating Pencil With Pen Lines

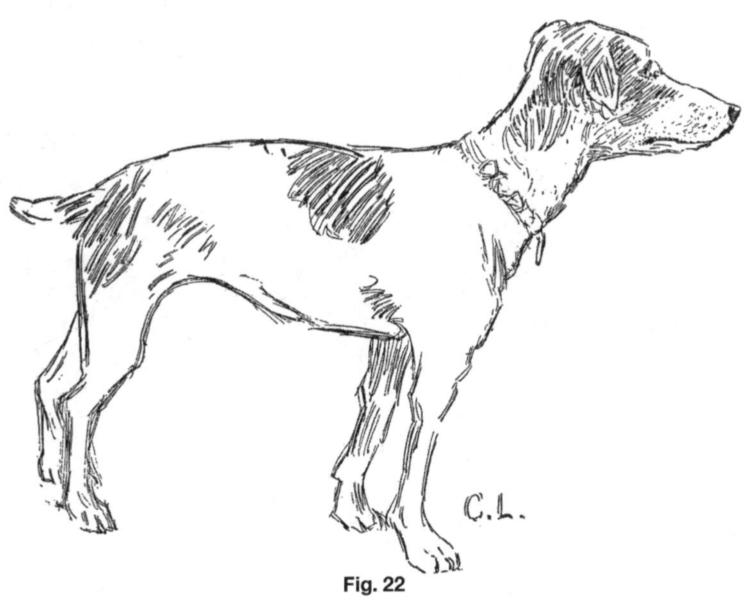

Fig. 22

Figs. 22 and 23 are pen-and-ink exercises, similar to Figs. 25 and 26, except that the drawings are not transferred, the pen drawings being made directly on the linen paper on which the soft pencil sketches were made.

In Fig. 22, the dog is drawn by means of two or more nearly parallel lines (and occasional closely placed dots) to represent the single broad lines made by the soft pencil. The pencil lines are then erased, leaving the peculiarly soft and pleasing effect shown. In this exercise it is advisable to use a new, finely pointed pen. In Figs. 23 and 24 the drawings are started the same as in Fig. 22, except that closely placed and carefully modulated dots are used to represent the pencil lines. When finished, erase the pencil lines. The faces

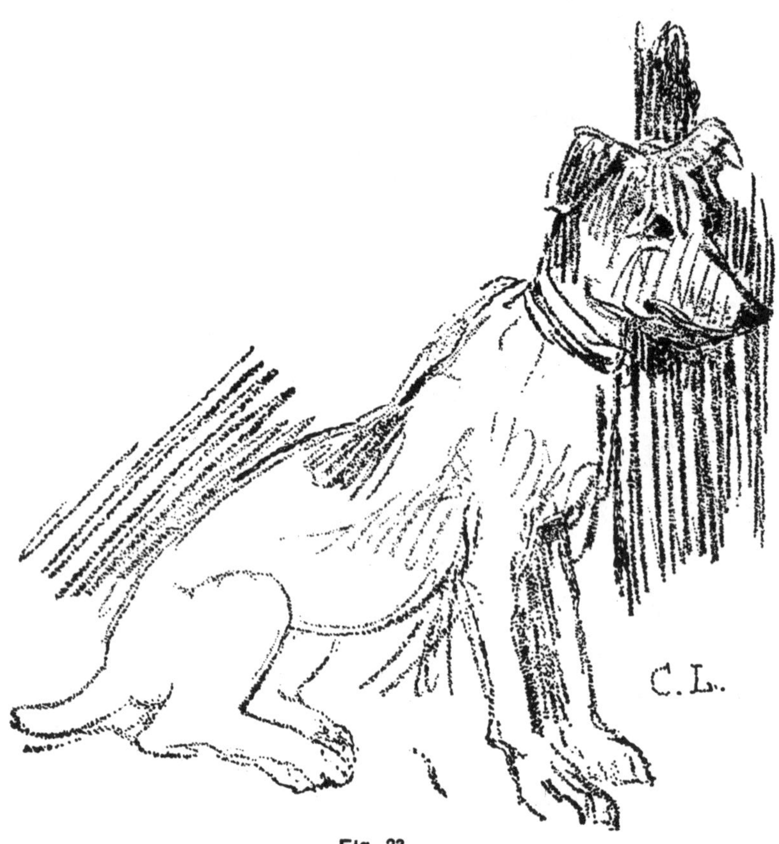

Fig. 23

in the lower part of Fig. 25 are stippled as in Fig 23. The result in each case is an effect similar to the original drawing. Drawings thus made are valuable chiefly for their permanence and adaptability in reproduction for printing purposes.

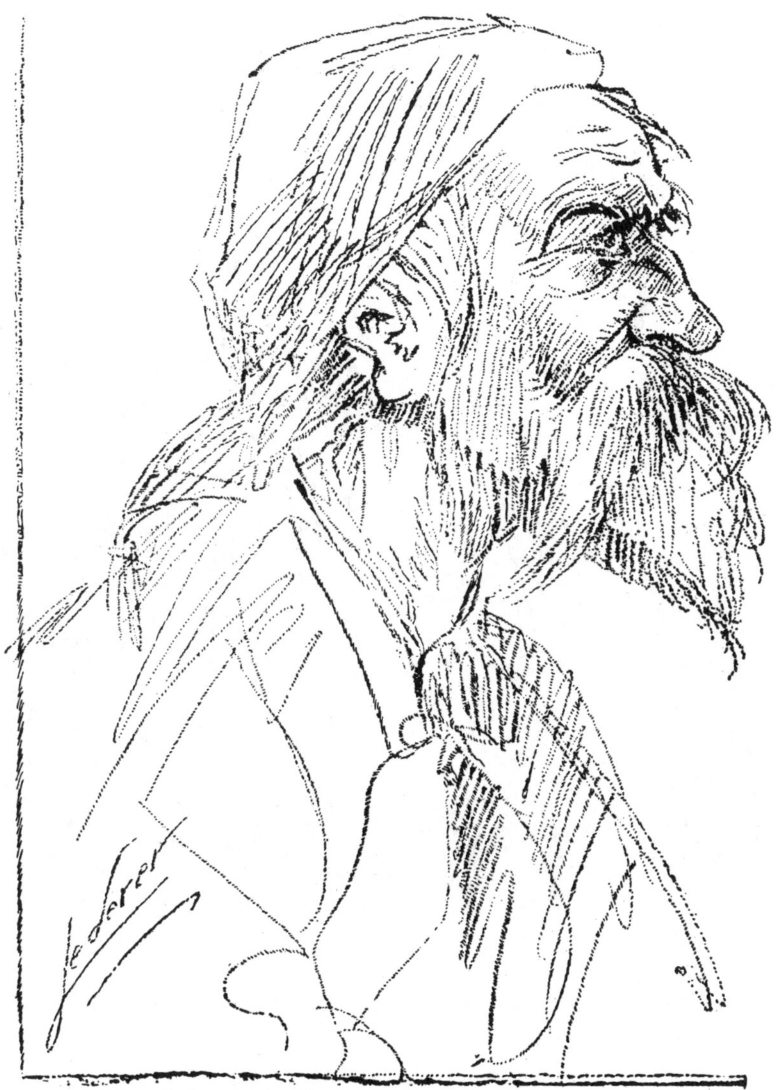

Fig. 24—Drawn by the Same Means as the Dog, Fig. 23

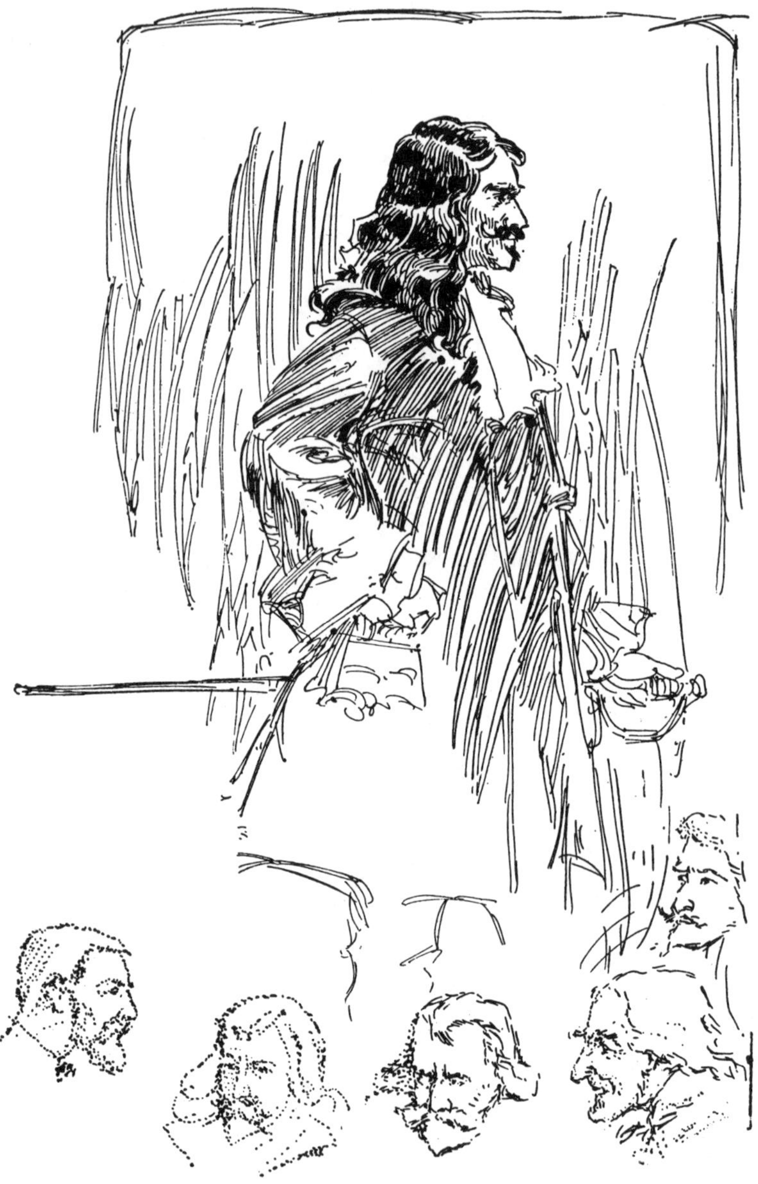

Fig. 25—The Principal Figure Drawn by the Same Means as the Dog, Fig. 23

Exercises in Ornamental Pen Drawing, shown in Figs. B and E (Figs. 26 and 27), are much less complex than would appear at first glance. The method of producing these examples of confusion in decorative design is as follows:

Make a drawing on thin, rough, linen paper of the motif in Fig. A. Then transfer in group form—one transfer over the other.

The pencil transfers will appear as at B, only the spaces will be dark. Then outline with ink but *do not cross the dark* spaces. When the ink is dry erase the pencil lines and the design will appear as in B.

As a preliminary exercise to the design, Fig. E, make a pencil drawing of the unit Fig. C and outline with ink. Erase pencil lines and the unit design D will appear. The design E is a repetition of the unit D, the only difference being that when the pencil transfers from C are made care must be taken not to cross with pen lines any of the dark transfer lines.

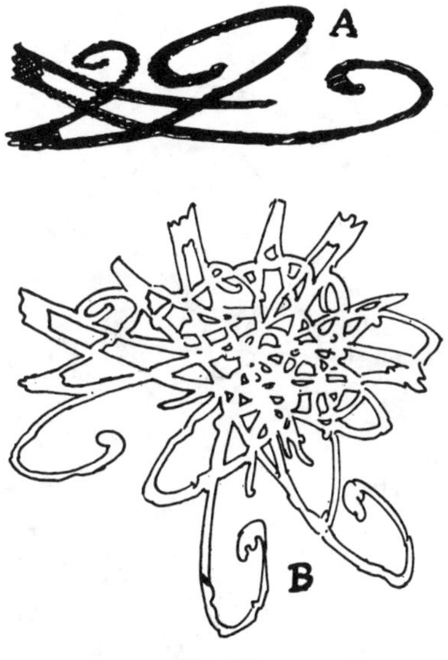

Fig. 26

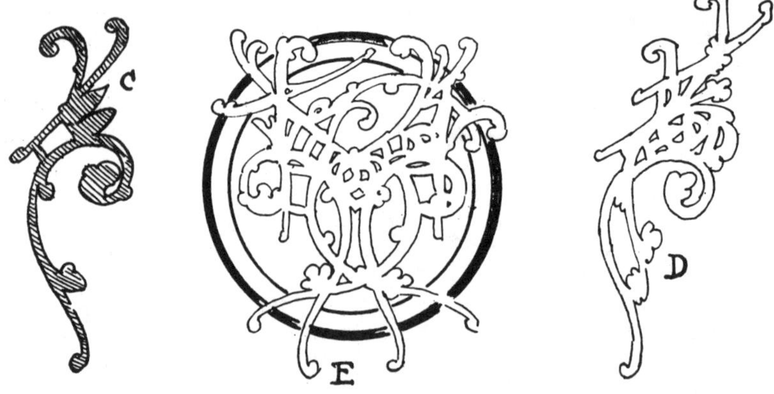

Fig. 27

The complicated design at the right is an example of what can be done with the cardboard curve shown on page 263.

The outlines of the cardboard curve, as shown on that page and reversed, were repeated several times with faint outlines. The outlines were then strengthened and accentuated until the accompanying design was developed. The operation is quite simple and quickly done.

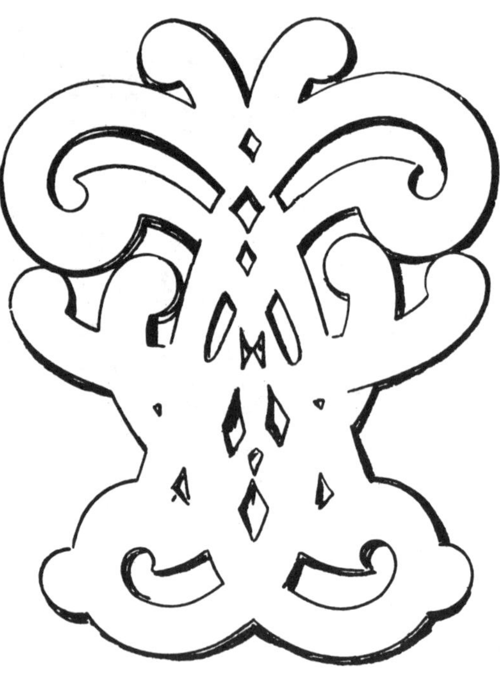

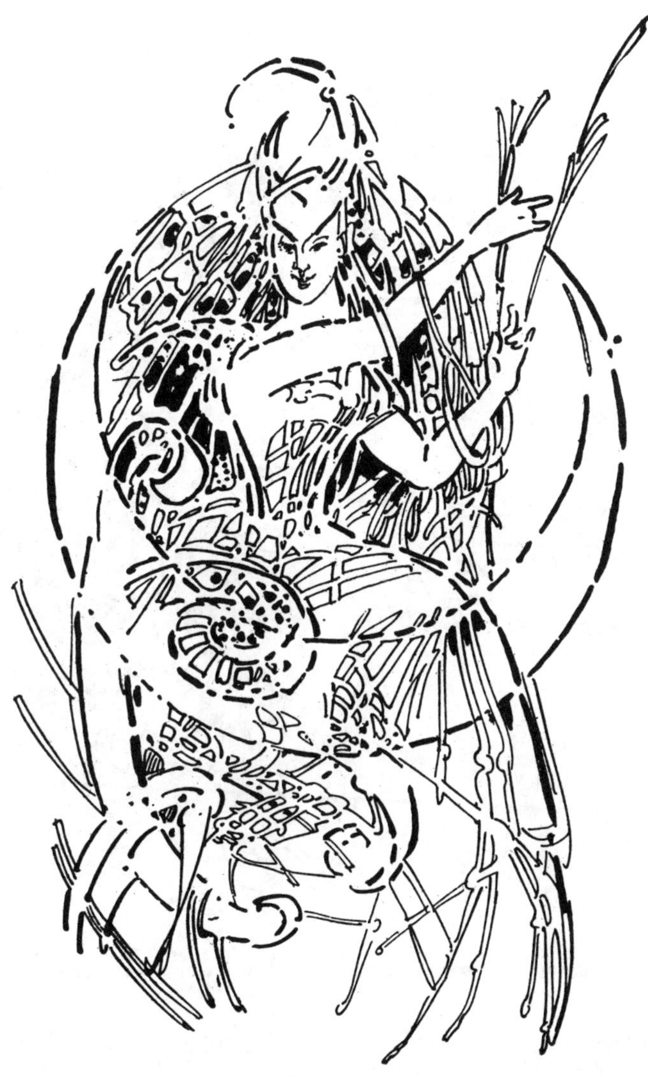

Fig. 28

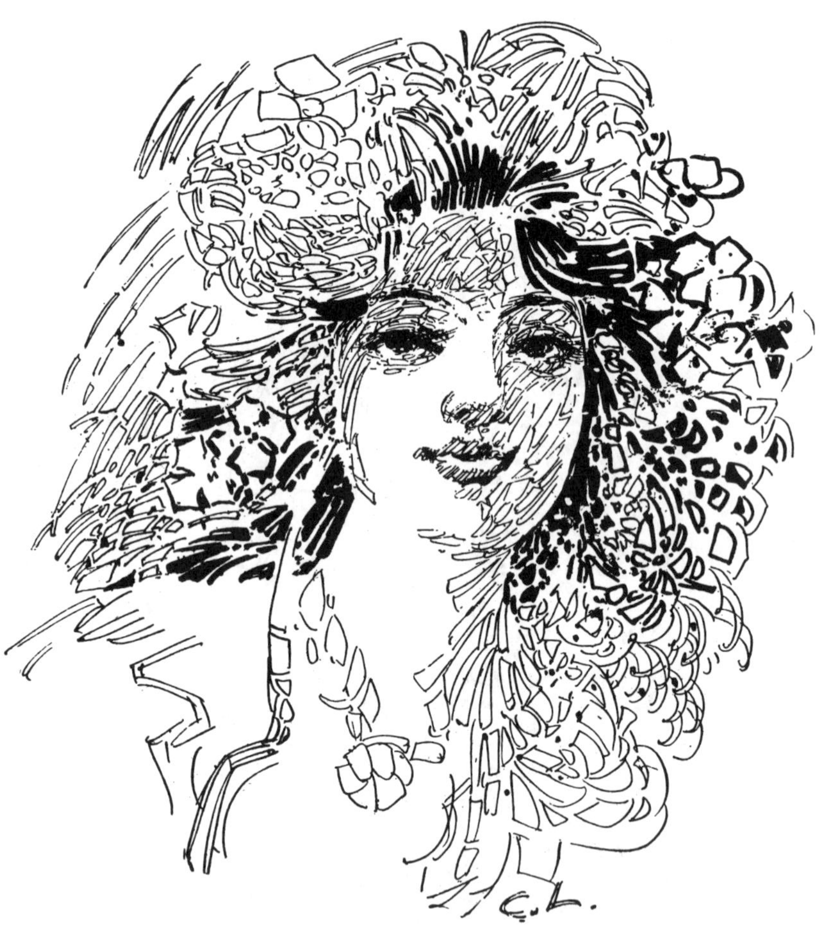

Fig. 29 is a combination of the human face and figure, coupled with decorative design, all executed according to preceding instructions.

Notes.—For subjects suitable for rendering in pen-and-ink see pages 48, 49, 50, 51, 52, 53, 54, 62, 66, 73, 77, 78, 81, 87, 88, 89, 90, 95, 99, 102, 111, 113, 115, 117, 119, 120, 124, 125, 126, 135, 136, 141, 141, 146, 150 to 157, 159, 160, 163, 164, 186, 190, all in chapter XXVII, pp. 222, 225, all in chapters XXIX, XXX, XXXI, XXXII, XXXIV.

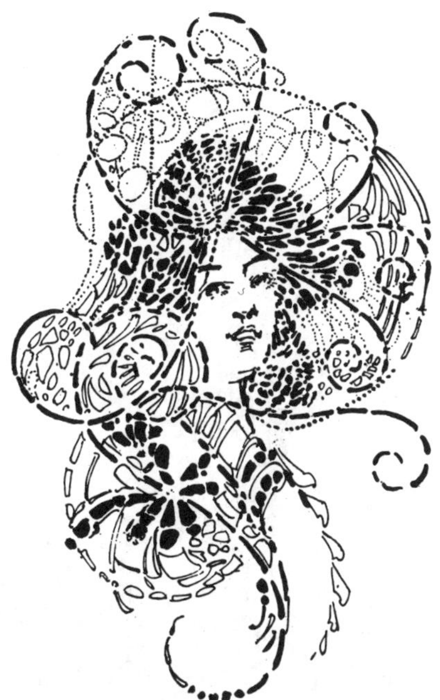

Fig. 30—This drawing is a more difficult example of the method followed in Figs. 26 and 27. The drawing is made with pencil on firm linen paper and then completed in the manner shown in Fig. 27. The accentuation, as shown by the solid black lines, may be made according to the artistic taste of the draftsman.

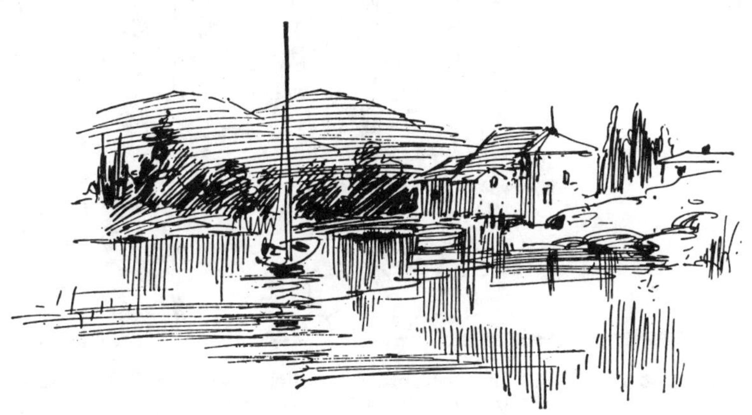

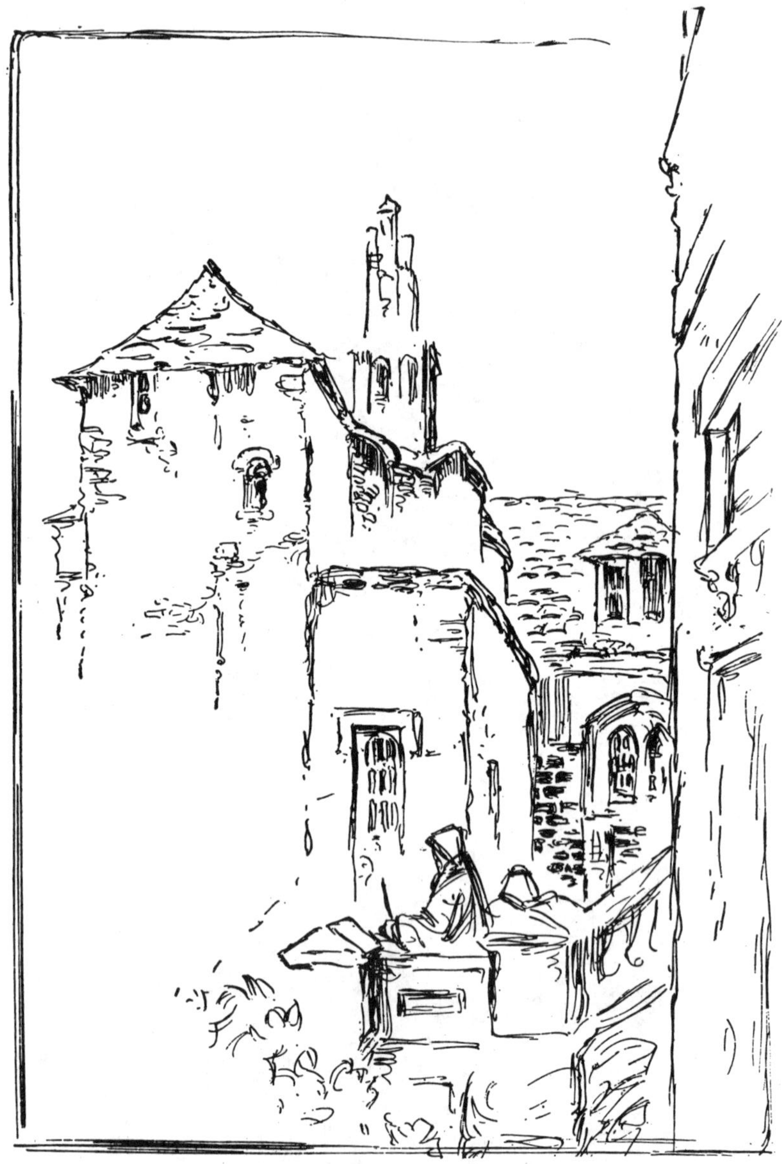

Fig. 31—Shows About the Amount of Penciling Necessary Before Beginning a Pen-and-Ink Sketch Such as Is Shown in Fig. 32

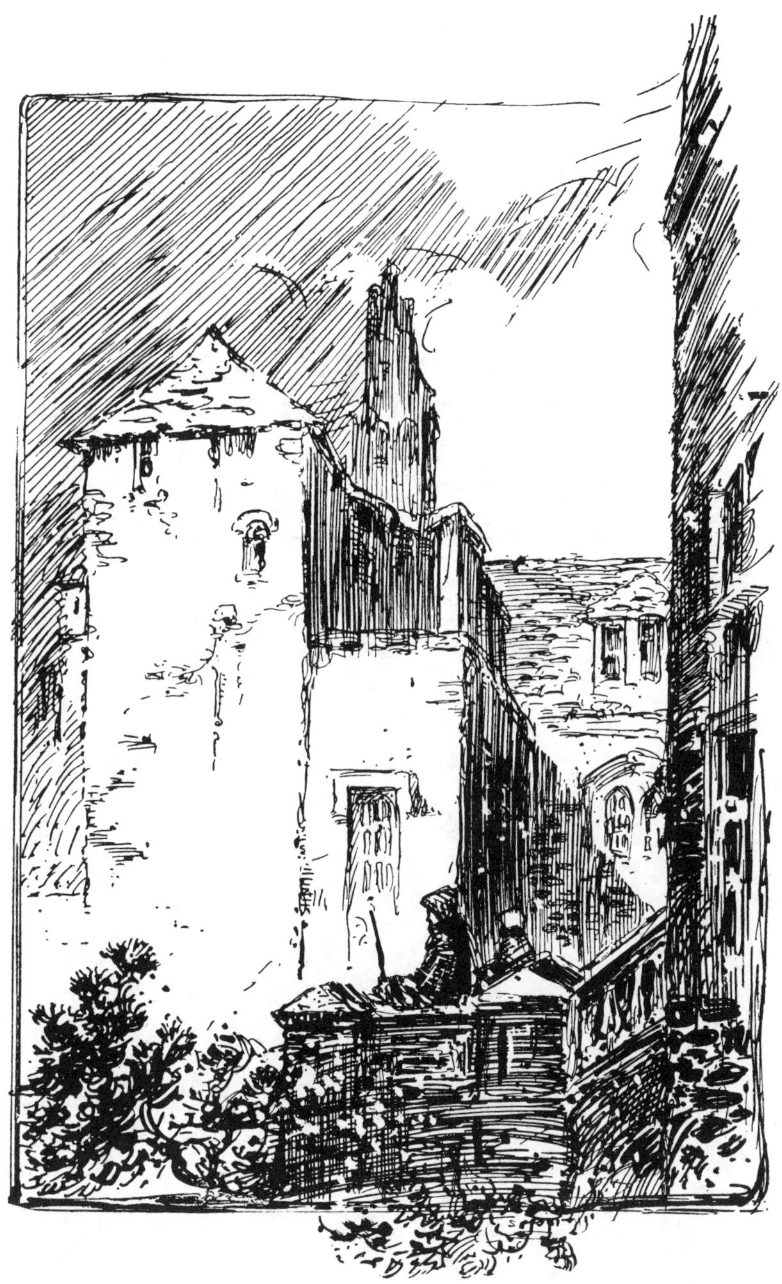

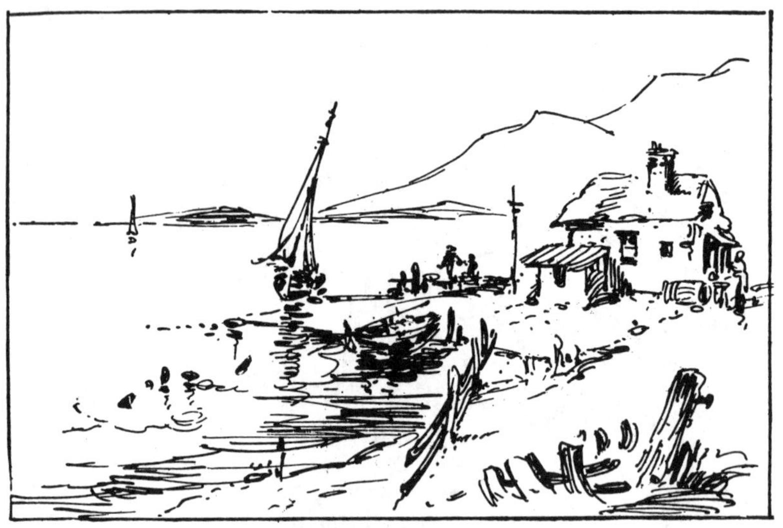

CHAPTER XXXIV

WORKING DRAWINGS

Working drawings are those from which objects can be constructed. They are also, and properly, called mechanical drawings, industrial drawings and construction drawings. They are necessary to guide the workman in nearly every branch of industry. A working drawing is made of two or more geometric views of the object. A geometric drawing shows an object in its simplest form; that is, having length or width, or showing but one face of the object. This can be represented on a flat surface by one drawing; then another must be made to represent the face, showing the thickness of the solid, and so on, until as many views have been made as there are dissimilar faces.

The Real Shape of the Surface cannot always be shown in these drawings, but simply the contour or outline when the surface is curved or oblique. The real shape, however, is readily understood by the position of the several views and the lines connecting them. When we know that certain angles and edges come in contact, we are enabled to understand the form that will result. Certain conventional lines are used in working drawings, and the knowledge of their use is necessary.

List of the Lines and Explanations.—Dotted lines connect different parts of different views that are in contact in the object.

Dot-and-dash lines are center lines, sometimes called construction lines. They are used when the object has a curved surface or is difficult to illustrate.

Dash lines represent invisible edges. Complete lines represent visible edges of surfaces.

In making working drawings the top view is usually placed directly over or under the front view, with corresponding points opposite. When more than two views are necessary, the side views are placed beside the front or upright, with the corresponding points exactly opposite.

Exercises in the Three Dimensions

Dimensions of a Line, which is known by its length.

Show, in a drawing, the length of a line twelve inches long, drawn to the scale of three inches to the foot (3=1); that is to say, each actual foot to be represented by three inches on the drawing, and every actual inch by a quarter of an inch on the drawing.

Dimensions of a Surface, which are known by its length and breadth.

Show, in a drawing, the length and breadth of a sheet of paper twelve inches long and six inches wide; i. e., 12″x6″. Scale, three inches to the foot; i. e., 3″=1′.

Dimensions of a Solid, the longest dimension being known by its length, the next longest by its breadth, while its shortest is known by its thickness.

Show, in a drawing, the length, breadth and thickness of a board 12x6. Scale, 3″=1′.

Exercises in Working Drawings.—Make working drawings of simple articles of furniture, like tables, chairs, bookshelves, etc. The measurements and views should be so plain that a workman would form a clear idea of the article and be able to construct one from the drawing.

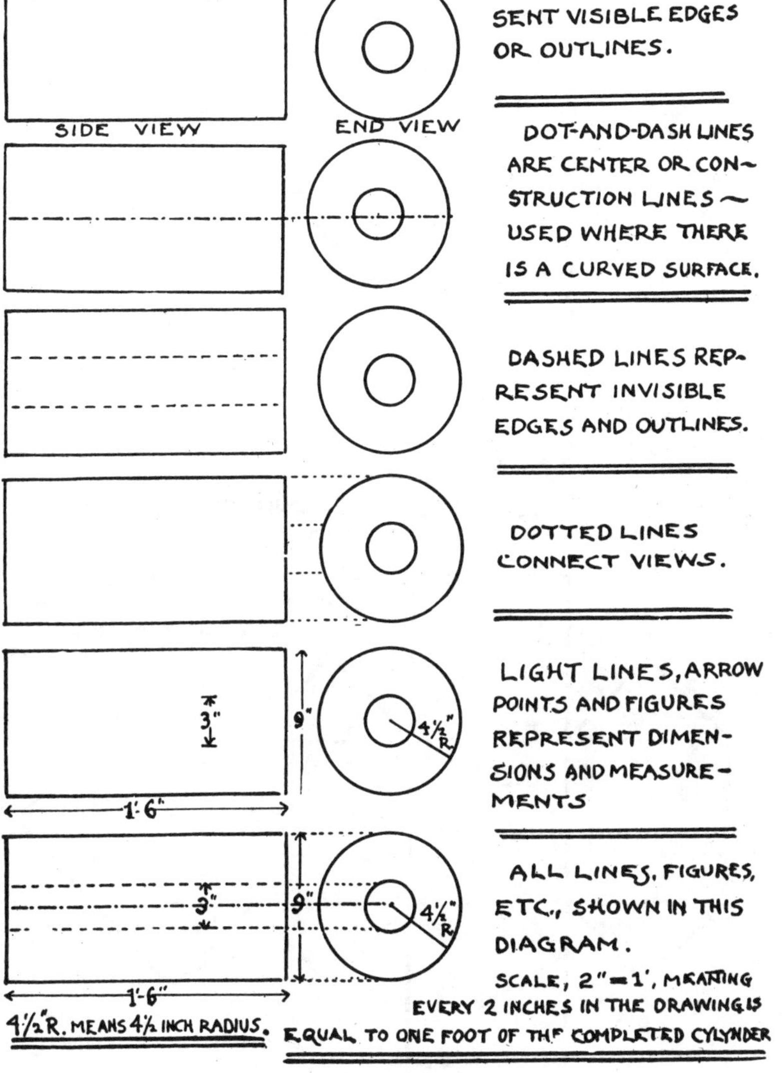
LINES, ETC., USED IN WORKING DRAWING OF HOLLOW CYLINDER.
SIDE VIEW
END VIEW
FULL LINES REPRESENT VISIBLE EDGES OR OUTLINES.
DOT-AND-DASH LINES ARE CENTER OR CONSTRUCTION LINES — USED WHERE THERE IS A CURVED SURFACE.
DASHED LINES REPRESENT INVISIBLE EDGES AND OUTLINES.
DOTTED LINES CONNECT VIEWS.
3"
9"
4½" R.
1'6"
LIGHT LINES, ARROW POINTS AND FIGURES REPRESENT DIMENSIONS AND MEASUREMENTS
ALL LINES, FIGURES, ETC., SHOWN IN THIS DIAGRAM.
SCALE, 2" = 1', MEANING EVERY 2 INCHES IN THE DRAWING IS EQUAL TO ONE FOOT OF THE COMPLETED CYLYNDER
4½" R. MEANS 4½ INCH RADIUS.

Fig. 1

Working drawings take the place of lengthy explanation, either written or oral. It is by such means that the dimensions are shown, dimension being an extent in any one direction,

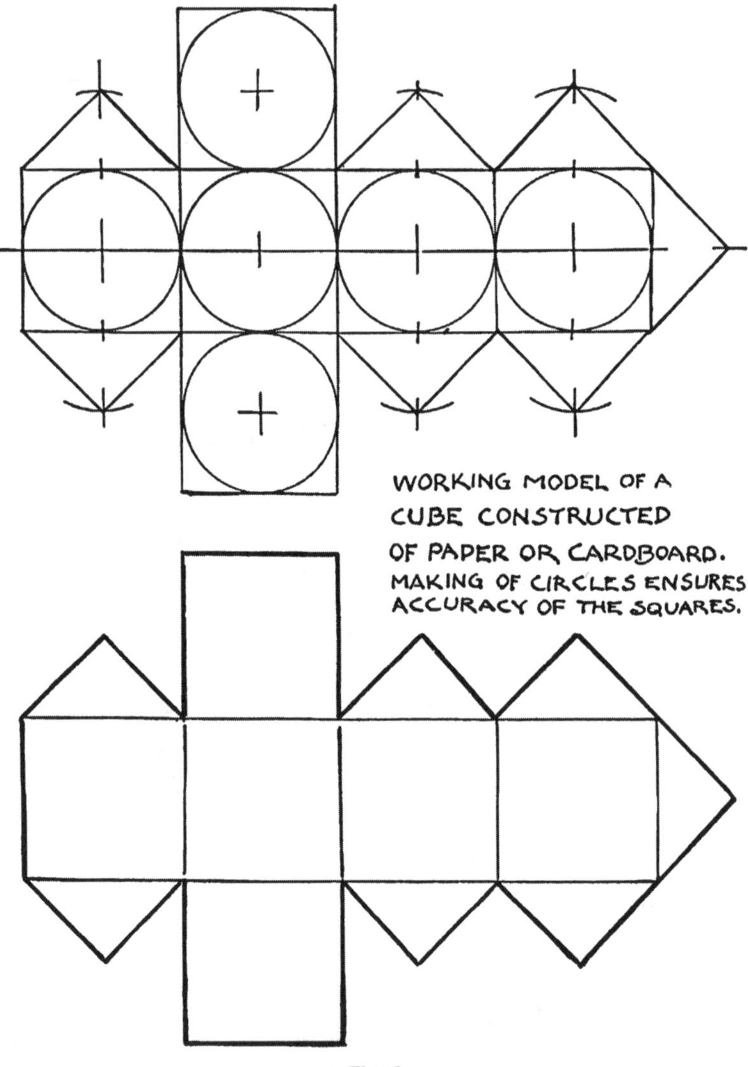

Fig. 2

and are three in number, length, breadth and thickness. These dimensions apply only to solids and not to hollow objects. They apply regardless to position.

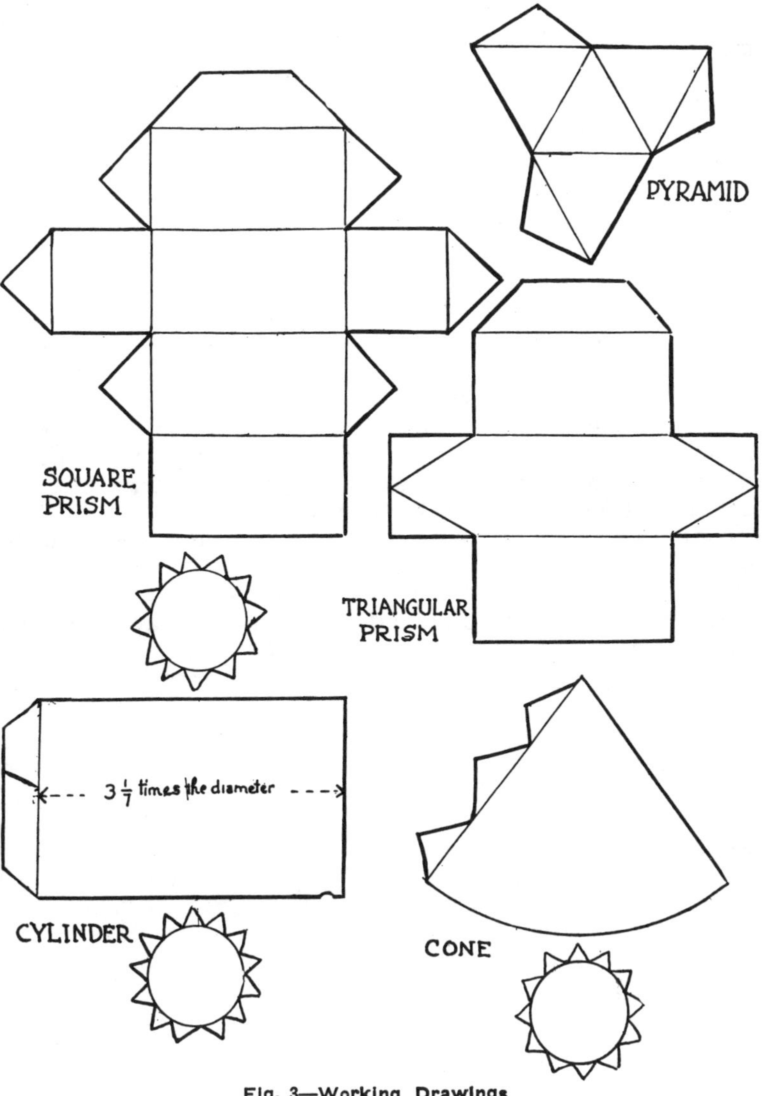

Fig. 3—Working Drawings

Lines, Etc., Used in Working Drawings

Working drawings show only the outlines of the object. The real shape is to be judged by the positions of the separate views and the lines connecting them. These lines tell us that certain angles, edges, and surfaces come in contact. By these means, we understand the form that will result.

The lines used arbitrarily define the things they represent. Besides the lines, certain characters are used as abbreviations, as for instance, in place of "feet" and "inches," ′ represents feet and ″ represents inches. The diagram on page 307 contains the lines used in industrial drawing.

Working Drawing of a Cube

The upper drawing on page 308 shows how a drawing is laid out from which to construct a cube. In the lower drawing the result is shown. The heavy lines only are the outlines, the fine lines indicate where the cardboard or paper is to be bent, and the triangles are the parts to be pasted.

First draw the central horizontal line; then the four circles in a row. Then draw two horizontal lines above and below the circles. Next, draw the short center lines intersecting the horizontals, including the short lines beyond, above and below. Now draw the perpendicular lines that form the cube, and the oblique lines. To establish the extent of the latter, describe segments of circles with the same radius as the others at the points of contact of horizontal and perpendicular lines with the circles.

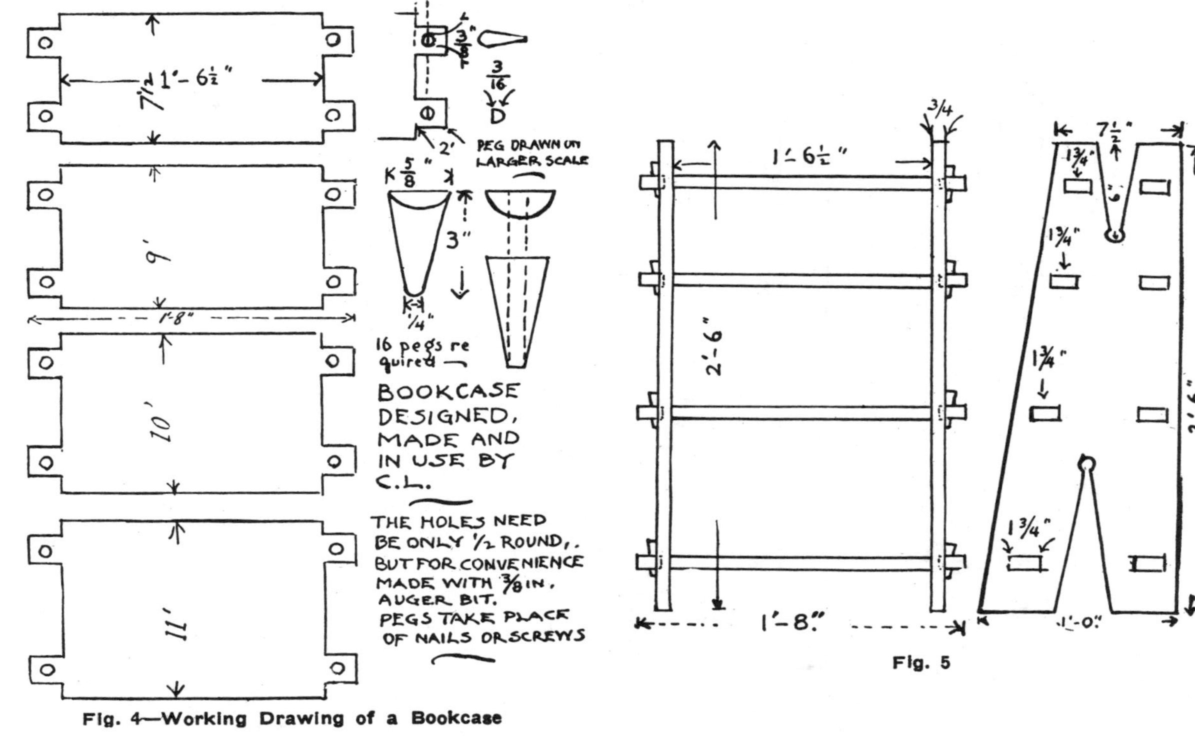

Fig. 4—Working Drawing of a Bookcase

Fig. 5

UNDER
SIDE
OF
TABORETTE
10"
1'-7½"
7/8"
8"
2"
10½"
1'-7"
3½"
1'
A
WORKING
DRAWING
OF
A
TABORETTE
A - WOODEN
PLUGS TO
HIDE SCREW-
HEADS

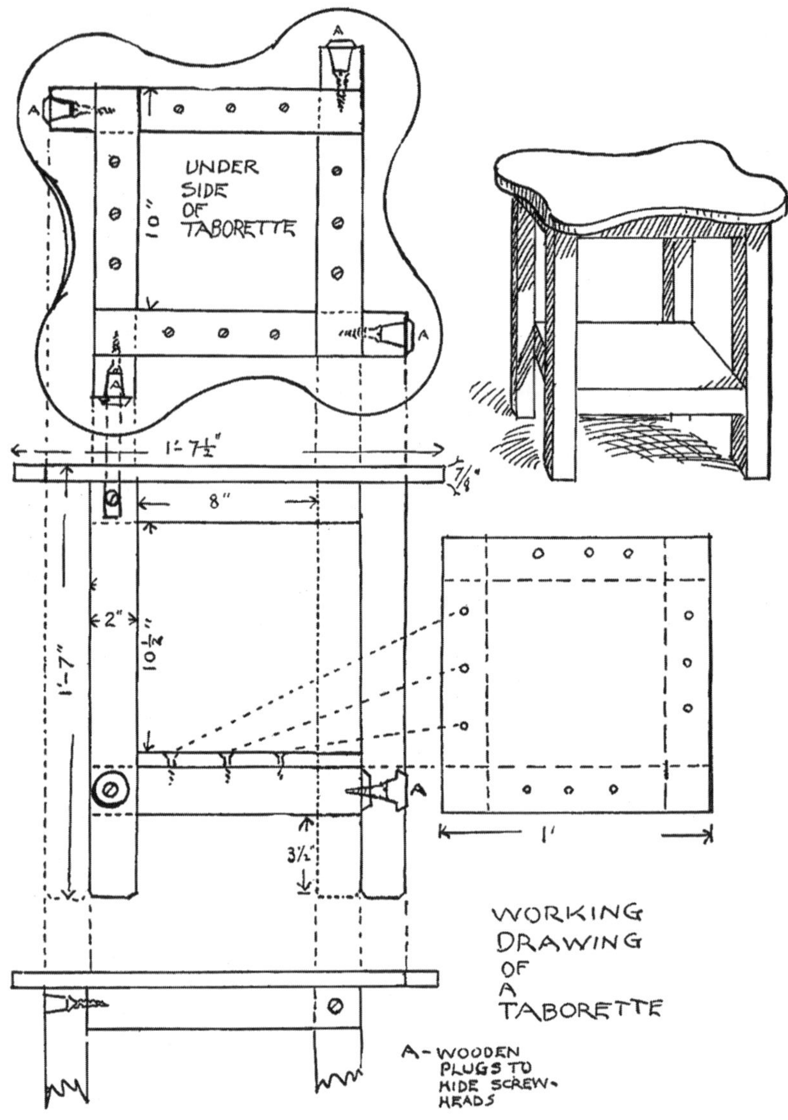

Fig. 6

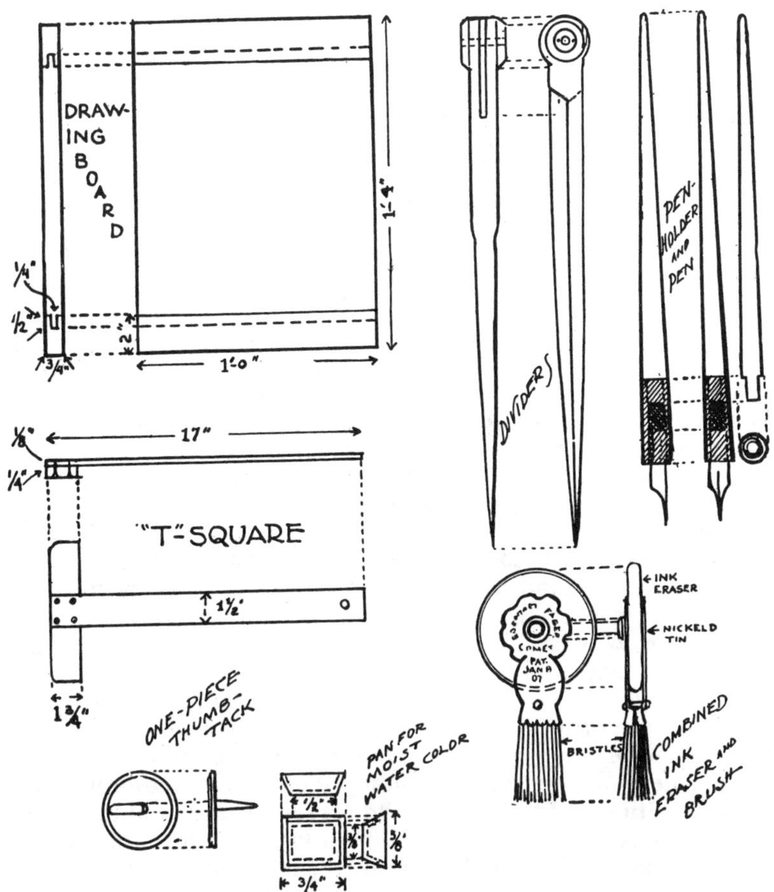

Fig. 7—Working Drawing

For exercise, make working drawings of a table, a chair, a music stand, etc.

Notes.—Subjects in this book suitable for working drawings: slate, p. 26; frame, p. 20; top, p. 38; vase, p. 77; stand and board, p. 172; boxes and cylinders, p. 225; candlestick, p. 235.

CHAPTER XXXV

WATER COLOR

Some teachers induce the belief that painting in oils or water color can be achieved without first having to learn to draw. This is about as absurd as if one were to study electrical engineering without first knowing the difference between a volt and an ampere. Painting cannot be separated from drawing. Painting is simply the art of drawing in color. Without understanding the elementary principles of drawing, color work will always show errors to the educated eye, if not to that of the untrained pupil. The study of color is a branch of drawing by itself and should not be considered separately.

Nature is a great teacher, but many of her rules are concealed and not readily found. To know some of her laws in advance will make instruction very much easier. Certain fixed rules, once memorized, will enable one to see nature with eyes of intelligence. Few errors of an artistic nature are greater than those made by the ambitious, but untrained, student of art, who goes to nature direct to solve the mysteries of her color scheme. It requires more than superficial observation to enable one to grasp the problem of harmonious color combinations and contrasts. Color intuition and perception often is innate, but it must be cultivated before one can approach an imitation of the subtleties of the tints and gradations that nature's pallette shows.

"If I only knew how to mix colors, I know I could paint," wails the tyro.

Yet mixing the colors is the easiest part after all. The great thing is the application. However, the "knowing how to mix them" should be learned first. Nature may inspire artistic feeling which is the impetus of true genius, but she cannot instill within the mind of the untutored that which is in itself a science almost separate and distinct. A knowledge of the rudiments of this science is needed even in the simplest work; without it, the time taken up in the exercise of painting is utterly lost.

The A, B, C of Color may be memorized readily, but it must be borne in mind that regular formulas for mixing pigments cannot be given as one would name the exact quantities in a medical prescription or the proportions in a recipe for making a salad. Only by practical operation of the brief instructions that are given in these pages will the student gain an understanding of the rules of color, contrast and harmony.

The Colors are divided into primaries (or elementaries), secondaries and tertiaries. In other words, first, second and third colors.

A primary color is one that cannot be produced by an admixture of others.

Yellow is a primary color, and stands first, for it is the nearest approach in color to light.

Red comes next, and is the intermediary between yellow and blue, which is the third and remaining primary color.

In theory, from these three colors alone, all other colors may be had.

Next to white, in color, we may class yellow, a primary intimately related to white as between light and color. Yellow, like white, is an advancing color, some form of it appears in nearly every palette.

From the primaries are formed the secondaries, orange (a mixture of yellow and red), green (a mixture of yellow and blue), and purple (a mixture of red and blue). The tertiary colors are:

Citron, made of orange mixed with green.

Russet (or brown), made of orange mixed with purple.

Olive, made of purple mixed with green.

Beyond this extent innumerable combinations are obtained by mixing the various tints and colors of varying inherent qualities.

WATER COLOR MATERIALS

The Beginner in the use of water colors should be provided with the following materials:

A box of water colors and two or three brushes.

A tablet of white water color paper (4½"x6").

A cup for water (one that is not easily tipped).

A piece of blotting paper.

A piece of cotton cloth (free from starch) for the purpose of drying the brush or taking up superfluous color and cleaning the color box.

A small sheet of white paper on which to try colors.

Water Color Paper.—In water color work, the paper best adapted for the purpose is that which is made of linen possessing a moderately rough surface, together with a good substance of body, that is to say, thickness.

If paper not in tablet form is used, before starting even the outline the paper should be slightly sponged on one side, and, before it has a chance to dry, the edges or margins, to the extent of a half inch, should be passed over with strong mucilage, paste or glue.

The paper should now be pressed firmly to the drawing board. As the paper dries it becomes stretched and is ready to receive the colors. When the work is completed cut the drawing within the lines where pasted. The paper must be *quite dry* before this is done.

Paper especially adapted for water colors already prepared in tablets can be secured, the sheets of which may be removed *after* the water color is completed. The drawing board need not then be used.

GENERAL INSTRUCTIONS

Position of the Tablet.—The tablet should be inclined at an angle of about 35 or even 45 degrees. This is for the purpose of letting colors flow downward, which is the general direction in which the brush should be manipulated.

Outlining the Design.—Make complete outlines of the subject to be painted before applying color. These outlines should be very light, so light as not to be observed, except on very close inspection, when the water color is completed.

Erasing.—Use the rubber eraser as seldom as possible, otherwise the rubber is apt to disturb the surface of the paper and cause the "washes" to appear streaked.

Parts to be Painted First.—As a general rule, put in the background tints first. Then the parts in the middle distance, and the foreground last.

Washes and How Applied

Water color painting is a series of washes. A wash is water tinted with color to be applied more or less evenly to the surface of the paper.

A flat wash is one in which there is no variation in tone. A wash may be light or dark—from a slight admixture of color to full strength; the latter being seldom used.

A graded wash is one where the wash varies from light to dark, or vice versa.

A broken wash is where the wash is divided by the outlines of other washes of another color.

A mixed wash is one where one color runs into another—as from yellow to green, etc.

A wash may represent a tint, hue or value.

A wash should be applied as follows: Dip the brush in water. Press it into one of the colors; extract the color with downward strokes; do not wiggle the brush backward and forward. When enough color has been taken up gently press the color from the brush into one of the compartments in the cover of the box. Then dip the brush into water again and mix the water with the color in the compartment. Stir gently and take up a brushful of the tint. Apply to the paper, renewing the color before the brush is dry. If the color runs too much, quickly dry the brush on the cloth and with the dry brush take up the superfluous color. A blotter may be used for the same purpose.

Parts to be Painted Last.—Parts that are in heavy color should always be put in last. Otherwise if additional washes are put in the background or middle distance the heavily painted portions will become dissolved and spread into the other parts. Thus, if the red chimney of a house were painted before the sky or clouds behind it were quite finished, and then a wash spread over the red chimney, the red would spread into the cloud or sky, spoiling the latter.

Let Light Tones Prevail.—In the beginning of water color exercises the prevailing tones should be light. Excessive color is productive of muddiness in texture. Purity of tone is more easily obtained and preserved by the application of tones few in number (or in combination) and light in quality. If more strength is found necessary, repeated washes, one over the other, each one being allowed to dry, will bring about the required result.

Neutral Foundation.—A pleasing effect is usually secured by making the variation in light and shade, especially in the foreground, and even middle distance, by means of grey or neutral tones, just as if the picture were to be composed of grey and white effects alone. Then the various local colors may be applied in transparent washes over the grey tones. The grey tones will show through the washes of color and produce much the same effect as if various grades of strength of color were used. It is the same principle as in coloring a photograph, except that the colorist has the advantage of adapting the strength of the underlying tones to suit the requirements of the subject; parts of a photograph usually being too dark for the superadded colors to show adequately.

When Backgrounds Are Unnecessary.—When painting single objects or simple groups, such as flowers, a book, a vase (almost any still life subject, in fact), it is not necessary to show the actual background. A broken tint is generally sufficient and less confusing in result.

Select Simple Subjects.—When drawing from nature in color as well as in black-and-white, simple subjects are best at first; the simpler the better. A stump of a tree, a fallen log, a group of rocks, a bunch of grass or weeds, an old water trough, an old shed or shanty; in fact, any single object or group is advisable rather than a widely distributed subject of an ambitious character.

Old and weatherworn subjects are better than new ones.

Terms and Definitions

The colors usually accepted as standard are the primaries, yellow, red and blue, and the secondary colors, orange, green and violet. Complementary colors are various proportions of the primary colors, such as olive, russet, etc.

Tone indicates any change of color. There are warm tones and cold tones.

Warm tones are those in which yellow and red prevail.

Cold tones are those in which blue and black are added sufficiently to produce a sense of coolness or dullness, such as russet, olive and grey.

Shades are the darker tones. **Tints** are the lighter tones of a color. The less color in proportion to the water used the lighter the tint becomes.

Hues are the intermediate tones between two intermingling tints or tones. Thus a green tone running into a yellow tone becomes a yellow-green hue.

Value is lightness or darkness of tone irrespective of color produced by its contrast with another.

Scale of color is the orderly series of tones; thus, yellow running from full strength to white, or from yellow to black.

Some Nevers

Never "scrub" with the brush or manipulate it any way so that the hairs of the brush become unevenly separated.

Never retouch a wet wash.

Never put one wash over another until the first one is dry.

Never work with a partly dry brush except to put in minor details to complete a water color.

Never put your brush aside without rinsing and drying it.

Never put the color box away without cleaning it.

Color on Color.—In working with water color, a better result is usually obtained by placing one color over the other when wishing to make a tint, rather than mixing the tint beforehand. Thus, for instance, if one wishes to produce a green, place an area of yellow on the paper, and after that is dry wash a tone of blue over it with a brush. The result thus obtained is a green of better value than could have been secured by first mixing the blue and the yellow. By the former method, while slower, a higher degree of transparency will be obtained. In painting landscapes, for instance, where one or the other of the first washes happens to show through, little accidental effects are secured which would otherwise be obtained with much difficulty.

SIMPLE COLOR EXERCISES

Only three colors are necessary at the beginning. More than three are inadvisable, and, in fact, make the study complex and difficult. For the purpose of the beginner, the three primary colors, yellow, red and blue, will produce every other color desired. In other words, all other colors contain combinations of two or three of these colors.

Mix blue and red, and you have purple or violet, or lilac, according to which of the two prevails.

Mix blue and yellow, and you have green.

Mix red and yellow, and orange is obtained.

Mix all three in *equal* proportions, and the result is a muddy brown.

Modifying the mixtures, for instance, three parts of red, two of blue and one of yellow produces a chocolate tint.

Notes.—Subjects suitable for simple and advanced water color: boat in p. 39, pp. 40, 41, 42, 43, 44, 48, 50, 51, 59, 60, 62, 66, 76, 81, 85, 90, 93, 102, 105, 106, 111, 114, 115, 116, 117, 120, 126, 135, 153, 154, 156, 164, 165, 166, 167, 170, 174, 176, 177, 178, 180, 181 and all in chapter XXV.

GLOSSARY

Accent. Emphasis of dark in an outline drawing; of light or of dark in a light-and-shade drawing; and of color or of light and dark in a color sketch.

Accessory. In a picture any part which is merely ornamental, or at least, not essential.

Acute Angle. One that is less than a right angle, or less than 90 degrees.

Angle. The difference in direction of two lines which meet or tend to meet.

Angular Perspective. Dealing with objects whose lines are either vertical or horizontal.

Anthiom. Spreading (flower) design in classic Greek ornament.

Apex. The summit or highest point of an object.

Arc. Any part of the circumference of a circle.

Arrangement. The orderly disposition of objects or forms.

Atomizer. In art, an instrument that will produce a vapor composed of a fixative that will "set" a drawing.

Axis. A straight line passing through the center of an object dividing it into two parts that balance each other.

Background. That part of any picture represented as farthest away from the eye.

Balance. The equality of parts, obtained by the proper distribution of lines or of light and dark; and of color or of light and dark in a color sketch.

Base. Usually the lowest side of any geometrical form. The plane surfaces of cylinders and cones.

Bisect. To divide into two equal parts.

Blend. To soften and bring together.

Blender. In pencil, crayon, pastel or charcoal drawing, anything used to blend with, such as a stump, soft rag or chamois leather. In oil painting the "blender" is a name given to a certain brush, used to blend the surfaces of freshly applied paint.

Blocking-in (lines). (Blocking-out.) The lightest and simplest suggestions of the leading lines and masses of a subject in which no heed is given to minor details; the essential directions of the lines or masses only being indicated.

Blue. One of the three primary colors. The others are yellow and red.

Border. As applied to ornaments, usually composed of units regularly repeated along a line. The outer edge of anything.

Bow Pen. Bow Pencil. Ordinary compasses being too large to make small circles, Bow Pens and Bow Pencils are provided with a center shank having a thread and thumb screw for changing the radius.

Breadth. Simplicity due to masses in which the details are subordinated to the spirit and effect of the whole.

Bristol Board. Named after Bristol, Eng., a fine calendered paste board used for pen-and-ink drawing.

Broken Wash. See Washes.

Cartoon. Originally applied to large drawings on walls or tapestry. Any large design on paper. Now applied to any drawing of a humorous character.

Cartoonist. One who makes cartoons.

Cast. An object, usually for purposes as a model, made of Plaster-of-Paris.

Cast Shadow. The shadow which one object throws upon another. It is sharper nearer the first object than farther away.

Center of Vision. See point of sight.

Chiaro-Oscuro. (Literally Clear-Dark.) The art of judiciously distributing light and shadows in a picture.

Cinquefoil. In ornamentation, a five-leafed design.

Circle. A plane figure bounded by a curved line, called circumference, all points of which are equally distant from a point called the center.

Circular. A face shaped like a circle.

Circumference. In art, the line that bounds a figure, especially a circle; the space included in a circle.

Citron. A greenish yellow, with a reddish tone; one of the tertiary colors. The others are olive and russet.

Cold Colors. Those in which blue predominates, such as blue, bluish green, violet, etc.

Colors. See Primary, Secondary and Tertiary Colors.

Complementary Colors. Certain colors are complementary to each other as green to red; orange to blue; violet to yellow. See primary, secondary and tertiary colors.

Compasses. Used for drawing circles and arcs of circles. Pen and pencil points are provided. See dividers.

Composition. The arrangements of the different lines, parts and masses of a subject.

Compound Curve. A concave and convex line joined without an angle.

Concave. An incurved line. Opposed to convex.

Construction. The making of any object.

Contrast. The effect due to the juxtaposition of different lines, different forms, different masses of light or dark or of different colors.

Contour. The outlines of the general appearance of an object.

Conventionalize. In art, to express the spirit and important truths of Nature by a subordination of less important features. For instance, formal or mechanically exact reproduction of the salient parts of a leaf or flower, which may be adopted as a unit for purposes of repetition.

Converge. To extend lines toward a common point; or planes toward a common line.

Convex. The opposite of concave. Rising or swelling into a spherical or rounded form.

Corner. The point of meeting of the edges of a solid.

Crayon. Any pencil made of chalk, pipeclay, charcoal or similar substance. Usually applied to the black crayon used for making black-and-white drawings and to the finer varieties of colored chalks. The name given to a crayon drawing—as, "It is a beautiful crayon." There are ordinary colored crayons, wax crayons and blackboard crayons.

Crayon Holder. Sometimes called Porte Crayon (Porte from French Porter, to carry). A holder to make the crayon more convenient for drawing.

Crayon Pencils. Similar to a lead pencil; a little larger. In place of graphite, substance like crayon is used.

Crayon Sauce. A very fine black substance used in connection with crayon drawing. It comes in sticks protected by tin foil. It is applied by means of the "stump."

Cross. Two bars, or parts, intersecting or crossing each other.

Cross-Hatching. In free-hand drawing, the use of lines crossing each other and producing light and shade effects.

Cube. A regular solid having six equal square surfaces.

Curve. A line in which no part is straight. A line bent without angles. Technically, a line no three consecutive points of which lie in the same direction.

Curves-Balanced. Pairs of curves that bend equally, but in opposite directions in every part. See Compound Curves.

Curve of Beauty. See Line of Beauty.

Cut Up. A drawing, design or painting having its effect destroyed by an excess or exaggeration of detail or unimportant objects.

Cylinder. A straight sided solid bounded by a curved surface and by two opposite faces called bases. Its length is greater than its diameter. Technically, a solid which may be generated by the rotation of a parallelogram around one of its sides.

Decorative. Adorning, embellishing. **Decorative Art.** Art which has for its purpose the pleasing of the eye.

Degree. The 360th part of the circumference of any circle.

Delineate. To mark out, to form by lines; to sketch, to portray, to picture.

Describe. To draw or make a line.

Design. To represent a thing in outline. Sketch. First idea represented by visible lines. Delineation.

Detail. A minute or particular part, as distinguished from a general plan or conception or from larger parts.

Details. Noun plural. The parts of a thing treated separately and minutely.

Device. That which is formed by design or invented. Anything fancifully conceived, as a picture. An emblem.

Diagonal. A straight line in any polygon which connects vertices not adjacent. A right line drawn from angle to angle.

Diagram. A drawing giving only the outlines or essentials, often crude.

Diameter. A right line passing through the center of a plane figure or solid, especially a circle.

Diffused Light. Scattered light. Spreading light. As the light seen in a mist or on a gray day. Starlight is diffused. The light in a room with the shades drawn is diffused. The light coming through an aperture and spreading fan-light is diffused. Light coming through a semi-transparent object is diffused.

Dimension. Extent in one direction.

Distorted. Different from the image in the eye, and producing frequently with purpose, as in comic drawing, a ludicrous impression of the object. When unintentional the effect is usually unsatisfactory.

Diverging Lines. Lines extending from a common point. Opposite of converge.

Dividers. Similar to compasses, but not provided with pen or pencil points; consist of two legs joined, the ends being sharply pointed.

Draftsman. Draughtsman. One who draws.

Drawing. Any representation of nature, imagination or by means of copying, of any object or group of objects done in outline. shade or color. The usual understanding of a drawing is one made in one tint or color, black being considered as such.

Drawing Pen. An instrument for ruling straight lines and curves that are not arcs of circles. It consists of two blades of steel fastened to a handle. Distance between pen points can be adjusted by thumb screws, thus regulating width of lines.

Dry Brush. The use of a brush almost devoid of moistness. A term used in connection with water color.

Easel. In art, a stand or frame, usually with three legs, to support a canvas, drawing board, blackboard, etc.

Edge. The intersection of two surfaces. A boundary line, straight or curved. Edges are represented by lines.

Ellipse. A plane figure bounded by a curved line, at every point of which the sum of the distances from two points within, called foci (plural of focus), is the same.

Equilateral. Equal sided.

Equilibrium. See Balance.

Face. One of the plane surfaces of a solid. It may be bounded by straight or curved edges.

Figure. (Abbreviation, Fig.) The form of anything as expressed by outlines.

Finicky. Extreme in trivial detail. Fussy.

Finishing. Completing a drawing after the lines have been determined, by erasing unnecessary lines and strengthening and accentuating where this is required.

Fixatif (or Fixative). A thin varnish, used in the form of a spray to render a drawing in pencil, charcoal or crayon impervious to ordinary rubbing or handling.

Flat Tint. One that is even throughout; showing no gradations.

Flatness. Evenness. Dullness. Insipidity.

Flat Wash. See Wash.

Fleur-De-Lis (French). In ornament, a flower resembling the lily, Plural, Fleurs-de-lis.

Foil. In ornament, a leaf. **Foilated.** In ornament, anything in the form of a conventional leaf or leaves, as trefoil, quatrefoil, cinquefoil.

Foreground. That part of any picture represented as being nearest to the eye. See Middle Distance and Background.

Foreshortening. Apparent decrease in length, due to a position oblique to the visual rays.

Formalize. To make in a stiff or precise manner.

Free Arm Movement. Movement of the arm from the shoulder.

Free-Hand. Executed by the hand, without the aid of instruments.

Geometrical Plane. The horizontal, projecting plane in perspective drawing.

Geometric Drawing. Showing an object in its simplest form; that is, having length and width, or showing but one face of an object.

Glossary. A dictionary or vocabulary explaining words which are difficult, peculiar, technical, obscure or local; a vocabulary giving the words of a book, author, dialect, science or art. If combined with a book, not necessarily confined to the words in that book.

Graded Wash. See Washes.

Gradation. A gradual change from light to dark, or from one color to another.

Graphite. Mineral form of the element carbon. Also known as plumbago, and as black lead, although lead does not at all enter into its composition. Graphite is the chief substance of the "lead" in pencils. Other substances give varying degrees of hardness.

Green. One of the secondary colors formed by mixture of yellow and blue. The others are orange and violet.

Ground Plane. Surface upon which objects in a picture are supposed to rest.

Gauche. See Opaque water color.

Guide-Lines. Faint lines made preliminary to a drawing for the guidance of the draftsman. They are analogous to the blue ruled lines on writing paper.

Half-Tint. The shading produced by means of parallel equidistant lines.

Handling. The way in which a medium is used. Relating to technic (or technique) which see. Same as **Rendering.**

Harmony. The pleasing arrangement of lines, light and dark, or color.

Height. The vertical measurement. Distance from top to bottom.

Heptagon. A plane figure of seven sides and angles.

Hexagon. A plane figure having six sides and angles.

High Light. One point of an object is frequently so situated that it reflects the ray which it receives directly to the eye. This point glitters, more or less, and is called the high light.

Horizon (horizontal line). In pictorial art, a horizontal line at the level of the eye.

Horizontal. Parallel to the surface of smooth water. In drawings, a line parallel to the top and bottom to the sheet is called horizontal.

Horn Centers. Small mask-like disks to protect paper, etc., from injury by the points of dividers or compasses.

India Ink. In sticks; made in China and Japan from fine lamp black and gelatin, perfumed and pressed into sticks. Liquid India: made in America; for sale in bottles ready for use; for pen-and-ink work.

Invert. To turn upside down.

Isometrical (projection). Method of drawing plans of machines, etc., whereby the elevation and ground plan are represented in one view. **Isometric.** Pertaining to equality of measure.

Juxtaposition. Nearness; contiguity; side by side.

Key. The scale of light and dark, or color.

Lateral. Pertaining to the side; as, a lateral view—i. e., a side view.

Legible. That which may be understood by visible marks or indications.

Length. Distance from end to end.

Limn (Lim). To draw or paint. To delineate.

Line. That which has extent only.

Linear Perspective. Treating of the appearance of objects expressed by outline.

Line of Beauty. A line, regarded as beautiful in itself, to which different artists have given different forms. Usually represented in the form of a very elongated letter S.

Longitudinal. In the direction of the length of an object.

Margin. The surrounding space of a drawing or design that is left uncovered.

Medallion. An ornamental figure, round, oval or even square in shape. (Practically the same as Rosette.) Strictly speaking, it is a term used in architecture and applies to such figures made in relief or stamped in metal. It has been adopted as a term in decoration generally.

Medium. The pencil, crayon, color or other material used to produce a drawing or painting; not applied to the paper or canvas itself.

Middle Distance. The part of any picture midway between the foreground and background.

Mixed Wash. See Washes.

Minute. Small.

Model. A form used for study.

Modeling. Production of form by building or fashioning of some plastic substance, as wax or clay. Used as a term in painting referring to manipulation or handling of represented form.

Modulate. To adapt; to proportion; to adjust.

Monochrome. Any design or drawing in which one color prevails.

Monotone. In one shade or tint.

Mosaic. Noun, meaning anything resembling mosaic work, which consists of an assemblage of substance such as small pieces of stone, glass, marble, etc., arranged so as to form a design.

Muddiness. Want of clearness or transparency in a tone or color.

Nonagon. A plane figure of nine equal sides and angles.

Oblique. Bending away from the perpendicular; neither horizontal nor vertical.

Oblique Angle. Either an acute or an obtuse angle as distinguished from a right angle.

Oblique Perspective. Deals with the lines oblique to the ground plane and the picture plane.

Oblong. A plane figure bounded by four straight lines and having four right angles, with opposite sides equal and parallel.

Obtuse Angle. Greater than a right angle, or more than 90 degrees.

Octagon. A plane figure of eight sides and angles.

Offset. A partial transfer from one surface to another, as from a tracing to drawing paper.

Olive. Greenish brown; one of the tertiary colors; the others are citron and russet.

Opaque (or Gauche) color. Pigment having a body which hides the surface (whether an underlying color or the paper) receiving the color. In transparent water colors Chinese white will render the pigments opaque.

Orange. One of the three secondary colors. The others are green and violet.

Ornament. In drawing. Decorative arrangement of line. Historic ornament; that designed in previous ages.

Orthographic Perspective. The science of determining the form of an object by means of perpendicular lines falling upon a geometrical plane.

Oval. A plane figure resembling the longitudinal section of an egg. Elliptical in shape.

Ovoid. An egg-shaped solid.

Palette. The article used by the painter, upon which to mix his colors. It may be a slab on a table, or a porcelain or wooden plate-like utensil carried in the hand, with a thumb-hole and space for the fingers, brushes and mahlstick. A term used to express an artistic range of colors; as, "His palette consisted ot only ten colors." Or, "He uses a warm palette," meaning he uses warm colors.

Panoramic (View). An entire view in every direction.

Parallel. Having the same direction and everywhere equally different, equally distant.

Parallelogram. A quadrilateral having its opposite sides parallel.

Pastel. A very soft colored crayon. They are made in a great many varying tints. Name given to a drawing made with pastels.

Pastel-Stenciling. Method of using stencils with dry colors. described in chapter under this title.

Pattern. A drawn or cut-out guide to determine form and dimensions of an object.

Perimeter. The boundary of a closed plane figure. In drawing usually used to describe the boundary of any conventional or distinctly outlined figure.

Perpendicular. At an angle of 90 degrees; at right angles to the plane of the horizon.

Perspective. The art of making upon a plane, called the picture plane, a representation of objects so that the lines of the drawing appear to coincide with the objects, when the eye is at one fixed point called the station point (or point of station).

Picture Plane. Represented by the flat surface on which a drawing is made.

Pigment. Any substance used as paint or color.

Plane. In art, the representation of a level surface, not elevated; a flat surface.

Plane Figure. A part of a plane surface bounded by lines.

Point. Usually the smallest mark that can be made.

Point of Light. The spot in an object where a brilliant light is concentrated. Usually a reflected light.

Point of Sight. That to which the eye of the spectator is supposed to be directed when he looks straight ahead.

Point of Station. In Perspective, the place where the artist is supposed to stand.

Polygon. A plane figure bounded by straight lines.

Porte Crayon. See Crayon Holder.

Poster. A modern word originally applied to printed bills or placards posted in a public place. When decorative, usually in colors, they are used as decorations in "dens" and bedrooms. Practically any large design to be tacked up unframed.

Primary Colors. Yellow, red and blue. See Secondary and Tertiary colors.

Prism. A solid bounded by two equal parallel polygons, having their equal sides parallel, and by three or more parallelograms.

Profile. The contour outline of an object.

Projection. In architecture and mechanics, jutting out.

Project. In art, to draw or exhibit as the form of anything. To construct; to delineate.

Protractor. A semi-circular mathematical instrument divided into 180 degrees for laying down and measuring angles on paper.

Pyramid. A solid of which one face, called the base, is a polygon, and the other faces, called lateral faces, are triangles having a common vertex, called the vertex of the pyramid. A pyramid is called triangular, square, etc., according as its base is a triangle, square, etc.

Quadrant. The space enclosed by one-quarter of the circumference.

Quadrilateral. A plane figure formed by four straight lines, such as the parallelogram, trapezium, trapezoid, rectangle, square, rhomboid and rhombus.

Quadrisect. To divide into four equal parts.

Quatrefoil. A figure composed of four leaf-like parts.

Radius. A straight line from the center to the circumference of a circle.

Recede. To move back; to fall away, as a vanishing line. Receding lines. Lines in a picture which appear to vanish.

Rectangle. A four-sided figure having all its angles right angles.

Red. One of the three primary colors. The others are yellow and blue.

Reflected Light. A light reflected to the dark side of an object by light objects opposite to the dark side of the first object.

Relief. In art, the appearance of projection and solidity. To stand out. In black-and-white, it is a word used to express contrast or strength in effect. Example: "The tree stands in relief against the sky."

Renaissance. The revival in the 15th century of the Roman and Greek art.

Rendering. Same as Handling.

Repetition. The arrangement of a unit on a line, around a center, about a line as axis, or upon geometric lines covering a surface, as for a wall paper or oil-cloth design.

Representation. Any kind of drawing, painting or sculpture.

Retreating Lines. See Recede.

Reverse. To turn to the opposite side.

Rhomboid. A quadrilateral whose opposite sides are equal and parallel, and none of its angles right angles.

Rhombus. A quadrilateral having four equal sides and no right angles. An equilateral rhomboid.

Right Angle. An angle formed by a right line standing on another perpendicularly or an angle of 90 degrees, measured by an arc which is one-quarter of a circle.

Right Line. A straight line.

Rosette. Strictly speaking, an ornamental figure in the form of a rose. Applied generally to any round or oval figure in ornament. It is sometimes called a medallion, which see.

Rubber-Erasers. There are several kinds—India rubber for pencil;

kneaded rubber for same purpose but softer, and sponge rubber still softer.

Ruling-Pen. See Drawing Pen.

Russet. Reddish brown; one of the tertiary colors; the others are citron and olive.

Sauce. See Crayon Sauce.

Secondary Colors. Green and violet and orange. Formed by mixtures of the primary colors, yellow, red and blue.

Section. A projection upon a plane parallel to a cutting plane which intersects any object. A distinct portion. A division.

Segment. Part of a circle.

Semi-Circle. Half a circle.

Semi-Diameter. Half a diameter.

Septangle (Heptagon). A plane figure of seven sides or angles.

Shade. Shadow. Shade and shadow have about the same meaning in drawing. Strictly speaking, shadow designates those parts of an object which are turned away from the direct rays of the light. Shade, in the strict sense, is applied to those surfaces which receive fewer direct rays and are intermediate in value between light and shadow. Generally speaking, opposite to light.

Shadow Cast. A cast shadow is one projected upon one object by another.

Silhouette (Sil-oo-et'). A dark profile against a white background. Usually applied to the human face, but sometimes used describing any dark object standing against the light, as "The mountain is silhouetted against the Western sky."

Sketch. Usually, but not necessarily, a hasty and unfinished drawing. **Time Sketch.** One made in a specified time. Sketch is frequently applied to the preliminary sketch upon which a finished drawing is based.

Sketch Block. A number of small sheets of paper fastened at the sides by means of glue. Separable.

Solid. A solid has three dimensions—length, breadth and thickness.

Sphere. A solid bounded by a uniformly curved surface every point of which is equally distant from the center.

Spheroid. (See Ellipsoid.)

Spill. See Stump.

Spiral (Curve). The path of a point revolved about a center, the distance of the point from the center constantly increasing.

Square. A plane figure bounded by four equal straight lines forming four right angles.

Stencil. An open-work pattern through which colors are passed, by brush (usually) to a surface underneath. To paint or color by means of a stencil.

Stippling. Filling in the space between hatching, or producing any certain effect by means of dots.

Study. In drawing, any carefully finished drawing or painting. Often one used as a model or to copy from.

Stump. A cigar shaped utensil for blending or spreading crayon, charcoal or pastel. It consists of tightly rolled leather or paper. Used also for applying "Crayon sauce." A small kind of stump is called a spill.

Stylus. In art, a pointed instrument, usually of agate, used for making transfers from one paper to another. Its point may be straight or curved.

Symbolism. The use of conventional forms to suggest ideas not inherent in the forms.

Symmetry. In design, a harmonious adjustment or adaptation of parts to one another and to the whole.

Technique (Technic). See Handling, Rendering.

Tertiary Colors. Olive, russet, citron and other shades made by admixtures of the secondary colors.

Texture. The character of the surface of a drawing of whatever kind, whether in black-and-white or in color.

Thumb Tacks. Used for fastening paper to a drawing board. They are easily put in and taken out.

Tint. A tone of color, produced by adding water to the color. In black-and-white, any specific gradation of tone between black and white.

Tone. Tone designates the changes which color undergoes by the addition of white, which lightens; or of black, which darkens its normal tone. **General Tone.** The prevailing shade or key prevailing in a picture.

Tracing Paper. A semi-transparent paper on which to trace drawings. **Tracing.** Term used to describe a drawing or sketch made on tracing paper.

Transparent Water Color. Watercolor which does not quite hide the surface receiving it. See Opaque Water Color.

Transverse. Running in a cross direction.

Trapezoid. A plane figure of four sides, two opposite sides of which are parallel.

Trapezium. A plane figure of four sides, no two of which are parallel.

Trefoil. A figure composed of three leaf-like parts.

Triangle. A plane figure bounded by three straight lines, and three angles.

Triangle. A triangular shaped flat instrument to make lines on paper; usually of 30, 45, 60 and 90 degrees.

Triangle Acute-Angled. A triangle having all acute angles.

Triangle Obtuse-Angled. A triangle having one obtuse angle.

Triangle Right-Angled. A triangle having one right angle.

Trihedron. An equilateral triangle, that is, having three equal sides.

Triangulation. Shaping or forming into triangles.

Trisect. To divide into three equal parts.

T-Square. A thin straight edge called the blade, fastened to a head at right angles to it. This forms a T, hence its name. **Swivel-Head T-Square.** One with an adjustable head, usually in conjunction with the fixed head: for purpose of making lines at any angle.

Unit of Design. Any figure repeated in a design or arrangement usually applied to ornament.

View. The object as seen by the eye. Views are called front, top, right or left side, back, or bottom, according as they are made.

Vanishing Points. Points in a picture at which receding (or retreating) lines appear to vanish.

Value. In color, the relative amount of light contained in different colors. The strongest are either the lightest or most brilliant. In drawing generally, value means the difference in effect due to any cause whatever, as color, light, atmosphere, shadow, etc.

Variety. The effect due to the combination of parts which are not alike.

Vertex. The highest point; the point in any figure opposite to and most distant from its base. The vertex of a solid is the point in which its axis intersects the lateral surface.

Vertical. Upright or perpendicular to a horizontal line or plane. Vertical and perpendicular are not synonymous terms, although frequently thus used.

Violet. One of the three secondary colors. The others are green and orange.

Wash. A term applied to the flowing of a color or tint over the surface of paper. "He put a wash of blue over the distant mountains."

Washes. Broken Washes. One which is broken or divided by others. Flat Wash. One which does not vary in tone. Graded Wash. One which varies. Mixed Wash. One which runs into another.

Warm Colors. Those in which red and yellow predominate.

Water Color Paper. In sheets, in eight sizes, Cap. 13"x17"; Demy, 15"x20"; Medium, 17"x22"; Royal, 19"x24"; Super Royal, 19"x27"; Imperial, 22"x30"; Double Elephant, 26"x40"; antiquarian, 31"x 52". It is usually made in three surfaces—"Cold Pressed" (C. P., having an ordinary surface with a slight grain; "Hot Pressed" (H. P.), having a smooth surface; "Rough" (R.), having a large, coarse open grain.

Width. Distance from side to side.

Working Drawing. One which gives all the information necessary for the workman to construct the object.

Zenith. The point in the heavens directly over the spectator's head.

INDEX